THE STOCK OPTIONS BOOK

18th Edition

ALISON WRIGHT
ALISA J. BAKER
PAM CHERNOFF

The National Center for Employee Ownership
Oakland, California

The Stock Options Book • 18th Edition
Alison Wright, Alisa J. Baker, and Pam Chernoff
Edited by Pam Chernoff
Indexed by Achaessa James
Book design by Scott Rodrick

The National Center for Employee Ownership
1629 Telegraph Ave., Suite 200
Oakland, CA 94612
(510) 208-1300 • (510) 272-9510 (fax) • Web: www.nceo.org

First printed May 1997; reprinted with revisions, January 1998, June 1998. Second edition, February 1999. Third edition, July 1999; reprinted with revisions, December 1999. Fourth edition, June 2001. Fifth edition, October 2002. Sixth edition, January 2004. Seventh edition, January 2006. Eighth edition, January 2007. Ninth edition, February 2008. Tenth edition, February 2009. Eleventh edition, February 2010. Twelfth edition, February 2011. Thirteenth edition, February 2012. Fourteenth edition, February 2013. Fifteenth edition, February 2014. Sixteenth edition, March 2015. Seventeenth edition, February 2016. Eighteenth edition, February 2017.

ISBN: 978-1-938220-49-4

Contents

Chapter 9: Tax Law Compliance Issues   165

Chapter 10: Basic Accounting Issues   189
Pam Chernoff and Elizabeth Dodge

Appendixes

Preface

Welcome to the 18th edition of *The Stock Options Book*. We continue to be amazed at the ever-evolving body of law and lore in our field. A version of this text has been on the shelves since 1997, but at the time of its first publication, no one could have predicted the extent to which the entire field of executive compensation in general, and equity compensation in particular, would become a cause célèbre. Attempts to rein in perceived executive greed have given rise to enormous changes since the inception of this publication, including major substantive revisions to the laws and regulations governing the tax, securities, accounting, and corporate treatment of equity-based compensation. It has been a wild ride.

The 18th edition continues our practice of fully updating and refining each prior year's materials. Alison Wright, a partner at the law firm Hanson Bridgett LLP, and Pam Chernoff, who has been editing the book since 2005, are responsible for updating the book, which was authored by Alisa J. Baker between 2002 and 2012.

As always, we hope you find this edition useful in your practice. Please continue to let the NCEO know which issues concern you the most and how you would like to see them addressed. You can send any comments to customerservice@nceo.org.

Alison Wright
Pam Chernoff
December 2016

Thanks to Susan Berry, CEP, for her invaluable contribution to the always-challenging "stock swaps" section of chapter 7; to Brennan Latham, CEP, for his help with the section on broker-assisted cashless transactions; and Ellie Kehmeier for her help with the tax accounting portions of chapter 10.

Introduction

This book is intended to give the reader a general overview of how stock options are used in the United States to reward employees for their participation in and commitment to the success of the employer corporation (referred to variously here as the "company" or the "employer"). Stock options are but one of several forms of equity incentives, which may range from restricted stock arrangements to outright gifts of stock. For the sake of keeping this discussion focused, these other forms of equity incentives are covered only briefly here.

There are two basic kinds of stock options: (1) "qualified" or "statutory" stock options, including incentive stock options (ISOs) and employee stock purchase plan (ESPP) options, which are specific creatures of the Internal Revenue Code of 1986 (the "Code"), as amended, and (2) all other stock options, called "nonstatutory" or "nonqualified" stock options (NSOs). This book carefully examines the tax aspects of employee stock options and cites appropriate authority on tax issues. However, the days when the equity compensation professional could feel free to review tax aspects of employee stock options in a vacuum are long past. Options are subject to a complex web of rules regarding their creation and exercise that are unrelated to the Code, including federal and state securities laws, accounting standards, and country-specific laws governing grants made to employees resident outside of the United States. Therefore, as appropriate, this book gives an overview of how non-tax rules apply and indicates the types of issues raised by the interaction of these rules. Readers should note that the discussion is intended to provide only general planning guidance; where appropriate, we have provided references to authoritative sources on these subjects.

The main body of this book is divided into three parts. Part I provides an overview of stock option plans, employee stock purchase plans, and, briefly, other forms of equity compensation, focusing on the tax aspects; Part II explores technical issues such as accounting (including 2016 amendments to Accounting Standards Codification Topic 718), securities, and tax compliance requirements; Part III looks at current ongoing regulatory issues, including the latest hot topics. Where helpful, illustrative tables are included. At the end of the book, there are supporting materials, including an article by NCEO cofounder Corey Rosen on designing a broad-based plan; primary sources; a glossary; and a bibliography.

As a caveat, it is important to remember that the use of equity incentives is under ever-increasing scrutiny by the Internal Revenue Service (IRS), the accounting profession (as represented by the Financial Accounting Standards Board [FASB]), the Securities and Exchange Commission (SEC), and Congress. When the original form of this text was first published in the early 1990s, stock option planning was a relatively esoteric function of tax and compensation design. Although this book generally describes current areas of ambiguity, the equity compensation professional must be aware that complex issues will continue to arise with respect to individual options and option plans. Each situation should always be reviewed carefully with legal and accounting experts to ensure compliance with the most current rules.

PART I
OVERVIEW OF STOCK OPTIONS AND RELATED PLANS

Chapter 1

The Basics of Stock Options

Contents

1.1 What Is a Stock Option?

Generally, when an individual is granted a compensatory stock option, that individual (the "optionee") receives a contractual right to purchase shares in a corporation for a fixed term at a fixed price—in most cases, the fair market value of the stock on the date the option was granted. Companies typically grant options to employees, consultants, or other persons providing services to the company to encourage their retention and participation in the success of the company. The optionee typically earns the right to the shares over a stated vesting period. Once the option vests, the optionee can choose when and if to exercise it (i.e., purchase the underlying shares). (Some plans allow for exercise prior to vesting, which is discussed in chapters 2 and 3.)

This book discusses stock options granted in connection with the performance of services only, as opposed to options purchased for investment purposes. The tax treatment of stock transferred pursuant to compensatory stock options is governed by the Internal Revenue Code (the Code). Sections 421 to 424 of the Code govern statutory options that are eligible for favorable tax treatment, while Section 83 of the

Code governs nonstatutory options. Different rules apply to determine the amount, character, and timing of the optionee's income inclusion as well as the availability of the corporate tax deduction when options are granted or exercised.

Most (although not all) compensatory options are granted pursuant to the employer company's stock option plan.[1] Companies generally adopt stock option plans that permit the grant of both incentive stock options (ISOs) and nonstatutory stock options (NSOs). NSOs are sometimes also referred to as nonqualified stock options and abbreviated as NQSOs. An ISO is a statutory option, subject to the technical requirements prescribed in Section 422 of the Code. ISOs may be granted only to employees of the issuing company (including employees of its parent and subsidiary corporations). Taxation of NSOs is governed by Section 83 of the Code. NSOs are *not* subject to special technical requirements for income tax purposes and may be granted to employees, consultants, nonemployee directors, or any other persons providing services to the company. They do not receive preferential tax treatment under the Code.

Employee stock purchase plans (ESPPs), which are another form of option plan employers can use to attract, retain, and motivate employees, may be either statutory (under Section 423 of the Code) or nonstatutory (under Section 83 of the Code). Because ESPPs are subject to distinct planning and tax considerations, they are discussed separately in chapter 5.

1.2   Legal and Regulatory Framework

As we will see throughout the book, the laws and regulations governing stock options are complex and ever-changing. Options are subject to tax and securities laws and regulations and accounting standards that often diverge in their requirements. In the federal tax and securities arenas, once a bill is signed into law, federal agencies are charged with interpreting and enforcing it.[2] Those agencies then promulgate binding regulations that govern the application of the laws. Proposed regulations generally go through a comment period during which interested

---

1.   When used for tax purposes, the term "compensatory option" may have a different meaning than when used for accounting purposes. See chapter 10, "Basic Accounting Issues."

2.   The legislative history of stock options is discussed in detail in chapter 13.

parties (such as stock plan professionals) can review them and make suggestions to the agency that is responsible for them. In addition, a body of case law has developed as various stock-option-related matters have been litigated. Recent developments in case law, as well as current agency rulings, are discussed in detail in chapter 15.

The accounting rules are unusual in that the Securities and Exchange Commission (SEC) has delegated its authority to set and interpret financial accounting standards to a private body called the Financial Accounting Standards Board (FASB).

In all three arenas (tax, securities, and accounting), compliance with complicated laws, regulations, or standards is sometimes made easier by the inclusion of a list of requirements called a "safe harbor." Companies that adopt safe harbor provisions are considered to have automatically satisfied the associated rule or law and are shielded from legal responsibility. Companies using a safe harbor may be sheltered from more complex compliance testing. For example, the SEC's Rule 144 is a safe harbor exemption that allows optionees who are not issuers, dealers, or underwriters to publicly resell stock (acquired on exercise) that otherwise would be restricted for securities law purposes under Section 4(1) of the Securities Act of 1933. To do so, the optionee must follow all of the rule's requirements.

In designing and administering stock option plans, practitioners must pay equally careful attention to tax, securities, and accounting issues, because they are distinct bodies of law and regulation. For instance, a transaction or plan design feature that is legitimate for tax purposes might not work for securities law purposes. An example of this arises when a company CEO wants to sell shares purchased by exercising an ISO. The CEO may well have satisfied the statutory holding period under the Code, making him eligible for preferential tax treatment on sale. However, he may nonetheless be barred from selling his shares by securities laws that do not allow him to buy or sell shares if he is in possession of "material nonpublic information" that would give him an advantage over other investors.

1.2.1 Tax Law

The Internal Revenue Service (IRS), an agency of the U.S. Department of the Treasury, is authorized to promulgate Treasury regulations that interpret and elaborate upon the Code. Thus, in many cases throughout the book, references to Code sections are interspersed with references to the corresponding Treasury regulations. While a specific section of the Code may be only a few pages long, the corresponding regulations can be much longer as they delve into much more detailed discussions of what the Code does and does not allow and in some cases offer examples of specific applications. For example, the portion of Section 422 of the Internal Revenue Code that describes the maximum value of stock options that may become exercisable in a given year and still be considered to be ISOs is just three short paragraphs, while the corresponding regulations take up four pages of the Code of Federal Regulations.

In addition to the Code itself and Treasury regulations, the IRS occasionally rules on specific circumstances. Its revenue rulings and revenue procedures officially interpret the Code and its related statutes and regulations. Taxpayers can rely on them in determining how to proceed on a specific issue. IRS *notices* are pronouncements that may provide substantive interpretations of the law and may provide guidance on the substance of forthcoming regulations. In addition, when a taxpayer has questions about how to handle a specific circumstance, it can request a private letter ruling (PLRs). These do not set precedent; they apply only to the taxpayers to whom they are addressed. However, they are often studied as an indication of the IRS's views on certain issues about which there has been little previous guidance. Other forms of IRS guidance are also available; these are described in more detail in section 15.1 of chapter 15.

1.2.2   Securities Law

The SEC is charged with oversight and enforcement of federal securities laws, which are designed to protect investors by ensuring that adequate information is available to them and by prohibiting fraud in the sale of securities. The primary securities laws that affect stock options are the Securities Act of 1933 and the Securities Exchange Act of 1934, which Congress passed in the hope of restoring investor confidence after the stock market crash of 1929. The 1933 Act requires that securities be registered with the SEC before they are sold unless they qualify for an exemption from registration. The 1934 Act is a far-reaching law that includes requirements for corporate reporting, proxy solicitations, tender offers, and trading by corporate insiders. Both have since been amended by subsequent legislation, most recently by the Dodd-Frank Act of 2010 and the Jumpstart Our Business Startups (JOBS) Act of 2012.

As the IRS does with tax laws, the SEC promulgates legally binding regulations that interpret the securities laws. Many regulations have built up around the 1933 and 1934 acts in the 75-plus years since their passage. The regulations that affect stock options and other forms of equity compensation are discussed in detail in chapter 8.

Regulations aside, the SEC has numerous avenues for making public pronouncements. The commission itself occasionally issues interpretive releases that reflect its views of legal and regulatory issues. Additionally, the commission's staff issues periodic legal bulletins that are not legally binding but may be indicative of their views on certain issues about which there has been little published guidance. In other cases, when an issuer of securities, such as a company granting stock options, asks the SEC for a ruling on a specific set of circumstances, the agency will issue a no-action letter saying that as long as the issuer does exactly what it proposes, the agency will not seek enforcement action for an alleged violation of securities laws.

The SEC has delegated regulatory authority for stock markets such as the New York Stock Exchange (NYSE) and Nasdaq to the Financial Industry Regulatory Authority (FINRA), which was created in 2007 to consolidate the regulation of U.S. exchanges with one body. FINRA is a self-regulatory organization, meaning it is a non-governmental entity with the power to create and enforce regulations.

In addition to federal securities laws, most states have their own securities laws that apply to private companies. These are known as "blue sky laws." The term apparently originated with judicial characterizations of "speculative schemes which have no more basis than so many feet of 'blue sky.'"

1.2.3 Accounting Rules

The Securities Exchange Act of 1934 gives the SEC the authority to set accounting standards, but the agency has historically delegated that authority to a private-sector organization. That organization, the FASB, is responsible for both establishing financial accounting standards and offering guidance on the implementation of those standards. The SEC retains the authority to veto FASB decisions and to punish companies that fail to follow FASB standards.

All of the authoritative pronouncements that make up U.S. generally accepted accounting principles (GAAP) are arranged by topic, subtopic, section, and paragraph in a codified system. In the case of stock options, the most notable FASB standard is Accounting Standards Codification Topic 718 (ASC 718). The portions governing compensatory equity granted to nonemployees are part of ASC 505.

The SEC's staff occasionally issues accounting bulletins that interpret accounting rules as they pertain to securities laws. For example, Staff Accounting Bulletin (SAB) Topic 14, Share-Based Payment (previously SAB No. 107 (SAB 107)), describes the SEC's interpretation of ASC 718 as it pertains to stock option valuation.

In 1984 FASB created the Emerging Issues Task Force (EITF), which is charged with addressing new issues that arise before widespread practice develops that complicates rulemaking. In the late 1990s and early 2000s, the EITF addressed many issues related to stock option accounting. However, because equity compensation accounting has been on FASB's front burner in recent years, the EITF has had little to do in the area of late.

Accounting standards updates (ASUs) give notice of changes to the codified standards. According to the FASB website, "An Update is a transient document that (1) summarizes the key provisions of the project that led to the Update, (2) details the specific amendments to the FASB Codification, and (3) explains the basis for the Board's decisions. Although ASUs will update the FASB Codification, the FASB does not consider Updates as authoritative in their own right." Once the comment period on an ASU has lapsed, any resulting modifications to authoritative GAAP are made within the codification system, regardless of the source of the updates or whether the changes are substantive or editorial.

1.2.4   Miscellaneous Laws

In addition to the rules described above that specifically address equity compensation, such as stock options, many other laws affect the use of stock in exchange for services. Federal and state labor laws, state employment laws, the federal Employee Retirement Income Security Act of 1974 (ERISA), state corporate and choice of law rules, and general common law contract principles all have a bearing on how and when equity can be used as compensation. The cases discussed in chapter 15 offer some insight into how these areas of the law interact with technical equity compensation issues.

Chapter 2

Tax Treatment of Nonstatutory Stock Options

Contents

Section 83 of the Code governs the tax treatment of property transferred in connection with services (as opposed to the payment of cash for services). For these purposes, the NSO transaction is no different than any other form of service-related property transfer: the service recipient (the company) receives services from the service provider (the employee, director, or contractor) in exchange for payment with property (in this case stock, but it also could be any other form of real or personal property). This chapter discusses the ways in which the general rule of Section 83 applies to NSOs.

2.1   Grant and Exercise Price

Who can receive grants? NSOs may be granted not only to employees, but also to outside directors and independent contractors who are not employees of the company. NSOs may be granted under an employee stock option plan or under a separate contract outside of a plan. In each case, the grant and exercise of NSOs will be subject to applicable securities laws (including blue sky laws). In privately held companies, NSOs granted outside of a plan are not eligible for state or federal securities law exemptions for sales made under an employee plan. Separate exemptions will need to be relied upon for such grants.[1] In publicly held companies, federal securities laws may apply to limit the exercise of options by public company "insiders" under Section 16(b) of the Securities Exchange Act of 1934, as further described in section 2.3 of this chapter.

What constitutes an appropriate exercise price? The federal income tax laws impose no statutory limit when it comes to setting the exercise price of an NSO. They may be granted at fair market value, at a premium over fair market value, or at a discount to fair market value without triggering a tax event at *grant*.[2] However, Section 409A of the Code provides a serious disincentive to granting NSOs at a discount by imposing steep taxes and penalties on the recipients of such options at vesting if the time of exercise is not fixed at the date of grant, as described below. Note, too, that there may be other limitations on setting the exercise price: for example, in a private company, state corporate and/or securities laws may place a limit on the NSO discount.

2.2   General Tax Rule

An individual service provider who has been granted an NSO will be subject to income tax only at the time the option is *exercised*, unless Section 409A of the Code applies (and other conditions are not met) or the option is exercised before it becomes vested (see below). The amount taxed will be the spread between the exercise price and the fair market value of the stock at time of exercise. As a general rule, the

---

1.   See, e.g., "the accredited investor" exemption in Section 4(6) of the 1933 Act; California Commissioner's Rules 25102(f) (personal knowledge exemption).

2.   Note, however, that if the exercise price is too deeply discounted, the IRS has indicated the grant could be considered to be an outright grant of stock and taxed at grant or vesting. In this case, the exercise price is not considered a barrier to stock ownership.

company will be entitled to take a tax deduction in an amount equal to the amount included in income by the optionee.[3]

For the optionee, any appreciation in the stock's fair market value between the exercise date and the sale of the shares acquired upon exercise will be treated as capital gain, which will be long-term if the shares are held for more than one year or short-term if the shares are held for one year or less. If the stock price drops between exercise and sale, the result will be a capital loss. The holding period for capital gain or loss purposes generally begins at the date of exercise (with the narrow exception of stock acquired one-for-one in a stock swap, described in chapter 7).

An exception to the general rule occurs when the NSO has a "readily ascertainable fair market value," as determined under Treas. Reg. § 1.83-7. In such rare cases, the option may be taxed on the date of grant. Ordinarily, an NSO will not have a readily ascertainable fair market value unless the option itself is publicly traded on an established securities market.

2.3 Application of Section 83 of the Code

As described above, the spread on exercise of an NSO represents compensation income to the optionee and accordingly is subject to the special rules of Section 83(a) of the Code that govern the timing of income inclusion for tax purposes. Under Section 83(a), the value of property (in this case, stock) received for services must be included in income in the year the optionee's rights to the property become "vested." Section 83(c) provides that vesting occurs at the first time an optionee's rights in the property are (1) transferable or (2) not subject to a "substantial risk of forfeiture." When a vested NSO is exercised, the property (in this case the stock acquired on exercise) is vested and is not subject to a substantial risk of forfeiture. Thus the optionee is taxed on the exercise of the NSO.

For these purposes, a substantial risk of forfeiture exists when the transfer of property (1) is conditioned on the performance or non-performance of substantial services in the future, or (2) is subject to a condition related to a purpose of the transfer and there is a substantial possibility of forfeiture if the condition is not satisfied. As a general rule,

---

3.   Section 83(h) of the Code; Treas. Reg. § 1.83-6(a).

the determination of whether a condition constitutes a substantial risk of forfeiture is based on the relevant facts and circumstances. However, under the regulations to Section 83(c) of the Code, a substantial risk of forfeiture exists if: (1) there is an expectation of regular and time-consuming future services; (2) the transfer of stock to an underwriter is conditioned on the successful completion of a public offering; or (3) return will be required if earnings of the company do not meet certain milestones.

A requirement for repurchase at fair market value, the risk that the value of the property will decline over a period of time, and nonlapse restrictions do *not* by themselves mean an award is subject to a substantial risk of forfeiture. Examples of conditions that *do not* create a substantial risk of forfeiture are: (1) a request for services in the future that may be declined by the employee; (2) a requirement that property be returned if the employee commits a crime (a clawback); (3) a covenant not to compete when there is little likelihood that it will need to be invoked or that it will be enforced; and (4) a requirement of future consulting services by a retired employee that is likely to be neither enforced nor fulfilled.[4]

Furthermore, with one important exception, "insider trading" restrictions that limit transferability after exercise do not constitute a substantial risk of forfeiture for these purposes. In Rev. Rul. 2005-48, the IRS ruled that a post-exercise lockup period that took effect eight months after grant did not present a substantial risk of forfeiture, notwithstanding the limitations imposed on the optionee by the company's insider trading policy. Under final regulations to Section 83 that were published in March 2014, the IRS further clarified that neither the potential that a company might claw back stock or options under some circumstances nor insider trading restrictions constitute a substantial risk of forfeiture.

A substantial risk of forfeiture does exist, however, for public company officers, directors, or more-than-10% shareholders within six months of grant, provided that the option grant and any exercise that occurs within those six months are subject to Section 16(b) of the Securities Exchange Act of 1934. Under Section 83(c)(3) of the Code, stock is considered to be restricted if its beneficial owner could be subject to suit upon sale of the stock under Section 16(b) of the Securities Exchange Act of 1934 and is not otherwise exempt. As described in

---

4.   Treas. Reg. § 1.83-3(c)(2).

chapter 8, the Exchange Act provides a six-month short-swing profits period during which time any insider who sells and purchases shares must disgorge any profit to the company. The insider is subject to suit by the company for any profit realized during the six-month period. Treas. Reg. § 1.83-3(j)(1) provides that, for purposes of Section 83(a), the Section 16(b) restriction lapse at the earliest of: (1) the end of the Section 16(b) six-month period, or (2) the first day that sale at a profit will not subject the holder to suit.[5]

2.4 Section 83(b) Election

Some companies allow optionees to exercise unvested NSOs. In such cases, the company retains a right to repurchase the shares for the lower of the option exercise price or the stock's fair market value at the time of repurchase until the stock becomes vested. When full vesting does not occur in the year of exercise, tax is deferred until the restrictions lapse. This means that if the value of the stock appreciates between the date of exercise and date of vesting, the optionee will be subject to tax on a greater spread than the spread at the date of exercise. The tax (and in the case of an employee, the associated withholding) will be due regardless of whether the optionee sells or otherwise disposes of the stock in order to finance the liability.

To avoid an unknown future tax event, an optionee who exercises unvested options may wish to file an election under Section 83(b) of the Code, which allows the optionee to "freeze" the compensation element of the spread (if any) on exercise and pay tax in the year of exercise as if the stock were already vested. If the election is filed timely, there will be no tax consequences as the stock vests. In other words, filing the election avoids ordinary income tax on any appreciation between the date of exercise and the date of vesting but does not avoid ordinary income tax on the excess of fair market value on the date of exercise over the exercise price. Exhibit 2-1 gives an example of taxation with and without a Section 83(b) election.

The drawback to a Section 83(b) election occurs if the stock is forfeited or depreciates in value after exercise of the option. In that

---

5. See also *Tanner v. Comm'r*, 117 T.C. 2001 (construing 16(b) restriction period for purposes of Section 83(c)(3)).

Exhibit 2-1. Understanding Vesting Restrictions

Assumptions
Stock price at grant: $1
Fair market value (FMV) at time of exercise: $1
Number of shares: 1,000
Total purchase price = $1,000
Vesting schedule: 5 years, 20% per year

Tax Consequences:
Without 83(b) election:
All options exercised on vesting date

Vesting date	FMV at vesting	Spread	Income
Year 1	$ 2.50	$ 1.50	$ 300
Year 2	5.00	4.00	800
Year 3	10.00	9.00	1,800
Year 4	20.00	19.00	3,800
Year 5	30.00	29.00	5,800

Total income taxed as compensation: $12,500
At the time of sale, the tax basis is $13,500, and any additional gain recognized on the sale is capital gain.

With 83(b) election:
All options exercised within 30 days of grant date

Purchase price	FMV at exercise	Spread	Income
$1	$1	-0-	-0-

Total income taxed as compensation: 0

At the time of sale, the tax basis is $1,000, and any additional gain recognized on the sale is capital gain.

---

case, the optionee may be in the unenviable position of having paid unnecessary tax on income with no available refund or capital loss treatment.

To make a Section 83(b) election, the optionee must file an election with the IRS office where he or she files his or her income tax return within 30 days of exercise. The optionee should also provide the company with a copy of the election so that tax withholding can be handled correctly.

Until 2016, taxpayers were required to attach copies of the election to their tax returns,[6] which effectively prevented them from filing their taxes electronically. In 2016, the IRS finalized regulations eliminating the requirement entirely for property transferred on or after January 1, 2016.[7]

The role of the company in filing the election should be carefully described in the materials given to the optionee, and it should be limited to administrative assistance only. Companies should take care to avoid assuming legal responsibility, and potential liability, for a Section 83(b) election. The ultimate responsibility for timely filing the election should remain with the individual optionee.[8]

Optionees must be advised to consult with their own tax advisors at the time of exercise of an unvested NSO to determine whether it is appropriate to file an election under Section 83(b). Failure to timely file cannot be corrected once the 30-day period has passed.

A Section 83(b) election may be revoked after the end of the 30-day period only if it was filed as a result of a genuine mistake of fact regarding the underlying transaction.[9] To do so, the taxpayer must file a formal request for a letter ruling[10] within 60 days of discovering the mistake. The reason for the request, the date the mistake first became known to the requester, and a copy of the election must be included. If the request is being made on or before the due date for the election, this should be noted.

The "mistake of fact" exception to the 30-day election period under Section 83(b) is very narrow indeed. A lack of understanding about tax consequences, risks of forfeitures, or other legal or contractual issues involved is insufficient. Mistakes about the value of the award or "the

---

6. Treas. Reg. § 1.83-2. There is no specific form for filing a Section 83(b) election, but the IRS did provide sample language in Rev. Proc. 2012-19.

7. Treas. Reg. § 1.83-2(c). Taxpayers had been allowed to rely on the proposed regulation for property transferred on or after January 1, 2015.

8. Notwithstanding the foregoing, the IRS Chief Counsel's office has approved the use of a consent form giving power of attorney to the employer for the purpose of filing the 83(b) election on behalf of an employee. *See* CCA 200203018 (January 18, 2002).

9. Rev. Proc. 2006-31.

10. Pursuant to Rev. Rul. 2006, 2006-1 IRB 1.

failure of anyone to perform an act that was contemplated at the time of transfer" are acceptable grounds for revocation. The mistake has to be based on "unconscious ignorance" of a fact material to the transaction. In Rev. Proc. 2006-31, the IRS provides an example in which an employee is issued restricted shares and files an election. He realizes after the end of the 30-day period that the company has two classes of stock and that the company has transferred the wrong kind of shares to him. So long as he files for a private letter ruling approving the revocation of the election with 60 days of first learning of this mistake, this request may be granted.

2.5   Application of Section 409A of the Code

Most NSOs are designed to be exempt from Code Section 409A. However, if the option's exercise price is less than the grant date fair market value, the award will be considered "deferred compensation" under Section 409A of the Code.[11] As such, the optionee (1) will be taxed at the time of vesting, *regardless of whether the award has been exercised;* and (2) will be subject to a 20% penalty tax in addition to ordinary income taxes at that time, unless certain other requirements of Section 409A are met on the date of grant. The IRS has stated that any technique that serves to provide a discount, including paying dividend equivalent rights upon exercise, will bring the grant into the scope of Section 409A.[12] Such rights may, however, be offered separately from the stock option award itself with proper planning.

The concept of "fair market value" is a tricky one, made even more so by the enactment of Section 409A. The regulations to Section 409A require that in order to support the position that a grant has been made at fair market value, privately held companies must either follow one of three specific safe harbor valuation methods or demonstrate that the valuation method actually used was reasonable. Depending on the stage of a company's lifecycle, the safe harbor could include using an independent appraiser, providing an in-house written valuation that satisfies certain specified criteria, or working with a non-lapse restric-

---

11.   Section 409A(d)(1) and Treas. Reg. § 1.409A-1(b)(5).

12.   Treas. Reg. § 1.409A-1(b)(5)(i)(D), (E).

tion based on a formula price. The IRS will respect a valuation based on a safe harbor unless the issuer's reliance is "grossly unreasonable."

A company that chooses not to use a safe harbor method must be prepared to show that its valuation is reasonable and made reference to the valuation factors set out in Section 409A, and there is no assurance that the IRS will agree that the method is reasonable for these purposes.[13] The burden of proving for tax purposes that a valuation does indeed represent fair market value lies squarely on the issuer if the safe harbors are not used.[14]

Given the severity of the penalties assessable under Section 409A, it's safe to say that few privately held companies will want to take chances with an unapproved valuation method and even fewer privately held or publicly held companies will wish to purposely grant discounted NSOs. For a more extensive discussion of the impact of Section 409A on options, see chapter 9.

2.6   Employer Deduction

Section 83(h) of the Code provides that a company is allowed to take a deduction for amounts included in income by a service provider in the taxable year in which the service provider's inclusion occurs or with which ends the taxable year of the service provider's inclusion. The amount included in income is generally the amount reported on the service provider's income tax return.[15] However, under the "deemed inclusion" rule, if the employer timely files a Form W-2 for an employee or Form 1099-MISC for a nonemployee, it need not show that the optionee actually included the spread in income in order to take the deduction.[16] For purposes of stock options, this means that an employer may take

---

13. Please note that the valuation methods in Section 409A are different from—and are used for a different purpose than—the "fair value" models required by ASC 718 for accounting purposes. See chapter 10.

14. Treas. Reg. § 1.409A-1(b)(5)(iv)(B).

15. Treas. Reg. § 1.83-6 (a)(1).

16. Treas. Reg. § 1.83-6 (a)(2).

a deduction for the spread on exercise so long as it timely reports the amount included in income by the optionee.[17]

Where a company merges with another or is acquired during the life of the option, the allocation of the deduction depends on the form of the acquisition. If the target survives the acquisition (e.g., as a wholly owned subsidiary), then only the target may take the deduction. However, if the acquisition is in the form of a merger in which the target is liquidated and the acquirer survives, then the acquirer is entitled to the deduction.[18]

In any case, under the regulations to Section 83(h), the employer deduction is predicated on meeting the reporting requirements and not on withholding, even when withholding is required under Section 3402 of the Code. However, note that compliance with Section 83(h) (including the deemed inclusion rule) will neither relieve the employer of any applicable payroll withholding requirements otherwise imposed with respect to the spread nor relieve it of penalties or additions to tax associated with failure to properly withhold. For more on NSO reporting and withholding, see chapter 9.

Beginning with transactions occurring in 2014, brokers will be required to give optionees a Form 1099-B reporting a cost basis equal to the amount paid for the stock when they exercise NSOs. This is discussed in further detail in chapter 9.

2.7   Accounting Treatment

Under Accounting Standards Codification Topic 718 (ASC 718), NSOs granted to employees at fair market value must be reported as an expense on companies' income statements. All NSOs must be valued using an option-pricing model; if the option is granted at a discount, the company must use a valuation model to estimate the value of the option, including the discount, expensed over the expected life of the award. See chapter 10 for a broader discussion of stock option accounting.

---

17. Note that such reporting will include compliance with the requirements set out in Sections 6041 and 6041A of the Code, as applicable.

18. Rev. Rul. 2003-98, 2003-34 IRB 378 (Aug. 25, 2003).

Chapter 3

Tax Treatment of Incentive Stock Options

Contents

Congress created the incentive stock option (ISO) in the Economic Recovery Tax Act of 1981. ISOs were intended to serve as a tax-advantaged investment vehicle for employees, with special benefits if a current employee committed to the investment in his employer for a combined holding period (the "statutory holding period") of (1) at least one year from the date of exercise *and* (2) at least two years from the date of grant. As a general rule, if an ISO satisfies all of the statutory requirements outlined below, the tax deferral benefit of ISO treatment remains the same today as it was in 1981. However, the rules governing the tax treatment of ISOs underwent numerous reviews and revisions between their inception and the most recent revisions, which became effective in 2006 (the effective date of final regulations issued in 2004).

3.1   Statutory Requirements for ISOs

ISOs are governed by the specific requirements prescribed in Section 422 of the Code and the general requirements for statutory options set out in Sections 421 and 424 of the Code. As a prerequisite to granting ISOs, the employer must have a written option plan that:

- sets forth the maximum number of shares that may be issued under options,
- identifies the employees (or class of employees) eligible to receive options, and
- is approved by the shareholders of the company within 12 months before or after the plan's adoption by the company's board of directors.

Assuming that the plan satisfies these requirements, the option grant also must conform to a number of statutory prerequisites under Section 422(b), including:

1. The option exercise price must be no less than the fair market value of the shares (as determined by the board of directors in good faith) on the date of grant.[1]

2. The option must be granted within 10 years after the earlier of the plan's adoption by the board or its approval by shareholders.

3. The option, by its terms, cannot be exercisable for a period longer than 10 years after the date of grant.

4. The option may be granted only to a person who is an employee of the company (or its parent or subsidiary) on the date of grant. For

---

1.   For a complete discussion of fair market value in the ISO context, see section 3.2.5 of this chapter.

this purpose, and that of all statutory options, "employee" is defined with reference to the common-law definition of employee as used for purposes of wage withholding under Section 3402 of the Code.[2]

5. The option must be exercised by the employee no later than three months after termination of employment except in cases of Code Section 22(e) disability, after which an ISO can be exercised for up to one year, or of death, for which the only statutory time limit for exercise by the estate is the option's original expiration date. Regardless of the reason for termination, the option term remains subject to the above-stated requirement that the option cannot be exercisable for a period longer than 10 years after the date of grant.

6. The option, by its terms, cannot be transferable (other than by will or laws of descent). During the employee's lifetime it can be exercised only by the employee.

7. If an option is granted to a more-than-10% shareholder of the company, its parent, or subsidiary, the exercise price can be no less than 110% of fair market value at the date of grant, and the option cannot be exercised for a period longer than five years after the date of grant.

Section 422(c)(4)(C) of the Code states that an option meeting the requirements of Section 422(b) shall be treated as an ISO if it is subject to any additional conditions, so long as such conditions are not inconsistent with the provisions of Section 422(b). Frequently, conditions include a right of the company to repurchase option shares upon termination of employment, or a right of first refusal to repurchase vested shares if the optionee proposes to transfer the shares to a third party. Other examples of permissible provisions include the right of an employee to pay the exercise price by executing a promissory note or with stock of the granting corporation.

The definition of "stock" includes capital stock of any class and with any combination of voting rights or no voting rights. Preferred stock and special classes of stock authorized only to be issued to employees also qualify (tracking stock in a division issued just to employees, for

---

2. Treas. Reg. § 1.421-1(h). See also IRS Notice 87-41, 1987-1 CB 296 (the "20-factor test").

instance, would presumably be an example of this), provided that this stock has the same rights and characteristics of capital stock.

The definition of an option includes warrants if they meet other requirements of the regulations. Warrants, like options, are financial instruments allowing the purchaser to buy shares at a fixed price for a defined period of time. Warrants are generally issued as investment vehicles, and rarely have compensation as their primary purpose; as such, they also usually carry a price at grant or purchase greater than fair market value. However, if a warrant otherwise meets the rules for an incentive option, the regulations allow it to be treated as an option for ISO purposes.

3.2   Analysis of Statutory Requirements

To qualify as an ISO plan, a stock option plan must contain certain terms and conditions prescribed by Section 422 of the Code, and must be adopted by the company's board of directors and approved by the shareholders within 12 months before or after such adoption. The plan must be in writing, which includes electronic format, provided such format meets prescribed regulatory requirements.[3]

The plan must state the maximum number of shares that can be issued under it as ISOs, even if it is a broad omnibus plan that allows for the issuance of several kinds of equity compensation, and must specify which classes of employees are eligible for option grants under it. If the plan is a broad equity compensation plan that allows for grants to nonemployees, then the class or classes of employees eligible for ISOs must be stated separately.[4]

Code Section 422(b)(1) requires that companies provide shareholders with information about the total number of shares subject to option under an ISO plan. The regulations clarify that this requirement applies for purposes of ISOs only. Companies may meet the requirement in a variety of ways, including by providing: (1) a specific number of shares

---

3.   Treas. Reg. § 1.422-2(b).

4.   Treas. Reg. § 1.422-2(b)(4). If the plan otherwise meets the requirements of Section 422, it may be structured in any way that is not inconsistent with the Code. See, e.g., PLR. 200513012 (ISO plan with ESPP-type structure still qualifies).

that can be granted as ISOs; (2) a percentage of shares outstanding at the date of adoption; or (3) a fixed number of shares increased relative to the number of shares outstanding at adoption based on a defined ratio. Note that for purposes of share counting, if outstanding shares are used to exercise an option, only the net number of shares issued to the optionee after the exercise is subtracted from the maximum number of shares available under the plan.

3.2.1   ISO Plan Must Be Properly Adopted

Shareholder approval must be by a method that would be treated as adequate under applicable state law in the case of an action requiring shareholder approval for the issuance of corporate stock or options. If state law does not prescribe a method and degree of shareholder approval for such issuances, then the plan must be approved by either (1) a majority of the votes cast at a duly held shareholder meeting at which a quorum is present either in person or by proxy, or (2) a method, and in a degree, that would be treated as adequate under state law for an action requiring shareholder approval (for example, unanimous written consent).[5]

An ISO plan adopted by the board of directors "subject to shareholder approval" *will be adopted on the date the plan is approved by shareholders.* If the board of directors stipulates a condition for adoption, the deemed adoption date is when that condition is satisfied.[6] Although the regulations do not specifically state that ISO grants made before shareholder approval will *never* be valid, it is best practice to obtain shareholder approval prior to the grant of any option subject to a stock plan.

In a corporate consolidation, the requirement for shareholder approval of the plan will be satisfied if the merger agreement fully describes the assumption of the plan. Separate shareholder approval is not required for assumption or substitution of statutory options in connection with a merger if such options were already granted under an approved plan.

---

5.   Treas. Reg. § 1.422-3. Note that this rule does not apply to Section 423 ESPPs.
6.   Treas. Reg. § 1.422-2(b)(2).

3.2.2   Amendment of ISO Plan Must Be Properly Approved

Changes to the number of shares authorized for issuance under an ISO plan or to the class of employees eligible to receive ISOs under the plan are treated as the equivalent of adopting a new plan, and thus must be approved by the board of directors *and* the shareholders of the company in accordance with Section 422(b)(1) of the Code. Under the Code, changes to an ISO plan that do not affect the number of shares available for issuance under option or the class of employees eligible to participate may be approved by the board of directors alone.[7] However, note that in publicly traded companies, a broader range of changes to a plan may be subject to shareholder approval under the listing require-ments of the exchange on which the company's stock is traded. For more details, see section 4.3

Shareholder approval will be required when there are changes to the shares to which the option applies, including changes related to the issuer. For instance, if a plan provides that a subsidiary's employees will receive statutory options in the subsidiary, and it is subsequently amended to permit grants from the parent, shareholder approval will be required within 12 months of the amendment. As noted above, ad-ditional shareholder approval is not required for validly granted ISOs assumed in a corporate transaction.

3.2.3   Options Must Be Granted Properly

The definition of "corporation" for ISO purposes includes not just C corporations but also any entity choosing to be taxed as a corporation under federal income tax rules, including S corporations, foreign corpo-rations, and limited liability corporations (LLCs). Corporations electing to be taxed as partnerships, including LLCs, limited liability partner-ships, and limited partnerships, are not considered to be corporations for these purposes. This definition makes it clear, for instance, that an employee of an LLC *taxed as a corporation* can receive ISOs.

ISOs (and all other stock options of the company) can be granted only by the board of directors or by an authorized subcommittee of the board. Options should be granted by formal board resolution,

---

7.   Treas. Reg. § 1.422-2(b)(1)(iii).

either at meetings or by written consent. This must be done pursuant to governance requirements that vary from state to state. For example, Delaware corporate law allows the board to delegate to an officer the authority to grant stock options pursuant to an option plan.[8] California corporate law, on the other hand, does not permit such delegation.

An option is generally deemed to have been granted on the date on which the board of directors or an authorized board subcommittee resolves to grant it. The regulations provide that the option will be considered to be granted *for tax purposes* in accordance with the intention of the corporation, even if there are "conditions" on the grant. Conditions that do not prevent a grant from being effective for tax purposes on the date of grant include shareholder approval of the plan and government approval or registration requirements.[9] (It is important to remember that this regulation governs for tax purposes (i.e., ISO purposes) only, and prior shareholder approval may nonetheless be necessary to establish a grant date for accounting and securities law purposes.) *At the time of grant,* all of the elements prescribed by Section 422 of the Code must be present or the ISO will be treated as an NSO.

3.2.4   ISOs Are Only for Employees

Unlike NSOs, ISOs can be granted only to persons who are employees rendering services to the company or who are employees of a "parent" or "subsidiary" corporation as such terms are defined in Section 424(f) of the Code. "Employee" is defined by reference to the common-law definition of employee as it applies for purposes of withholding under Section 3402 of the Code. Thus, ISOs generally cannot be granted to persons who serve as independent contractors, consultants, or outside directors to the company since they are not employees. A question that frequently arises is whether ISOs may be granted to employees of a corporate entity in which the granting corporation has a "joint venture" interest. The Code is clear on this point: unless the corporation's stake is at least 50% (i.e., the joint venture satisfies the statutory definition

---

8.   See Delaware General Corporation Law, Section 157 (as amended, July 1, 2001).

9.   Treas. Reg. § 1.421-1(c)(2).

of subsidiary), the joint venture employees are not eligible to receive ISOs under the granting corporation's plan.[10]

In addition, to receive ISO tax treatment, the optionee must be an employee of the company at the time of exercise or have terminated employment with the company no more than three months before the date of exercise (or 12 months in the case of a person whose employment was terminated by permanent and total disability within the meaning of Section 22(e) of the Code). In the case of a leave of absence, the regulations provide that for ISO purposes the employment relationship will terminate after three months of leave unless the individual has the right to continued employment with the company under either contract or statute (e.g., the Family and Medical Leave Act or Uniformed Services Employment and Reemployment Rights Act of 1994). Accordingly, persons whose employment with the company is terminated will be able to exercise ISOs only for a limited period of time.[11] If the employee dies, the Code places no time limit on exercise by the estate other than the option's existing expiration date. Note that these are statutory maximums. The company granting the option is free to set more restrictive limits on post-termination exercise, so long as it is not subject to other statutory limitations such as state corporate or securities law limits. For example, the California rules state that when termination occurs other than for cause, an optionee must have a minimum of 30 days (and, in the case of death or disability, a minimum of six months) within which to exercise an option post-termination.[12]

In the case of an assumption or substitution of an ISO pursuant to a corporate transaction, both current employees and former employees who are still within the three-month post-termination exercise period will qualify to receive ISOs in connection with the transaction. Optionees on leave pursuant to a statute or contract that provides for continuing rights of re-employment also continue to be considered employees for these purposes.

---

10. Section 424(f) of the Code; Treas. Reg. § 1.424-1(f)(2).

11. Section 421(b) of the Code (employment requirement); Treas. Reg. § 1.4211(h) (2) (leave of absence).

12. Rule 260.140.42(g) under the California Corporate Securities Law of 1968.

3.2.5   Option Exercise Price for ISOs

The concept of "fair market value" is very important for ISO purposes under Section 422, just as it is for NSO purposes under Section 409A.[13] To qualify as an ISO, an option cannot be granted at an exercise price lower than the fair market value of the optioned stock on the date the option is granted (without regard to any restrictions on the stock that will expire at some future time).[14] Further, an employee who owns stock possessing more than 10% of the total combined voting power of all classes of stock of the company (or of any parent or subsidiary of the company) cannot be granted an ISO at an exercise price less than 110% of the fair market value of the underlying stock on the date the option is granted.

The regulations to Section 421 of the Code state that "any reasonable valuation" (including the valuation methods permitted under the estate tax regulations) may be used to determine the fair market value of a statutory option.[15] Regardless of the valuation method used, fair market value must be determined without regard to any restriction other than a restriction that, by its terms, will never lapse.[16] In other words, vesting requirements in and of themselves do not factor into fair market value.

The importance of pricing the option at the grant date fair market value was highlighted in 2006 and 2007 as numerous companies came under investigation for possibly having "backdated" their stock options—meaning set the exercise price at an earlier date's fair market value. Optionees who were told they had received ISOs, but whose grants were backdated, in fact held discounted NSOs. Such grant timing issues are discussed in detail in chapter 4.

Setting fair market value is the responsibility of the board of directors, and there is no definitive rule as to the proper means of determining the fair market value of stock that is not publicly traded. The stakes are high because setting fair market value too low could result in an ISO being treated as an NSO, which in turn could mean penalties for both employer and employee for failure to withhold and pay over taxes at

---

13. See chapter 2.

14. Section 422(b)(4) of the Code.

15. Treas. Reg. § 1.421-1(e)(2); Treas. Reg. § 1.422-2(e)(1).

16. Section 422 (c)(7).

the time of exercise and a tax liability for the optionee under Code Section 409A. Section 422(c)(1) of the Code addresses this problem by providing a safe harbor: if the board makes *a good-faith attempt* to set a valuation at the time of grant, that valuation will be treated as fair market value for ISO purposes even if such value is subsequently challenged by the IRS.[17]

In this context, what constitutes a good-faith attempt? When stock is publicly traded, valuation based on a method using market quotations will be presumed to be in good faith.[18] Shares in privately held companies present a more difficult challenge. In setting the value of such stock, the board of directors should look to the prices at which recent sales of the same or similar classes of stock have been made. An independent appraiser may also provide a good estimate of the stock's value.[19] To this end, a non-public company can successfully establish a good-faith attempt to meet the option price requirements by demonstrating that fair market value was based on an average of the fair market values for a specific grant date as "set forth in the opinions of completely independent and well-qualified experts," under Treas. Reg. § 1.422-2(e)(2)(iii). However, regardless of whether the stock is publicly traded, there will *not* be a good-faith attempt unless the fair market value of the stock on the date of grant is determined both with regard to nonlapse restrictions and without regard to lapse restrictions.[20]

Notwithstanding the flexibility of the "good faith" ISO valuation rules, the cost of making a mistake in pricing is increasingly worrisome

---

17. Section 422(c)(1) also applies to safeguard fair market value calculations for purposes of the $100,000 first-exercisable rule under Section 422(d).

18. Treas. Reg. § 1.4222(e)(3).

19. Valuation problems frequently arise when private companies grant stock options to employees at a time when the company is simultaneously raising capital through the sale of similar stock to outside investors at a considerably higher price. The board should be advised that granting an option at a low price in such a situation might result in the option not qualifying as an ISO, thereby depriving the optionee of ISO tax benefits and subjecting the person to penalties under Section 409A of the Code. This is one of many reasons that a company is advised to sell a different class of stock (i.e., preferred stock) when raising capital from nonemployee third parties.

20. Treas. Reg. § 1.422-2(e)(2)(iv).

to issuers. As a general rule, best practice counsels reliance on the more rigorous Section 409A valuation standard whenever possible.

3.2.6 Limitation on Size of Option

Under Section 422(d) of the Code, an ISO may be first exercisable only as to $100,000 worth of stock in any calendar year, based on the stock's fair market value on the grant date. "First exercisable" is defined to mean the calendar year in which the option can first be exercised, which is normally, but not always, the year of vesting. An ISO will not fail in its entirety simply because it exceeds the $100,000 limitation. Instead, the amount in excess of $100,000 will be automatically treated as an NSO, without any negative effect on the ISO portion of the option. The first share that takes the amount over the $100,000 threshold is disqualified from ISO treatment.

Moreover, there is no limit on the aggregate value of stock that may be subject to an ISO grant. Thus, for example, an employee could receive an ISO for $500,000 worth of stock, as long as the ISO was first exercisable in no more than $100,000 increments annually. Of course, the first exercisable rule does not require that the optionee actually exercise any portion of the ISO in the year it first becomes exercisable. In this example, the employee would be entitled to wait until the entire ISO became exercisable and then exercise for $500,000 worth of stock in one installment. However, note that if the exercise schedule under the option were accelerated at any time during its term, the first exercisable rule would come into play. Continuing the example, assume in year three the option is accelerated to allow exercise of the $100,000 increment originally set to become exercisable in year four. In year three, $200,000 worth of stock is now first exercisable, $100,000 of which qualifies for ISO treatment and $100,000 of which is now treated as an NSO. In year five, the remaining $100,000 worth of stock would still qualify for ISO treatment.

Furthermore, if the $100,000 limit is exceeded because multiple grants vest in a year, then for purposes of determining which options retain their ISO status and which are disqualified, the options are taken in the order in which they were granted, with the earlier grant taking precedence. Options that are not ISOs when issued do not count toward the limit.

If an option is disqualified from ISO treatment by a modification or cancellation before the year in which it would have become exercisable, then it is not considered when calculating the $100,000 limit. But if the modification or cancellation happens any time in the year the option would have become exercisable, the option is counted for purposes of the limit for that year.[21] Disqualifying dispositions, meaning those in which shares are sold before the statutory holding period has elapsed, do not prevent those options from being counted toward the $100,000 limit.

Acceleration of the vesting of an ISO does not disqualify the option, but accelerated options are counted toward the $100,000 limit in the year of acceleration. This can get tricky if a change of control trigger or performance trigger allows exercise if a change of control occurs before vesting or disallows exercise until a performance target is met. If there is such an acceleration provision, then options first exercisable during a calendar year pursuant to an acceleration clause do not affect the application of the $100,000 rule for options exercised before the acceleration provision was triggered. All of these prior options can be exercised, up to the $100,000 limit, even if the accelerated options are exercised in the same year. However, any options from the accelerated group that are in excess of $100,000 minus the fair market value at grant of the previously exercised options that year are disqualified as ISOs and must be treated as NSOs.

Note that Treas. Reg. § 1.422-3(e) states that calculation of fair market value for these purposes may be made by any "reasonable method," including independent appraisals and valuation in accordance with the gift tax rules.[22]

3.2.7   Limitation on Term of Option

Generally, Section 422(b)(3) provides that an ISO may be exercisable for no more than 10 years. However, in the case of an employee who owns stock representing more than 10% of the total voting power of all classes of stock of the company, the term of an ISO is limited to

---

21. Treas. Reg. § 1.422-4(b)(5).

22. See section 3.2.5.

five years under Section 422(c)(6). The company may, of course, grant options with shorter terms than the maximum permitted by the Code.

3.2.8 Payment for Option Shares

ISOs may provide for payment of the exercise price in cash, with a promissory note, with shares of the company's stock, or with other noncash consideration. The form of consideration should be set forth in the stock option plan, the option grant, or in the board resolutions granting the ISO. Any amendment to an ISO to add a permissible form of consideration that was not previously established at the time of grant is a modification to the ISO. See section 3.5 below.

If the board of directors and applicable state corporate law permit an employee to exercise an ISO by payment of a promissory note, the terms of the promissory note must be carefully structured so as to avoid adverse tax consequences to the employee or the company. In nearly all cases, the note should be a full-recourse note bearing interest at a rate governed by Treasury regulations under Sections 483, 1274, and 7872 of the Code. If a nonrecourse note is used, there is a risk that the purchase of the stock will be treated for tax purposes as if it were the grant of an NSO. The result of such treatment is that the employee will recognize ordinary income when he or she pays off the note in an amount equal to the difference between the value of the stock on the date the note is paid and the actual purchase price of the stock. Moreover, if the rate of interest on the note is not high enough to satisfy the regulations, the IRS will impute additional interest for tax purposes. This can result in additional taxable interest income to the company without a corresponding receipt of cash, as well as causing the employee's ISO to be treated as an NSO. Moreover, the creation of a deemed discount option may result in additional unanticipated liability under Section 409A of the Code. Chapter 7 treats these financing issues in more detail.

3.3 Taxation of ISO Stock

The principal federal income tax benefit of an ISO to an optionee is that there will be no income tax at the time of exercise unless the alternative minimum tax rules apply, as discussed in section 3.4 below. Further, no payroll tax withholding of any kind is required upon the exercise of an ISO. Exercise does, however, trigger reporting under Code Section 6039, as described in section 9.3.

The sale of ISO shares held for the statutory holding period is called a "qualifying disposition," under Section 421 of the Code. In a qualifying disposition the entire gain or loss ultimately realized upon the sale is treated as long-term capital gain or loss rather than as ordinary income. Such gain or loss is equal to the difference between the amount received in the qualifying disposition and the amount paid upon exercise of the ISO. If the optionee realizes a loss on the disposition, the optionee's basis in the ISO shares is adjusted and a capital loss is taken, as necessary. Exhibit 3-1 illustrates the tax consequences to the optionee of exercising an ISO and holding the ISO shares for the statutory holding period.

Exhibit 3-1. Comparison of ISOs Versus NSOs: Consequences to Optionee

Assumptions:
Option price: $1
Fair market value at exercise: $5
Sale price: $10
All options are vested at time of exercise

	NSO	ISO
Include in income:		
At exercise	$4 ordinary income New "adjusted basis" in stock equals option price plus spread = $5 Subject to withholding	$0*
At sale	$5 capital gains (Difference between sale price and adjusted basis: $10 – $5 = $5)	$9 Qualifying disposition: $9 long-term capital gains Disqualifying disposition: $4 ordinary income $5 capital gains

*Possible tax preference item for AMT purposes, but no ordinary income or capital gain or loss.

ISO shares sold before the end of the statutory holding period are said to be sold in a "disqualifying disposition" under Section 421 of the Code. A disqualifying disposition literally disqualifies the option from beneficial ISO tax treatment and instead causes the option to be treated similarly to an NSO. The optionee will be required to include the spread on exercise in ordinary income in the year of sale, and any subsequent appreciation in value between the exercise and disposition of the shares will be characterized as capital gain. However, the tax treatment of the disqualified shares differs from NSO tax treatment in three important respects:

1. *Timing of income recognition:* If the option were an NSO, the ordinary income tax would in most cases be due for the year of exercise; however, since exercise timing isn't a factor in determining whether a disqualifying disposition has occurred, the income tax liability upon a disqualifying disposition of an ISO occurs in the year in which the shares are sold.

2. *Applicability of payroll taxes:* ISO shares are exempt from FICA and FUTA taxes regardless of whether they are disposed of in a qualifying or disqualifying disposition.

3. *Amount of income recognized:* Section 422(c)(2) limits the recognition of gain on disposition of ISO shares to the shareholder's *actual gain.* Accordingly, in the case of a disqualifying disposition:

    - If the share price drops between the exercise date and the sale date, but still exceeds the exercise price, then the profit on the sale (i.e., difference between the sale price and the exercise price) is treated as ordinary income.

    - If the share price drops below the exercise price, then the difference between the exercise price and the sale price is treated as a capital loss. No ordinary income is reported. Exhibit 3-2 illustrates both of these outcomes.

    Note that this limitation rule does not apply if the disposition is a sale or exchange with respect to which a loss (if sustained) would not be recognized by the individual, for example in a "wash sale" under Section 1091 of the Code, a gift or other non-arm's length transaction, or a sale between related persons.[23]

Furthermore, in one important respect—the ability to file an 83(b) election—ISOs exercised for unvested stock are not treated as NSOs upon a disqualifying disposition. This means that if an ISO is "early exercised"—i.e., exercised prior to vesting—and subsequently disquali-

---

23. Treas. Reg. § 1.422-1(b)(2)(ii).

fied, the optionee will recognize the ordinary income that would otherwise have been recognized at vesting under Section 83.[24] The Section 83(b) election will, however, affect the alternative minimum tax (AMT) calculation discussed in section 3.4 below.

Upon a disqualifying disposition, the employer is entitled to a compensation deduction in the amount of the spread included in the optionee's income.[25] The company is not required to withhold on a disqualifying disposition of an ISO in order to qualify for the deduction. Exhibit 3-1 illustrates the tax consequences of a disqualifying disposition. Note that brokerage fees cannot be deducted from the reportable spread.

Exhibit 3-2. Comparison: ISO Taxation with Volatile Stock Prices

Assumptions:
Option price: $5
FMV at exercise: $10
Spread at exercise: $5 ($10 - $5)

	Qualifying disposition		Disqualifying disposition	
Sale prices	$8	$4	$8	$4
Taxable amount:				
Upon exercise*	$0	$0	$0	$0
Upon sale:				
Ordinary income	$0	$0	$3	$0
Capital gain or loss	$3 capital gain	$1 capital loss	$0	$1 capital loss

*Possible tax preference item for AMT purposes, but no ordinary income or capital gain or loss.

3.4 Alternative Minimum Tax Issues

The spread on exercise of an ISO is subject to alternative minimum tax (AMT) in the year of exercise unless the stock is sold in the same calendar year. Although the specific application of the AMT is too complex to summarize here, generally AMT is exactly what its name suggests: an alternative to the regular tax system. AMT is imposed on alternative minimum taxable income (AMTI) as computed under Sections 56

---

24. See section 2.3.
25. Treas. Reg. § 1.83-6(a)(2).

through 58 of the Code.[26] To arrive at AMTI, the taxpayer computes regular taxable income (as defined in Section 55(c) of the Code) and then adjusts that amount by any adjustments or "tax preference items" (i.e., items that reflect certain deductions and tax deferral benefits allowed under the regular tax system) taken in the taxable year. The spread on exercise of an ISO is treated as a tax preference item.

Under Section 55 of the Code, AMT is computed on the amount of AMTI in excess of the applicable exemption amount ($82,100 for married taxpayers filing jointly and $52,800 for single taxpayers in 2014).[27] If the AMT exceeds the taxpayer's regular tax in a given year, the taxpayer must pay the AMT amount rather than the regular tax amount. The difference between AMT and regular tax in any year is allowable as a credit against regular tax in future years when no AMT is due pursuant to Section 53 of the Code. Thus, for taxpayers who are not regularly subject to AMT, the payment essentially serves as a prepayment of regular tax and accordingly offsets any deferral benefit that the taxpayer would otherwise enjoy in a year when AMT exceeds regular tax.

3.4.1 Effect of AMT on ISOs

Section 56(b)(3) of the Code (relating to adjustments applicable to individuals in computing AMTI) states the following:

> (3) Treatment of incentive stock options—Section 421 shall not apply to the transfer of stock acquired pursuant to the exercise of an incentive stock option (as defined in section 422). Section 422(c)(2) shall apply in any case where the disposition and the inclusion for purposes of this part are within the same taxable year and such section shall not apply in any other case. The adjusted basis of any stock so acquired shall be determined on the basis of the treatment prescribed by this paragraph.

Under this special provision, an ISO is not considered to be a statutory option (accorded special treatment under Section 421 of the Code)

---

26. The relevant statutory provisions are found in Sections 53 through 59 of the Code.

27. AMT rates are constantly changing. For 2016, the rate was generally 26% of the first $186,300 of AMTI in excess of the exemption for married people filing jointly and 28% above that amount. Special rules also apply to limit the maximum capital gains rate to 28%. However, the exemption amount is reduced as income goes up.

for AMT purposes. The effect of this language is to treat ISOs for AMT purposes as though they were NSOs subject to the rules of Section 83 of the Code. Accordingly, as further discussed below, employees who exercise ISOs that are not fully vested at the time of exercise should be advised regarding whether to file a Section 83(b) election for AMT.

3.4.2 Effect of Disqualifying Dispositions on AMT

A disqualifying disposition of an ISO has no effect on the optionee's AMT liability unless the liability arises in the same calendar year as the disqualifying disposition. In other words, if the taxpayer makes a disqualifying disposition in the same calendar year as exercise, the AMT liability will be canceled.

Before 2006, some optionees had begun to take advantage of the fact that in a declining market, a disqualifying disposition could offer a better tax benefit than holding for the full statutory holding period: e.g., if the spread on exercise was $100 and the gain on sale was only $50, it might be better to sell and pay tax on $50 than hold and pay AMT on $100. They would sell in a disqualifying disposition, pay ordinary income tax on the gain, and then buy similar stock on the open market shortly thereafter. The new regulations clarified that this transaction qualifies as a "wash sale" under Section 1091 of the Code. Accordingly, if the sale and purchase occur within 30 days of each other, the sale is treated as never having occurred, and the optionee is required to pay tax on the full spread at exercise (in the example, $100).

3.4.3 When to File a Section 83(b) Election for ISO AMT

Under Section 83 of the Code, the optionee who exercises an NSO must pay ordinary income tax on the difference between the purchase price and the fair market value of the shares (the "spread") on the *later of* the date of exercise or the date of vesting. The Section 83(b) election is a technical device that allows the optionee to minimize his or her tax liability if the spread is greater on the date of vesting than on the date of exercise. Filing the election within 30 days of exercise "freezes" the spread and limits the optionee's ordinary income tax to the value at the date of exercise. Any additional gain is treated as capital gain (or any loss is a capital loss).

Although as a general rule, ISOs are not subject to Section 83 of the Code, that section does apply to an ISO that is exercised for unvested stock for purposes of computing the AMT. As such, the regulations allow the optionee to file a Section 83(b) election for AMT purposes—i.e., to freeze the gain includible in the AMT computation to the spread on exercise. The 83(b) election for an ISO *applies only to the AMT* for these purposes. This makes sense because for AMT purposes, an ISO is treated as if it were an NSO.[28]

The same risk factors described above that apply on filing a Section 83(b) election for NSOs apply for filing a Section 83(b) election for AMT. If the optionee makes a disqualifying disposition of the stock, the 83(b) election for AMT will not protect him from the ordinary income tax consequences of early exercising without an 83(b) election.

The decision to file an 83(b) election is highly individual to each optionee and must take into account all of the factors influencing the optionee's tax position. In particular, the disqualifying disposition issue puts an additional gloss on planning considerations when exercise of an ISO produces AMT in the year of exercise. If, in such a case, the optionee believes that the ISO shares will appreciate considerably before vesting and the optionee intends to hold the stock for the statutory holding period, a Section 83(b) election should be filed for AMT. If, however, the optionee intends to make a disqualifying disposition of the ISO shares in the year of vesting, it may be disadvantageous to make a Section 83(b) election at the time of exercise. Making such an election will accelerate the AMT into the year of exercise, and there will be no opportunity to effectively cancel AMT by making a disqualifying disposition in the year of vesting. Of course, if the optionee has no intention of making a disqualifying disposition of the ISO shares, a Section 83(b) election would be advisable in an up market. Accordingly, where appropriate, optionees should file Section 83(b) elections for AMT within 30 days of the time ISOs are exercised for restricted shares.

3.4.4 Background on the AMT

When the technology-fueled stock market bubble popped in 2000, many optionees who had failed to focus on the effects of the AMT were

---

28. Treas. Reg. § 1.422-1(b)(3), Example 2.

unpleasantly surprised to see substantial tax bills despite the fact that the value of their stock had subsequently declined below the exercise date price.[29] At that time, the newspapers were full of stories about Silicon Valley executives who had held onto stock acquired at the height of the boom without considering the AMT consequences. In the down market, these executives found themselves with huge AMT bills and insufficient assets to satisfy the liability.

Later in the decade, Congress offered some relief from this situation. Beginning with the 2007 tax year, certain taxpayers could claim old, unrecovered AMT credit, even if it meant getting a refund that exceeded the current year's taxes. The Tax Relief and Health Care Act of 2006 allowed a refundable credit for a prior year AMT liability after a period of years. Specifically, the act provides that if an individual has a long-term unused minimum tax credit for any taxable year beginning before January 1, 2013, the applicable credit limitation for the taxable year at issue will not be less than the AMT refundable amount.

Further, after years of lobbying, Silicon Valley executives were able to persuade Congress to include AMT relief in the Emergency Economic Stabilization Act of 2008 (EESA) passed in October 2008. That financial rescue legislation included significant relief for individuals who exercised ISOs and experienced negative tax consequences because of AMT with respect to an ISO spread that disappeared when the value of the underlying stock plummeted during the dot-com crash of the early years of the century. Section 103 of EESA provided for a complete abatement of ISO-related AMT, interest, penalties, and liabilities incurred prior to October 4, 2008. In addition, it increased the AMT refundable tax credit (for amounts already paid) by the *greater of* 50% of the unused minimum tax credit for the preceding years, or 100% of the AMT credit determined with respect to the prior tax year, regardless of the person's income. The new law effectuated these changes through amendments to Section 53 of the Code.

The experience of the dot-commers emphasizes the need to respect the special rules for ISOs in regard to AMT and disqualifying dispositions. These rules require careful consideration of potential effects that the AMT rules will have on filing Section 83(b) elections for ISO

---

29.   See discussion of timing considerations for dispositions below. See also Ashlea Ebeling and Janet Novack, "Killer Tax," *Forbes Magazine*, April 1, 2002.

purposes when the option is "early exercised." It is advisable for many employees who exercise unvested ISOs to file Section 83(b) elections exactly as though they were exercising NSOs. Moreover, the tax rules will apply to trigger certain planning possibilities as well as pitfalls for optionees who expect to make disqualifying dispositions of their ISO stock in a year other than the year of exercise.

3.5 Modifying Statutory Options

With few exceptions, Section 424(h) of the Code and its regulations provide that a "modification" of an ISO or an option granted under a Section 423 employee stock purchase plan (discussed in detail in chapter 5) will require that the exercise price of the option be adjusted to match the fair market value of the option stock on the date of amendment, if that price is higher.[30] For purposes of the statutory option provisions of the Code, a modification is defined to mean a change in the original terms of the option that gives the optionee *additional benefits* under the option. Not all significant changes represent "additional benefits" for these purposes. For example, a change to the length of an ESPP offering period may or may not be an additional benefit.[31] Examples of modifications cited in regulations include: extending the period for exercise, adding an alternative to the exercise of the option (such as a stock appreciation right), providing an additional benefit upon exercise (such as a cash bonus), and making an offer to change the terms of the grant if that offer remains outstanding for more than 30 days or if it is accepted.[32]

If an ISO is modified only with respect to a portion of the optioned shares, or if the modification is solely for the purpose of increasing the number of shares under option, only the portion of the ISO relating to such shares will be deemed modified for these purposes. The affected

---

30. For modifications of ESPP options, the regulations provide that fair market value will be the higher of the fair market value on (1) the original grant date, (2) the date of the modification, or (3) the date of any intervening modification. Treas. Reg. § 1.424-1(e)(3).

31. See, e.g., PLR 200418020 (April 30, 2004) (suspension of offering period followed by an extension to permit exercise was not a modification).

32. Treas. Reg. § 1.424-1(e)(4)(i), (ii).

options will be considered to be newly granted options.[33] If a company inadvertently modifies its ISOs, it can undo the modification without disqualifying the option as long as the modification is reversed by the earlier of the last day of the calendar year when the change was made or the date of exercise of the option.[34]

Accordingly, if an ISO exercisable at $1 per share is amended at a time when the underlying stock has a value of $5 per share, the option exercise price will have to be increased to $5 per share to maintain the ISO status of the option. Options that are not repriced in the event of a modification are treated as NSOs. If an ISO is modified, the grant date is deemed to be the date of the modification rather than the date of the original grant. This will mean that the optionee's statutory holding period must be extended for an additional two years. Note that even if the modification occurs in a down market without repricing (because the exercise price is greater than current fair market value), the statutory holding period will re-start on the date of the modification.

A change in option terms by virtue of a "corporate transaction" will not be treated as a modification for these purposes. "Corporate transactions" include mergers, consolidations, reorganizations, and liquidations; changes in the corporate name; and other changes as may be prescribed by the Internal Revenue commissioner. Stock splits and stock dividends are not modifications so long as they are proportionate and do not result in more than minor changes to the value of the awards. For example, if a company conducts a 2-for-1 stock split in which every share become two shares, each of which is worth half of the pre-split share price, then outstanding option grants could be adjusted accordingly—the size of each outstanding grant could double and the exercise price could be halved without jeopardizing the ISO treatment or requiring remeasurement of the $100,000 limit.

Section 424(h)(3) of the Code states that each of the following types of changes to a statutory option will be an exception to the general rules regarding modifications: changes attributable to the issuance or assumption of an option pursuant to a corporate reorganization under Section 424(a), changes to permit the option to qualify under Section

---

33. Treas. Reg. § 1.424-1(e)(4)(v).

34. Treas. Reg. § 1.424-1(e)(4)(viii).

423(b)(9), and changes to accelerate the time within which an option may be exercised.

A change in the terms of the option to accelerate the time within which the option may be exercised is not a modification.[35] However, this begs the question of whether acceleration of vesting—which also results in an acceleration of exercisability—constitutes a modification. IRS rulings on this issue suggest that vesting and exercisability are considered the same for these purposes, but the issue has never been directly addressed by the IRS.[36] Note, however, that the *addition* of a provision to accelerate on a change of control will result in a modification, but this is clearly distinguishable from a provision that simply provides for acceleration.[37]

In the context of a corporate transaction, Section 424 makes it easy for the parties to avoid modifying statutory options by simply following certain mechanical rules. Section 424(a) provides that "issuing or assuming an option" for these purposes includes both substitution (i.e., an acquirer cancels old options in the target and grants new ones in the new company) and assumption (i.e., an acquirer assumes old options in the target on their current terms, but the exercise of those options may be for stock in a different company). Options assumed or substituted must meet all of the following tests:

1. *Spread Test:* The aggregate spread of the shares subject to option immediately after the transaction cannot exceed the aggregate spread of the shares subject to option immediately before the transaction.[38]

2. *Ratio Test:* On a share-by-share comparison, the ratio of the option price to the fair market value of the shares subject to the option immediately after the transaction must not be more favorable to the optionee than it was immediately before the transaction.[39]

3. *No Additional Benefits:* The assumed or substituted option may not include additional benefits that the optionee did not have before

---

35. Section 424(h)(3)(C) of the Code and Treas. Reg. § 1.424-1(e)(4)(ii).

36. See Rev. Rul. 74-504, 1974-1 C.B. 105; PLR 89094011.

37. See PLR 8330103.

38. Section 424(1)(1); Treas. Reg. § 1.424-1(a)(5)(ii).

39. Treas. Reg. § 1.424-1(a)(5)(iii).

the transaction (e.g., extended exercise period, new tandem stock/ SAR rights etc.).[40]

So, for example, Employee E holds an option in Company S to purchase 60 shares of S stock at $12 per share. Company S is acquired by Company P in a transaction that satisfies Section 424(a) of the Code at a time when the fair market value of a share of S is $32. P cancels E's option and substitutes a new option to purchase 80 shares in Company P at $9 per share. Immediately after the transaction, the fair market value of a share of P stock is $24. The above tests apply as follows:

1. *Spread Test:*
   Aggregate spread before: $1,200 ([$32 − $12] x 60 shares)
   Aggregate spread after: $1,200 ([$24 − $9] x 80 shares)
   Passes spread test

2. *Ratio Test:*
   9/24 is not greater than 12/32 (both equal 3/8)
   Passes ratio test

3. Additional benefits: None

Accordingly, the substitution satisfies Section 424(a) and does not constitute a modification under Section 424(h)(3).[41]

Note that most transactions raise the question of what to do with fractional shares and still fall within the exceptions to Section 424(h) (3). In general, the safe way is to round up the exercise price and round down the number of shares so that the spread and ratio tests are satisfied and no fractional shares are involved. Other methods have included paying cash in lieu of fractional shares at the time of exercise[42] or canceling the portion of the option exercisable for a fractional share and reducing the aggregate exercise price of the remaining options pro-rata.[43] Note that although the last two methods should not trigger Section 409A when used in connection with a qualifying change in control, it

---

40. Section 424(a)(2).

41. This example is found in Treas. Reg. § 1.424-1(a)(10), Ex. (6).

42. See, e.g., PLRs 8726026, 8720033.

43. See, e.g., PLR 8448024, 7741022.

is always important to check with counsel to ensure no surprise adverse tax consequences.

Certain exercises of discretion will not be treated as modifications so long as such discretion has been previously authorized, including the exercise of corporate discretion to (1) modify an option with respect to the payment of employment or withholding taxes, and (2) pay a bonus, make a loan, or offer the right to tender previously owned stock when an option is exercised. Note that if such discretion has not been previously authorized, the exercise of such discretion will be treated as a modification.

No amendment to or modification of a statutory option should be made without careful tax consideration, because such changes can result in significant tax problems that must be understood fully by both the employee and the company. Further, note that modifications can carry accounting consequences. See chapter 10 for a detailed discussion of accounting issues.

Plan Design and Administration

Contents

As we have seen, the technical requirements governing stock option plan design are detailed and numerous. As such, companies should give themselves the broadest possible flexibility when they design equity compensation plans. This chapter looks at the broader issues companies should consider when designing and operating their plans as well as the more specific issues to be considered when choosing whether to offer ISOs or NSOs.

4.1   General Considerations for the Company

The adoption of a broad, flexible equity compensation plan will permit a company to grant ISOs or NSOs to employees and NSOs to outside directors and consultants who are not employees. Such a plan may also provide for the grant of other types of equity rights, such as restricted stock, stock appreciation rights (SARs), restricted stock units, and performance-based grants. This is called an "omnibus plan" or, less commonly, an "umbrella plan."[1] A well-drafted omnibus plan provides two important kinds of flexibility: first, for the plan itself and second, for the individual grants made under the plan.

Companies that grant multiple kinds of awards out of a single plan increasingly use "fungible share pools" in which different kinds of awards deplete the pool of shares available under the plan at different rates. A publicly traded company may be required to use a fungible share pool in order to secure approval of the plan from the company's institutional shareholders. It is less common for privately held companies to use fungible share pools.

Generally, stock options and other awards that give recipients the equivalent of the appreciation in value of a share of stock deplete the share pool by one share, whereas restricted stock, restricted stock units, and other awards that give the recipient most or all of the value of a full share deplete the share pool faster. For example, a plan might consider each exercised option to reduce the number of shares that can be issued

---

1.   While this chapter focuses on stock options, many of the issues discussed also apply to other forms of equity compensation grants, which are discussed briefly in chapter 6. For in-depth analyses of restricted stock, performance-based grants, phantom stock, and SARs, see Corey Rosen, et al., *Equity Alternatives: Restricted Stock, Performance Awards, Phantom Stock, SARs, and More,* 15th ed. (Oakland, CA: NCEO, 2017).

under the plan by one share, but count each share of a restricted stock award as reducing the pool by 1.5 shares.

4.1.1 Plan Perspective

A plan may be drafted to give the plan sponsor room to anticipate legal issues without requiring constant updates to the document. As we have seen, the rules regulating stock option plans are complex and subject to frequent change for legal and political reasons. Response to such *external* changes may be facilitated by writing the plan document in such a way that it can be interpreted using the broadest parameters permitted under current law. An important example of this is ensuring that tax restrictions set out in an omnibus plan apply only where necessary. An oft-overlooked mistake can occur when omnibus plan language inadvertently applies ISO limitations to all grants, NSOs as well as ISOs. A common example of this mistake is language that sets a post-termination exercise period of three months for all options. While this is an ISO requirement, it does not apply to equity grants that are not tax-qualified and may unnecessarily tie the plan administrator's hands.[2] Other examples of this mistake include generic restrictions on transferability, pricing requirements, and overbroad application of U.S. law to international grants.

Similarly, plan provisions that are governed by *internal* substantive company policy should refer to such policies *as in effect from time to time* without incorporating them into the plan specifically; this acknowledges that it may be legally permissible for such policies to change at the company's discretion. Examples of policies best adopted outside the plan include fair market value methodology, hiring and performance grant matrices, and global plan administration.

However, in some arenas specificity within the plan can prevent legal disputes with plan participants. The plan document itself should clearly lay out, for example, whether options continue to vest during a leave of absence and what happens upon a change of employment

---

2. The specific ISO rules required to be set out in the plan are discussed in detail in chapter 3.

status, even if it refers to company policy outside the plan as to what constitutes a legally protected leave or termination "for cause."[3]

Just as well-defined terms in the plan document can avoid disputes with plan participants, a well-written plan document is the appropriate place to ensure grants do not create inadvertent complications for the company. For example, in order to be exempt from overtime calculations, equity compensation (including stock options, SARs, and Section 423 plan options) granted to a nonexempt employee under a bona fide employee plan is subject to a variety of restrictions under the Fair Labor Standards Act (FLSA). Exempt rights may not be exercisable for at least six months after grant and (like Section 423 plan options) they may not be priced at less than 85% of the fair market value of the stock or the stock equivalent, determined at the time of the grant. While these restrictions generally pose no problems for employee plans, note that a Section 423 ESPP with an exercise period of less than six months will not be eligible for the FLSA exemption from overtime calculations, nor will options with vesting schedules of less than six months. Companies that grant equity to nonexempt employees should be careful to set vesting schedules accordingly.

4.1.2   Grant Perspective

From the individual grant perspective, an omnibus plan may be drafted to give the plan administrator a range of alternative terms and conditions when granting equity incentives. Generally, this means that the plan will contain sufficient information to provide for a "default" grant if interpretation is warranted, but sufficient flexibility to allow the plan administrator to devise specific solutions in a wide variety of granting situations. For example, a reasonable strategy would be for the plan document to set forth a generic vesting and exercise schedule for option grants, even though there's no legal requirement the company do so. The goal of this strategy is to protect the company from litigation over inadvertent clerical mistakes, such as leaving a vesting schedule off of an option grant. However, whenever a generic schedule is included in

---

3.   For a more complete discussion of plan administration issues, see "Administering an Employee Stock Option Plan" by Mark A. Borges and Christine Zwerling in *Selected Issues in Equity Compensation*, 14th ed. (Oakland, CA: NCEO, 2017).

the plan, it's vital that the document clearly delegate authority to the plan administrator (which may be accomplished through the approval of a standard grant document) to provide for variations on vesting and exercise so long as such variations are not inconsistent with the other terms of the plan. In other words, the generic schedule would apply if—and only if—an individual grant did not state specific terms, or if the specific terms stated were in conflict with the plan document. Without this clear delegation, much of the flexibility of the omnibus plan will be undermined.

As we have already noted, an equity incentive grant is a contract between the grantor (the company) and the grantee (the grant recipient). The complete contract is made up of the individual notice of grant/exercise documents plus the plan itself. Generally, the grant document should incorporate the plan by reference, state that the individual document controls *unless it is inconsistent with (or in conflict with) the terms of the plan* (in which case the default provisions of the plan control), and then set out specific terms of the grant, such as:

- the number of shares subject to the award,
- the exercise price,
- the vesting and exercise schedule (including such variations as early exercise and performance vesting),
- contract rights of the company (e.g., rights of first refusal),
- nonstatutory definitions related to termination or severance (e.g., constructive termination), and
- limitations on forms of consideration for exercise.

Exhibits 4-1 and 4-2 set out basic guidance regarding the types of plan provisions that should be included in (or excluded from) the plan document.

4.1.3 Grant Acceptance

Since the grant is a contract, does the notice of grant need to be executed by the optionee to be valid? As a rule, the grant itself is unilateral—i.e., the terms are as stated by the company and are not subject to negotiation, nor do they expire if the optionee doesn't execute the notice. The

Exhibit 4-1. Basic Plan Features

Feature	Purpose	Notes
Discretionary plan scope	Permit administrator to exercise broad discretion in awarding equity grants in a variety of compensation situations.	
Statutory provisions	Tax rules for ISOs (and 423 plans)— set out in Code Sections 421–424; administrative requirements for exclusion under Section 162(m); deferred compensation concerns under Section 409A.	*Tax code requires specific language, approvals and $ limitations for valid ISO plans and for avoidance of $1 million cap on compensation deductions attributable to options for some top employees in public companies; adverse tax consequences for discounted options or options that permit deferral of compensation.*
Change of control provisions	Provide guidance for plan termination and/or acceleration on acquisition.	*Note effect of Code Section 280G regulations for factoring options into "golden parachute" definition of reasonable compensation; required shareholder approval of "golden parachute" payments; deferred compensation concerns under Section 409A for severance arrangements.*
Limitations on value of stock grants	Plan must state maximum number of shares that may be awarded under plan and maximum number that may be awarded as ISOs.	*Code Sections 422 and 423 require shareholder approval of total number of shares in plan and impose certain $ value limitations; Code Section 162(m) safe harbor requires a stated maximum number of shares available to any individual at a public company.*
Basic corporate governance	ISO plans and ESPPs require shareholder approval for number of shares and certain material provisions; plans sponsored by companies listed on major stock exchanges also require approval; shareholders vote on executive compensation plans.	*Public company SEC disclosure requirements have widened, as have stock exchanges' shareholder approval requirements. Shareholders vote on executive pay.*
Federal securities law requirements	Sale of stock under any plan, private or public, requires federal securities law compliance. Language generally incorporated in disclosure documents rather than plan itself, but some exceptions.	*Rules 701 and 144 generally explained in investor representations to pre-public company investors; Section 16 for public company insiders is transactional and so generally included in disclosure docs rather than plan document. Ever-increasing SEC reporting requirements for equity compensation.*
State securities law requirements	"Blue sky" rules differ from state to state—some states require very specific language to take advantage of permits or exemptions, others require notice only.	*Note that some state registration requirements differ from federal registration requirements.*
Leaves of absence	Effect of general LOA policies under plan—does vesting stop? Partial vesting?	*Also applies to change in status; e.g., does vesting change if employee goes from full time to part time or from employee to consultant?*

Exhibit 4-2. Policies Outside of the Plan

Feature	Description	Notes
Grant policies	Provide employment grade matrix for hire grants, reload options, retention grants.	Particularly useful for routine grants delegated to committee; have board adopt and approve from time to time.
Vesting policies	Default vesting schedule adopted for all grants.	Performance vesting used as incentive on a case-by-case basis.
Repricing/ regrant policies	Guidelines to avoid accounting issues.	Shareholder approval required for public company repricings if not specifically allowed for in plan document; proxy advisory service ISS requires shareholder approval of repricings.
Tax planning	No withholding on ISOs; provide for FICA/FUTA withholding for NSOs.	Monitor legislation for new developments.
Adding shares to plan	Long-term planning for additional shares—requires shareholder approval.	With recent reluctance of investors, the fewer times company needs to ask shareholders for more shares the better.*
Global plan administration	Decisions about when to adopt specific country subplans; approvals.	Need to assess importance of tax advantages in each country.

*Some publicly traded companies have had recent success in seeking shareholder approval of the share reserve on a more regular basis (including annually). Some institutional shareholders appreciate a company's ability to plan and justify the use of stock awards based on shorter planning periods.

fact and date of the grant are memorialized in formal corporate records (i.e., minutes of the board or the committee charged with administering the plan). Thus, the only reason for requiring an optionee's execution is that it provides for an acknowledgment of receipt of the grant. Failure to consent to the terms may result in rejection of the grant altogether, but does not change the grant agreement itself.

The risk is that if a signature is required and not obtained, the optionee could (in theory, at least) argue that he was unaware of the terms of the grant and take the position that he was relying on oral promises with respect to his equity grants that differ from the terms in the actual grant. Such arguments, while rarely successful, still give rise to a small risk of litigation. From a practical standpoint, this is more of an issue for grants of restricted stock awards and units, which can vest and be paid without the award holder ever accepting the terms and conditions of the award. With respect to stock options, however, even if the optionee does not accept the grant notice or grant agreement, the company may still require acceptance of all of the terms and conditions of the option as a prerequisite to exercise.

The issue of award acceptance can be minimized or exaggerated by the use of electronic delivery. Many companies now deliver award documents to employees and other service providers via e-mail or through an intranet or extranet. Companies have developed different strategies and there is no one-size-fits-all solution. Some companies no longer require award acceptance; however, this position can increase litigation risk and may create additional issues for awards granted outside of the United States. Other companies delay vesting or payment until the award holder has accepted the award.

4.2   ISOs or NSOs?

Many companies have found that ISOs are a useful tool for providing tax-advantaged incentives to key personnel. With ISOs, if the statutory holding periods and other rules are met, the optionee incurs no tax liability upon exercise (unless the optionee is subject to AMT), but instead incurs tax liability only upon the sale or other disposition of the shares, and even then the employee is taxed at long-term capital gains rates rather than at ordinary income rates, which are historically higher. However, because ISOs are statutory creatures, they must be granted and exercised in accordance with the technical conditions of Section 422 of the Code and the IRS regulations thereunder. The grant and exercise of ISOs are also regulated by state and federal securities laws and state corporation laws. A further drawback is that, assuming the optionee complies with all the ISO rules, the employer will not be entitled to receive a compensation deduction as a result of either the grant or exercise of an ISO. Chapter 3 sets out the details of using ISOs.

In contrast, the grant of an NSO is not limited by federal income tax laws as to the number of shares, length of term, or identity of the recipient (although the company's plan usually will stipulate the eligibility requirements for an NSO). As detailed in chapter 2, upon the optionee's exercise of the NSO, the company is entitled to receive a compensation deduction in the amount of the spread between the option price and the value of the stock at time of purchase. The tax consequences of an NSO, however, are generally less advantageous to the employee than those of an ISO, and the employer has a withholding obligation on the spread at the time of exercise.

Exhibits 4-3 below and 3-1 in chapter 3 set out the relative advantages and disadvantages of using NSOs and ISOs.

Exhibit 4-3. Comparison: ISOs Versus NSOs: Consequences to Company

	ISOs	NSOs
Option price	Must be no lower than fair market value at date of grant; "good faith" valuation necessary.	Should be no lower than fair market value at date of grant or Section 409A consequences may apply; state corporate law may govern.
Qualification requirements	Must meet all requirements of Section 422 at time of grant; must be granted under qualified ISO plan.	None; may require state corporate securities permit or exemption if issued under a plan.
Who is eligible	Employees only	Employees, consultants, directors, other independent service providers.
Limitations	(a) $100,000 first exercisable per year; (b) grant and plan both have 10-year term only; (c) more-than-10% shareholders subject to special limitations.	No tax limitations (but watch for Section 162(m) cap, which is also applicable to ISOs); discount options will cause tax consequences under Section 409A.
Corporate deduction	None if optionee holds for ISO holding period; deduction for spread if optionee makes disqualifying disposition and report timely filed by company.	Deduction for spread in year of exercise provided income included (or "deemed included") by optionee.
Withholding obligation	None	At a minimum, withhold at supplementary rates (income tax and FICA) at exercise by employee.
Reporting	Section 6039 reporting in year following year of exercise and disqualifying disposition tracking (W-2, W-2(c))	W-2, 1099

4.3 Plan-Level Shareholder Approval Considerations

In recent years, the hurdles for obtaining shareholder approval for equity compensation plans have become higher and higher. Plan sponsors would be well-advised to think carefully about strategies for obtaining shareholder approval of their equity compensation plans before embarking on any major changes or increasing the share reserve, and before taking their plans to shareholders for a vote. Plan sponsors must also design executive compensation plans with an eye toward shareholder votes on the compensation packages of the named executive officers whose compensation is disclosed in their proxies—the so-called say-on-pay vote.

Privately held companies that anticipate becoming publicly traded should design their plans to conform with the equity compensation plan requirements of the exchange on which they expect their shares to be listed and on the executive compensation approval and disclosure requirements that affect publicly traded companies, and are discussed in further detail in chapters 8 and 13.

4.3.1   When Is Shareholder Approval Required?

The authorization to use shares in an ESPP or employee stock option plan may require shareholder approval under tax, corporate, and stock exchange rules, or under all three. In the rare case that a private company sponsors a nonqualified ESPP, it should check state securities laws to determine whether shareholder approval is required.[4]

The Code requires that shareholder approval of statutory option plans (both ISO plans and Section 423 ESPPs, which are also tax-qualified plans) be obtained within 12 months of the date the board of directors authorizes the allocation of shares under the plan.[5] An ISO plan adopted by a company's board of directors "subject to shareholder approval" *is considered adopted on the date the plan is approved by shareholders,* e.g., if the board stipulates an adoption condition, then the deemed adoption date is when that condition is satisfied. In contrast, the 10-year limit on the company's ability to grant statutory options from a plan is counted from the *earlier* of adoption by the board of directors or shareholder approval. Although Treasury regulations do not specifically state that ISO grants made before shareholder approval will *never* be valid, a lesson from the stock option backdating scandals—which frequently focused on questions regarding the timing of corporate approvals—is that the

---

4.   See, e.g., California Corporations Code Section 25100, et al.

5.   Section 422(b)(1) (ISOs); 423(b)(2) (ESPPs). See also PLR 9312035 (approving an increase of the ESPP share limit in the middle of the offering period). ISO plans may also be approved by shareholders 12 months in advance of board authorization; however, this rule rarely comes into play.

best practice is to obtain shareholder approval prior to the grant of any option subject to a stock plan. Note that this rule does not apply to Section 423 plans.

Furthermore, corporate and state securities laws generally require initial plan approval, and, depending on the state, also may require approval of additions to the pool.[6] Finally, each stock exchange has its own rules regarding shareholder approval and the degree to which it must be obtained for employee option plans. This means that shareholder approval is usually necessary for nonstatutory as well as statutory plans, and it is always necessary for ISO plans and Section 423 ESPPs.

In addition to plan approval, public company shareholders must be allowed a nonbinding vote on the pay of named executive officers at least once every three years.

4.3.2   Stock Exchange Rules

Companies listed on the New York Stock Exchange and the Nasdaq must receive shareholder approval for all equity compensation plans, with certain very narrow exceptions, and, under rules adopted pursuant to the Dodd-Frank Act of 2010, must use compensation committees comprising only independent directors and allow those committees the authority to choose compensation consultants and hire independent legal counsel.

4.3.2.1   *Shareholder Approval of Plans*

The NYSE rules governing shareholder approval are contained in Section 303A(8) of the Listed Company Manual. The Nasdaq rules are NASD Rules 4310(c)(17)(a) and 4320(e)(15)(A). Inconsistencies between the two sets of rules are minor; probably the most significant is that the NYSE rules require the company to submit in writing to the SEC the reasons why it is relying on one of the material modification exemptions if it wishes to avoid seeking shareholder approval of a change to a plan. A summary follows.

---

6.   California is a notable example of a state that requires shareholder approval on both plan adoption and addition of shares. See California Commissioner's Rules § 260.140.41–45.

1. *Scope:* All equity compensation plans, and any material revisions to these plans, must be approved by shareholders, with certain narrow exceptions outlined below. Equity compensation plans that are subject to board approval must be recommended to the board by a committee made up of "independent directors," as described below.

2. *Equity Compensation Plans Defined:* An equity compensation plan includes any plan or other arrangement to deliver securities, including options, to employees, directors, or other service providers. The term does not include dividend reinvestment plans, or plans that allow employees, directors, or other service providers to buy shares on the open market for current fair market value.

3. *Material Modification:* "Material" is not defined by the rules, although it specifically does not include the limitation of rights and benefits associated with a plan; only modifications expanding employee rights and benefits are covered. In 2016, the NYSE amended its FAQ section to specify that "an amendment to a plan to provide for the withholding of shares based on an award recipient's maximum tax obligation rather than the statutory minimum tax rate is not a material revision if the withheld shares are never issued, even if the withheld shares are added back to the plan." (This was in response to a rule change that ended the requirement that plans that allowed share withholding at greater than the statutory minimum tax rate must use liability accounting.[7]) The list of covered modifications includes:

    a. A material increase in the number of shares available, other than for stock splits, corporate reorganizations, and similar arrangements. Evergreen plans require approval for each increase unless the plan has a term of not more than 10 years. If the increase is not pursuant to a formula, then each increase must be approved by shareholders. A requirement that grants be made out of treasury or repurchased shares will not, in itself, be considered a formula.

    b. An expansion of the types of awards available under the plan or of the class of employees, directors, or other service providers eligible to participate.

---

7. For details on the accounting rule change, see chapter 10.

    c.   A material extension of the term of the plan.

    d.   A material change in the method of determining the strike price of options, such as changing the fair market value from the closing price on the date of grant to the average of the high and low prices on the date of grant.

    e.   The deletion or limitation of any provision prohibiting repricing.

4.   *Repricings:* A plan that does not specifically permit repricing is considered to prohibit it. Any actual repricing is thus considered a material modification. Cancellation of an option and substitution for a new award pursuant to a merger, acquisition, spin-off, or similar transaction is not included.

5.   *Employment Inducement Awards:* If the company's independent compensation committee approves them, inducement awards to new hires may be made without shareholder approval. Companies must disclose in a press release, and in written material for the NYSE, a description of the award, its terms, the number of shares, and its recipient. The term "new hires" includes rehires of previous employees following a "bona fide" period of non-employment.

6.   *Mergers and Acquisitions:* Shareholder approval is not required to replace options or other awards in a transaction. Shares available for award of a closely held company that is acquired may be used in post-acquisition grants provided the plan existed prior to the merger or acquisition being contemplated. The time the shares are available cannot be extended after the transaction. Under the Dodd-Frank Act, shareholders must be allowed a nonbinding vote on any agreements under which payments will be made to named executive officers in the event of a corporate change in control—assuming they have not already had an opportunity to vote on those payments.

7.   *Qualified Plans:* Employee stock ownership plans, other Code Section 401 plans invested in company stock (401(k), profit sharing, and stock bonus plans), and Section 423 ESPPs do not require approval under the stock exchange rules. Tax-qualified ESPPs do, however, require shareholder approval under Section 423 of the Code.[8]

---

8.   See section 5.1.

8. *Parallel Excess Plans:* These are plans that provide additional company contributions or employee deferrals into qualified plans that limit the total amount of compensation that can be considered or place ceilings on the total amounts that can be contributed. Companies sometimes make up the difference that would be allowed if these ceilings did not exist; the contributions or deferrals are not tax favored. Investments in equity in these plans are exempted from shareholder approval requirements. The plan must cover all or substantially all affected employees, its terms must be the same for those covered, it must parallel the terms for the qualified plans, and no one can receive compensation in excess of 25% of cash compensation.

9. *Broker Voting:* Broker-held shares ("street name" shares) cannot be voted by proxy by brokers unless the beneficial owner provides specific instructions. This includes votes on equity compensation plans, votes for directors, and votes on executive pay packages.

4.3.2.2   *Independence of Compensation Committee and Advisors*

The national securities exchanges' listing standards require that the committee that makes recommendations with respect to, among other forms of compensation, equity plan-related compensation to a publicly traded company's board of directors be made up entirely of independent directors. The board's determination of director independence must take into account compensation a director receives from the company, its parent, or subsidiaries for work that is not related to the director's service on the board.

Under the NYSE's requirements, this committee is responsible for making "recommendations to the board with respect to non-CEO executive officer compensation, and incentive-compensation and equity-based plans that are subject to board approval." For this purpose, "executive officer" means the president; principal financial officer (the "CFO"); principal accounting officer (or, if there is no principal accounting officer, the controller); any vice president of a principal business unit, division, or function (such as sales, administration, or finance); any other officer who performs a policy-making function; or any other person who performs similar policy-making functions.

The compensation committee must have sole discretion to hire compensation consultants or independent legal counsel. Companies are required to provide for the funding for such advisers, but the committees themselves are directly responsible for the appointment, compensation, and oversight of the advisors' work. They are required to assess whether their outside advisors are genuinely independent based on other services they provide the company, the percentage of total revenues that come from the company, business or personal relationships that might be pertinent, and other factors. The use of compensation consultants and any conflicts must be disclosed in the company's proxy statement. As a result, those who advise a company on matters related to equity compensation may be required to meet these independence standards in order to avoid proxy disclosure, as they may in fact be deemed to be advisors to the compensation committee that administers the equity compensation plan. This is a facts and circumstances test that must be applied to each company's circumstances. These requirements do not apply to companies that qualify as smaller reporting companies.

The stock exchanges' independence standards went into effect with respect to any advice received or advisors hired after July 1, 2013.

4.3.3 Proxy Advisor Influence

Proxy advisory firms such as Institutional Shareholder Services (ISS) and Glass Lewis exert a great deal of influence over the design of equity incentive plans. Proxy advisors advise institutional shareholders on whether to vote for or against equity compensation plans established by publicly traded companies. To gain a favorable recommendation from the proxy advisors, companies will design their plans to fit within the proxy advisors' guidelines. For example, these guidelines might dictate the use and design of post-vesting holding periods and change-in-control provisions or prefer some performance metrics over others. Some commentators have remarked that proxy advisory firms have an outsized influence on the design of equity compensation plans, and many companies will work directly with their major shareholders to consolidate support for their equity compensation plan proposals and thus attempt to circumvent the proxy advisors.

4.4   Say-on-Pay Votes

Under the Dodd-Frank Act, public company shareholders must have the opportunity to register their nonbinding votes on compensation packages offered to top executives, but not directors, at least every three years, with a frequency that is itself subject to shareholder vote at least every six years.

Under the rules, the votes are based on the company's Compensation Discussion and Analysis (CD&A), compensation tables, and related narrative disclosures in the proxy statement.[9] Companies are required to discuss in their CD&As how their compensation policies and decisions have taken the results of say-on-pay votes into account and to explain to shareholders whether the company regards the votes as non-binding. They must also disclose whether they intend to abide by the shareholders' wishes for the frequency of say-on-pay votes.

Under the Jumpstart Our Business Startups (JOBS) Act of 2012, "emerging growth companies" are exempt from say-on-pay and say-on-frequency voting until at most one year after they pass certain thresholds and are no longer considered an emerging growth company. "Emerging growth companies" are described in section 8.2.

Shareholders are also allowed advisory votes on compensation that would be paid to named executive officers in connection with changes in corporate control such as mergers or acquisitions, unless such arrangements have already been voted on in a regular say-on-pay vote. Companies must also disclose these amounts, as well as any tender offers or transactions designed to take a company private, in their proxies. Under the SEC's rules, which went into effect in April 2011, such votes will occur at any meeting where shareholders are asked to approve a change in control. Emerging growth companies are also exempt from this requirement.

Brokers are not allowed to vote uninstructed shares on any of these matters.

For the most part, shareholder say-on-pay votes have been generally positive with respect to executive compensation. However, negative votes are more and more frequently showing up with respect to smaller public companies. In situations in which shareholders register

---

9.   These are discussed further in section 8.6.

a less than enthusiastic vote, some public companies may choose to change their compensation strategies in order to appease shareholders. However, companies are not required to makes changes based on the say-on-pay vote (since the vote is nonbinding). Some companies may choose to ignore the implications of the vote, but should be aware that many institutional shareholders will begin to withhold votes on compensation committee members or the full board of directors if they perceive that the company is not responding to a negative say-on-pay vote in an appropriate manner.

4.5   A Note on Plan Amendments

The adoption of an equity compensation plan for employees is, of course, discretionary to the employer. However, once adopted, the terms of the plan—incorporated by reference in each individual grant—constitute an enforceable contract between the company and its optionees. Although most well-drafted plans include a reservation of discretion to the board or plan administrator, no amount of reservation will support a unilateral diminishment of existing grant rights. In other words, while the board will generally be free to amend the plan (subject, in some cases, to shareholder approval or other governance requirements), most such amendments will be prospective only. This means that a plan may be amended to change or diminish benefits for future equity grants or grantees, but—barring express agreement of the grantees—outstanding grants remain subject to their original terms and conditions. What constitutes "diminishment" is, of course, a tricky factual issue that must be resolved by company counsel on a case-by-case basis. For example, while increasing the kinds of consideration acceptable on exercise of an option under the plan looks like a benefit, it could result in an ISO modification—a diminishment—if applied to outstanding grants.[10] On the other hand, changing the plan language to make it easier to exercise (e.g., by using electronic notice rather than paper notice) is unlikely to require any additional agreement from outstanding grantees.

This issue frequently comes up in the context of mergers in which the target company plan includes a guarantee of acceleration or other immediate benefits for optionees on a change in control. Companies

---

10.   ISO modifications are discussed in section 3.5.

that try to alter the benefit of the guaranteed acceleration (for example, by placing the cash value of the unvested options into escrow and paying it out over a vesting period post-merger) are most likely breaching their contracts with the optionees; an invitation to litigation.

Attempts to amend individual option grants raise the same issues as attempts to amend existing plan provisions, but are even more risky. Employees who are pressured into "agreeing" to an amendment they view as detrimental to their vested interests may have state employment law claims as well as basic breach of contract and reliance claims.[11] Even when the parties actually do agree to an amendment, they must be careful to avoid the potentially negative tax, accounting, and/or corporate consequences that can accompany option modifications, as discussed at length elsewhere in this text.[12]

4.6   International Planning Considerations

When stock options first became popular in the United States, U.S. companies that operated globally were faced with practical, as well as technical, concerns about whether to offer the same equity incentives to their international employees (i.e., non-U.S. employees resident in foreign countries) as they offered to their U.S. employees. For the most part, throughout the 1980s and well into the 1990s stock options were perceived as a dubious benefit at best in all but a few European countries.[13] Many international employees were accustomed to receiving compensation packages that included fringe benefits (such as car and housing allowances) as well as state-mandated retirement and leave payments. Culturally, equity was not considered to be a particularly

---

11. For example, we are aware of multiple threats of litigation arising from situations in which companies attempted to unilaterally force optionees to accept repriced options as a result of corporate misdating.

12. See, e.g., sections 3.5 and 12.1.

13. Notable exceptions to the rule were the United Kingdom (England, Ireland, and Scotland) and France, where versions of tax-qualified option plans have long been available. However, holding periods and other requirements for buying stock under these plans are far more restrictive than those imposed under the Code.

valuable or prestigious component of the compensation package, particularly if offered in lieu of more traditional benefits.

Further, the regulatory environments found in most foreign countries were not conducive to use of securities as compensation. Many countries imposed punitive tax or regulatory schemes on stock options, or had ambiguous rules that were difficult for either U.S. or local counsel to interpret with confidence. For example, until the late 1990s, the Scandinavian countries and the Netherlands imposed substantial taxes on both the grant and exercise of stock options. However, the most common concerns throughout the world (especially in Asia, including China and Japan) were corporate, securities, and exchange control laws that prevented local country corporations from granting employees equity at all. For multinationals operating through local subsidiaries, or attempting to transfer parent stock through such subsidiaries, these regulatory controls could be major stumbling blocks.

Because worldwide stock option plans can be a potent tool for creating a companywide ownership spirit that bridges cultural gaps, U.S. multinationals have continued to find ways to extend equity compensation to international employees wherever possible. In some cases this has involved simply adapting the U.S. plan to meet global needs; in others, an assessment of local tax and corporate issues result in adoption of mirror plans or subplans for individual country use. Companies will sometimes grant equity awards with mandatory cash settlement to avoid issuing shares to employees in countries that either do not allow direct share ownership or limit the amount of money or shares that can come into or go out of the country.

Communicating the benefits of options has become easier with the increased mobility of the international workforce and accordingly higher levels of interest in and awareness of equity compensation worldwide. In addition, as foreign-based companies with U.S. employees have sought to add employee stock plans, they have worked with their governments to amend local country rules to enable their use. Most countries now tax employee options on exercise, rather than on grant.[14] In any case, deci-

---

14. See the Baker & McKenzie Global Equity Matrix at www.bakermckenzie.com/ nlnagescountrymatrix, or "GPS: Global Stock Plans" (Santa Clara, CA: Certified Equity Professional Institute, 2009) at www.scu.edu/business/cepi/gps_published_research.cfm.

sions regarding whether and how to grant to international employees must be subject to a careful review of the issues, including (without limitation): local country securities, corporate, and employment law/ social tax requirements; exchange control regulations; the tax impact on employees; the tax impact on the company in the U.S. and locally; requirements for tax-approved or other government review status; the effect on (or necessary amendments to) design of the overall plan; and the perceived benefit/value to local country employees vs. the cost of compliance.

With respect to the tax treatment of compensatory stock options for purposes of qualified cost-sharing (transfer pricing) arrangements between U.S. companies and their foreign affiliates, all costs attributable to stock-based compensation must be taken into account in determining the controlled participant's operating expenses.[15] The spread on a statutory stock option, even if not otherwise includable in employee compensation, will nonetheless be shared for these purposes. U.S. multinationals need to work carefully with their tax advisors to ensure compliance with these complex rules when extending equity compensation to the non-U.S. workforce.

A complete discussion of international plan issues is beyond the scope of this book, although where appropriate, the text flags areas of concern for global equity planners. A growing number of resources and professional organizations are devoted entirely to exploration of these issues, and the reader is encouraged to seek them out for general information and guidance.[16] Before designing or implementing any global features in an equity plan, however, companies are best advised to consult both U.S. and local country counsel.

4.7   Grant Timing

In 2006 and 2007, newspapers, commentators, and ultimately the government turned their attention to a suspicious trend among public companies: that of granting options (frequently to top executives) at the lowest fair market value available during any option granting cycle.

---

15. T.D. 9088.

16. See the Global Equity Organization (GEO) at www.globalequity.org.

Although company plans and SEC filings consistently represented that these options were granted at fair market value on the date of grant, a 2006 academic paper[17] questioned whether such disproportionately employee-favorable results could be reasonably expected to have occurred without manipulation of grant dates. As of November 2006, the *Wall Street Journal* (which had broken the story early that year) was reporting that more than 120 companies had been subject to option backdating investigations by internal audit committees and/or the SEC,[18] with more than 50 companies under investigation by the Department of Justice (DOJ) for possible criminal conduct. As a result, by late 2006 more than 40 executives had been fired or resigned in connection with option backdating, employee exercises under many stock plans had been suspended, and numerous shareholder derivative actions had been filed on this issue.[19]

Throughout 2007 and 2008, companies found themselves subject to both external investigations by regulators and internal investigations by independent committees appointed by their own boards. Lawsuits continued to be filed by the SEC and investors. Hewlett-Packard reached a $117.5 million settlement with institutional holders of Mercury Interactive shares. (H-P had earlier acquired Mercury Interactive.) An equally high-profile case—between Apple, Inc., and its investors—settled for $14 million in 2008. Then, in 2010, Apple further agreed to pay $16.5 million plus an additional $4 million in attorneys' fees to settle

---

17. Randall Heron and Erik Lie, "What Fraction of Stock Option Grants to Top Executives Have Been Backdated or Manipulated?" July 14, 2006, available at www.biz.uiowa.edu/faculty/elie/Grants-11-01-2006.pdf; and Erik Lie, "On the Timing of CEO Stock Option Awards," *Management Science,* May 2005, available from www.biz.uiowa.edu/faculty/elie/Grants-MS.pdf. Lie and Heron estimate that manipulations occurred in at least 30% of executive grants between 1996 and 2005.

18. See "Perfect Payday Options Scorecard," which was regularly updated until September 2007 by the *Wall Street Journal* with news and information on companies and executives under investigation. The scorecard continues to be available online at online.wsj.com/public/resources/documents/info-optionsscore06-full.html.

19. Employee lawsuits were just beginning to emerge. See Kathleen Pender, "Hidden Victims of Stock Option Backdating," *San Francisco Chronicle,* October 26, 2006.

backdating-related claims in a class-action lawsuit led by the New York City Employees' Retirement System.

Ultimately, only a handful of criminal charges came out of the backdating scandal, resulting in 12 criminal convictions, only five of which resulted in prison time.[20]

With the perspective offered by time, it is apparent that in most (although not all) cases backdating problems turned more on a question of poor corporate record-keeping than on intentional misconduct. To be sure, the focus on backdating gave rise to increased—and appropriate—attention to valuation methodology (in tandem with the development of best practices under Section 409A) and grant timing practices. Although subsequent legal and regulatory developments have made improper grant timing less likely to occur, companies are well-advised to ensure they have and follow appropriate grant timing procedures.

4.7.1　What Is Option Backdating?

The phrase "option backdating" has historically referred to the practice of representing that an option was granted at an earlier date than the actual date of grant so as to take advantage of the lower fair market value on that earlier date. In other words, the plan committee—either the board of directors or its compensation committee—would complete the action required to grant the option (e.g., the corporate resolution or unanimous written consent) on a later date than the fair market value date, but would knowingly date—and price—the option grant as of the earlier date when the fair market value was lower.

> **Example 1:** *Intentional Backdating.* Company's plan states that all options will be granted at fair market value determined as of the date of grant. In January, management recommends a list of employee options with a strike price of $10 per share, the fair market value on January 1. The compensation committee meets on the 30th of each month. On January 30, when the fair market value is $12 per share, the committee approves the list of options with a unanimous written consent. The consent states that the approval is "as of" January 1, and the option grant date is stated as January 1, with a strike price of $10 per share.

20.　See Peter Lattman, "Backdating Scandal Ends with a Whimper," *New York Times*, November 11, 2010.

Variations on intentional backdating may include: approval with the date left blank and filled in once the lowest price is ascertained; approval for a group of unallocated options that are treated as granted on the date of approval or the date of allocation, depending on when the share price is lower; or approval for new-hire grants on a date prior to the actual first date of employment.

Option backdating need not be intentional, however. Many of the option backdating investigations determined that sloppy administrative procedures frequently led to backdated grants that were neither intended by nor obvious to the plan committee. Such procedures include waiting long periods between the date of approval and the date of documentation; mistakenly leaving eligible optionees off of the granting list but including them anyway when the approval and grants are papered; and getting approval at random times from a one-person plan administration committee.

> **Example 2:** *Inadvertent Misdating.* Company's plan states that all options will be granted at fair market value as of the date of grant. The plan committee is a single-member committee appointed by the board. Management provides the plan committee on January 15 with a written consent dated that day that lists optionees who started employment during the previous month. The fair market value on January 15 is $10 per share. The plan committee gets around to signing off on the list on February 1, when the fair market value is $12 per share, and returns the list to the plan administrator for documentation. The plan administrator, seeing that the consent was dated January 15, generates option documents with a January 15 date and a $10 per share strike price, even though the actual grant date is February 1.

Another technique that caused trouble when it came to light was looking back over a 30-day window period, selecting the lowest fair market value during the window, and using that value as the strike price for all options granted during the window. In the 1990s, Microsoft adopted this practice and, although this method was ultimately rejected by the IRS, it was picked up by other companies and (unless expressly authorized by the company's plan) is a form of backdating.[21] Another variation on price averaging was to use a trailing 30-day average to

---

21. Note that originally Deloitte & Touche approved this 30-day window method, but then withdrew its approval in 2005. Micrel, Inc., which used this form of pricing, settled a lawsuit against Deloitte in February 2007. See Eric Dash,

determine fair market value, even when the plan called for fair market
value *on the date of grant.*

> **Example 3**: *Price Averaging.* Company's plan states that all options will be
> granted at fair market value determined as of the date of grant. As a general rule,
> at the end of each calendar month, management provides the plan commit-
> tee with a list of option grants for new employees hired during the preceding
> month. Company's stock is volatile, and can vary widely over a 30-day period.
> Accordingly, the plan committee has a practice of granting monthly options
> at the trailing average closing price over the preceding 30-day period. During
> the month of January, closing prices range from $10 to $18, with the trailing
> average price at $13.50. On January 30, the closing price is $15. All new-hire
> grants are priced at $13.50 per share.

4.7.2   Grant Timing: Spring-Loading, Forward-Dating, and Bullet-Dodging

In cases of "spring-loading," "forward-dating," and "bullet-dodging,"
the plan committee purposefully times option grants to points in the
trading cycle when it assumes that the fair market value will be com-
paratively low. Spring-loading refers to granting options prior to the
anticipated announcement of good news, while bullet-dodging is the
reverse: granting options after the announcement of bad news. Forward-
dating refers to approving an option in advance of its stated grant date,
anticipating that the fair market value will have dropped as of that
grant date. In each of these instances, the strike price is demonstrably
the fair market value on the date of grant. These approaches are not
inherently problematic, but they must be disclosed to shareholders
under the SEC rules on executive compensation and related-persons
disclosure, which require disclosure of granting philosophy.[22] Through
the eyes of institutional investors (and from a shareholder-relations
perspective), these techniques may appear unduly generous to employees. However, there is no reason that grant-timing techniques in
and of themselves—if observed consistently, documented properly,

---

"Inquiry into Stock Option Pricing Casts A Wide Net," *New York Times,* June
19, 2006.

22. See section 8.6.

and disclosed to shareholders—should be considered to be on a par with intentional backdating.

> **Example 4**: *Grant Timing.* Company's plan states that all options will be granted at fair market value as of the date of grant. Management annually recommends performance grants for all employees in September, prior to the announcement of third-quarter earnings, when trading in company's stock is historically at its calendar year low. On September 15, when the fair market value of the stock is $10 per share, the plan committee approves the grants. On October 15, third-quarter earnings are released and the stock price rises to $15 per share. There is no question that $10 per share was the fair market value on the date of grant and that the plan committee approval (and all option grants) were properly documented.

4.7.3   Consequences of Backdating

As discussed throughout this text, option backdating may cause a domino effect of serious problems for the issuer. Those problems can be tracked through as follows:

- *Invalid Options:* Most plans—as approved by the stockholders— require options to be priced at fair market value (or at a specific maximum discount from value) on the date of grant. If options are not so priced, they are invalid under the plan and may (in many cases) be subject to rescission.

- *Corporate Governance Violations:* From the corporate governance perspective, the shareholders have approved the plan on its stated terms. A failure to follow those terms results in a governance violation. In other words, even if it is permissible to grant a discount option under the plan, granting such an option by subterfuge would not be permissible. Any method that misrepresents the fair market value at grant (either through using a date other than the date on which the plan committee action was completed, or using price averaging to determine fair market value) would be unauthorized for corporate governance purposes.

- *Adverse Tax Consequences:* Options granted at a strike price lower than fair market value—if such price is not set in good faith—will be disqualified from treatment as ISOs for tax purposes, and, if classified as discount NSOs, will be subject to adverse tax consequences for the optionee and disallowed tax deductions for the company. Furthermore, discounted NSOs can result in penalty taxes imposed on the service provider under Code Section 409A.

- *Adverse Accounting Consequences:* Backdating may result in account-ing errors that cause material misstatements of the company's financial statements, requiring the company to restate financials for years previously filed with the SEC.

- *Securities Law Violations:* The requirement to restate prior financials generally leads to late (or suspended) filing of current SEC reports (10-Qs, 10-Ks, etc.). A period of late or suspended SEC filings will result in any documents that incorporate such SEC filings by reference—in particular, the S-8 registration statement covering the option plan—to be invalid until all restatements (and SEC investigations) are complete, leading to a "bad" S-8 registration statement and subsequent blackout of employee option exercises under the plan.

- *Lawsuits:* Finally, all of the affected constituencies—regulators, stock-holders, and optionees—can be expected to pursue legal remedies for the problems raised by backdating, including criminal actions, shareholder derivative suits, and optionee civil suits (in contract and fraud claims).

This section briefly discusses the tax, accounting and securities laws issues raised above.

4.7.3.1   *Tax Consequences*

The backdating practices above may implicate one or more of three tax Code provisions: Section 162(m), Section 422, and Section 409A.

- *Section 162(m):* As further discussed in chapter 9, Section 162(m) imposes a $1 million cap on corporate deductions for compensa-tion paid to certain executive officers. As a general rule, options granted at no less than fair market value on the date of grant will qualify for the performance-based exception to the cap. However, options that are determined to be discounted, regardless of whether the discounting was intentional, are not eligible for this exception, leading the IRS to disallow previous deductions if such discounted options would have resulted in compensation in excess of the $1 million cap.

- *Section 422:* As further discussed in chapter 3, Section 422 requires that ISOs be granted at no less than fair market value on the date of grant. Although Section 422(c) sets out a safe harbor for good-faith determinations of fair market value, valuations based on intentional backdating are unlikely to be viewed by the IRS as having been made in good faith. If an ISO is disqualified and treated as a discounted NSO, optionees may have complicated tax consequences (including recapture—if possible—of pre-paid AMT, back taxes to the year of exercise, and even capital gains recalculations). From the company's perspective, there may be back withholding taxes due (as well as lost corporate tax deductions due to improper reporting that may not be able to be captured). Former employees are unlikely to cooperate in correcting these issues.

- *Section 409A:* As further discussed in chapter 2, Section 409A treats options granted at a discount as "nonqualified deferred compensation" that is subject to both regular taxes and a 20% excise tax at the time the option vests. The company will have reporting and withholding obligations with respect to the amounts subject to Section 409A. The IRS, in Notice 2008-113, offered limited relief for companies that unintentionally grant discounted stock options as long as the exercise price is corrected by the end of the calendar year following the year in which the option was granted. If the optionee is a Section 16 insider, the exercise price must be corrected before the end of the calendar year in which the grant was made.

4.7.3.2   *Accounting Consequences*

Under ASC 718, the backdating would be reflected in the fair value of the option grant. As described further in chapter 10, both exercise price and grant date fair market value of the stock are inputs into the option pricing models used to value stock options for accounting purposes, meaning a discounted option would have a higher fair value than one granted at the current FMV. A company that failed to correctly value the options would be in danger of materially misstating its financials.

4.7.3.3   *Securities Law Consequences*

The potential impact of materially misstating financial statements could include invalid registration statements, suspension of trading, stock exchange de-listing, enforcement of CEO/CFO clawback requirements, and criminal investigations based on information revealed in the disclosure process. The most significant potential securities law consequences include faulty SEC filings, CEO/CFO certification issues, and Form S-8 registration problems.

- *Issues with SEC Filings:* As discussed above, most employee plans provide that options must be granted at fair market value. Generally, if discounted grants are authorized in a plan, the maximum discount from fair market value is specifically limited (e.g., to 15%) and subject to the requirement that it be disclosed at the date of grant. If a shareholder-approved plan does not authorize discount options, then any backdated options granted by the company must be treated for securities law purposes as having been granted outside of the plan. In addition, if backdating led to material misstatement of financials, any public disclosures of the company that included those financials (i.e., all periodic reports, proxy statements, and registration statements), as well as reports of changes in beneficial ownership by insiders, may have been inaccurate or misleading. Any one of these issues alone could lead to the severe consequences noted above.

- *CEO/CFO Certification Issues:* The CEO and CFO are required to certify that the financial statements accompanying their companies' 10-Qs and 10-Ks are accurate in all material respects. False certifications by these officers open them up to securities and criminal law sanctions and clawbacks of incentive compensation.

- *Form S-8 Registration Statement Issues:* Like all other filings that incorporate financial statements by reference, the validity of a stock plan's S-8 registration will be called into question as a result of backdating. Further, if public filings are delayed or suspended, it is likely that no other exemption from registration (such as Rule 144) will be available to permit option exercises under the plan. Accordingly, a company may believe it is necessary to suspend all activity under its employee equity plans until the backdating issues are resolved and SEC filings are brought into compliance. This action, even when authorized by the compliance provisions of the plan, raises legal issues for optionees who are unable to exercise their vested options because they leave (or are terminated) during the self-imposed blackout period.

4.7.4 Suggestions for Avoiding Backdating in the Future

Companies are well advised to scrutinize their plan administration procedures. The best approach is to establish clear, consistent granting procedures that are not subject to discretionary variation and that make it easy to identify specific grant dates. In the event variation from the norm occurs, it should be clearly documented and the underlying reason for the variation should be explained.

Best practices for these option-granting purposes might include:

- *Establish Written Granting Policy:* In connection with SEC disclosure rules, work with the compensation committee (or plan committee) to prepare a description of the underlying principles for option granting at all levels under the company's equity compensation plans.

- *Require Observance of Specific Corporate Formalities:* These could include delegation of granting authority to a committee of more than one uninterested director, obtaining of consent in a meeting rather than as a unanimous written consent, immediate documentation of the resolutions adopted by the committee, and having a policy of communicating information to the plan administrator as soon as possible after the grant has been completed.

- *Establish Regular Granting Schedule:* Adhere to a normal schedule (monthly, quarterly, annually, etc.) for specific types of grants (e.g., new hire, performance). Deviate from the schedule only infrequently, and even then only with full explanation. If grant timing concerns are a trigger point for shareholders, it may be necessary to ensure that the schedule minimizes the possibility of spring-loading or bullet-dodging.

- *Establish Specific Written Criteria for Setting Fair Market Value:* There may be very little discretion here, however, depending on what the plan itself says about how fair market value must be determined. Authority and manner of setting the price should be clearly delineated.

- *Ensure That Stock Administration Procedures are Reliable:* Immediate reconciliation of stock plan records—in both database and minute books—is essential. Any red flags should be explored with counsel immediately. Timely issuance of paperwork is key, as are tracking and paying attention to all Section 16 reporting requirements.

- *Implement Ongoing Audit Procedures:* Companies should monitor their own granting activities with an internal audit on no less than a quarterly basis. Such audits will ensure that granting guidelines are being followed, reports timely filed, reconciliations made, and issues flagged on a real-time basis.

Employee Stock Purchase Plans

Contents

An employee stock purchase plan (ESPP) is a special form of employee stock plan that operates like a subscription purchase plan but is treated for tax purposes like a stock option plan. It may be used in conjunction with or as an alternative to a discretionary equity compensation plan. ESPPs are typically designed to allow employees to make regular, ongoing purchases of employer stock through accumulated after-tax payroll contributions, usually at a substantial discount from fair market value on the date of purchase. The majority of domestic ESPPs are tax-qualified plans that adhere to the limitations and requirements of Section 423 of the Code. Such ESPPs are referred to as "423 plans" or "Section 423 plans." However, in some cases employers adopt ESPPs that do not meet the requirements of the Code. These "non-Section 423 ESPPs" or "nonqualified ESPPs" are also discussed briefly below.

Public company planners will discover that they have a great deal of flexibility to tailor an ESPP to meet both corporate and employee needs, even when the ESPP is subject to the special tax limitations set out in Section 423. As with any stock-based compensation plan, a company that implements an ESPP must be careful to comply with state and federal securities laws, which are discussed in chapter 8. As always, securities counsel should be consulted to determine the applicable rules.

Because of the high degree of tax and administrative complexity inherent in a typical ESPP, such plans generally are not adopted by private companies. In particular, most ESPPs are designed around an ongoing, automatic calculation of fair market value and an automatic purchase technique that is not practical for the non-publicly traded company. ESPP administration (including reporting and tracking) is frequently handled by the company's broker or transfer agent, an alternative not available to a privately held company. Moreover, employees are unlikely to choose to make ongoing, automatic after-tax investments when there is no guarantee that there will ever be a public market for sale of the stock. Finally, in many states, local securities laws do not provide an exemption from registration for shares acquired under ESPPs, which poses another substantial hurdle.

This chapter discusses planning and design considerations and techniques that have developed over the years for ESPPs.

5.1   Statutory Requirements for Section 423 Plans

Section 423 plans are governed by the specific requirements prescribed in Section 423 of the Code and its regulations, as well as the general requirements for statutory options set out in Sections 421 and 424 of the Code.[1] As with an ISO plan, the employer must have a written Section 423 plan that sets forth the maximum number of shares that may be issued under the plan and the employees (or class of employees)

---

1.   The Treasury Department finalized updates to the Section 423 regulations in November 2009. Those regulations apply to grants made on or after January 1, 2010, although companies were able to rely on them before that date.

who are eligible to receive options under the plan.[2] The plan must receive shareholder approval within 12 months of its adoption by the company's board of directors.[3] Further shareholder approval is needed if there is a change in the shares being issued or a change in the granting corporation. As with an ISO plan, any changes to the number of shares or class of employees eligible to receive shares under the plan require additional shareholder approval. Companies may include an "evergreen provision" that provides for an annual increase the maximum aggregate number of shares available for grant under the plan by a specified percentage of the authorized, issued, or outstanding shares at the date of the adoption of the plan, as long as the plan specifies a maximum number of shares that may be added to the reserve under such provision and the evergreen provision is approved by shareholders.

However, unlike an ISO plan, administration of a Section 423 plan is subject to specific limitations on employee eligibility, participation, and availability. In order for options granted under an ESPP to be eligible for statutory option treatment, the plan must adhere to strict nondiscrimination rules, including a requirement that it be offered on a nondiscriminatory basis to all employees of the company who do not qualify as highly compensated under the Internal Revenue Code and that shareholders who own 5% or more of the company be excluded from participation. These rules are intended to ensure that Section 423 plans are not used as a vehicle for executive compensation. In fact, employers may wish to simply exclude top executives from participation entirely in order to ensure that the plan benefits only employees who do not ordinarily receive discretionary option grants under the company's stock option plans. This is an acceptable strategy under Section 423, which prohibits discrimination *in favor* of highly compensated employees, but does not prohibit discrimination *against* such employees.[4]

Specifically, the statutory prerequisites set out in Section 423(b) of the Code include:

1. Options may be granted only to employees of the employer corporation or its designated parent or subsidiary corporations to

---

2.   Treas. Reg. § 1.423-2(c)(3), (4).

3.   Treas. Reg. § 1.423-2(c)(1), (2).

4.   Section 423(a)(3), (5) of the Code; Treas. Reg. § 1.423-2(d), (e).

purchase stock in any such corporation. For these purposes, and for all statutory options, "employee" is defined with reference to the common-law definition of employee as used for purposes of wage withholding under Section 3402 of the Code.[5]

2. The plan must be approved by the shareholders of the granting corporation within 12 months before or after the plan is adopted.

3. Under the terms of the plan, no employee may be granted an option if such employee, immediately after the option is granted, would own stock having 5% or more of the voting power or value of all classes of stock of the employer or its parent or subsidiary corporations.[6]

4. Under the terms of the plan, if any options are granted to any employees, they must be granted to all employees of the corporation[7] with the exception of:

    a. employees employed less than two years,

    b. employees whose customary employment is 20 hours or less per week,

    c. employees whose customary employment is for not more than five months in any calendar year, and

    d. "highly compensated" employees as defined in Section 414(q) of the Code.

5. Under the terms of the plan, all participants must have the same rights and privileges, except that the amount of stock that may be purchased by any employee under an option may bear a uniform relationship to the employee's total compensation or his or her basic or regular rate of compensation, and a limit may be placed on the maximum number of shares that an employee may purchase under the plan. The key to satisfying the "equal rights and privileges" rule is to apply any administrative rules uniformly to all participants

---

5. Treas. Reg. § 1.421-1(h). See also IRS Notice 87-41, 1987-1 CB 296 (the "20-factor test"). The definitions of "parent" and "subsidiary" for statutory option purposes are set out in Section 424 of the Code.

6. Section 423(b)(3) of the Code. The rules for determining the percentage of stock ownership are set out in Section 424(d) of the Code.

7. Section 423(b)(4) of the Code.

in a single offering period. For example, the plan may define compensation to include only base salary or may also include bonus or overtime compensation, so long as the same definition applies to all. Another example: if the plan imposes administrative limitations on the number of shares that may be purchased during any offering period—such as an overall cap on the number of shares, a cap determined by formula, or a maximum percentage of payroll—these limitations must apply across the board.[8] Companies are free to set different rules for different offering periods that apply to different corporate entities within these constraints by, for example, excluding different groups of highly compensated employees from different offering periods under a single plan.

6. Under the terms of the plan, the option price may not be less than the lesser of 85% of the fair market value of the stock determined either (a) at the time of grant of the option or (b) at the time of exercise of the option.

7. Under the terms of the plan, options may not be exercised after the expiration of (a) five years, if the option price is not less than 85% of fair market value on the date of exercise, or (b) 27 months, if the option price is the lesser of 85% of fair market value on the date of grant or exercise.

8. Under the terms of the plan, no employee may be granted an option that permits his or her rights to purchase stock under all Section 423 plans of the employer company (and its parent and subsidiary corporations), to accrue at a rate that exceeds $25,000 worth of stock on the basis of fair market value at the time of grant. This limit is determined cumulatively for each calendar year in which such option is outstanding at any time.[9]

9. Under the terms of the plan, options may not be transferable except by will or the laws of descent and distribution, and must be exercisable during the employee's lifetime only by such employee.

---

8. Treas. Reg. § 1.423-2 (f).

9. Section 423(b)(8) of the Code; see also Treas. Reg. § 1.423-2(i) and the examples in Treas. Reg. § 1.423-2(i)(4).

5.2 ESPP Design

5.2.1 ESPP Design Vocabulary

The unique ESPP form has spawned its own special vocabulary to describe plan design and operation. An understanding of the following terms is essential before working through all of the design elements of an ESPP:

1. *Offering Period:* The period during which rights to purchase stock under an ESPP are outstanding. The period begins for all participants on the offering date and ends on a predetermined exercise date.

2. *Offering Date* or *Enrollment Date:* The first day of the offering period.

3. *Grant Date:* The same as "offering date" for tax purposes so long as the plan includes a limit on the number of shares that a single participant can purchase during an offering period—whether an absolute number or formula. (This requirement is *not* satisfied by a statement of the $25,000 limit.) If the maximum number of shares that may be purchased during the offering period is not determinable until the exercise date, then the grant date does not occur until that date.

4. *Participant or Optionee:* Employee who enrolls in an offering period.

5. *Option:* The participant's right to participate in an offering period. For tax purposes, a Section 423 plan option begins on the offering date and has a term equal to the duration of the offering period.

6. *Exercise Date* or *Purchase Date:* Predetermined date or dates upon which stock is purchased for all participants during an offering period. There is always an exercise date at the end of the offering period. There may also be interim exercise dates at the end of multiple purchase periods during a single offering period.

7. *Purchase Period:* A period during the offering period that is shorter in duration than the offering period. There is always an exercise date at the end of a purchase period. Although the first day of a purchase period may not be the offering date, the use of the term "purchase period" generally indicates that the exercise price will be determined with reference to the first day of the offering period rather than with reference to the first day of the purchase period.

8. *Exercise Price* or *Purchase Price:* The price paid for a share of stock purchased at the end of a purchase period, generally determined

as of the exercise date (frequently by applying a discount to the lower of the fair market value on either the offering date or the exercise date).

9. *Overlapping Offering Periods:* Offering periods that run concurrently, but have different offering dates (and accordingly, may have different exercise prices).

10. *Reset Provision:* A plan provision under which an offering period automatically terminates as of any exercise date on which the fair market value of a share of stock is lower than it was on the offering date. The new offering period has the same end date that the terminated offering period would have had if the reset had not been triggered.

These terms are used in connection with ESPPs throughout this book.

5.2.2   Statutory Design Limits for Section 423 Plans

As the above list of requirements shows, while Section 423 plans are a type of statutory option plan, they differ significantly from plans that allow for the grant of ISOs. First, eligibility is strictly controlled under Section 423(b): while *all* employees must be eligible (subject to the specific exclusions set out above) if any are to be eligible, an employee who owns 5% or more of the employer's stock immediately becomes ineligible as of the date he or she crosses the 5% threshold or would cross it if he or she were allowed to remain in the plan.[10] Second, the term "option" for purposes of a Section 423 plan generally refers to the right to participate in an offering period under the plan, rather than to an individual option grant.[11] All option grants are uniformly subject to a limitation on how much stock can be optioned by a single participant on a calendar-year basis, and the maximum number of shares under an option for any offering period must be determinable on the offering date. Third, the plan may not be drafted or operated in any manner that would result in different classes of employees having unequal "rights and privileges" within a single offering period.[12]

---

10. Section 423(b)(4); Treas. Reg. § 1.423-2(d), (e).

11. Treas. Reg. § 1.421-1(a)(2).

12. Section 423(b)(5); Treas. Reg. § 1.423-2(f).

It can be very challenging to ensure that both the plan design and its operation comply with all of these rules. For example, the application of uniform rules with different results will not violate the "equal rights and privileges" requirement. This means that if a plan provides that all participants may set aside up to 10% of compensation for purchases under an offering period, the fact that employees with different levels of income will accordingly be able to purchase widely different amounts of stock does not violate the rule. The regulations allow "equal rights and privileges" to be measured offering by offering, and allow the exclusion of different groups within the parameters of Section 423. For example, a parent company can prohibit its officers from participating in the plan while allowing a subsidiary's officers to participate, or it can make employees of the parent company wait longer than employees of the subsidiary before becoming eligible to participate in the plan.

One difficult application of the rules arises from the $25,000 limitation, because of the complexities of computing the annual limit on an accrual basis. Under Section 423(b)(8) and its regulations, the option value is measured when the option first becomes exercisable, i.e., on the offering date. The key to the calculation is *accrual in accordance with the annual $25,000 limit*, not purchase in accordance with the limit.

If the plan permits, a participant could purchase zero shares in the first year of a 24-month offering period with no interim purchase periods, and $50,000 worth of stock (computed as of the offering date) in the second year of the offering period. If the 24-month offering period had one purchase date in year one and another in year two, the participant could purchase up to $25,000 in stock in year one and then in year two be eligible to purchase $50,000 worth of stock minus whatever amount was purchased in year one.

However, the reverse of this is not true—i.e., the unaccrued right to purchase $50,000 worth of stock may not be anticipated in the first year of the offering period. Further, if the employee is participating in more than one offering period at any time, the total accrual under all offering periods will be added together to determine when the limit has been reached. However, amounts accrued under one offering period may not be used in a subsequent (or concurrent) offering period, even if the limit has not been exhausted with respect to any particular calendar year.

By way of illustration, assume that the offering period is 24 months and the offering date is January 1. If the stock was worth $10 per share on the offering date, each January 1 a participant may buy up to 2,500 shares of stock for each calendar year of the offering period (subject to whatever percentage or other limitations have otherwise been imposed by the company). However, now assume that a new offering period begins every six months, and the price on July 1 is $15 per share. For the offering period beginning on January 1, a participant has an option to purchase up to 2,500 shares. However, assume that he is only actually able to purchase 1,000 shares (shares with a value of $10,000) by the end of the first offering period, leaving a 1,500 share deficit. The unused portion of the January 1 option—1,500 shares—terminates on the last exercise date of the offering period (June 30), and may not be carried over to any subsequent offering period. For the offering period beginning July 1, the participant's available maximum would be the difference between $25,000 (the total calendar year maximum) and $10,000 (the amount of value purchased), over $15 (the value of a share on the second offering date), or 1,000 shares. This calculation can become even more complicated when short offering periods straddle two calendar years.

In practice, companies need to ensure that the pool of shares allocated to the ESPP does not get used up too quickly and that the plan can be administered without excessive attention to arcane calculations. This is particularly important during a downturn in the market, when the discounted price of shares drops and the number of shares purchasable with participant funds rises accordingly. The best way to handle this may be threefold: (1) cap the percentage of compensation that may be contributed to the plan, (2) cap the total number of shares that may be purchased during the offering period, notwithstanding percentage, and (3) carefully observe the $25,000 limit.

Note, too, that Treasury regulations effectively force companies that do not set the purchase price on the first day of the offering period to explicitly cap the total number of shares that may be purchased during the offering period.[13] Under these rules, the grant date does not occur for tax purposes until the maximum number of shares that can be purchased by each participant during the offering period is known.

---

13. Treas. Reg. § 1.423-2(h)(2), (3)

Thus, shares purchased under a plan that has a look-back feature but does not cap the number of shares an employee can purchase during an offering period will be deemed to have a grant date that occurs on the date on which the shares are purchased.

It is easy to see that the interplay of these limits means that employers must take special care when designing a Section 423 plan. The regulations provide a safety net by generally protecting options exercised during an offering period that complies with Section 423, even when the terms of the plan itself are noncompliant. Further, a single noncompliant offering period will not contaminate any other offering period that is compliant. Nonetheless, failure to comply fully with the rules can result, at best, in disqualification of a single option from Section 423 plan status and, at worst, in disqualification of an entire offering period.[14] For example, pursuant to the regulations, only the affected option will be disqualified if initially granted to a participant who is ineligible to participate in the plan under Section 423(b)(4), or subsequently rendered noncompliant during the offering period (either operationally or by virtue of the participant becoming ineligible). On the other hand, an entire offering period may be disqualified if an individual who is eligible to participate in the offering period is not permitted to participate, if an option is priced below the minimum pricing requirements of Section 423(b)(6), if an offering period exceeds the durational limits of Section 423(b)(7), and if the purchase (or right to purchase stock) during an offering period accrues at a rate in excess of that permitted in 423(b)(8). Such inadvertent disqualification can result in serious adverse tax consequences to employees who were expecting to be eligible for the tax benefits of Section 423.[15]

5.2.3   Typical Structure of an ESPP: Payroll Deduction Plans

As detailed above, Section 423 sets out a laundry list of requirements for tax qualification under the Code. However, although one would assume that non-Section 423 ESPPs offer greater possibilities for plan design, employers have been able to develop remarkably flexible plans for employees within the confines of the rules. By incorporating Sec-

---

14. Treas. Reg. 1.423-2(a)(1), (4)

15. Treas. Reg. § 1.423-2(i).

tion 423 compliance into ESPP planning, employers have been able to provide plan participants with a substantial discount from market price (as well as tax deferral). In practice, non-Section 423 ESPPs often look identical to Section 423 plans—but they can operate without concern for statutory limitations. For example, like most Section 423 plans, most non-Section 423 ESPPs are designed to be payroll deduction plans. However, the company may limit or expand eligibility, vary the types of benefits extended to different participants, and extend or reduce the length of offering periods. In their simplest form, ESPPs may be "open-market plans" that offer little or no discount to the participant but provide an ongoing investment vehicle for regular stock purchases.

Companies that have ESPPs that do not conform with Section 423 can offer share-price discounts, but should be careful to determine the purchase date at or before the beginning of the offering period so that stock purchased under the plan is not deemed to be deferred compensation subject to Code Section 409A, which would subject participants to immediate taxation and penalties at vesting. In practice, most ESPPs have a predetermined purchase date, which satisfies this requirement.

The most widely used form of ESPP has been the Section 423 payroll deduction plan, pioneered largely by Silicon Valley companies in the early 1980s. When designing a Section 423 ESPP, the employer must consider two levels of issues: (1) the enrollment procedure/participation level permitted for participants, and (2) the overall structure of the offering period. The limitations of the Code act as an overarching framework to the design, but administrative convenience will generally govern the operation of the plan.

5.2.3.1   *Enrollment Procedures/Participation Level*

A major administrative asset of an ESPP is its automatic purchase feature. This is made possible by establishing participant accounts that are prefunded through after-tax payroll contributions. Alternatively, plans can provide for purchases via cash payment or promissory note. However, few ESPPs have this feature because of the administrative difficulty of obtaining timely payment from participants on the exercise date.

To become a participant, each employee completes a subscription or enrollment agreement before the offering date of the first offering period that they are eligible to join. The enrollment agreement states the percentage of after-tax earnings that the participant wishes to set aside for use in purchasing stock under the plan. The cap on the percentage is purely discretionary to the company, although typical caps are in the 10%–15% range.

During the offering period, the company accumulates the deducted amounts in accounts for the plan participants. Unless a participant withdraws from the plan before the exercise date, his or her option is exercised automatically by the company on the purchase date. The number of shares purchased is the maximum number of shares that may be purchased with the accumulated payroll contributions in the participant's account at the applicable option price, up to the overall number of shares subject to the option (as determined on the offering date). The exact number is computed by dividing the actual amount in the participant's account by the exercise price, and then applying any additional caps (e.g., company-imposed per-participant offering cap, $25,000 limit) to that number.

If there are not enough shares available under the plan to be purchased at the end of a purchase period, the balance of the payroll contributions can be returned to the participants (with or without interest at the discretion of the company). Most plans contain language providing that if the share pool is depleted before the end of an offering period, participants will receive pro-rata allocations rather than their full allotment of shares on the exercise date. Payroll contributions can also be returned if the amounts accumulated in a participant's account would provide for a purchase that exceeds the per-participant limits under the plan. Plans should not allow withheld payroll contributions to carry over from one offering period to another or other participants in the plan will have to be allowed to make direct payments into the plan to make up the difference between their own contributions to the plan and the largest carryover amount allowed in that period.[16] (Amounts that would purchase fractional shares can be carried from one offering period to the next without triggering a requirement to allow others to contribute an equal amount.) Note that this is where the difference between offering period and purchase period becomes important. In a

---

16. Treas. Reg. § 1.423-2(f)(5).

long offering period, "excess" payroll contributions will always be carried over to the next purchase period (unless otherwise withdrawn by the participant), even if re-enrollment and return of funds is required for subsequent offering periods.

At the discretion of the company, the initial enrollment agreement may stay in place indefinitely until withdrawn by the participant or the participant may be required to file a new enrollment agreement for each offering period.

There are a variety of ways of dealing with withdrawals or percentage changes under the plan, particularly in a down market when employees may want to reduce their investment in company stock so as to diversify their portfolios. Plans should always permit the participant to withdraw completely from an offering period, or options granted under that offering period may be deemed to be exercised for tax purposes on each date that payroll contributions are accumulated in the participant's account.[17] Otherwise, there are no statutory restrictions on how employee contributions must be handled: it is purely a matter of administrative design for the company. Some employers permit participants to make withdrawals and changes in their election percentages at any time during the offering period, while some limit the number of times that changes can occur, or permit withdrawals and percentage decreases but not increases during a purchase period.

A well-designed plan will also include provisions for automatic withdrawal in certain circumstances. The best example of this is automatic withdrawal from the plan (and return of all contributions) when a participant terminates employment during an offering period. This ensures that the plan does not actually authorize disqualification based on employment-related requirements. For example, an individual option will always be disqualified if permitted to be exercised more than three months after termination of employment. More worrisome, under the "equal rights and privileges" rule either the offering period or the whole plan could be disqualified if some—but not all—participants are afforded the right to participate after termination.[18]

---

17. Treas. Reg. § 1.421-1(f).
18. Sections 421(a) and 423(b)).

5.2.3.2 *Offering Period Structure*

In a typical ESPP, the employer first decides whether it will establish long or short offering periods, and whether such offering periods will be consecutive or concurrent.

A short, consecutive offering period structure has the advantage of being straightforward and easy to administer. It has a single exercise date, after which the offering period ends and a new offering period, with a new offering date price, begins. If the plan has a "look-back" feature, the exercise price for each option is computed as the lower of 85% of fair market value on the offering date or the purchase date. At the purchase date, the number of optioned shares that may be purchased with the funds credited to the participant's account for that period are purchased. If the participant has withdrawn from the offering period prior to the purchase date, his or her option terminates on the date of the withdrawal, and all payroll contributions that have been withheld so far in the offering period are returned to him or her. The plan as a whole may be easily terminated without adversely affecting any individual participant's rights to purchase stock, since there are no concurrent offering periods. Because the offering period is short, the stock price is unlikely to undergo large fluctuations between offering date and purchase date, making it possible to realistically predict the number of shares needed to fund the plan on an ongoing basis.

A long offering period may be more administratively complex, but it has the advantage of providing exceptional price benefits to employees and as such will be perceived very favorably as an employee benefit. Such an offering period might last as long as two years and include multiple purchase periods: for example, a 24-month offering period might have four 6-month purchase periods. During the offering period, participants who were enrolled on the offering date have an option to make four purchases (one on each purchase date). The exercise price for each purchase is computed as the lower of 85% of fair market value on the offering date or the purchase date. Although the purchase date price may change, the offering date price remains constant.[19] Exhibit 5-1 illustrates the difference between four consecutive six-month offering periods and a single two-year offering period with four interim purchase dates.

---

19. Section 423(b)(7) of the Code.

Exhibit 5-1. Comparison of Short Consecutive Offering Periods with Long Offering Period and Interim Purchase Periods

Date	Stock price	85% of stock price	Purchase price in plan with consecutive 6-month purchase periods	Purchase price in plan with 2-year offering period and 6-month interim purchase periods
June 1, 2008	$10	$8.50	N/A	N/A
December 1, 2008	$15	$12.75	$8.50	$8.50
June 1, 2009	$12	$10.20	$10.20	$8.50
December 1, 2009	$9	$7.65	$7.65	$7.65
June 10, 2010	$16	$13.60	$7.65	$8.50

Employers who establish long offering periods can either set them up as overlapping, concurrent offering periods so that new employees may participate in a full-length offering period from the start, or they can allow employees to join the plan at the start of each purchase period within the long offering period. In either case, the plan administrator must be aware that in an up market, there will be multiple exercise prices on any given exercise date. If new offering periods start, say, every six months and last for two years, then each offering period will look back to its own starting date fair market value. In plans with interim purchase periods, those who join after the offering period is under way will look back to the first day of the first purchase period in which they participated. In a down market, the number of shares purchasable in any offering period will increase as the price drops. In a worst-case scenario, this can result in the plan running out of stock mid-offering period.

Plan designers should be aware that, while the regulations permit complicated accruals in plans that have long offering periods, the plan itself may be designed to avoid complexity. For example, a plan could limit the amount of stock value that may be accrued under all plans of the company during any six-month period to $12,500 worth of stock, notwithstanding the $25,000 annual cap. Or a plan with concurrent offering periods could provide that eligible employees may participate in only one offering period at a time (so long as this rule is applied uniformly to everyone who is eligible to participate in the plan).

Obviously, in an up market, the discount from fair market value at the date of grant can increase dramatically with the fair market value of the shares under an ESPP with a long offering period. Assume, for example, that the fair market value of the stock is $20 at the date of grant and that, with a 15% discount, the purchase price would be $17 (85% of $20). Assume further that at month 24 the fair market value of the stock is $40. By allowing an employee to purchase the shares at 85% of the lesser of date of grant or date of exercise, the 15% discount would increase, in this example, to a discount of 42.5% of the value on the date of purchase.

However, what happens in a down-market scenario? The cash amount reserved to the participant's account remains the same, but as the stock price decreases, the number of shares purchasable with the static cash reserve will increase. Ironically, in a falling market participants are unlikely to want to purchase more stock. They are more likely to choose to withdraw from the offering period (after the end of the purchase period) and immediately re-enter at a different percentage on the next offering date, so as to lock in the lower price being set for subsequent offering periods.

One way to address this problem, albeit one that has declined in popularity is automatic withdrawal as part of a reset provision. This feature provides that on any exercise date where the stock price is lower than the offering date price, the plan automatically withdraws participants and enrolls them in a new offering period beginning on the day after the exercise date and ending on the date when the offering period otherwise would have ended. This provision needs to be included in the plan prior to the beginning of the affected offering period. Unfortunately, reset provisions have come to be viewed as dilutive by nonemployee stockholders. Moreover, under Accounting Standards Codification Topic 718, this feature carries negative accounting consequences for the company because the withdrawal and re-enrollment are treated as a modification.[20] This negative accounting treatment is unfortunate, because participants are always free to withdraw from an offering period and re-enroll in a later period: in other words, the automatic withdrawal technique is really just for administrative convenience. Moreover, in plans that limit the number of times that changes can occur, the reset

---

20. Modification accounting is discussed in chapter 10.

may be the only way to avoid penalizing employees who have a higher offering date price because of seniority. Of course, it's not necessary for the company to "rescue" employees from unfavorable stock prices (and it is noteworthy that in this type of ESPP, an "underwater" offering date price will be ignored in favor of a discount from the exercise date price anyway). Exhibit 5-2 provides an illustration of overlapping offering periods that include multiple purchase periods and a reset feature.

Exhibit 5-2. ESPP Offering Periods

Overlapping two-year offering periods (OP) with four six-month exercise periods (EP) and a reset. Each purchase price (PP) is the lower of 85% FMV on offering date (OD) or exercise date (ED).

	1/1/06	7/1/06	1/1/07	7/1/07	1/1/08	7/1/08	1/1/09	7/1/09	1/1/10
FMV	$20	$10	$5	$10	$20	$30	$35	$30	$40
OP1	OD1	*ED--------ED----------							
PP($)		$8.50	$4.25						
OP2		OD2 -------*ED-------							
PP($)			$4.25						
OP3			OD3 ------ ED	---------- ED	-------- ED	--------- ED			
PP($)				$4.25	$4.25	$4.25	$4.25		
OP4				OD4--------ED	-------- ED	-------- ED	--------- ED		
PP($)					$8.50	$8.50	$8.50	$8.50	
OP5						OD5 -----ED	--------- ED	--------- ED	--------- ED
PP($)							$17.00	$17.00	$17.00	$17.00

*Because of the reset, OP1 and OP2 terminate on any ED when ED price is lower than OD price, automatically purchasing shares and then enrolling all participants in next OP.

Offering period structure also may become an issue in a corporate transaction situation. If the employer corporation is acquired in the middle of an offering period, the employer may choose to terminate the offering period (and the ESPP) in advance of the acquisition, and such flexibility should be built into the plan design. In this scenario, the final purchase date under the ESPP will occur in advance of the effective date

of the acquisition. The exact timing of the purchase should allow the
employer to address the administrative issues that may arise in connection with the final purchase and the impending corporate transaction.

5.2.4   Participating in a Section 423 Plan After Termination

Most Section 423 plans are designed to automatically withdraw former
employees from participation on the date they terminate employment.
As noted, participants must, at all times during the period beginning
with the offering date and ending on the day three months before the
exercise date, be employees of the sponsoring corporation (or its parent
or subsidiary). In theory, an employee who terminates employment less
than three months before the end of a purchase period could be allowed
to remain in the plan through the next purchase date. However, there
are serious risks to this alternative. First, if the post-termination period is
actually longer than three months, the offering period may be disqualified for all participants because of the participation of a nonemployee.
Second, in order to comply with the "equal rights and privileges" requirements of Section 423, the right to exercise post-termination would
need to be extended to all participants and could not be awarded on a
case-by-case basis (as, for example, with a discretionary stock option).
Failure to offer a benefit on a nondiscriminatory basis may also result
in disqualification of the offering period or even the entire plan.

5.3   Tax Consequences

The tax consequences of ESPP options, like the tax consequences of stock
options generally, depend on whether they are statutory stock options.
ESPPs intended to qualify under Section 423 of the Code are statutory
stock option plans, and in addition to the specific rules set out in Section
423 are governed (along with ISO plans) by Sections 421 and 424 of the
Code. As a general rule, the same rules apply to modifications of Section
423 plan options as apply to ISO modifications.[21] However, note that—unlike an ISO—an ESPP right that is modified, renewed, or extended must

---

21. See discussion on "Modifying Statutory Stock Options" in section 3.5.

be priced at the higher of fair market value at the date of grant, the date of modification, or the date of any previous modification.[22]

ESPP options that are not granted under a Section 423 plan are NSOs for tax purposes, and as such are governed by Section 83 of the Code (discussed more fully in chapter 2). Accordingly, in the year of exercise, the participant will be required to include in ordinary income the difference between the exercise price and the fair market value of the stock on the exercise date. As a general rule, the employer will be entitled to take a tax deduction in an amount equal to that included in income by the participant.[23] Gain recognized on the disposition of ESPP shares will be treated as long-term capital gain if the shares were held for more than one year from the exercise date. The mechanics of reporting and withholding on the exercise of an NSO are described in chapter 9, "Tax Law Compliance Issues."

5.3.1 Employee Income Taxes

If a plan satisfies all of the Section 423 requirements, the ultimate tax consequences depend on the actions of the employee and the option price of the stock purchased in relation to its fair market value. A plan participant will not recognize income for federal income tax purposes either upon the grant of an option (the offering date) or upon the exercise of an option (exercise or purchase date) under the plan. Instead, all income tax consequences will be deferred until the participant sells the stock or otherwise disposes of the shares.

If stock granted at less than fair market value is held for the statutory holding periods (more than one year from exercise date and more than two years after the offering date), or if the participant dies while owning the shares, the participant will realize ordinary income on a sale (or a disposition by way of gift) to the extent of the lesser of: (1) the difference between the fair market value of the stock and the option price at the *date of grant,* or (2) the actual gain (the amount by which the market value of the shares on the *date of sale or disposition* exceeds the purchase price). All additional gain upon the sale of stock is treated

---

22. Section 424(h)(2) of the Code; Treas. Reg. § 1.424-1(e)(3).

23. Section 83(h) of the Code; Treas. Reg. § 1.83-6(a).

as long-term capital gain. If the shares are sold and the sale price is less than the purchase price, there is no ordinary income, and the difference between the sale price and the purchase price is a long-term capital loss for the employee.[24] To get the benefits of a qualifying disposition, the ESPP participant must be an employee of the corporation granting the option (or of a parent or subsidiary corporation of the employer corporation) at all times during the period beginning with the date of grant and ending on the purchase date, or in the case where a terminated employee is allowed to purchase under the plan, ending on the day three months before the option is exercised.[25]

Different rules apply on disposition of statutory option stock as a result of death.[26] Further, a person who is required to sell ESPP stock for purposes of complying with federal conflict of interest laws is treated as satisfying the statutory holding period regardless of how long the stock was held.[27]

If the maximum number of shares that can be purchased by any one participant during the offering period is not established before the beginning of the offering period, then the grant date is not considered to occur until the purchase date. (A statement of the $25,000 limit does not satisfy this requirement.) In such a case, for ordinary income tax purposes, the grant date discount would be measured on the date of purchase, not the first day of the offering period. Exhibit 5-4 describes the tax consequences of a grant date that does not occur until the purchase date.

If the participant makes a disqualifying disposition of Section 423 plan stock, the participant recognizes ordinary income at the time of sale or other disposition taxable to the extent of the spread on exercise—i.e., the difference between fair market value and purchase price on the *exercise date*. This excess will constitute ordinary income in the year of sale or other disposition even if no gain is realized on the sale or if a gratuitous transfer is made. The difference, if any, between the proceeds of sale and the fair market value of the stock at the exercise date is a

---

24. Section 423(c) of the Code; Treas. Reg. § 1.423-2(k).
25. Section 421(a) of the Code.
26. See chapter 11.
27. Section 421(d) of the Code.

capital gain or loss (which is long-term if the stock has been held more than one year). Ordinary income recognized by an employee upon a disqualifying disposition constitutes taxable compensation that must be reported on a W-2 form.[28]

Separately, brokers are required to furnish plan participants with Forms 1099-B that reflect a cost basis equal to the amount paid for the shares purchased. This requirement has some problematic aspects for ESPP participants. The new requirement is discussed more fully in section 9.2.3.

Exhibits 5-3 and 5-4 illustrate the tax consequences of exercising Section 423 options. Note in exhibit 5-3 that if the grant date for tax purposes did not occur until the purchase date (for example, because the plan did not specify a maximum number of shares each participant could purchase in an offering period), then in a qualifying disposition, the ordinary income would be $3 per share and the long-term capital gain would be $18.50.

Exhibit 5-3. 423 Plan Options—Illustration: Gain on Disposition

Fair market value	*Exercise price*
First day (grant date): $10.00	Lesser of 85% first or last day: $8.50
85% of first day: $8.50	Sale price: $30.00
Last day: $20.00	Exercise price: $8.50
85% of last day: $17.00	

	Qualifying	Disqualifying
Gain	$21.50	$21.50
Ordinary income	$1.50 (15% at grant)	$11.50[a]
Capital gain	$20.00 long-term capital gain	$10.00[b]

[a]Ordinary income on discount at exercise

[b]Long-term capital gain or short-term capital gain, depending on holding period

---

28. Section 421(b) of the Code; Treas. Reg. § 1.83-6(a)(2). Compare this treatment to the treatment of a loss on a disqualifying disposition of ISO stock described in section 3.3 of chapter 3.

Exhibit 5-4. 423 Plan Options—Illustration: Loss on Disposition

Fair market value
First day (grant date): $10.00
85% of first day: $8.50
Last day: $20.00
85% of last day: $17.00

Exercise price
Lesser of 85% first or last day: $8.50
Sale price: $5.00
Exercise price: $8.50

	Qualifying	Disqualifying
(Loss)	($3.50)	($3.50)
Ordinary income	-0-[a]	11.50[b]
Capital loss	($3.50) long-term capital loss	($15.00)[c]

[a]Lesser of discount at offering date or actual gain
[b]Discount at exercise
[c]Short-term or long-term capital loss (sale price minus fair market value at exercise)

5.3.2   Employer Taxes

Neither income tax nor payroll tax withholding is required on a disqualifying disposition of ESPP stock.[29] On a disqualifying disposition only, the employer company is entitled to take a deduction for federal income tax purposes to the extent that a participant recognizes ordinary income, subject to any limitations otherwise imposed by the Code.[30] The company is not entitled to a deduction if the participant meets the statutory holding period requirements—even when the employee must recognize ordinary income on part of the gain.

The employer should set up administrative parameters to track dispositions of ESPP stock, including, for example, requiring participants to notify the employer company in writing of the date and terms of any disposition of stock purchased under the plan. Further, the employer will be unable to take the deduction connected with a disqualifying disposition unless it has been properly "tracked." The mechanics of reporting and withholding on ESPP shares are further described in chapter 9, "Tax Law Compliance Issues."

---

29. The American Jobs Creation Act of 2004 settled a 33-year dispute between employers and the IRS over whether withholding was required by specifically stating it is not.

30. For example, the limitations on deductions in Sections 162(m) and 280G of the Code. See sections 9.6 and 9.7.

The Form 1099-B requirements may serve to confuse plan participants who will receive forms reflecting a cost basis equal to the purchase price of the shares, which does not accurately reflect the cost basis they must report on their taxes. Plan sponsors may wish to remind participants that their tax basis will include any "spread" included in income at the time of (or prior to) the sale. This, too, is described more fully in chapter 9.

5.3.3 Quirky Tax Outcomes for Section 423 Plans in Down Markets

Notwithstanding the general tax treatment described above, the operation of the Section 423 rules can produce some surprising results in plans that have look-back features in which the purchase price is computed as a discount from the fair market value at either offering date or purchase date, whichever is lower. In a rising market, we assume that the market value of the stock at the purchase date will be higher than it was at the offering date, and thus the purchase-price discount will be taken from the fair market value on the *offering date*. In a down market, however, it works the other way: the purchase-price discount is taken from the fair market value on the *purchase date*.

If the participant satisfies the statutory holding period requirements, Section 423(c) treats as ordinary income the portion of the gain equal to up to 15% of the offering date price, *regardless of the actual purchase price for the stock*. This contrasts with tax treatment on a disqualifying disposition, which characterizes *only the spread at exercise* as ordinary income.

Thus, in a down market, it is possible to get a better tax benefit from a disqualifying disposition than from a qualifying disposition. Although counterintuitive, the participant's tax outcome may be improved by selling earlier, particularly if the shares were held just long enough for the capital gains to be taxed at the lower long-term rates (i.e., more than one year from purchase but not two years from grant).

In the down-market scenario, participants benefit from knowing that they may control tax consequences by timing the disposition. Exhibit 5-5 illustrates this strange tax result.

Exhibit 5-5. Dispositions in a Down Market

Facts: 6-month offering period, 85% FMV pricing

Offering date FMV: $20; 15% discount = $3 (85% = $17)

Exercise date FMV: $10; 85% (actual exercise price) = $8.50; 15% discount = $1.50

Sale prices: (a) $50 (b) $15 (c) $5

Scenario 1: Qualifying dispositions (QDs): The lesser of the difference between option price and FMV on date of grant and actual amount of gain on sale is included in ordinary income (OI). The remainder is capital gain (CG) or capital loss (CL), which is either long-term (LT) or short-term (ST). For these purposes, the first day of the offering period is the date of grant even if the price is not yet determinable, and the option is treated as having been exercised on that date.

Scenario 2: Disqualifying dispositions (DDs): Apply Section 83 on exercise date to difference between FMV and option price.

(a) *$50 sale price*
    QD: Discount at offering date: $3
           Gain on sale: $50 − $8.50 = $41.50
           Lesser of $3 or $41.50 = $3.
           OI =$3, LTCG = $38.50.
    DD: OI on discount at exercise date: $1.50
           CG on sale: $50 − $10 = $40

(b) *$15 sale price*
    QD: Discount at offering date: $3
           Gain on sale: $15 − $8.50 = $6.50
           Lesser of $3 or $6.50 = $3
           OI = $3, LTCG = $3.50
    DD: OI on discount at exercise date: $1.50
           CG on sale: $15 − $10 = $5

(c) *$5 sale price*
    QD: Discount at offering date: $3
           Gain (loss) on sale: $5 − $8.50 = ($3.50)
           Lesser of $3 or ($3.50) = ($3.50)
           OI = $0, LTCL = $3.50
    DD: OI on discount at exercise date: $1.50
           CL on sale: $5 − $10 = ($5)

5.4   International Planning Considerations

Although a detailed discussion of international ESPP issues is beyond the scope of this chapter, it is important to note the key question of when—and whether—to include international employees as participants in the plan. Companies that employ non-U.S. employees (both resident and nonresident) should be aware that even when Section 423 provides no tax benefits to such employees, they must nevertheless (in general) be eligible to participate in the company's plan if not otherwise excluded under Section 423(b) of the Code. Companies are allowed to conduct separate offering periods that, while they must comply with Section 423, can include differing terms. This rule eases situations in which local law requires employees to receive special treatment that is not otherwise available to U.S. employees under the plan: i.e., that otherwise would result in a violation of the "equal rights and privileges" requirement set out in the regulations. For example, an offering to U.S. employees could exclude employees who work less than 20 hours a week while a European offering under the same plan may be required to include part-time employees under local law. Under this approach, "equal rights and privileges" are measured offering period by offering period, not in terms of plan operation in its entirety.

However, failure to extend participation to non-U.S. employees who would otherwise be eligible to participate in the plan or an offering period—and to take such employees into account for purposes of Section 423 nondiscrimination rules—can result in disqualification of the individual option, the plan, and/or the offering period. This means that there may be circumstances when companies must extend ESPP participation to employees in countries where it is expensive, time-consuming, and of little benefit to employees to do so. There are, however, two notable exclusions for determining eligibility of non-U.S. employees: such employees may be excluded if they reside in a jurisdiction where participation would be expressly illegal, or where the company's compliance with the foreign jurisdiction's laws would disqualify the plan or offering as a whole under Section 423.[31] Moreover, while an ESPP must be offered to all employees of "designated companies" if it is offered to any employees of such companies, even under the final regulations, it is never necessary to designate every subsidiary for participation in an offering or the plan as a whole. In fact, unless a parent or subsidiary is specifically designated, the employer is not required to extend participation to its employees. This design element may help global companies that employ non-U.S. employees through foreign subsidiaries, as it provides one permissible way to avoid raising eligibility and nondiscrimination issues with respect to such employees.

---

31. Treas. Reg. 1.423-2(e)(3).

Such a design will offer no relief, of course, if a company's international employees are not employed by separate entities.[32]

32. Plan sponsors should consult their legal advisors before making decisions with regard to international plan matters. For general information on international plans see, e.g., the Baker & McKenzie Global Equity Matrix at www.bakermckenzie.com/nlnagescountrymatrix, or "GPS: Global Stock Plans" (Santa Clara, CA: Certified Equity Professional Institute, 2009), at www.scu.edu/business/cepi/gps_published_research.cfm. Current updates on international issues are readily available online at www.naspp.com and www.globalequity.org.

Chapter 6

Trends in Equity Compensation: An Overview

Contents

Over the past decade, discussions of equity compensation have expanded beyond stock options to include grants of tax-restricted stock awards and units, stock appreciation rights (SARs), and phantom stock. The forces contributing to the increasing popularity of these instruments have been varied and have led to restricted stock units (RSUs) and restricted stock awards (RSAs) becoming popular enough to rival stock options as a vehicle for broad-based equity compensation.[1]

---

1.   See the National Association of Stock Plan Professionals' "Domestic Stock Plan Design Survey" and Equilar's "Equity Trends Report."

RSAs and perhaps to a greater degree RSUs have gained in popularity for several reasons. For one thing, accounting rules that favored stock options over other forms of equity compensation were replaced in 2005.[2] For another, corporate governance trends and shareholder approval rules have led companies to look for forms of equity-based compensation that appear at first glance to be more palatable to shareholders—who must approve most public company equity compensation plans and who tend to prefer plans that give out fewer actual shares. This trend continues to evolve in various ways, including through institutional shareholders requiring employers to count "full-value awards" differently than stock options for purposes of calculating the dilutive effect of an equity compensation plan. In addition, the extreme stock market volatility of the past several years has made awards that cannot fall underwater more attractive and easier to communicate to employees. Companies that grant equity compensation are not abandoning traditional stock options wholesale, but these other vehicles for sharing equity with employees—RSUs in particular—are increasingly relevant to discussions of equity compensation.

This chapter discusses recent trends for tying equity compensation to shareholder interests and provides a brief overview of some of the available alternatives to stock options. Our discussion is intended to give the reader a survey of the landscape only.[3]

6.1   Aligning Equity Compensation with Shareholder Interests: Some Trends

In recent years investors have gained more tools for addressing the perceived a gap between one of the stated goals of equity compensation—aligning employee and shareholder interests—and reality. Certainly, at the top executive level, windfall compensation from equity grants has not served any useful performance-related purpose. In response, an increasing number of public companies had already adopted stock ownership policies for executives and directors that directly addressed

---

2.   For more on this, see chapter 10.

3.   For fuller explanations of these vehicles, see Corey Rosen et al., *Equity Alternatives: Restricted Stock, Performance Awards, Phantom Stock, SARs, and More*, 15th ed. (Oakland, CA: NCEO, 2017).

the issue of aligning employee and shareholder interests even before the Dodd-Frank Act of 2010 mandated that companies allow shareholders advisory votes on executive pay. Since stock ownership policies must be disclosed under SEC compensation disclosure rules, quite a bit of information on this important trend has become available.

6.1.1 Stock Transaction Policies

These policies limit the ability of executives and/or directors to buy and sell stock acquired pursuant to equity compensation awards. The philosophy is that in order for employee stockholders' interests to be aligned with those of other investors, they must genuinely be at risk (i.e., they must not be able to cash out as soon as their awards are in the money). One or more policies regarding ownership may be combined. Companies must be careful to keep such policies from being so restrictive that they discourage employees from acquiring the shares through stock option exercises or otherwise undermining the value of the stock award as an incentive. They should also be sufficiently flexible to address estate planning, tax withholding, and hardship considerations. The policies should be in writing and must be disclosed as part of the Compensation Discussion & Analysis disclosure in the proxy statement.[4]

Examples of such policies include:

- *Holding Policies.* Require employee stockholders to retain stock for a certain period of time (e.g., for a specified number of years or until termination) or until the achievement of certain performance milestones.

- *Minimum Ownership Policies.* Require employee stockholders to retain stock until a minimum ownership level is reached and to maintain that ownership level during the employment period. This may be a specified amount, a percentage of total shares acquired under an award (or under all awards), or a total stock value equal to a multiple of base salary.

- *Anti-Hedging Policies.* Prohibit employee stockholders from limiting risk with respect to stock purchased under equity awards by engaging

---

4. See section 8.6.

in hedging transactions (e.g., zero-cost collars, forward sale contracts etc.). These policies can be included in companies' insider trading policies. Note, however, that in 2009 the SEC issued a rule allowing employees to use vested options as collateral for the purchase of call options on employer stock, a result that is out of sync with the philosophy inherent to corporate anti-hedging policies. The Dodd-Frank Wall Street Reform and Consumer Protection Act of 2010 requires companies to disclose in their proxy statements any policies allowing employees or directors to hedge employer stock.

6.1.2   Clawbacks

In this context, a clawback is a contractual right to recover realized equity compensation upon the occurrence of certain events. The Sarbanes-Oxley Act authorizes SEC enforcement of forfeiture of compensation by the CEO and CFO in the event of certain securities law violations (e.g., those giving rise to financial restatements, such as backdating).[5] The Dodd-Frank Act broadens this to include current and former officers and applies to incentive compensation when vesting is based on stock price or other financial reporting metrics. This includes performance-vested equity compensation received in the three years leading up to a restatement that results from material noncompliance with SEC rules. The Dodd-Frank provision will go into effect once the associated regulations, which were proposed in mid-2015, are finalized and the national securities exchanges issue listing standards that follow the SEC regulations.[6]

Because the Dodd-Frank Act does not require that compensation be clawed back solely from those who were involved in the financial misstatements, it potentially has a much broader application than the Sarbanes-Oxley provision. However, in 2016 the Ninth Circuit Court of Appeals took a broader view of the clawback provisions of the Sarbanes-Oxley Act when it upheld the SEC's argument that Sarbanes-Oxley allows clawbacks from CEOs and CFOs who have certified false

---

5.   Sections 304 and 1103.

6.   The proposed regulations are discussed in chapter 13.

and misleading financial statements that are later restated—even if the restatement was not caused by the misconduct of the CEO or CFO.[7]

Prior to passage of Sarbanes-Oxley, companies typically sought to use clawbacks as a way of enforcing post-termination noncompete clauses, although some states do not allow their enforcement under those circumstances.[8] That being said, there is an ongoing trend of broadening contractual clawback provisions to allow for reclamation of compensation upon termination for cause or disloyal acts that the board of directors determines to be against the best interests of the company. The trend is fueled in part by proxy advisory services' favorable view of clawback policies, which they take into account when assessing companies' executive compensation proposals. Other companies are adopting clawback policies that more closely follow the statutory language of the Dodd-Frank Act in anticipation of those rules going into effect.

6.1.3 Performance-Contingent Long-Term Incentives

As with stock-selling policies, performance-contingent long-term incentives place limits on the executive's ability to realize gains from equity compensation that might be seen as out of alignment with the results realized by nonemployee stockholders. Providing for performance-based awards makes for an appealing Compensation Discussion and Analysis (CD&A) in the proxy disclosure, can minimize expense under Accounting Standards Codification Topic 718, and aids in establishing deductibility under Section 162(m) of the Code.[9] However, as with stock-selling policies, companies must carefully weigh the benefits of improving investor optics against the very real potential for undermining the value of the equity grant to employees if the goals are perceived as unreasonable or unachievable. In particular, performance-vested grants that use metrics tied to share price or other financial reporting metrics, including relative TSR, would be covered under proposed clawback rules under the Dodd-Frank Act. Examples include:

---

7. *SEC v. Jensen*, No. 14-55221 (9th Cir. Aug. 31, 2016).

8. For an analysis of the enforceability of noncompete-related clawbacks under state law, see section 12.2.

9. This limit is discussed in section 9.6.

- *Capped-Value Awards.* The terms of these awards limit the amount of appreciation that can be realized on exercise. The cap may be stated in terms of a dollar amount or a percentage (e.g., 125%) of the strike price. Exercise will be triggered on the date when the underlying stock hits the cap.

- *Premium-Priced Awards.* The exercise price of the award is at a premium to the fair market value on the date of grant—i.e., the award is "underwater" on the date of grant. In addition, the terms of the award generally state that it may not be exercised until the underlying stock reaches the level of the premium price and in some cases remains at or above that price for a stated period of time.

- *Performance-Vested Awards.* Vesting of equity awards is based not on a period of years (i.e., continuing employment) but rather on the achievement of specific performance goals. The goals may be personal, companywide, or a combination of the two. Some companies combine performance and time-based vesting by specifying that awards will vest on the earlier of a set date or the achievement of a performance goal. Alternatively, some companies add a time-based vesting restriction on awards that are granted only upon the achievement of performance goals.

- *Relative TSR Plans.* Vesting or grant of additional equity awards is based on "total shareholder return" (TSR) as a long-term relative performance measure: i.e., TSR is measured relative to the performance of peer-group companies. As an incentive device, this plan design should work if executives are given a realistic corporate performance target that can be reasonably influenced vis-á-vis the peer group/industry. The success of this approach requires picking the right group of comparable companies, arriving at a rational metric, and communicating it in a way that makes sense to both executives and shareholders.

6.2   Restricted Stock Awards (RSAs)

Under restricted stock award plans, companies grant shares to employees or nonemployees but restrict them for a time after grant. The recipients, who may or may not have to pay anything for the shares, cannot take possession of them until the specified restrictions lapse, and thus are not taxed until they receive the shares. The most common restriction requires the employee to continue to work for the company for a certain number of years, often three to five. This time-based vesting may occur all at once or gradually. The company is free to choose the restrictions. It could, for example, restrict the shares until certain corporate, departmental, or individual performance goals are achieved. The shares are issued at grant and held in escrow until vesting. As a result, the company will generally pay dividends even on unvested shares. It may also provide voting rights or give the employee other benefits of being a shareholder before the restrictions lapse.

In most cases, a company will grant fewer shares of restricted stock than it would options because the restricted stock has value to the recipient even if the share price drops after the grant date.

In this scenario, "restricted stock" means stock that is restricted for tax purposes. However, in other cases the "restricted" aspect of restricted stock may be a securities law restriction. For example, the stock may be unregistered and thus subject to securities laws governing whether it can be transferred to someone else. Or the term can refer to restrictions imposed by the company. For example, companies often limit executives' trading or impose special blackout periods when they aren't allowed to sell their shares. Nonprofessionals are frequently unclear about what they mean by "restricted stock"; equity compensation professionals would be wise to clarify the nature of the restrictions desired by the company before designing a restricted stock plan.

For the purposes of tax-restricted stock, Section 83 of the Code applies to require the recipient to include the difference between the price paid for the shares and their fair market value on the vesting date as compensation income at the time of vesting, and the employer is entitled to a tax deduction in the year the recipient must include that amount in his or her income taxes. Subsequent changes in value are capital gains or losses.

Award recipients who want to avoid being taxed at the time of vesting have the right to make Section 83(b) elections, much as they can for stock options. If they make the election, they are taxed at ordinary income tax rates on the "bargain element" of the award at the time of grant. If the shares are simply granted at no cost to the employee, then the bargain element is their full value. If the employee does have to pay for the shares, then the tax is based on the difference between what is paid and the fair market value. If the recipient must pay the full price of the shares, there is no tax. Any future increase in the value of the shares until they are sold is then taxed as capital gains, not ordinary income.

A Section 83(b) election carries some risk. If the employee makes the election and pays tax, but the restrictions never lapse, for example because the employee leaves the company before the shares vest, then he or she will have paid unnecessary taxes that are not refundable.

As for the employer, it can take a tax deduction only for amounts on which award recipients owe income taxes, regardless of whether a Section 83(b) election is filed.

RSAs are exempt from taxation as deferred compensation under Code Section 409A as long as the payment of the stock is not deferred past vesting. However, the same is not true of restricted stock units (RSUs), discussed below.

6.3   Restricted Stock Units (RSUs)

RSUs are similar to RSAs, except that the company does not issue the shares until the award is vested and paid out, which means they are slightly different from a tax perspective. RSUs have steadily gained in popularity since 2003, when Microsoft announced it would discontinue granting stock options in favor of RSUs in an effort to limit dilution. They now rival stock options in terms of popularity.

From the company's perspective, waiting until vesting and payout to issue the shares eliminates the need to predict repurchases of unvested shares for accounting purposes. It also means that RSUs do not come with voting or dividend rights prior to vesting, although the employer can choose to make separate dividend equivalent payments on the shares.

From the employees' perspective, the fact that the stock is not transferred until it is already fully vested and paid out means no Section 83(b) election is available. However, most employees will be able to finance the income taxes due upon payout by cashing out part of the award at that time. The company, of course, is entitled to a corresponding tax deduction for each vested RSU that is paid out.

Because RSUs are not exempt from Code Section 409A, any deferral of receipt of the shares after vesting should be structured with that section's limits in mind.

Exhibit 6-1 shows a comprehensive comparison between stock options, restricted stock, and RSUs.

Exhibit 6-1. Restricted Stock vs. Stock Options vs. RSUs

	Restricted Stock	ISOs	NSOs	RSUs
Is employee taxed at grant?	No, unless 83(b) election is made; otherwise, ordinary income tax paid when restrictions lapse.	No.	No.	No.
Is employee taxed at vesting?	Yes, unless employee makes 83(b) election.	No.	No.	Yes if award is paid out at vesting. If award is subject to deferral beyond vesting date, the income tax event is deferred and the awards must meet the requirements of Section 409A.
Is employee taxed at exercise?	N/A	No.	Yes.	N/A
Can award receive capital gains tax treatment?	Yes, if an 83(b) election is made, any gain between grant date and sale is taxed as capital gain, without 83(b), any gain between vest date and sale is capital gain.	Yes, any gain on shares received on exercise is taxed as capital gain, provided holding period rules are met.	Only for gain on shares held after exercise.	No. Full value of stock award at vesting/transfer is taxed at ordinary income rates. Capital gain only on subsequent appreciation (if any).

Exhibit 6-1. Restricted Stock vs. Stock Options vs. RSUs

	Restricted Stock	ISOs	NSOs	RSUs
Can tax be deferred until sale?	Yes, if 83(b) election made.	Yes, if requirements met.	No, unless purchase of unvested shares is permitted.	No.
Can alternative minimum tax apply?	No.	Yes, to spread on exercise if shares not sold in year of exercise.	No.	No.
Does the employer get a deduction?	Yes, for amount recognized as ordinary income by employee.	Only for disqualifying dispositions for amounts taxed as ordinary income.	Yes, for amount recognized as ordinary income by employee.	Yes, for amount recognized as ordinary income by employee.
Does the employee get dividends?	Generally yes.	Not until shares are actually purchased.	Not until shares are actually purchased.	No direct dividends before vesting, but dividend equivalents can be paid.
Voting rights for employees	Can be attached before vesting.	Not until shares are actually purchased.	Not until shares are actually purchased.	Not until shares are actually transferred.
Is there value if the share price drops below grant price?	Yes.	No.	No.	Yes.
Do the awards affect dilution and EPS calculations?	Yes, but fewer restricted shares than options are normally issued because of their downside protection.	Yes, even if the awards are underwater.	Yes, even if the awards are underwater.	Yes, but fewer shares than options are normally issued because of their downside protection.

Exhibit 6-1. Restricted Stock vs. Stock Options vs. RSUs

	Restricted Stock	ISOs	NSOs	RSUs
Can employees delay exercise or receipt of shares after vesting?	No, shares belong to employee when restrictions lapse.	Yes, under terms of option.	Yes, under terms of option.	Yes, receipt of shares can be deferred after vesting, but should be compliant with Section 409A.
How is value affected by volatility?	Better in less volatile companies.	Better in more volatile companies.	Better in more volatile companies.	Better in less volatile companies.

6.4 Stock Appreciation Rights (SARs)

A SAR is much like a stock option. It is a contractual right that allows the holder to elect to receive the appreciation in the value of a set number of shares of stock between the grant date and the exercise date. SARs may be paid in cash, stock, or a combination of the two as prescribed in the grant documents. As with options, the holders of SARs usually have the right to choose when to exercise the award and receive the payment.

6.4.1 Tax Issues: Employees

SARs trigger income tax for the employee when they are exercised.[10] SARs that are exercised for stock are taxed under Code Section 83, which also governs NSOs. Those that are exercisable for cash, however, are not taxed under Code Section 83 because they are considered to be unfunded and unsecured promises to pay money rather than property.[11] Instead, the recipient is taxed under the constructive receipt rules of Code Section 451. Similarly, a stand-alone SAR that is subject to a cap on appreciation payable will be considered to be constructively received

---

10. Rev. Rul. 80300, 1980-2 C.B. 165, *as amplified by* Rev. Rul. 82121, 1982-1 C.B. 79.

11. Treas. Reg. § 1.833.

at the time the cap is reached and will be taxed at that time under the rules of Code Section 451.[12]

SARs are specifically excluded from deferred compensation treatment under Code Section 409A as long as their exercise price is no lower than the stock's fair market value on the grant date and other requirements are met. This applies to SARs settled in both cash and stock. Cash-settled SARs, however, receive unfavorable accounting treatment compared with stock-settled SARs.

6.4.2   Tax Issues: Employers

The employer is entitled to a compensation deduction in the year the SAR is exercised by the employee.[13] If the SAR is exercised for cash, the IRS takes the position that the timing of the deduction is governed by Section 404(a)(5) of the Code. That section provides for a deduction in the employer's taxable year in which or with which the employee's taxable year of inclusion ends.[14] Note that the effect of Section 404(a)(5) is to give an employer whose fiscal year is not the calendar year a deduction in a different calendar year than the one in which the employee recognizes the income. The employer is required to withhold taxes on exercise of the SAR.[15]

6.4.3   Tandem SARs

In some cases, SARs are issued in tandem with an option that has the same vesting schedule. In a tandem option/SAR, the exercise of one right typically cancels out the complementary right. For example, an employee may be granted a tandem SAR/NSO for 2,000 shares. The employee could choose to exercise 1,000 SARs, and as a result, the complementary 1,000 NSOs would be canceled. Thus, the employee could avoid conducting a cashless exercise by simply exercising the SAR

---

12. Treas. Reg. § 1.4512. See generally PLR 9904039; PLR 9903037 (tandem option/SARs).

13. Code Section 162(a).

14. See, e.g., PLR 8230147. Treas. Reg. § 1.404(a)12(b)(1).

15. Code Section 3402.

instead of the option. Or the employee might choose to partially exercise for stock with cash obtained by exercising the appropriate number of shares as SARs. With careful planning, the employee may be able to use the SAR to avoid investing any out-of-pocket cash in the stock *and* have cash in hand for paying tax on the spread as well.

The IRS has specifically provided that a tandem ISO/SAR is a "permissible provision" for purposes of the ISO rules, so it is also possible to have a tandem ISO/SAR as long as they have identical exercisability provisions.[16] A tandem ISO/SAR gives the optionee the chance to make a determination at the time of exercise as to whether he or she wants an immediate (taxable) cash award, or a long-term investment in the stock. If the optionee is looking for the investment rather than the cash and chooses to exercise the option and hold the stock, he or she will still get the benefit of preferential ISO tax treatment even though the SAR would not have been eligible for such treatment had it been exercised instead of the ISO.

6.5   Phantom Stock

Phantom stock plans provide bonuses based on the value of a stated number of shares, to be paid out at the end of a specified period. The bonuses are almost always paid in cash. Where they are paid out in stock, they are frequently referred to as RSUs, rather than as phantom stock.

Unlike most SARs, phantom stock is considered to be deferred compensation. When the payout is made, it is taxed as ordinary income to the employee as long as the details of the plan follow the requirements of Code Section 409A and the corresponding regulations. As with other forms of equity compensation, the employer is entitled to deduct from its taxes the amount the employee must include as income in his or her own taxes.

If the terms of the award do not comply with the deferred compensation rules, the recipient suffers adverse tax consequences in which all amounts considered deferred are immediately taxed as income unless they remain subject to a substantial risk of forfeiture and have not been taxed previously. The recipient must also pay a 20% penalty tax on the

---

16. Treas. Reg. § 1.422-5(d)(3).

amount taxed, and pay cumulative interest at the IRS underpayment rate plus one percentage point.

Some phantom plans condition the receipt of the award on meeting certain objectives, such as sales, profits, or other targets. These plans often refer to the phantom stock as "performance units." Phantom stock can be given to anyone, but if it is given out broadly to employees and is designed to pay out only upon or after termination of employment, there is a possibility that the plan will be considered a retirement plan and will be subject to the Employee Retirement Income Security Act of 1974 (ERISA). Careful plan structuring can avoid this problem.

PART II
TECHNICAL ISSUES

Chapter 7

Financing the Purchase of Stock Options

Contents

For the optionee, receiving a grant is only the first step in realizing the compensation aspect of equity compensation. To get the benefit of an option, the optionee must actually purchase the underlying stock. Compensatory stock options may always be exercised by tender of cash in the amount of the exercise price stated in the option grant. However, most companies provide their employees with financing mechanisms to assist in option exercises. This chapter discusses several of the most popular alternatives, including same-day sale arrangements for public companies, net exercises, stock swaps, and company-provided loans.

In all cases, authorized exercise methods must be specified in the company's stock option plan as well as in the option grant itself. If the plan and agreement do not allow for non-cash exercise methods, the company will find itself severely limited as to what alternatives it can legitimately offer to optionees. Moreover, if a company allows an employee to exercise an ISO using a method other than cash when that method has not been authorized in both the award agreement and plan document, the exercise will result in a Section 424(h) modification of the ISO at time of exercise. If the ISO is not repriced at that time, it will be treated as an NSO for tax purposes. Finally, adding an allowable exercise method to an already granted option carries accounting consequences that are discussed in chapter 10. Plan administrators need to be aware that these issues will arise if the board decides to amend an option to allow for new forms of payment.

7.1   Broker-Assisted Cashless Transactions

The most common form of exercise, a broker-assisted cashless exercise allows an optionee to exercise an option for stock in a public company with the proceeds from the sale of stock acquired under the option. Essentially, the exercise is financed by selling, through a securities brokerage firm, the number of option shares necessary to pay the full exercise price of the option being exercised plus any withholding taxes due on the date of exercise. For practical purposes, it gives the same result as a stock swap with less complication: the appreciation on the stock is used to finance the exercise of the option, and the employee does not have to come up with cash for the exercise. This entails a short-term extension of credit by the broker, which is authorized under the Federal Reserve Board's Regulation T.[1] Regulation T applies to any receipt of securities pursuant to an employee benefit plan that is registered with the SEC

---

1.   Note that same-day sale transactions are facilitated by the Federal Reserve Board Amendment to FRB Regulation T (January 25, 1988).

on Form S-8, meaning it is available to employees and nonemployees (e.g., consultants and nonemployee board members) who participate in such plans.

Broker-assisted cashless exercises take two primary forms: same-day sales and sell-to-cover exercises. In a same-day sale exercise, the broker sells all of the shares acquired upon exercise of the option, remits the exercise price and any taxes due upon exercise to the company, and deposits the remainder of the proceeds from the sale in the optionee's account. In a sell-to-cover exercise, the broker sells just enough shares to cover the exercise price and any taxes due and deposits the remaining shares from the exercise in the optionee's brokerage account. In either scenario, the optionee could choose to pay cash to the company to cover the taxes, but in practice this rarely happens.

Note that brokers are not required to file 1099-Bs for same-day sale transactions so long as the company certifies in writing that it intends to report compensation from the sale (measured using the actual sale price) on the service provider's W-2 or Form 1099, as appropriate.[2]

7.1.1   Tax Issues

A broker-assisted cashless exercise is fairly straightforward from a tax standpoint, as illustrated in exhibit 7-1. Note that the use of ISO shares will necessarily constitute a disqualifying disposition of those shares because the ISO holding period will not be satisfied. The proceeds from this sale are remitted to the company.[3] No withholding is required on ISOs even in the case of a disqualifying disposition.

Also, payment of the exercise price must occur no later than the settlement date or there is a risk that the broker's margin loan will be deemed an interest-free loan under Section 7872 of the Code.[4]

---

2.   Rev. Proc. 2002-50.

3.   For a discussion of the administrative and tax reporting issues presented by same-day sales see "Administering an Employee Stock Option Plan" by Mark A. Borges and Christine Zwerling in *Selected Issues in Equity Compensation*, 14th ed. (Oakland, CA: NCEO, 2017).

4.   For more on employer loans generally, see section 7.4.

Exhibit 7-1. Cashless exercise

Exercise of NSO for 200 shares

Exercise price: $20

FMV at exercise: $50

Total amount needed to exercise 200 shares: $4,000

Number of shares sold to cover exercise price: 80

Taxable amount at time of exercise: $6,000 ($30 per share spread x 200 shares)

Tax withholding at 25% supplemental income rate: $1,500

Shares sold to cover tax liability: 30

Amount issued to optionee if sell-to-cover: 90 shares

Cost basis of 90 issued shares: $4,500 (90 shares times $50 per share)

Amount issued to optionee if same-day-sale: $4,500

In the case of an ISO, the use of a cashless exercise technique raises the Section 424(h)(3) modification issue discussed throughout unless the technique is permitted in the ISO grant or the company is not a party to the same-day sale agreement. If the company is not party to the transaction, it should not be deemed to be giving additional benefits to the optionee, and the result should be the same as if the optionee secured a third-party loan to finance the transaction. Furthermore, the addition of a same-day sale program to an already granted stock option constitutes a modification of the option.[5]

7.1.2   Insider Issues

Restrictions on employer loans (i.e., "extensions of credit") to directors and executive officers under Section 402 of the Sarbanes-Oxley Act of 2002 generally operate to prevent cashless exercise by insiders if the transaction is directly with the company rather than through a broker.[6] However, under the act, third-party loans are not prohibited so long as the company does not participate in arranging for the extension of credit. When Sarbanes-Oxley was passed, there was some concern that the restrictions on credit would prevent insiders from conducting broker-assisted cashless exercises, but that worry has essentially proved unfounded. Although cashless exercises historically involved short-

---

5.   Treas. Reg. § 1.424-1(e)(4)(i).

6.   See section 7.4 below.

term margin loans, in practice they seldom do anymore. Instead, most brokers treat the purchase of shares obtained upon exercise and sale of the shares as happening simultaneously. Note, however, that the SEC has not provided any guidance on the impact of Sarbanes-Oxley on broker-assisted cashless exercises.

7.2 Net Exercise

In recent years, the exercise financing technique popularly known as "net exercise" or "immaculate exercise" has become an attractive alternative to broker same-day sales. These are similar to same-day sales except that the company itself, not the broker, withholds shares to cover the exercise price. For practical purposes, a net exercise permits the optionee to buy shares with no cash down; instead, the optionee agrees that the issuer will withhold (at exercise) that number of shares with a value equal to the full exercise price. The optionee receives only the balance of the shares and pays ordinary income tax on the full spread on exercise: i.e., the difference between the amount paid for the issued shares and their fair market value at exercise.

In addition, the company may withhold additional shares to cover the taxes due. But because no cash is generated by a net exercise (and the IRS doesn't accept shares to cover withholding), the company may want to require that sufficient shares be sold on the market to provide for tax withholding, or that the optionee provide a check for the withholding at the time of exercise, otherwise the company is required to generate the cash to cover the withholding. Optionees may appreciate the opportunity to reduce their brokerage fees by using this method rather than a same-day sale. Note that the net exercise technique for ISOs is unsettled. The net exercise feature may result in a disqualification of the whole ISO. On the other hand, employers and employees may take the position for tax purposes that the shares held back to cover the exercise are never issued, and the ISO maintains its tax-qualified status.

When using the net exercise technique, it is important to check share counting procedures to ensure that net shares are properly counted under the pool. Finally, if amendments to the plan are required to allow for net exercise, consult with counsel regarding any Section 409A modification or shareholder approval requirements.

A similar, but not identical, method is called a "pyramid exercise." An optionee conducting a pyramid exercise must pay the funds necessary to exercise a minimum number of options and then tender the shares to the company to serve as the basis for a series of stock swaps that ultimately result in all of the shares under option being exercised. The result is the same as a stock-settled SAR: i.e., the number of shares purchased will be equivalent to the total spread at the date of exercise divided by the fair market value of a share on the date of exercise, and the full value of the purchase price is taxable at ordinary income rates.

7.3 Stock Swaps

If the company has made multiple grants to employees, it may wish to allow them to exercise their options with previously owned stock. This form of exercise is called a "stock swap." The rules governing the tax consequences of stock swaps are extremely complex, and the following discussion only touches upon the key issues. The general principles regarding "like-kind exchanges" under Sections 1036 and 1031(d) of the Code apply to swaps of both NSOs and ISOs. Swaps involving ISOs are specifically authorized by Section 422(c)(4)(A) of the Code. Both the FASB and the SEC look favorably on swaps, but companies should be aware that securities issues may arise when using this technique.

For those options under which stock swaps are permitted, the key to analyzing the tax consequences is to focus on three separate levels of stock purchases: (1) the original purchase of the shares that will be exchanged in the swap, (2) the purchase of shares under the current option, and (3) the character of the sale of the acquired stock. The following discussion considers all levels of a stock swap when (1) an ISO is exercised, and (2) an NSO is exercised.

For convenience, this discussion uses the following terminology in describing stock swaps:

- *"Swapped shares"* or *"Swapped-in shares"*: Shares that were acquired previously and are swapped or surrendered to exercise a new option.

- *"Replacement shares"*: Shares that are received in the swap in a one-to-one like-kind exchange for the swapped shares (pursuant to Section 1036 of the Code), i.e., that directly "replace" the swapped-in shares.

- *"Additional shares"*: Shares that are received in excess of the replacement shares (and that constitute the compensation element of the swap).

The term "basis," as used in this discussion, is the amount a taxpayer is deemed to have paid for the shares. Generally, the employee will take a "carryover basis" in the replacement shares under Section 1031(d) of the Code—i.e., a basis equal to his or her original cost basis in the swapped shares—*increased* by any amount included in income as compensation under Code Sections 421 through 424 or Code Section 83 as a result of the swap.

The examples in this section (exhibits 7-4 to 7-8) describe the tax treatment of swaps of NSOs and ISOs in many combinations. All examples assume that 90 previously owned shares are used to effect the exercise of 150 shares, meaning the stock swap results in 90 replacement shares and 60 additional shares. The shares used to effect the swap are described in exhibit 7-2. Whether the swapped-in shares themselves are ISOs or NSOs is addressed in each example, as is the character of the newly exercised shares. Exhibit 7-3 explains the basic calculation behind the swap itself. The examples ignore the effect of tax withholding on the transactions described.

Exhibit 7-2. History of 90 Swapped-in Shares

Exercise price: $2,250 ($25 x 90 shares)

FMV at exercise: $3,600 ($40 x 90 shares)

Taxable gain included in basis (applies only to examples in which swapped-in shares are not tax-qualified): $3,600 ($15 spread x 90 shares)

Exhibit 7-3. Explanation of Swap

Per-share exercise price of shares exercised in swap: $45

Stock's FMV at time of swap: $75

Spread on exercise: $30 ($75 FMV at time of swap minus $45 exercise price—this will be relevant in only some of the below examples)

To exercise 150 options with an exercise price of $45, the optionee must pay a total of $6,750. To raise that amount, the optionee turns in 90 already owned shares that have an FMV of $75 per share and an aggregate value of $6,750.

7.3.1   Using Nonqualified Shares to Exercise an NSO

The rules with respect to stock swaps for NSOs are fairly straightforward. For the shares swapped in, the employee will have included and paid tax on the spread between the exercise price and fair market value of the stock in ordinary income as compensation at the time of exercise. At the time of the swap, the employee takes a carryover basis in the replacement shares and a basis equal to the fair market value of the shares on the date of exercise.[7] See exhibit 7-4.

Exhibit 7-4: Nonqualified Shares Used to Exercise NSOs

The shares described in exhibit 7-2 are swapped as described in exhibit 7-3. All shares are nonqualified. The tax consequences of the swap are:

*   90 replacement shares
    *   — Amount includable in income at time of swap: $0
    *   — Cost basis: $3,600 (Carry-over cost basis of $40 per share from exercise of swapped-in shares times 90 shares)
*   60 additional shares
    *   — Amount includable in income at time of swap: $4,500 ($75 FMV on exercise date times 60 shares)
    *   — Cost basis going forward: $4,500 (amount included in income)
*   Total amount included in income at time of swap: $4,500

7.3.2   Using Tax-Qualified Shares to Exercise an NSO

An NSO may be exercised with statutory option shares even if the employee has not held the shares for the statutory holding period. The stock swap is not considered to be a disqualifying disposition, and the employee continues to hold the same number of ISO shares as were swapped. The swap, accordingly, does not result in a change in basis or an extra inclusion in income. The employee is permitted to tack his or her holding period for the swapped shares to the holding period for the replacement shares under Section 1223(1) of the Code. See exhibit 7-5.

---

7.   See Sections 1036 and 1031(d) of the Code and Revenue Ruling 80-244.

Exhibit 7-5. ISO Shares Used to Exercise NSOs

An optionee holds 90 tax-qualified shares that were acquired by exercising an ISO using the prices described in exhibit 7-2. The optionee uses those tax-qualified shares to exercise NSOs, as described in exhibit 7-3. The tax consequences of the swap are:

- 90 replacement shares
  - Amount includable in income at time of swap: $0
  - Amount includable for AMT purposes if shares held through the end of the taxable year: $4,500 ($75 FMV on the swap minus $25 ISO exercise price times 90 shares)
  - Cost basis: $2,250 (Carry-over cost basis of $25 per share the optionee paid to exercise the ISOs times 90 shares)
  - Tax status: ISOs, with a holding period that is counted from the original grant and exercise of the ISO, not from the swap date
- 60 additional shares
  - Amount includable in income at time of swap: $4,500 ($75 FMV on exercise date times 60 shares)
  - Cost basis going forward: $4,500 (amount included in income)
  - Tax status: NSOs
- Total amount includable in income at time of swap: $4,500

7.3.3   Using Nonqualified Shares to Exercise an ISO

An ISO may be exercised using stock of the granting corporation so long as all other ISO requirements are met and the option plan and the award agreement allow exercise with stock.[8] ISO shares acquired with stock are subject to the statutory holding period,[9] which starts (for ISO purposes) at the date of the swap. The employee may not "tack" (add) his or her holding period in the swapped-in shares onto the statutory holding period of the new ISO replacement shares, no matter how long he or she has held the swapped shares. However, for purposes other than the statutory holding period, the employee's holding period in the swapped shares may be tacked onto the replacement shares (i.e., for computation of short-term or long-term capital gain on a disqualifying disposition).

The optionee will not include any amount in income as compensation upon exercise of an ISO with swapped nonqualified shares. Instead, he or she will defer recognition of the income and tax on such

---

8.   Code Section 422(c)(4)(A).

9.   Treas. Reg. § 1.422-5(b)(2).

income until the time that he or she disposes of the ISO shares. Where nonqualified shares are used to exercise an ISO, the employee will take a "carryover basis" in the replacement shares under Section 1031(d) of the Code—i.e., a basis equal to his or her original cost basis in the swapped shares.

Exhibit 7-6. Nonqualified Shares Used to Exercise ISOs

The tax consequences of the swap are: An optionee holds 90 nonqualified shares that were acquired by exercising an NSO using the prices described in exhibit 7-2. The optionee uses those shares to exercise an ISO under the circumstances described in exhibit 7-3.

- 90 replacement shares
  - Amount includable in income at time of swap: $0
  - Amount includable for AMT purposes if shares not sold before end of calendar year: $2,700
  - Cost basis: $3,600 (the carry-over cost basis of the NSOs used to effect the swap)
  - Tax status: ISOs, with a holding period that is counted from the date of the swap
- 60 additional shares
  - Amount includable in income at time of swap: $0
  - Amount includable in AMT calculation if shares not sold before end of calendar year: $1,800 ($30 per share spread on exercise times 60 shares)
  - Cost basis: $0
  - Tax status: ISOs, with a holding period that is counted from the date of the swap
- Total amount includable in income at time of swap: $0
- Total amount includable in AMT calculation if replacement and additional shares held through end of calendar year: $4,500

If all 150 shares are later sold for $90 per share ($13,500 total):

- Qualifying disposition
  - Ordinary income: $0
  - Long-term capital gain: $9,900 ($13,500 minus the replacement shares' cost basis of $3,600)
- Disqualifying disposition:
  - Ordinary income: $7,200 ($2,700 total spread on exercise of the 90 replacement shares plus the $4,500 fair market value of the 60 additional shares)
  - Capital gain: $2,700
  - To determine long-term vs. short-term capital gain:

    Replacement shares: count from the exercise date of the swapped-in NSOs
    Additional shares: count from swap date

The exercise of an ISO with previously acquired stock results in the taxpayer taking a zero basis in the additional shares acquired in the swap. See exhibit 7-6.

The regulations provide that in the event of a disqualifying disposition of the shares received in the swap, the employee is deemed to have disposed of the shares with the lowest basis first (i.e., the zero basis additional shares). Thus, for example, if the optionee in the example sold 110 shares in a disqualifying disposition the person would be considered to have sold the 60 additional shares plus 50 of the replacement shares.

7.3.4   Using Tax-Qualified Shares to Exercise an ISO

Special rules apply if the stock has been purchased pursuant to an ISO or Section 423 plan (referred to here as "statutory option shares"). The equity plan professional should study Treas. Reg. § 1.422-5(b)(1) and the examples in Treas. Reg. § 1.422-5(e) for a detailed explanation of the IRS position on stock swaps of statutory options.[10]

Treas. Reg. § 1.422-5(b)(3) provides that exercise of an ISO with previously acquired stock is a tax-free exchange under Section 1036 of the Code to the extent that old shares are exchanged for an equal number and kind of replacement shares.

7.3.4.1   *Using Tax-Qualified Shares for Which the Holding Period Has Been Met*

As a rule, the optionee will not include any amount in income as compensation upon exercise of an ISO with swapped shares. The exception to this occurs when ISO shares that have been held for the full ISO holding period are used to effect the exchange, and the new ISO shares are subsequently disposed of in a disqualifying disposition. In that case, the optionee will take a "stepped-up basis" in the replacement shares equal to the fair market value of the shares on the date of the swap for purposes of computing ordinary income under Section 421(b) of the

---

10. Rev. Rul. 80244, 19802 C.B. 234 (original application of stock swap principles to qualified stock options). See also PLR 99901006 (stock swap does not result in constructive receipt under trust formed to fund plan).

Code. For all other purposes (i.e., computing capital gain with respect to the replacement shares), the optionee takes a carryover basis.

Regardless of the kind of stock used in the swap, the employee will take a zero basis in the additional shares (i.e., the non-replacement shares received in the swap). See exhibit 7-7.

Exhibit 7-7. ISO Shares Held for Full Holding Period Used to Exercise ISOs

The tax consequences of the swap are:

- 90 replacement shares
  - Amount includable in income at time of swap: $0
  - Amount includable for AMT purposes if shares not sold before end of calendar year: $2,700 ($30 spread on exercise at time of swap times 90 shares)
  - Cost basis: $2,250 ($25 exercise price of swapped-in shares times 90)
  - Tax status: ISOs, with a holding period that is counted from the swap date
- 60 additional shares
  - Amount includable in income at time of swap: $0
  - Amount includable in AMT calculation if shares not sold before end of calendar year: $1,800 ($30 spread on exercise at time of swap times 60 shares)
  - Cost basis: $0
  - Tax status: ISOs, with a holding period that is counted from the date of the swap
- Total amount includable in income at time of swap: $0
- Total amount includable in AMT calculation if replacement and additional shares held through end of calendar year: $4,500

If all 150 shares are later sold for $90 per share ($13,500 total):

- Qualifying disposition
  - Ordinary income: $0
  - Long-term capital gain: $11,250 ($13,500 gain on sale minus $2,250 cost basis of replacement shares)
- Disqualifying disposition:
  - Ordinary income: $4,500 ($30 spread on exercise at time of swap times 150 shares)
  - Capital gain: $6,750

    90 replacement shares: long-term capital gain of $4,050
    60 additional shares: capital gain of $2,700, which is short-term if shares sold less than one year after swap, otherwise long-term

7.3.4.2 Using Tax-Qualified Shares for Which the Holding Period Has Not Been Met

When statutory option shares that have not been held for the full ISO holding period are swapped for new ISO shares, the swap constitutes a disqualifying disposition of the swapped-in shares under Section 424(c) of the Code. The employee must include in income as compensation the difference between his or her original purchase price for the statutory option shares and the fair market value of those shares at time of exercise (the spread on the original exercise). Accordingly, his or her basis in the replacement shares will be equal to his or her original cost basis in the statutory option shares *plus* the amount included in income as a result of the swap. See exhibit 7-8.

Exhibit 7-8. ISO Shares Not Held for Statutory Holding Period Used to Exercise ISOs

An optionee holds 90 tax-qualified shares that were acquired by exercising an ISO using the prices described in Exhibit 7-2. The optionee has not satisfied the ISO holding period on these shares. The optionee uses those shares under the circumstances described in Exhibit 7-3. Because the holding period has not been met, the swap is a disqualifying disposition of the swapped-in shares. The tax consequences of the swap are:

- 90 replacement shares
  - Amount includable in income at time of swap: $1,350 ($15 spread at time of original exercise of swapped-in shares times 90 shares)
  - Amount includable for AMT purposes if shares not sold before end of calendar year: $2,700 ($30 spread on exercise at time of swap times 90 shares)
  - Cost basis: $3,600 ($40 FMV of swapped-in shares on date of exercise of swapped-in shares times 90 shares)
  - Tax status: ISOs, with a holding period that is counted from the date of the swap
- 60 additional shares
  - Amount includable in income at time of swap: $0
  - Amount includable in AMT calculation if shares not sold before end of calendar year: $1,800 ($30 spread on exercise at time of swap times 60 shares)
  - Tax status: ISOs, with a holding period that is counted from the date of the swap
- Total amount includable in income at time of swap: $1,350
- Total amount includable in AMT calculation if replacement and additional shares held through end of calendar year: $4,500

If all 150 shares are later sold for $90 per share ($13,500 total):

- Qualifying disposition
  - Ordinary income: $0
  - Long-term capital gain: $9,900 ($13,500 sale proceeds minus replacement shares' cost basis of $3,600)
- Disqualifying disposition:
  - Ordinary income: $7,200 ($2,700 total spread on exercise of the 90 replacement shares plus the $4,500 fair market value of the 60 additional shares)
  - Capital gain: $2,700, which is long-term if the sale occurs more than one year from date of swap

7.3.5   Procedure for Stock Swaps

While the optionee can actually deliver shares at the time of exercise, the more common way is to initiate the transaction electronically through the system regularly used for initiating stock option exercises. No notarization is required to support constructive delivery in this type of paperless exercise.[11] Where electronic initiation of an exercise is not available, the IRS and the SEC have expressly sanctioned the use of a certification/attestation process for constructive delivery of the swapped shares. If the shares are held in street name, the IRS suggests that the optionee give a notarized statement attesting to the number of shares owned that are intended to be used in the swap.[12]

The company will have to develop its own criteria and instructions for determining the fair market value of the swapped shares on the exercise date. The criteria adopted will differ for private and public companies.

7.4   Employer Loans

Another alternative available to employers to help employees finance the exercise of their stock options is an employer-provided loan. However, the type of loan used may have serious securities, accounting, and tax consequences. If a promissory note is found to be insufficient, the

---

11. See PLR 200207005 (approving paperless exercise of ISOs using e-mail).

12. In PLR 9736040, the IRS stated that "this procedure is sufficient to constitute the constructive exchange of stock for federal income tax purposes." See also PLRs 9628028, 8650045, and 8210098.

employee may be unpleasantly surprised to find that neither the tax nor securities holding periods on the stock have begun to run until the loan is paid off. Further, under the Sarbanes-Oxley Act of 2002, issuers are prohibited from making personal loans to the most common recipients of stock options: top executives who are public company insiders.[13] Before providing for any loan arrangements, the following issues must be explored in depth by the equity plan professional.

7.4.1 Recourse Notes

Companies typically wish to provide the most favorable terms possible when making a stock purchase loan to employees. Although a note may legally be drafted to limit the lender's recourse in the case of default (for example, recourse against the underlying property only), there are many reasons why limited or nonrecourse notes are unwise. First, as a corporate and securities law matter, when offered to officers or insiders such notes appear self-dealing and may raise fiduciary and governance issues for the stockholders. As noted above, under the Sarbanes-Oxley Act of 2002, public companies are prohibited from making any personal loans to insiders. Second, for tax purposes, company-provided loans for stock purchases must put the optionee at risk for the underlying property. A statutory option that is exercised with a promissory note will not be considered to have been exercised at all "unless the optionee is subject to personal liability" on the loan under Treas. Reg. § 1.421-1(f). Similarly, for NSOs, Treas. Reg. § 1.83-3(a)(2) provides that the purchaser must show that he or she has taken on the rights and obligations of an investor, including risk of loss, with respect to the property. The purported purchase of property using a nonrecourse note will be considered to be an option. In either case, stock paid for with a nonrecourse note will not be considered to be transferred until the note is fully paid or collateralized.[14]

---

13. Section 402 of the Sarbanes-Oxley Act.

14. However, what constitutes sufficient recourse to avoid characterization as "nonrecourse" for these purposes? Treas. Reg. § 1.833(a)(2) sets out some factors for weighing risk, but as a rule the IRS will not give guidance on whether a transfer has occurred when property is acquired with partial recourse debt. See, e.g., Rev. Proc. 2002-3, 2002-1 IRB 117 § 3.01(3) (January 17, 2002). Tax

7.4.2 Collateral

For tax purposes, collateralizing a recourse loan to purchase stock with the underlying stock will suffice to trigger the capital gains holding period. However, for securities law purposes, the holding period under Rule 144, which offers a safe harbor for the sale of stock that is subject to securities-law restrictions and is explained in detail in chapter 8, will not start unless and until shares are fully paid or collateralized with security other than the underlying stock.[15]

7.4.3 Authorization in ISO Plans

The IRS specifically permits employer-provided loans for statutory option exercises.[16] However, the modification issue discussed in section 3.5 will arise if the loan provision is added to the grant at the time of exercise. Note that a third-party loan (e.g., a broker loan) arranged without the involvement of the employer will not constitute a modification to the ISO.

7.4.4 Providing Adequate Interest

Employer-provided loans for employer stock are subject to the rules respecting "below-market" loans for seller-financed transactions under Sections 483 and 1274 of the Code.[17] If a seller-financed loan is deemed

---

lawyers generally suggest that the underlying property be valued at no less than 25% of the face value of the note, but this is based on anecdotal evidence rather than IRS guidance.

15. Rule 144(d)(2).

16. Treas. Reg. § 1.421-1(b)(2).

17. Section 483 applies to seller-financed sales greater than $3,000 and up to $250,000, where some or all payments are due more than one year after sale or exchange. Section 1274 applies to seller-financed sales over $250,000 where some or all payments are due more than six months after the date of sale or exchange. In the case of publicly traded stock, the "original issue discount" rules of Section 1273 of the Code govern to produce similar results. Employer-provided loans that are not for seller-financed property are governed by Section 7872. With respect to third-party loans for employees, Section 7872 of the Code establishes rules for taxing any loan made in connection with the performance of services that is (1) not for a seller-financed sale (under Sections 483 and 1274) and (2) deemed to

to be below market because it carries insufficient stated interest terms, the principal of the loan will be recharacterized by the IRS and adequate interest will be calculated based on that principal. The chief impact of such recharacterization for both ISO and NSO purposes will be that the employee will be deemed to have paid less than fair market value for the stock at exercise. Accordingly, the option will be treated as a discount NSO under Section 409A, subject to the tax and penalties at vesting.[18] If the option is an ISO, it will also be disqualified from statutory option treatment under Section 421 of the Code. Treas. Reg. § 1.422-2(e)(2)(v) specifically provides that amounts treated as interest are not includible in the ISO exercise price. Furthermore, the regulation states that a fair market value set by adjusting the option price to reflect amounts treated as interest will not be a "good-faith attempt" and thus will result in a discount option.[19] In either case, the employee's basis in the optioned stock will be reduced because the imputed interest will be subtracted from the total amount paid under the note.[20]

The rules regarding imputed interest are exceedingly complex and are far beyond the scope of this chapter. For tax purposes the issue will never arise if all promissory notes include an interest rate equal to the applicable federal rate (AFR) prescribed under Section 1274(d) of the Code (published monthly by the IRS).[21]

---

be a "below-market loan" (BML). If an employee loan is a BML, the difference between the amount of interest paid and the amount that should have been paid (pursuant to the rules described below) is treated as "forgone interest" that has been transferred from the lender/employer to the employee/borrower, and then retransferred from the employee/borrower back to the lender/employer. The forgone interest amount is taxable as compensation and may result in an adjustment to the loan principal. Section 7872 and its extensive set of regulations are extremely complicated, but the basic gist of the rules is that employee loans will not be BMLs if they (1) carry market interest rates and (2) such rates are not entered into with a principal purpose of tax avoidance.

18. See chapter 2.

19. See chapter 3.

20. Treas. Reg. § 1.83-3(g). See also Treas. Reg. § 1.422-2(e)(2)(v) (below-market loan results in disqualified ISO).

21. For seller-financed sales, Sections 483 and 1274 of the Code generally provide that AFR is the lowest rate for the relevant term as between the month of sale and the two preceding months. Loans for an amount below $2.8 million are

7.4.5   Loan Forgiveness

Privately held companies that wish to encourage executives to exercise their options and hold option stock will sometimes provide for loan forgiveness, either in the loan contract itself or as a side agreement. Typically such arrangements set out a forgiveness schedule tied to continued employment, underlying vesting (e.g., same vesting schedule as stock) or other performance milestones. Companies may also agree to forgive stock-related loans when the underlying stock is valued well below the original purchase price.[22]

Loan forgiveness provisions, regardless of where stated, raise a number of issues that must be carefully considered by the company and the borrower. For tax purposes, the amount of the forgiveness is ordinary income, which must be recognized as received, withheld upon, and reported by the company on the optionee's Form W-2.[23] The employer company is entitled to a corresponding tax deduction in the amount included in the employee's income. If forgiveness is in installments, so is the tax liability. A final comment: after Sarbanes-Oxley, as noted above, public companies are essentially prohibited from making loans to insiders.

7.4.6   Recommendations

Employer-provided stock option loans, while seemingly attractive to the employee, raise an inordinate number of issues for the company

---

subject to a maximum AFR of 9%. However, it is unclear under Section 7872 of the Code and its proposed regulations whether these special minimum AFR rules will apply to a note issued by an employee for the purchase of employer stock. The safest course in most cases will thus be to use the monthly rule (described above) to avoid any risk of selecting a below-market rate. See note 17 above for more on the operation of Section 7872.

22. This issue got a lot of attention in the wake of the technology crash of 2001. Executives with loans and AMT liabilities for underwater stock were anxious for quick solutions, without full awareness of the tax consequences described below. See also discussion of AMT in chapter 3. The sensitivity to executive compensation surrounding the stock market crash of 2008 appears to have limited the use of this technique in 2009.

23. Treas. Reg. § 1.83-4(c).

(particularly the public company). Given the increasing number of constraints on such loans, a better alternative might be for the company to assist the employee in obtaining a third-party loan. Such loans frequently include favorable terms (e.g., nonrecourse, secured by underlying stock), and they avoid the issues described above. From the tax perspective, the company's involvement with third-party loans should not trigger tax: this is essentially the same mechanism as obtaining a third-party broker loan for a same-day sale.[24] However, given the lack of guidance from the SEC, public companies should tread carefully when considering providing insiders with access to third parties, as even the "arrangement" of such access may violate Section 402 of the Sarbanes-Oxley Act.

---

24. See section 7.1 of this chapter.

Overview of Securities Law Issues

Contents

This chapter briefly looks at some of the substantive provisions related to stock plans under state and federal securities laws, as well as related securities law reporting requirements, including equity compensation-related disclosures for public companies. Attention to this area of the law has been intense for the past decade, beginning with the passage of the Sarbanes-Oxley Act of 2002, which in the words of the White House, "imposes tough penalties to deter and punish corporate and accounting fraud and corruption, ensures justice for wrongdoers, and protects the interests of workers and shareholders." Regulations and interpretations of this law have followed in the ensuing years. The Dodd-Frank Act of 2010 further altered disclosure and other requirements in ways that are still being determined as of this writing. Updated sources should always be consulted before relying on the rules described below.[1] As noted throughout this book, the grant of a stock option may be unlawful if the option plan has not been properly qualified (e.g., registered) under or exempted from applicable securities laws. If an option grant is unlawful due to securities law violations, the optionee may have the right to rescind any stock purchase made under his or her option and to demand repayment of the purchase price with interest, as well as other rights under applicable state laws.

8.1   State Blue Sky Laws

As a general rule, public companies are eligible for stock-exchange-related exemptions from state securities laws and regulations (these laws and regulations are commonly referred to as "blue sky laws") for granting employee options. *Non-public companies, however, must check carefully with counsel to determine whether permit and/or notice requirements are imposed by any states in which the company intends to issue options.* In addition, public companies that are traded on foreign stock exchanges should be equally cautious, as not all states provide a blanket exemption for companies traded on non-U.S. exchanges.[2]

---

1.   News of congressional action (including links to current activity in both houses) may be obtained from www.usa.gov, among other resources. Information on and copies of the latest SEC releases may be obtained from the SEC website at www.sec.gov.

2.   See, e.g., the California Commissioner's Rules, which impose a variety of restrictions on plans sponsored by privately held corporations pursuant to Section 25102(o) of the law and Reg. §§ 260.140.8, 41-45, as amended effective July 9, 2007. See also Kristy Harlan, "State Securities Law Considerations for Equity Compensation Plans," *Selected Issues in Equity Compensation*, 14th ed. (Oakland, CA: NCEO, 2017).

8.2   Classification of Companies

The nature of the company that grants equity compensation affects what it must do to comply with federal securities laws and regulations. Publicly traded companies that are listed on a stock exchange or that are subject to the registration requirements of the Securities Exchange Act of 1934 have the greatest number of disclosure requirements to meet, but are generally able to register their shares using a simplified registration statement called a Form S-8. Most private companies are not subject to the disclosure requirements, but the holders of stock in these companies can sell it only pursuant to an exemption from registration.

The Jumpstart Our Business Startups Act of 2012 (JOBS Act) created an interim category of company called an "emerging growth company." This designation applies to private companies and newly public companies that have total annual gross revenues of less than $1 billion. This designation does not apply to companies that registered shares on or before December 8, 2011. Such companies are exempt from some of the disclosure requirements of the 1934 Act. Emerging growth companies are allowed to retain that status until the earlier of:

- the last day of the fiscal year of the issuer during which it had total annual gross revenues of $1 billion or more;

- the last day of the fiscal year of the issuer following the fifth anniversary of the date of the first sale of common equity securities of the issuer pursuant to an effective registration statement under the Securities Act of 1933;

- the date on which such issuer has, during the previous 3-year period, issued more than $1 billion in non-convertible debt; or

- the date on which such issuer is deemed to be a "large accelerated filer," which means it had an aggregate worldwide market value of common equity held by nonaffiliates of $700 million or more and has been subject to the Exchange Act's filing requirements for at least a year.

Emerging growth companies are not subject to as many disclosure rules as other public companies. The status does not affect whether the shares are required to be registered (or whether an exemption from registration must be found), but does allow emerging growth companies that are contemplating in IPO to file a confidential draft registration statement for review by the SEC and reduces the disclosures required in the annual proxy statement for emerging growth companies that are public companies.

8.3 Federal Securities Rules: Rules 144 and 701

Before securities can be offered or sold to employees (or other service providers), they must either be registered under the Securities Act of 1933, as amended, or qualify for an exemption from registration. Obviously, an exemption will always be necessary to permit a privately held company to offer options on or sell its securities since by definition such securities are not registered under the 1933 Act. Securities (including options) issued to an employee or other purchaser pursuant to an exemption are referred to as "restricted securities." Restricted securities held by employees are most commonly acquired from the issuer (or from an affiliate) in one of the following situations: (1) a private placement by the issuer;[3] (2) a negotiated sale by an insider; (3) an option exercise under a stock option plan before the company goes public; or (4) a corporate reorganization in which the acquiring company issues stock under Section 4(2) rather than pursuant to a registration statement.

Any company that has more than $10 million in assets *and* either 2,000 or more total equity holders or 500 or more nonaccredited equity holders must register its securities and will be subject to reporting requirements under the Exchange Act. The JOBS Act raised the equity holder limit from 500 to 2,000, and, even more significantly, specifies that employees who received their unregistered equity securities through a compensation plan do not count toward the 2,000-shareholder limit.[4] The definition of "employee compensation plan" remains to be written by the SEC.

---

3.   Section 4(2) nonpublic transaction.

4.   Shareholders who acquire their shares in a crowdfunding transaction that totals less than $1 million also do not count toward the 2,000 shareholder limit. Crowdfunding, however, is outside the scope of this discussion.

But what happens to restricted securities *after* an IPO? It's up to the issuer. In many cases, the issuer will immediately register restricted securities issued under its employee plan (for example, on a Form S-8 registration statement), thus removing the restrictions and making the stock (in general) freely tradable. However, it's not always the case that registration occurs, particularly when it comes to restricted securities that were issued outside of a plan. When not registered, restricted securities remain restricted even once the issuer's stock is trading on the public market: i.e., such securities may be sold into the market only in reliance on an exemption. The most commonly used exemptions for compensation-related restricted securities are Rule 144, which is available to individuals, and Rule 701, which is available to companies. Both are described below. Note that in all cases, resales of restricted securities in reliance on an exemption must be cleared with company counsel prior to transfer, and appropriate notice and disclosure filings must be made with the SEC upon sale. Typically, in the case of restricted securities bearing restrictive legends, company counsel will issue an opinion letter to the issuer's transfer agent authorizing the transfer of the securities (which were generally issued pursuant to Rule 144 or Rule 701), with a copy to the selling brokerage firm.

8.3.1   Rule 144 Generally

Rule 144 is a safe harbor exemption created by the SEC to permit public resales of restricted securities under Section 4(1) of the 1933 Act by persons who are not issuers, dealers, or underwriters of the stock—i.e., by persons who are not making a market in the stock.[5] The underlying exemption in Section 4(1) of the 1933 Act allows securities to be sold by any person *other* than an issuer, underwriter, or dealer (as such terms are defined in the 1933 Act and its regulations) without registration of the shares with the SEC and without delivery of a prospectus in a form approved by the SEC. Such persons are categorized as either "affiliates" or "nonaffiliates." Rule 144(a)(1) defines "affiliate" to mean a

---

5.   Application of the rule is extremely complex; this chapter is not intended to provide detailed guidance on its application. For a comprehensive current treatise on all aspects of the rule, refer to J. William Hicks, *Resales of Restricted Securities,* 2012 ed. (Eagan, MN: Thomson West).

person who directly or indirectly controls, is controlled by, or is under common control with the issuer. All persons who are not affiliates are nonaffiliates for these purposes. As a rule, executive officers and directors are deemed to be affiliates.

Rule 144 sets out a list of requirements that must be met by a holder of restricted securities in order to satisfy the safe harbor. If the safe harbor has been met, the holder may freely sell unregistered stock into the public market (subject to the limitations of the rule). The rules include:

- Restricted securities held by affiliates and nonaffiliates for a minimum holding period of six months from purchase are eligible for public resale by the holder so long as the issuer has met the reporting requirements imposed under the Securities Exchange Act of 1934 (the Exchange Act).[6] For non-reporting companies, nonaffiliates may resell securities after a year, which is also true for affiliates, but with some restrictions.

- The number of securities that can be sold in any three-month period for most publicly traded companies is limited to the greater of 1% of the outstanding stock of the issuer or the average weekly trading volume during the four calendar weeks preceding the receipt of the order to execute the transaction. The volume sale limitations are measured over a three-month rolling period.[7]

- Restricted securities must be sold in a "broker's transaction" or directly to a "market-maker" in the stock.[8] Solicitation of potential buyers is allowed, but if the company solicits buyers, then it may sell shares only to those the company and the seller reasonably believe to be "qualified institutional buyers."

- Resales of restricted securities must be reported to the SEC on Form 144.[9]

---

6. Rule 144(d).

7. Rule 144(e).

8. Rules 144(f) and 144(g).

9. Rule 144(h). 1933 Act Reg. § 203.144. For specific instructions see Form 144, SEC Release No. 52231 (1975), as amended.

Upon sale, Rule 144(h) requires that three copies of Form 144 be filed with the SEC for any affiliate who relies upon Rule 144 to sell more than 5,000 shares during any three-month period *or* who sells shares having an aggregate sales price of more than $50,000. If the shares are listed on a stock exchange, a Form 144 must also be filed with the listing exchange. Rule 144(c) also requires that the issuer provide current public information (pursuant to the reporting requirements of the Exchange Act) in order for the seller to take advantage of the rule.

As long as a sale of restricted securities is made in full compliance with Rule 144, the seller (whether affiliate or nonaffiliate) may rely on the exemption to sell such securities after satisfying the holding period described above. Nonaffiliates can resell restricted securities of non-reporting companies freely after one year. Affiliates will always be subject to the full compliance requirement, regardless of how long they hold their stock.

If Rule 144 is unavailable or undesirable, other exemptions may be useful. For example, private sales that do not comply with Rule 144 may be eligible for an exemption under Section 4(1) or "Section 4(1½)," a term used for a hybrid exemption using some of the criteria from both Section 4(1) and Section 4(2) of the 1933 Act. Public sales may also be exempt under SEC Regulation A, Rule 145, or Section 3(a)(10) of the 1933 Act. However, there are many requirements for such exemptions, and no sales should be made in reliance on any exemption without consulting counsel.[10]

8.3.2 Rule 144 Decision Tree

The following three-point decision tree may be used as an initial step in determining how (or whether) Rule 144 applies:

---

10. Note that both the seller and the broker in a Rule 144 transaction have a vested interest in ensuring that the sale fully complies: the seller, because without the exemption the sale may be unwound (i.e., be subject to rescission); and the broker, because without Rule 144 compliance, the Rule 4(4) exemption underlying the broker's side of the transaction may not be available. Although SEC enforcement actions are rare, both civil and criminal liabilities may be imposed if the SEC believes there has been abuse.

1. *Is the Seller an Affiliate?*

    • If yes, then securities must be sold in reliance on an exemption. Rule 144 may offer safe harbor protection for public sales relying on Section 4(1) (or a different exemption may apply for private sales); go to step 3.

    • If no, then go to step 2 to determine whether an exemption will be necessary.

2. *Are the Securities "Restricted Securities"?*

    • If yes, then securities must be sold in reliance on an exemption. Rule 144 may offer safe harbor protection for public sales relying on Section 4(1) (or a different exemption may apply for private sales); go to step 3.

    • If no, then securities may be resold into the public market without an exemption. No further testing is necessary.

3. *How Will Sales Be Made?* (Note: must be a trade, not a "distribution.")

    • *Public Sales*: By affiliates: Must always rely upon Rule 144 and satisfy all of its requirements prior to public resale. By nonaffiliates: May sell without restrictions after meeting holding period.

    • *Private Sales:* If sale is private (i.e., not made on a public market), the hybrid "Section 4(1½)" exemption mentioned above may apply (i.e., as if the seller were an issuer making a private placement) or Rule 144A may apply (to institutional investors only). The JOBS Act expands Rule 144A to cover sales by means of general solicitation or advertising so long as the shares are sold to persons reasonably believed to be institutional investors; however, limitations apply that may limit the practical use of this expansion of the rule.

By working through the decision tree, one can see that sales of *unrestricted securities* by a *nonaffiliate* will never be required to comply with Rule 144. On the other extreme, sales of *any securities* (regardless of whether they are restricted securities) by an *affiliate* will always be required to comply with either Rule 144 or another exemption.

8.3.3 Rule 701

As described above, Rule 144 provides a safe harbor exemption from registration under the 1933 Act for *persons* who wish to resell restricted securities. In contrast, Rule 701 provides a safe harbor exemption from registration under the 1933 Act for nonreporting companies with respect to offers and sales of restricted securities to nonaffiliate participants under an employee stock plan. For these purposes, a written compensation agreement between the issuer and a single employee will still be a plan. Rule 701 covers securities acquired under an eligible plan that are held by employees, directors, general partners, trustees (if the issuer is a business trust), officers or consultants and advisors, and their family member transferees. The definition of "consultants and advisors" for Rule 701 purposes is quite restrictive. They must: (i) be natural persons (i.e., not corporate entities); (ii) provide bona fide services that are not capital-raising (i.e., no securities promoters); and (iii) have an "employment relationship" with the issuer—the services must be of the type that have "significant characteristics of employment" even if performed by a nonemployee (i.e., no independent agents or franchisees).

The offer to acquire such securities (e.g., options) must be made at the time the recipient is actually providing services to the company in order for Rule 701 to apply, even if the exercise occurs after termination of the services. If its conditions are satisfied, Rule 701(c) permits securities acquired under the plan by covered offerees to be sold as soon as 90 days after the IPO (subject, of course, to any lockup or market stand-off requirements contractually imposed by the underwriter).

The issuer's ability to rely upon Rule 701 turns on whether *before the IPO*, the issuer satisfied certain mathematical tests with respect to securities sold or optioned under its employee plans. Under Rule 701, in any given 12-month period the sum of (1) the exercise price of outstanding options plus (2) the aggregate dollar amount of sales made in reliance on Rule 701 during the preceding 12 months cannot exceed the greater of (a) $1 million; (b) 15% of the company's total assets, measured at the issuer's most recent balance sheet date (if no older than its last fiscal year end); or (c) 15% of the outstanding securities of the same class of stock being offered and sold in reliance on Rule 701, measured at the issuer's most recent balance sheet date (if no older than its last fiscal year end). In order to ensure post-IPO availability of Rule 701, privately held companies need to track stock and option issuances on a rolling basis during the life of the employee plan. After the first time the thresholds are exceeded, Rule 701 will be unavailable for subsequent grants (although shares that previously came in under the thresholds will still be eligible to use the exemption).

The issuer must deliver to investors a copy of the employee plan. In addition, if the aggregate sales price or amount of securities sold during any consecutive 12-month period exceeds $5 million, the issuer is subject to additional disclosure requirements before the date of sale. Under Rule 701(e), such disclosure obligations include:

1. If the plan is subject to ERISA, a copy of the summary plan description;

2. If the plan is not subject to ERISA, a summary of the material terms of the plan;

3. Information about the risks associated with investment in the securities sold pursuant to the compensatory benefit plan or compensation contract;

4. Financial statements required to be furnished by Part F/S of Form 1-A under Regulation A (§§ 230.251–230.263) as of a date no more than 180 days before the sale of securities in reliance on this exemption (including financial statements of parent if the parent's assets are used to compute the asset test); and

5. If the sale involves a stock option or other derivative security, the issuer must deliver disclosure a reasonable period of time before the date of exercise or conversion.[11]

Exhibit 8-1 provides a sample Rule 701 tracking worksheet.[12]

---

11. 1933 Act Reg. § 203.701(e).

12. For more information on Rule 701, see Eric Orsic, "Federal Securities Law Considerations for Equity Compensation Plans," *Selected Issues in Equity Compensation*, 14th ed. (Oakland, CA: NCEO, 2017).

Exhibit 8-1. Rule 701 Test Sheet

I.   Information needed for the calculations:

   A.   *Dollar amount* of aggregate sales price for securities offered or sold under Rule 701 in the last 12 months (sum of all cash, property, notes, cancellation of debt, or other consideration received by or to be received by the issuer for the sale of the securities. Value options at exercise price of the option on date of grant): $____

   B.   *Number of securities sold* under Rule 701 in the last 12 months (treat the securities underlying all currently exercisable or convertible options, warrants, rights, or other securities, other than those issued under this exemption, as outstanding): ____

   C.   *Total company assets* as of last balance sheet date: $____

   D.   *Outstanding securities of the class* at the end of the last fiscal year (the "class" being the securities being sold under Rule 701, e.g., common), including securities of that class issuable pursuant to exercise of outstanding options, warrants, rights, or convertible securities that were not issued under Rule 701 as of last balance sheet date: ____

II. Rule 701 qualification tests (to qualify under Rule 701, the company need satisfy only one of the three tests):

   1.   *Dollar Cap Test*
      Does A exceed $1 million? Yes ____ No ____
      If "no," then company is qualified under this test.

   2.   *Assets Test*
      Does A exceed 15% of C? Yes ____ No ____
      If "no," then company is qualified under this test.

   3.   *Stock Test*
      Does B exceed 15% of D? Yes ____ No ____
      If "no," then company is qualified under this test.

8.4   Federal Securities Rules: Section 16

Under Section 16 of the Exchange Act, officers, directors, and more-than-10% shareholders of a public company are considered to be "insiders." Public company insiders are subject to special restrictions on their ability to buy and sell company stock, including the obligation to publicly disclose all stock holdings and transactions on reports filed with the SEC. Most importantly, under Section 16(b) of the Exchange Act such insiders are subject to the "short-swing" profits rule. This rule gives the company the right to sue to recover any "profits" (as defined in the statute) realized by an insider from any purchases or sales of the issuer's securities within a six-month period. Purchases and sales are "matched" during the six-month period, and "profit" is measured with respect to all transactions, not merely transactions involving the same shares.[13] For stock option purposes, the six-month period begins on the date of grant unless the grant is exempt (as further discussed below). Once a non-exempt transaction occurs, it is matched against any other non-exempt purchase or sale that occurs within six months (i.e., within the period beginning six months before the transaction and ending six months after the transaction).

Because the rules provide a choice of transactional exemptions, most public company insiders can participate in stock option plans without running afoul of the Section 16 limitations.[14] Generally, Rule 16b-3 provides that a grant will be exempt from the operation of Section 16(b) if: (1) it has been approved in advance by the issuer's board of directors; (2) it has been approved in advance by a committee comprising solely two or more "non-employee directors" (a term that has a specific definition under Rule 16b-3); (3) it has been approved in advance or subsequently ratified by the issuer's shareholders; or (4) neither the option nor the underlying shares are disposed of within six months of the date of grant.[15] Further, so long as the grant itself is exempt, the exercise of the grant is a non-event for purposes of Rule 16b-3. This is because the acquisition of a derivative security (the option grant) is considered to be the acquisition of the underlying equity for purposes of Section 16.[16]

The sale of shares acquired upon exercise is also subject to Section 16(b) and the exemptions in Rule 16b-3, one of which exempts sales and purchases that are directly with the issuer.

Section 16 also includes Section 16(a), which sets out comprehensive reporting requirements for Section 16 transactions. These requirements are discussed briefly below in section 8.5.

---

13. Section 16(b)(3) of the Exchange Act.

14. This is a brief overview of a complicated area of the law and is not intended to provide definitive guidance. For in-depth discussion, see Peter J. Romeo and Alan L. Dye, *Section 16 Treatise and Reporting Guide,* 3d ed., available online at www.section16treatise.net. See also Orsic, "Federal Securities Law."

15. Release No. 34-37250 (1996); Rule 16b-3(c),(d). A different exemption may apply for Section 423 plan options, as discussed in section 8.6 below.

16. Rule 16b-6.

8.5 Securities Law Information and Reporting Requirements

The securities laws impose various reporting obligations with respect to option plans and transactions under such plans. These obligations (along with many others unrelated to options) were significantly expanded by the Sarbanes-Oxley Act of 2002, enacted July 30, 2002,[17] and further expanded with the Dodd-Frank Act of 2010. The JOBS Act of 2012 rolled back some of the new disclosure requirements for emerging growth companies.

The SEC continues to be engaged in a long, complex rulemaking process under all of these laws, and only time and experience will flush out outstanding issues yet to be settled or even commented upon. The history of rulemaking under Sarbanes-Oxley began with the first SEC releases in 2002, and has continued through the proposed rules regarding (among other things) accelerated filing in 2005 and 2007, the final executive compensation disclosure rules, effective November 7, 2006, and the amendments to those rules finalized in late 2009. The extensive rulemaking process required under the Dodd-Frank Act of 2010 has barely begun as has rulemaking under the JOBS Act. Accordingly, the following reporting information is intended as a basic summary only. Before any securities reporting is attempted, careful consultation must be undertaken with legal counsel to determine the status of the law.[18]

8.5.1 1933 Act: S-8 Prospectus

Assuming that the issuer is not relying on Rule 701 to provide an exemption from registration for shares issued under its employee stock plan, the issuer will generally register such shares on a Form S-8, which is available to public company employers that have complied with all required reporting obligations in the 12 months immediately prior to

---

17. P.L. 107-204.

18. Please note that this section does not discuss the executive compensation and stock option disclosure requirements under the Exchange Act, nor does it analyze the Section 16(a) reporting obligations. For an in-depth analysis of the latter rules, see Romeo and Dye, referenced above.

its filing.[19] Companies that have been subject to the reporting requirements for less than a year can use Form S-8 so long as they are current
in their reporting.

By using the Form S-8, the issuer may take advantage of a simplified prospectus delivery requirement with respect to the registration of
shares of stock to be issued under such plans. The prospectus does not
have to be filed with Form S-8, but instead can be included by reference.
Further, participants need not receive a "prospectus" per se; instead,
they may have access to a number of documents that provide material
information regarding the plan, its operations, and the securities to be
issued; provided, however, that each such document must be labeled as
a prospectus and include other specific securities law disclaimers. Specifically, Form S-8 requires that participants be furnished with (among
other things): the name of the plan and the registrant, the administrator's telephone number, information about the plan's administration, a
description of the securities being offered under the plan, the rules for
eligibility, the manner of determining the price, the tax consequences,
any restrictions (including restrictions on resale), and forfeiture events.[20]

Generally, employers satisfy the prospectus requirements by incorporating the company's public documents by reference and providing a
detailed, "user-friendly" plan summary (including a copy of the plan)
to all employees. The SEC has ruled that if e-mail is used in the "ordinary course" of employee business, an alternative is provided for those
who do not otherwise access e-mail, and paper versions are available
to those who do not have electronic access, then electronic delivery of
these documents is a satisfactory way of meeting the prospectus delivery requirement. This analysis may be logically extended to Internet or
intranet (intra-company website) delivery if access is readily available
to all employees.[21] In companies where e-mail and intranets are used,
this method of disseminating the prospectus is both efficient and cost-
effective.

---

19. See general instructions to Form S-8, Section A. The Rule 701 exemption may
    apply to permit sales of restricted stock optioned under an employee stock
    plan before the issuer's IPO. See section 8.2.3 above.

20. See Form S-8, Items 1, 2.

21. SEC Release No. 33-7288, IV, Example (1).

8.5.2   Exchange Act: Section 16(a) Filings

Under Section 16(a) of the Exchange Act, public company insiders must file information reports with the SEC disclosing their holdings of, and transactions in, the equity securities of their companies. Although most of the transactions discussed here will be exempt for Section 16(b) purposes, they may still be subject to reporting under Section 16(a), as follows:

- *Form 3:* To report equity holdings the first time a person becomes subject to Section 16;[22] filed within 10 calendar days of event that triggers the insider status. If the filing is triggered by an IPO, then Form 3 must be filed on or before the date when the company becomes public.

- *Form 4:* To report non-exempt transactions (including any occurring during the six months after terminating insider status), exercises and conversions of derivative securities (whether or not exempt), and certain acquisitions.[23] Form 4 is required to be filed before the end of the second business day after the transaction was executed.[24]

- *Form 5:* To report exempt transactions other than those covered by Form 4.[25] Form 5 must be filed within 45 calendar days after the end of the company's fiscal year. The kinds of transactions that may qualify as reportable on Form 5 include gifts of stock, transfers to family members for estate planning purposes, and small acquisitions of less than $10,000 that are not directly from the company.

For each form, the insider is required to electronically file three copies: one with the SEC, one with each applicable stock exchange, and one with the company. The filer must keep a manually signed copy for five years after filing. Both the SEC and the issuer are required

---

22. Rule 16a-3(a).

23. Rule 16a-3(f), 16a-6.

24. Sarbanes-Oxley Act of 2002, Section 403(a). As mandated by the act, the SEC adopted final rules for implementation of the Section 16(a) amendments as of August 29, 2002, in SEC Release No. 34-46421 (Aug. 27, 2002).

25. Rule 16a-3(a), 16a-3(f).

to post Section 16 statements on publicly accessible websites no later than the end of the business day following the filing and to keep them accessible for at least a year.[26] Forms filed electronically and posted on the website are deemed filed with the exchanges and Nasdaq without additional filings.

For its part, the company must report any delinquent filings in its annual proxy statement pursuant to Item 405 of Regulation S-K. An issuer may not assume that its timely receipt of a Form 4 from an insider (i.e., within three calendar days of the transaction) is an indication that the form was also timely filed with the SEC (i.e., within two calendar days). Instead, the issuer is required to monitor all insider electronic filings to be sure they have been timely filed.

8.6   Exchange Act: Equity Compensation Disclosure Rules

In addition to the Section 16(a) rules described above, the Exchange Act imposes extensive disclosure and reporting obligations on public companies, including obligations with respect to equity compensation awarded to employees and consultants. In 2001 and 2002, the SEC responded quickly to public outcry over perceived corporate failures to adequately disclose executive compensation. After many initiatives and statements, the SEC adopted its final rules on executive compensation and related-person disclosure in 2006, and further amended the rules in 2009. In addition, the Dodd-Frank Act of 2010 requires SEC rulemaking on a number of new executive compensation disclosure provisions, which will further alter the disclosure landscape. The JOBS Act, on the other hand, limits the required disclosures for emerging growth companies.

The current rules are complex and only the highlights are summarized in this section. The intention of the rules is to illuminate the rationale behind, as well as the amount and form of, the executive compensation program provided by a company to its executives, and to do so in a comprehensible manner. The adopting release, issued in accordance with the SEC's "plain English" requirements, is extensive and illuminating;

---

26. Section 403(a) of the Act (new Section 16(a)(4)); SEC Release No. 33-8230 (May 7, 2003).

in addition to consulting counsel, any professional who is engaged in preparing proxy disclosures and other executive-compensation-related filings would be well advised to study the rule in full.[27]

8.6.1 Executives Covered by Reporting Requirements

The chief executive officer (CEO), chief financial officer (CFO), and three other highest-paid executive officers (ranked on the basis of total compensation) are subject to individual disclosure requirements. They are termed the "named executive officers" or "NEOs." Total compensation is determined for these purposes without regard to pensions or deferred compensation.

For smaller reporting companies, meaning generally those with less than $75 million of publicly traded stock, and emerging growth companies, the NEOs include only the CEO and to next two most highly compensated employees.

8.6.2 Compensation Discussion and Analysis

Companies are required to include a narrative and tabular report of the required disclosure items. In addition, companies must include a plain-English Compensation Discussion and Analysis (CD&A). In general, the CD&A greatly expands the amount of information that was formerly required to be included in the board compensation committee report. Rather than simply reporting the result of the board's compensation decisions, the CD&A is intended to provide shareholders with analysis that explains the reasoning behind these decisions. At minimum, the CD&A must include the following points with respect to each of the NEOs:

- Objectives of the compensation program
- Reason for the type of incentives provided

---

27. The rule can be found at www.sec.gov/rules/final/2009/33-9089.pdf. For a more extensive summary, and a deskbook copy of the rules and tables, see the *Executive Compensation Disclosure Handbook,* 2010 ed., by Danielle Benderly, et al. (Chicago: R.R. Donnelley), as updated May 2010. It can be downloaded from www.perkinscoie.com/news/pubs.aspx.

- Details of each specific element of the program
- How compensation is structured, determined, and paid
- Equity award grant procedures, including stock option timing issues

The key to the CD&A is that it should be the compensation committee's answer to the questions: What results are we trying to accomplish for each NEO with our executive compensation program? How are we hoping to objectively see those results? And what are the actual policies and procedures we are applying to do so?[28] To answer these questions, many companies also provide executive summaries that highlight changes from previous years. We can expect that the SEC and reporting companies will continue to explore these issues as time goes on through the use of the comment letter process.

Smaller reporting companies and emerging growth companies are not required to file a CD&A.

8.6.3 NEO Executive Compensation Disclosure Tables and Related Narrative Disclosures

Tabular disclosure of executive compensation has been a proxy requirement since 2002. However, the tables have been expanded and modified, along with the requirement to provide additional narrative disclosure (in addition to the CD&A described above). Under Item 402 of Regulation S-K, the following separate tables are required whenever relevant (along with narrative discussion of those tables):

- Summary Compensation
- Outstanding Equity Awards at Fiscal Year End
- Option Exercises and Stock Vested
- Pension Benefits
- Nonqualified Deferred Compensation
- Grants of Plan-Based Awards
- Director Compensation

---

28. The SEC has set out a lengthy discussion of topics that may be reviewed in the CD&A if the company believes they are material and helpful to shareholders' understanding of the program's principles.

The information contained in the tables generally falls into the following categories:

- *Current Compensation:* Compensation (i.e., salary; bonus; nonequity incentives; and perks) earned during the most recently completed fiscal year and two preceding fiscal years (as applicable) in the Summary Compensation table. The Summary Compensation and Director Compensation tables also must include the full grant date fair value of equity incentives granted in the covered fiscal year, as calculated under ASC 718.[29] Supplemental information on plan-based awards granted during the most recently completed fiscal year, including the full grant date ASC 718 fair value of each equity compensation award, is reported in the Grants of Plan-Based Awards table. The Dodd-Frank Act of 2010 requires disclosure of the relationship between executive compensation and the company's financial performance. It also requires disclosure of the ratio by which the CEO's pay exceeds the total compensation of all other company employees.[30] Both provisions are not yet required as they are subject to rulemaking that is not completed.

- *Current Equity Holdings and Earnings:* Outstanding equity holdings as of the fiscal year end in the Outstanding Equity Awards at Fiscal Year End table and earnings realized on equity holdings during the most recent fiscal year in the Option Exercises and Stock Vested table.

- *Post-Employment Compensation:* Retirement and other post-employment compensation (including pension plans) in the Pension Benefits table, deferred compensation plans in the Nonqualified Deferred Compensation table, and, in a separate section, a narrative disclosure of any other post-employment payments (e.g., relating to separation, retirement, and change in control transactions).

Smaller public companies and emerging growth companies are exempt from some of these disclosure requirements. Companies must

---

29. Before the SEC's 2009 revisions, companies were required to include the amount recognized that year under ASC 718 in the Summary Compensation and Director Compensation tables instead of the full grant date fair value.

30. For a fuller discussion of the Dodd-Frank Act, see section 13.2.4.

file Summary Compensation tables that cover only the last two fiscal years, Outstanding Equity at Fiscal Year-End tables, and Director Compensation tables. They need not file the other disclosures. In lieu of filing a CD&A, they can provide a narrative description of information necessary to understand the Summary Compensation table.

In 2009 the SEC expanded the scope of the executive compensation disclosures to require companies to specifically disclose whether their incentive compensation plans encourage employees to take excessive risks, but only if the risks are "reasonably likely to have a material adverse effect on the company." This requirement applies to all employees, not just NEOs.

8.6.4   Special Disclosure Regarding Stock Options

The options-related tables described above must also include the following *for each outstanding award*:

- Grant date
- Grant date fair value
- ASC 718 grant date[31]
- Closing market price on grant date, if higher than strike price
- Date action taken to grant award, if different than grant date

The narrative disclosure accompanying these tables must generally discuss the company's option-granting practices and philosophies, including the role of the compensation committee in setting these practices and establishing any grant-related policies. It must also discuss any material factors related to the individual grants, such as repricings, modifications, employment agreement terms, and performance goals for vesting, etc.

8.6.5   Form 8-K Reporting Requirements

Public companies are required to report certain events related to NEOs within four business days after their occurrence on Form 8-K under

---

31. In 2009, the Financial Accounting Standards Board created a codified numbering system for authoritative accounting literature. Under it, FAS 123(R) became ASC 718.

Item 5.02. As a general rule, companies must report the following compensation-related events under Item 5.02 of the Form 8-K:

- Departure (retirement, resignation, termination) of any of the following "specified officers": principal executive officer, president, principal financial officer, principal accounting officer, principal operating officer, person performing similar functions, or any NEO.

- Compensatory arrangements with new directors or specified officers, including brief description of same.

- Any material amendment to a material compensatory arrangement with an NEO, including a brief description of same (but not including broad-based compensation arrangements).

- Any salary or bonus amounts previously omitted (because not calculable) from the Summary Compensation table.

Note that in accordance with an FAQ published by the SEC, changes to equity compensation plans that include executive officers but are not material as to the individual officer need not be disclosed prior to the time the plan would normally be filed.[32]

The 2009 SEC rules require companies to report the outcome of proxy votes on a Form 8-K, which accelerates the disclosure of results.

8.7   ESPP Securities Law Considerations

Generally, ESPPs are subject to the same securities laws as those described above with respect to stock options. However, a few distinctions should be noted. These distinctions may apply to non-Section 423 employee stock purchase plans as well if they are designed as broad-based plans but simply do not satisfy all of the requirements of the Code.

8.7.1   Securities Act of 1933

Section 423 plans are subject to the federal securities laws described above. However, because most companies offer Section 423 plans only

---

32. This 2004 FAQ, which is still useful in interpreting the rules, can be found at http://www.sec.gov/divisions/corpfin/form8kfaq.htm.

after going public, sponsors typically register ESPPs with the SEC on Form S-8.[33] Accordingly, Rule 144 will apply (to sales by affiliates) only on a limited basis.

8.7.2   Securities Exchange Act of 1934

With respect to Section 16(b), the SEC rules provide a specific exemption for transactions under a "tax-conditioned plan." For these purposes, Rule 16b-3 provides that a tax-conditioned plan is an employee benefit plan that meets the coverage and participation requirements of Sections 423(b)(3) and 423(b)(5) of the Code. This means that, as a general rule, any Section 423 plan transaction (other than the disposition of stock acquired under the plan) will be exempt from Section 16(b) and its filing requirements.[34] An insider who acquires shares under a Section 423 plan should add those shares to his or her next Form 4 (or Form 5) filing in the column titled "amount of securities beneficially owned following reported transaction" and include a footnote detailing the nature of the increase in owned shares. Dispositions, of course, must always be reported on the Form 4, as must the rare transaction that does not qualify for an exemption (e.g., cancellation of a portion of a fixed-price option).[35] The only exception to this broad exemption arises if a transaction is considered to be a "discretionary transaction" under Rule 16b-3(b)(1). Generally, discretionary transactions will occur only in the context of a retirement plan.

Nonstatutory ESPPs are not eligible for "tax-conditioned plan" status. Such plans will need to comply with a different Section 16(b) exemption, as discussed in section 8.3 above.

8.8   International Securities Law Issues

Non-U.S. employees who receive securities in U.S. companies are generally subject to U.S. securities laws with respect to transactions in such securities. However, additional issues may arise if local country law

---

33. For information on Form S-8, see section 8.5.1 above.

34. Rule 16a-3(f)(1)(i)(B).

35. See Rule 16b-3(b)(5). For detailed information, consult Romeo and Dye and see above.

limits or restricts ownership of U.S. securities by residents, or if the U.S. issuer is required to comply with local country permit rules. Foreign countries frequently impose disclosure and reporting requirements on transfers of employee-owned securities (regardless of where the issuer is located). Exchange/currency controls are also common, including restrictions on sending currency outside of the country for the purposes of purchasing securities. As always, both U.S. and local country counsel must be consulted to ensure compliance before grant.

Tax Law Compliance Issues

Contents

Income recognized by an optionee on the exercise of an NSO or disqualifying disposition of an ISO may be subject to federal income and payroll taxes, including Social Security and Medicare (FICA) and unemployment (FUTA), and in many cases state income taxes as well. Option-related income is subject to a variety of reporting and disclosure requirements under the Code, and the employer may be entitled to take a compensation deduction with respect to such income in the year of inclusion by the optionee. This chapter reviews the relevant requirements for withholding, reporting, disclosing, and deducting income realized in connection with stock options.

9.1   Tax Withholding for Stock Options

The compensation element (the spread) on exercise of an NSO by an employee or former employee constitutes wages subject to federal income tax withholding under Section 3402 of the Code (and where applicable, state income tax withholding). The spread is treated as "supplemental wages" for withholding purposes.[1] Supplemental income can be subject to different withholding rates than regular or base salary income. Supplemental payments of $1 million or less can be withheld at 25% or the employee's regular withholding percentage; supplemental payment amounts that exceed $1 million are withheld at 39.6%. (Note that these rates change from time to time.) Exhibit 9-1 summarizes the current withholding rules for NSOs. Note that federal withholding is not permitted on exercise by a nonemployee who is not a former employee of the company, and in fact if shares are withheld to cover taxes for a nonemployee, for example a nonemployee director, liability accounting is triggered.

No payroll tax withholding is imposed upon the exercise of a statutory stock option.

Exhibit 9-1. Withholding Information for NSO Exercise

	FIT/SIT Withholding	FICA/FUTA Withholding	Form
1. Employee	Spread on exercise	Spread on exercise	W-2[a]
2. Former employee			
(a) Year of termination	Spread on exercise	Spread on exercise	W-2
(b) Subsequent years	Spread on exercise	Spread on exercise	W-2[b]

---

1.   See Rev. Rul. 82200, 19822 C.B. 239; Rev. Rul. 67257, 19672 C.B. 359. See also Treas. Reg. § 31.3402(g)1 (supplemental wage withholding generally). See Treas. Reg. § 31.3401(a)-1(a)(5); see also chapter 12.

Exhibit 9-1. Withholding Information for NSO Exercise

3. Retiree: same as former employee[c]			
4. Estate			
(a) Calendar year of death	None	Spread on exercise[d]	W-2
(b) Subsequent years	None	None[e]	1099-MISC
5. Nonemployee former spouse (NEFS)[f]			
(a) Employee employed	Spread on exercise: NEFS	Spread on exercise withheld from payment; imputed to employee	1099-MISC: NEFS (FIT) W-2: Employee (FICA)[g]
(b) Former employee: calendar year of termination	Spread on exercise: NEFS	Spread on exercise withheld from payment; imputed to employee	1099-MISC: NEFS (FIT) W-2: Employee (FICA)
(c) Former employee: subsequent years	Spread on exercise: NEFS	Spread on exercise: employee	1099-MISC: NEFS W-2: Employee (FICA)
6. Transferee[h]			
(a) Employee employed	Spread on exercise: employee	Spread on exercise: employee	W-2: employee[i]
(b) Former employee: calendar year of termination	Spread on exercise: employee	Spread on exercise: employee	W-2: employee
(c) Former employee: subsequent years	Spread on exercise: employee	Spread on exercise: employee	W-2: employee
7. Change to consultant status	Allocate spread on exercise across years of service; withhold on amount attributable to years as employee[j]	Allocate spread on exercise across years of service; withhold on amount attributable to years as employee	W-2 for employee years; 1099-MISC for consultant years
8. Change of residence			
(a) To foreign country from U.S.	If U.S. citizen, entire spread taxed in U.S.; if U.S. tax resident, allocate spread on exercise across years of service; exclude if IRC § 911 applies, otherwise withhold on spread[k]	If U.S. citizen, entire spread taxed in U.S.; if U.S. tax resident, allocate spread on exercise across years of service; exclude if totalization agreement requires social security payments to foreign country only[m]	W-2

Exhibit 9-1. Withholding Information for NSO Exercise

(b) To different state	Allocate spread on exercise as required by rules of each state for state income tax purposes; FIT not affected[n]	Spread on exercise	W-2

Notes to Exhibit 9-1

a. Sections 3401(a) and 3121(a) of the Code. The spread on exercise is wages for both FIT and FICA purposes.

b. Note that Treas. Reg. § 1.83-6(a)(2) provides that a deduction is available as long as reporting is made, including using a 1099-MISC for a former employee. However, Section 3401 of the Code and its regulations specifically provide that the employment relationship giving rise to a withholding obligation is not dependent on whether the payment is made at the time of the relationship.

c. For these purposes, there is no difference between a retired employee and an employee who has terminated for other reasons. Payments to retirees are excluded only in certain limited situations: some payments from and to qualified plans and certain deferred compensation payments (for which FICA withholding has already occurred). Sections 3401(a) and 3121(v)(i) of the Code.

d. Rev. Rul. 86-109.

e. Section 3121(a) of the Code.

f. Note that generally this will apply only in community property states (unless the plan permits transferability).

g. Rev. Rul. 2002-22; Rev. Rul. 2002-31.

h. Note that this will apply only if the option is transferable.

i. Section 83 of the Code.

j. Sections 83, 3402, and 3121 of the Code. No withholding is required for independent contractors, so the analysis here is the same as for any former employee, subject to allocation.

k. Sections 83 and 1441 of the Code. The spread is allocated between U.S. source income (i.e., attributable to years resident in the U.S.) and foreign source income, based on where the services were performed. Withholding would ordinarily be required on U.S. source income. PLR 8711107. However, Section 911 may provide an overall exclusion that will trump the withholding requirement.

l. Section 3121 of the Code. The same rules apply, except that certain tax treaties (totalization agreements) may allocate the Social Security payment differently.

m. Each state has different rules. Most states require source income to be allocated on the same basis as USSI/FSI. See section 9.7.

9.2 Tax Reporting for Stock Options

9.2.1 Nonstatutory Options: Form W-2 or Form 1099

Generally, the spread on exercise of an NSO should be reported on the employee's or former employee's Form W-2 for the year in which the exercise occurred. Reporting for nonemployees is on a Form 1099.[2] As noted above, if the optionee is an employee at the time of the grant, the spread will generally be subject to withholding of income taxes, FICA, and FUTA at exercise.

9.2.2 Statutory Options, Code Sections 422 and 423: Form W-2

No tax withholding is required on the spread on exercise of a statutory option by an employee or former employee. However, if an employer intends to take a tax deduction with respect to a disqualifying disposition of statutory option stock, deductibility is subject to compliance with Section 83(h) of the Code, which provides that the employer may deduct an amount equal to the amount included by the employee in income. As more fully described in section 2.6, if the employer timely reports the includible amount on the employee's Form W-2, the employer may rely upon the "deemed inclusion" rule and deduct the amount reported regardless of whether it has actual proof of the employee's inclusion. Although the Code does not require federal income tax withholding at the time of sale or disposition, it imposes Form W-2 information reporting requirements on any remuneration payments ultimately made to employees which, in the aggregate, exceed $600 annually.[3] For purposes of deductions with respect to a disqualifying disposition, the deemed inclusion rule will be satisfied if the Form W-2 or W-2c (as applicable) is filed by the employer on or before the date on which the employer files

2. Typically, this amount has been reported in the "other" or "misc" box on either form. However, from time to time the IRS prescribes the use of various codes, and employers should check for the most up-to-date rules annually under Treas. Reg. § 1.83-6(a)(2).
3. Treas. Reg. § 1.6041-(2)(a)(1).

its tax return claiming the deduction.[4] Employers are required to use a "V" code on the Form W-2 when reporting disqualifying dispositions.[5]

Income resulting from the sale or disposition of ISO and Section 423 ESPP shares is exempt from FICA and FUTA.

9.2.3 Form 1099-B

For option exercises and ESPP purchases after the start of 2011, the IRS requires brokers to furnish optionees with Form 1099-B reflecting the cost basis of the securities. Only the amount paid for the shares is stated on the form, a requirement that has the potential to lead to over-reporting or even double reporting on the part of plan participants. Prior to 2013, the amount reported could be increased by any amount the optionee had to include in income, which meant the holders of NSOs could receive forms reflecting their true cost basis in the shares.[6] However, the final regulations issued in 2013 provide that only the exercise price of options or the purchase price of ESPP shares may be reported on Form 1099-B.[7]

Participants in Section 423 ESPPs are particularly likely to be confused by the forms. The reporting requirement is triggered by the purchase of shares—before the amount that must be included in income is known. The ordinary income element of Section 423 plan shares is affected by drops in stock price after the purchase date and by the character of the disposition of shares.

The requirement for the new form was included in the Energy Improvement and Extension Act of 2008, and final rules were published in April 2013. Companies are well advised to communicate to employees the fact that the amount brokers are reporting to optionees is seldom the same as the taxable income that the optionees themselves must reflect on their taxes. Participants should be advised to carefully calculate their own tax basis for purposes of their individual tax returns and not rely upon cost basis reported on the Form 1099-B. Wherever possible, plan sponsors should remind participants that tax basis (as opposed to cost

---

4.   Treas. Reg. § 1.83-6(a)(2).

5.   See IRS Announcements 2002-108, 2002-49 IRB 952; 2001-92, 2001-39 IRB 301.

6.   IR-2010-104.

7.   T.D. 9616.

basis) includes exercise price plus any amounts included in ordinary income. Participants should also be encouraged to consult with their tax advisors prior to reporting capital gains (or losses) on ESPP stock.

9.2.4 FATCA Reporting

The Foreign Account Tax Compliance Act of 2010 (FATCA) added a new set of reporting requirements that affect U.S. taxpayers who receive stock options from non-U.S. companies. Under new Code Section 6038D, the holders of stock in non-U.S. companies (including stock that was acquired upon the exercise of a stock option) must report those holdings to the IRS on Form 8938 if the aggregate value exceeds $50,000. This provision went into effect beginning with the 2011 tax year. A taxpayer who fails to file the form can be fined $10,000. The penalty can increase to a maximum of $50,000 if the taxpayer does not file even after being informed by the IRS that the form is due. Unlike the requirements discussed above, the responsibility for filing this form lies solely with the employee. Employers should consider whether they wish to alert affected employees to the requirement. Unvested awards are not subject to reporting unless a Section 83(b) election has been filed.

9.3 Section 6039 Information Reporting for Statutory Options

Section 6039 requires information returns be furnished in writing to optionees and the IRS upon exercise of an ISO or "first transfer" of ESPP stock. The ESPP reporting obligation had historically been triggered by the sale of the stock, and Section 6039 reporting previously was on a less formal information statement that went only to employees. The IRS released final forms 3921 (for ISO exercises) and 3922 (for ESPP share transfer) on November 8, 2010.

Failure to satisfy the reporting obligation will result in penalties to the employer company under Section 6722 of the Code (see section 9.3.3 below).

9.3.1 Information Required to Be Reported to Optionee

The employer must satisfy the Section 6039 reporting obligation early in the year following the year in which the ISO exercise or ESPP stock "transfer" occurred. In the case of ESPP stock, the obligation applies only on the first transfer of ESPP stock by its original owner; that is, the company will not be required to report on interim or subsequent transfers. The 2010 final regulations redefined "first transfer" to include transfer to a brokerage account, meaning that in most cases, the reporting obligation arises at the time of purchase, when the shares are deposited into the employee's brokerage account, instead of the time of sale. However, if shares are issued directly to the participant or held in book entry form by either the company or a transfer agent, no transfer will be deemed to have occurred upon purchase. The reporting requirement will be triggered by the subsequent sale of the shares or transfer to a brokerage account.

The specific reporting requirements set out in the final Section 6039 regulations provide that the statement furnished to the optionee upon exercise of an ISO (the "transferor") and to the IRS on a Form 3921 contain the following information:

1. The name, address, and employer identification number of the granting company;

2. The name, address, and employer identification number of the company whose stock is being transferred, if it is different than the granting corporation;

3. The name, address, and identifying number of the transferor;

4. The date the option was granted to the transferor;

5. The exercise price per share;

6. The date of exercise;

7. The fair market value of a share of stock on the exercise date; and

8. The number of shares to which title was transferred pursuant to the exercise.

In the case of the first transfer of ESPP shares, the final Section 6039 regulations on a Form 3922 require reporting of the following information:

1. The name, address, and identifying number of the transferor;

2. The name, address, and employer identification number of the company whose stock was transferred;

3. The date the option was granted to the transferor;

4. The stock's fair market value on the grant date;

5. The exercise price per share;

6. The exercise price per share determined as if the option were exercised on the date the option was granted to the participant;

7. The date of exercise;

8. The fair market value of a share of stock on the exercise date;

9. The date the legal title of the shares was transferred by the transferor; and

10. The number of shares to which legal title was being transferred.

A statement is considered to be furnished to the transferor if it is mailed to the person at his or her last known address or, with the transferor's consent, delivered electronically.[8] The returns are required to be furnished to the employee no later than January 31 of the year following the calendar year of the transaction. The deadline for filing the forms with the IRS depends on whether the company is filing them electronically. Electronic transmission to the IRS through the Filing Information Returns Electronically (FIRE) system is required for any form for which the company must file 250 or more copies.[9] For example, a company that must file 260 Forms 3921 and 200 Forms 3922 will be required to file only the Forms 3921 electronically. Companies filing paper forms must file them with the IRS by February 28 of the year following the calendar year of the transaction, those filing electronically have a March 31 deadline.

9.3.2 Tracking ESPP Qualifying Dispositions

Despite the Section 6039 reporting requirement, limited attention has traditionally been paid to tracking qualifying dispositions of ESPP stock. However, the newly strengthened reporting requirements make it essential that companies do track dispositions. Moreover, the IRS has

---

8. Treas. Reg. § 1.6039-1(d) (mail); § 1.6039-1(f) (electronic).

9. IRS Publication 1220, Rev. Proc. 2009-20.

stated in Publication 15-B that employers should track all qualifying and disqualifying dispositions. A "qualifying disposition" is a disposition of ESPP stock that occurs either after the applicable holding periods have expired or upon the death of the employee. As noted above, companies are not entitled to a tax deduction on a qualifying disposition, although the amount included in ordinary income under an ESPP option must be reported by the company on the optionee's W-2.[10] Because there is no perceived tax benefit to the employer in tracking qualifying dispositions, many companies have automatically assumed that there is also no requirement to do so. The final regulations under Section 6039 require companies to report the difference between the share price on the grant date and the amount for which the shares would be purchased if the exercise price were based on the stock's FMV on that date. This effectively provides both the employee and the IRS with the amount that must be included as ordinary income in the year of qualifying disposition of the shares. The reporting obligation for the qualifying disposition—when properly tracked by the company—is on Form W-2.

The challenge of Section 6039 for ESPP purposes has always been not only the paperwork required for adequate reporting but also the timing of its requirements. Prior to the final regulations, tracking was problematic because, by its terms, a qualifying disposition must occur at least two years after grant of the option (or upon death of the optionee); thus, it was not unusual for the employee to have left the company long before the disposition took place. Because the final regulations allow the reporting requirement to be triggered when the stock is deposited in a brokerage account, this issue under Section 6039 will be far less challenging than it was in the past. Of course, in the rare cases that an ESPP transfer is made directly to the employee, the stock plan administrator or transfer agent will still be required to recognize that the transferred stock is ESPP stock regardless of whether the transferor is still an employee of the company.

---

10. Section 423(c). For ISO purposes, information reporting with respect to the year of exercise would be necessary (although not specifically required) regardless of Section 6039, so as to give optionees the ability to compute AMT. As a practical matter, for public company stock transactions the transfer agent/ broker will ordinarily issue an information report to the optionee at the time of exercise.

9.3.3 Penalties for Noncompliance

Section 6721 of the Code applies generally to impose penalties for failure to furnish information returns (including failure to furnish returns required under Section 6039) to the IRS. Section 6722 applies to impose separate penalties in the same amounts for failure to furnish information returns to employees, meaning a company that fails to file a return with the IRS and to furnish one to an employee will be fined twice. In 2015, the IRS announced a significant increase in penalties beginning with information returns due in 2016. The penalties are graduated depending upon how late the forms are. For 2016, the penalties are:

- $50 per information return if the forms are correctly filed within 30 days of the due date (by March 30 if the due date is February 28), with a maximum penalty of $500,000 per year ($175,000 for small businesses);

- $100 per information return if the forms are correctly filed more than 30 days after the due date but by August 1, with a maximum penalty of $1.5 million per year ($500,000 for small businesses); and

- $250 per information return if the forms are correctly filed after August 1 or are not filed at all, with maximum penalty of $3 million per year ($1 million for small businesses).

In cases in which the forms are not filed due to willful disregard of the requirement, the penalty is at least $500 per information return with no maximum penalty.

9.4 Procedure for Withholding with Stock

To assist optionees in providing for tax withholding on exercise of an NSO, many companies allow optionees to elect to provide for withholding by instructing the company to retain shares of stock on exercise of the option. Both the IRS and the SEC have approved stock withholding for tax withholding purposes.[11]

---

11. See, e.g., PLRs 9736040, 9629028, and 8650045 (withholding for stock swap); Ralston Purina Company, SEC No-Action Letter (April 23, 1991); and Cravath,

To withhold federal, state, or local taxes with stock, the company simply computes the tax due on the spread and retains shares with a fair market value equal to such amount on the employee's exercise of the option. The company's grant documents should state that the company will withhold on exercise as applicable either by collecting cash from the employee, by withholding from the employee's compensation, by withholding stock, or by a combination of methods.

For U.S. participants, the IRS allows withholding at either the supplemental payment rate or at a rate based on the participant's W-4 instructions. Until 2016, liability accounting was required for grants for which shares could be withheld at more than the minimum statutory rate (generally the supplemental rate). However, Accounting Standards Update 2016-09 allows for withholding at the maximum statutory rate if allowed under the plan. In response, the NYSE added language to its Frequently Asked Questions on Equity Compensation document stating, "an amendment to a plan to provide for the withholding of shares based on an award recipient's maximum tax obligation rather than the statutory minimum tax rate is not a material revision if the withheld shares are never issued, even if the withheld shares are added back to the plan."[12]

In practice, withholding at the supplemental rate for payments of $1 million or less is more practical than applying each participant's W-4 rate, and the rate required for payments above $1 million is the current U.S. maximum of 39.6%. The change to accounting rules has more practical application for companies with participants outside the U.S. than for domestic participants, as determining the minimum statutory rate had proved challenging in some jurisdictions.

The company must deposit federal income taxes with the IRS within the next business day for any transactions if the cumulative tax liability exceeds $100,000. An exception to this that applies only to NSOs exercised using a same-day sale allows companies to remit taxes within one day after settlement from the brokerage firm (generally the day after T+3)

Swaine & Moore, SEC No-Action Letter (May 6, 1991). Note that this is a different scenario than broker-assisted withholding (e.g., same-day sales), which is not considered to be stock withholding for these purposes.

12. https://www.nyse.com/publicdocs/nyse/regulation/nyse/equitycompfaqs.pdf.

was laid out in a 2003 IRS field directive.[13] The field directive does not apply to other forms of equity (for example, restricted stock transfers) or to other methods of exercise, even if, like net exercises, they have similar outcomes to same-day sales. Notwithstanding the IRS guidance and the long-term tradition of T+3, the SEC voted in September 2016 to propose a rule amendment that would shorten the standard settlement period for most broker-dealer securities transactions to T+2. The SEC will review public comments before taking any further steps to adopt a rule change.

9.5 Internal Revenue Code Section 409A

Under Internal Revenue Code Section 409A, any compensation deferred under a "nonqualified deferred compensation plan" (NDCP) is currently taxable unless it is subject to a substantial risk of forfeiture (i.e., using the principles of Section 83 of the Code) or satisfies the rigorous requirements of Section 409A summarized below. For purposes of Section 409A, nonqualified deferred compensation generally does *not* include: (1) qualified benefit plans, such as employee stock ownership plans (ESOPs) or 401(k) plans; (2) sick leave, death benefits, or similar arrangements; (3) statutory stock options (i.e., ISOs and ESPPs); (4) NSOs granted at fair market value (subject to certain limitations and requirements); (5) restricted stock awards taxed under Section 83 of the Code; and (6) non-discounted SARs (as with NSOs, subject to certain limitations and requirements). All other forms of nonqualified deferred compensation, it can be assumed, are subject to the design and operational requirements of Code Section 409A, *including:* (1) nonqualified employee stock purchase plans that include a discount feature; (2) nonstatutory options and SARs that include a deferral feature (i.e., allow an employee to defer receipt of the award after it has already been exercised) or don't otherwise meet the requirements for exemption; and (3) phantom stock, restricted stock units, performance shares, and similar plans.

The deadline for compliance with Section 409A was December 31, 2008. Stock rights that were granted before April 10, 2007, can comply

13. The field directive can be found at www.irs.gov/businesses/article/0,,id=171226,00. html.

with transitional guidance issued in 2005, the regulations as they were initially proposed, or the final regulations. Rights granted after that date should comply with the final regulations or with additional regulations proposed in June 2016, which the IRS allows companies to rely on even though they are not yet final

9.5.1   General Application

If compensation deferred under an NDCP is not otherwise subject to a substantial risk of forfeiture, it will be taxed at the time of deferral unless the following conditions are satisfied:

1. The initial election to defer (including the time and form of payment) is made before the start of the year in which the compensation is earned. An election to defer "performance-based" compensation (as defined under Code Section 409A) may be made up to six months before the end of the performance period.

2. Any additional election to defer receipt of deferred compensation must be made at least 12 months before the date the deferred compensation would otherwise have been received, and in most cases the deferred compensation must be further deferred for at least five years after the original payment date.

3. Distributions may be permitted only upon separation from service (for certain "key employees" of public companies, this includes a six-month waiting period); at a specified date or dates (under a fixed schedule); or upon disability, death, change in control, or unforeseeable emergency, in each case as such terms are defined by Section 409A and its regulations.

4. No acceleration of payments is permissible, unless the acceleration is specifically permitted under Section 409A and its regulations.

Note that short-term deferrals (i.e., where payment is made no later than 2½ months after the close of the year the substantial risk of forfeiture lapses) are exempt from the application of Section 409A, but even here strict rules must be followed. Under the 2016 proposed regulations, however, short-term deferrals may be deferred beyond the original payment date if necessary to avoid violating federal securities laws or other applicable law.

Section 409A and the Section 409A rules are extremely complicated. Failure to comply with these rules triggers severe and adverse tax consequences for the employee or other service provider who is eligible to receive the deferred compensation. As noted above, the participant's total deferrals under the NDCP are immediately taxed as income except to the extent it is subject to a substantial risk of forfeiture (and not previously taxed). In addition, there is a 20% penalty tax on the amount of the deferral and any earnings attributable to it, plus cumulative interest at the underpayment rate plus 1% on the tax that should have been paid on the original deferral and any related earnings.

9.5.2   Specific Application of the Rules to Equity Awards

As we have noted, many equity and equity-based awards are exempted from the Section 409A definition of NDCP, either as a result of the statutory language or the Section 409A rules. The following discussion summarizes the IRS interpretation of Section 409A as it applies to SARs, restricted stock, and NSOs.[14]

9.5.3   NSOs and SARs

The Section 409A rules clarify that both NSOs and SARs ("stock rights") will be exempt from Section 409A so long as (1) the exercise price can never be less than the fair market value of the underlying stock on the date of grant; (2) the stock right is exercisable for "service recipient" stock, a definition that applies only to *common stock* of the employer or its parent or subsidiary; (3) the stock right includes no deferral features other than deferral of income until exercise; and (4) the stock right is not modified in a way that would otherwise subject it to Section 409A.

As with the other exempt forms of compensation, stock rights may be thrown into the purview of Section 409A if they are coupled with features that would otherwise be classified as payments under a

---

14. Note that awards that were earned and vested as of December 31, 2004, are exempt from Section 409A regardless of their terms (so long as such terms were not materially modified after October 3, 2004).

NDCP. Note that generally, NSOs assumed or substituted in a merger or acquisition will not trigger deferred compensation treatment if the conditions of Section 424 governing the transfer of statutory options in a corporate transaction are met. In addition, the regulations make it clear that acceleration of vesting will not (in and of itself) cause an option to fall into Section 409A.

For purposes of setting the exercise price, Section 409A provides that fair market value may be determined using "any reasonable valuation method" and the regulations elaborate on this concept. With publicly traded companies, determination of fair market value is rarely a problem. However, privately held companies must pay special attention to the hurdles inherent in setting fair market value so as to avoid inadvertently granting NSOs or SARs at a discount.[15]

Modifications are treated as the grant of a new stock right, which will result in a discount if the fair market value of the underlying stock has increased since the original date of grant. Moreover, even when there is no increase in price, many common modifications are viewed as adding a feature providing for additional deferrals for purposes of Section 409A. The final regulations contain an important exception for extension of the post-termination exercise period of a stock right. Such an extension will not be considered a modification so long as the option expires no later than the earlier of: (1) the end of its original maximum contractual term, or (2) 10 years from the date of grant. In addition, if the stock right is at-the-money or underwater (i.e., has an exercise price equal to or greater than the fair market value of the underlying stock at the time of the extension), then the stock right may be extended without being subject to the above limitations.

The IRS has established a corrections program available to companies that have granted discounted options as the result of an operational failure, so long as the company has established procedures to ensure that it does not happen in the future. Under IRS Notice 2008-113, options are eligible for relief only if the grant documentation indicates the award was intended to be granted at or above FMV on the grant date, and the option holder is not under investigation by the IRS.

---

15. See sections 2.2 and 2.5 of chapter 2 for more details on setting fair market value under Section 409A.

Corrections must be made before the options are exercised. If the option holder is a Section 16 insider, the company has until the end of the calendar year to correct pricing errors; if the option holder is not an insider, the company has until the end of the calendar year following the grant.

9.5.4 Restricted Stock and RSUs

Restricted stock awards (whether or not vested at grant) are subject to Section 83 of the Code rather than to Section 409A. However, the Section 409A rules note that a plan under which a service provider obtains a legally binding right to receive property in a future year may provide for the deferral of compensation and thus become an NDCP. A restricted stock unit, for example, will fall into Section 409A and accordingly must satisfy the general requirements to avoid early taxation (i.e., no deferral of delivery after vesting or deferral that meets Section 409A's requirements on the timing of deferral elections).[16]

9.6 Limit on Deductions: $1 Million Cap (Code Section 162(m))

Section 162(m) of the Code provides that a public company may not take a tax deduction with respect to compensation in excess of $1 million paid to the CEO and top three highly compensated employees ("covered employees"), excluding the CFO. The exclusion of the CFO arose in 2007 as the result of a wording difference between new executive compensation disclosure requirements and the wording of Section 162(m). Thus, CFOs are automatically included in the disclosure and automatically excluded from the Section 162(m) cap.

The value of employee stock options will be factored into the $1 million cap calculation unless they are considered to be "performance-based compensation." Section 162(m) and its complex regulations provide a special safe harbor for options in this regard, although the rules for use

---

16. For information on the application of Section 409A to restricted stock, see Barbara A. Baksa, "Restricted Stock Awards, Units, and Purchases," in *Equity Alternatives: Restricted Stock, Performance Awards, Phantom Stock, SARs, and More,* 15th ed. (Oakland, CA: NCEO, 2017).

in computing the limitation set out a veritable maze of definitions and exclusions. As an alternative to using the safe harbor, stock options may be designated as "performance based" under the general rules of Section 162(m)(4)(C) of the Code (requiring disclosure of material terms of performance goals), which has numerous requirements. However, notwithstanding its complexity, the safe harbor generally provides an easier route for most companies.[17]

Generally, options granted to covered employees will be excluded from the $1 million cap if the plan under which options are issued satisfies the following requirements:

1. The plan is administered by a committee of outside directors. For these purposes, an "outside director" may not be a current or former employee of the company (or its affiliates) during the taxable year, must never have been an officer, and must not receive any remuneration from the company other than as a director. This definition differs from that used for Section 16 and other securities law purposes, and accordingly the company may choose to have a special committee in place purely for the purpose of making Section 162(m) grants.[18]

2. The plan specifies who is eligible to participate, and this is disclosed to the shareholders.

3. The plan states a maximum number of shares that may be granted to any single participant, and this is disclosed to the shareholders.

4. Options are granted at no less than fair market value.

5. The plan, as disclosed, is approved by the shareholders.

Any broad-based option plan that is designed to include ISOs will necessarily satisfy requirements 2 and 5. Requirement 3 can be met by drafting the plan to state a per-person maximum annual grant. In 2015, the IRS finalized a rule requiring plans meant to qualify as performance-based to specify and disclose a per-person maximum, thus ending an

---

17. Treas. Reg. § 1.162-27(e)(2).

18. Section 162(m)(4)(C); Treas. Reg. § 1.162-27(e)(3). See also PLR 9811029 (compensation committee appropriate for 162(m) purposes).

earlier practice of allowing ISO plans' stated share pool limit to be deemed to set out an annual per-person limit equal to the total number of shares available under the plan.

Note that under the regulations, repriced options will be double-counted (i.e., both the original option and the repriced option will be counted separately) in computing the per-person limit.[19] Requirements 1 and 4 require an affirmative intention on the part of the company to observe the criteria for the exclusion and are operational rather than a function of the plan itself.

Under Rev. Rul. 2008-13, compensation does not qualify for the performance-based exemption if it is designed to be payable automatically upon voluntary or involuntary termination even if the performance goals have not been met.[20] This applies to any year in which such an award is outstanding—not just the year of termination. While many stock options were unaffected by Rev. Rul. 2008-13, because such grants rely on the safe harbor described above, it is important to keep an eye on this issue for options that do not comply with the safe harbor. Problems can arise, in particular, when severance is negotiated at the time of an executive's termination from employment. In order to retain their performance-based exemption, options in the severance package that are not in compliance with the safe harbor may not be accelerated or cashed out prior to the actual achievement of their related performance goals.

Note, too, that compensation does not fail to qualify as performance-based under Section 162(m) merely because the plan allows it to be payable upon death, disability, or change of ownership or control, although compensation actually paid on account of those events before the attainment of the performance goal would not qualify as performance-based.

Options, SARs, and RSAs granted by a publicly held corporation before the corporation was publicly held and before the expiration of the transition period described below are not subject to the Section 162(m) deduction limit. Under regulations finalized in 2015, the IRS confirmed that RSUs and phantom stock do not qualify for the same exception under Section 162(m). Therefore, RSUs and phantom stock

---

19. Treas. Reg. § 1.162-27(e)(2)(vi)(B).

20. Rev. Rul. 2008-13 applies to performance periods that begin after January 1, 2009. It does not apply to contracts that existed before February 21, 2008.

granted after March 31, 2015, are counted toward the deduction limit unless they are distributed or pay out during the transition period.[21]

Corporations that conduct an IPO may rely on the exemption until the earliest of: (i) The expiration or material modification of the plan or agreement; (ii) the share pool is depleted; or (iii) the first shareholder meeting that occurs after the end of the third calendar year following the calendar year in which the IPO occurs or, in the case of a privately held corporation that becomes publicly held without an IPO, the first calendar year after the calendar year in which the corporation becomes publicly held.[22] Plan administrators should be alert to the type of grant made, and the manner in which it is granted, to any officer whose compensation might fall under Section 162(m). Concern about performance-based options was ratcheted up even further in 2006, when the option backdating scandal broke and companies were forced to review previously granted options to ensure that they had actually been granted at fair market value. Among the many issues raised by option backdating was the validity of the 162(m) calculation. In 2009, the IRS office of chief counsel issued a memorandum affirming that if an option is found to be discounted, the tax deduction attributable to its exercise will not be excludable from the $1 million cap even if the backdating was unintentional and the executive reimburses the company for the discounted amount.

In the past few years, two laws reduced the amount of compensation deductible in specific industries. The Emergency Economic Stabilization Act of 2008 (EESA) limited the deductible amounts for financial companies that accepted money under the Troubled Asset Relief Program (TARP), and the Patient Protection and Affordable Care Act of 2010 limited deductible compensation in health-care companies.

Under EESA, new Code Section 162(m)(5) specified that public and private companies that received money under TARP and had not yet repaid it to the government could deduct no more than $500,000 in executive compensation earned in the current year, including amounts paid in a later year, with no exception for "performance-based" compensation. This limit applied not only to those covered by the remainder of Sec-

---

21. Prior rules contained no such transition relief for RSUs or phantom stock.

22. Treas. Reg. § 1.162-27(f)(2).

tion 162(m), but also to the CFO as well as any individual who would have been a "covered employee" for the purposes of Section 162(m)(5) during the taxable year, regardless of their status at the end of such year.

Whereas EESA limited the deduction available under Section 162(m) for companies that accepted help under TARP, the Patient Protection and Affordable Care Act of 2010 created stricter compensation deductibility limits for health-insurance companies. New Section 162(m)(6) limits covered health-insurance providers to deducting $500,000 in compensation paid to *any* officer, director, employee, or service provider. Like Section 162(m)(5), it contains no exception for "performance-based" compensation. The new code section went into effect in 2013 and covers compensation paid for services performed after 2009.

9.7 Limit on Deductions: Golden Parachute Rules

Under Sections 280G and 4999 of the Code, certain employees and consultants ("disqualified individuals") who receive payments, including additional or accelerated stock options, contingent on a "change in control" of the payor company (or its related company) may suffer adverse tax consequences, along with the payor. If such payments are deemed to be "parachute payments," the disqualified individual is permitted to receive an aggregate payment of up to three times his "base amount" without penalty. However, if the present value of the amounts paid is equal to or greater than three times the base amount, the difference between the payment and one times the base amount will constitute an "excess parachute payment." Section 280G disallows a tax deduction to the payor in the amount of the excess parachute payment paid and Section 4999 imposes a 20% excise tax on the payee (in addition to normal income tax) with respect to the excess parachute payment received.[23] The Dodd-Frank Act of 2010 includes a requirement that

---

23. The golden parachute rules are highly technical, and each of the terms set off in quotes is specifically defined by the Code and its regulations, along with numerous other definitions. Consideration of options in parachute payments constitutes only one part of the extensive regulatory scheme. See Treas. Reg. § 1.280G-1. For a detailed technical and historical review of Section 280G and its regulations, see Bill C. Wilson and Diane M. McGowan, Tax Management Portfolio 396: *Golden Parachutes* (Washington: BNA).

change-in-control provisions be subject to a non-binding shareholder vote. That requirement is discussed further in chapter 13.

Any but the most rudimentary overview of these complicated rules is beyond the scope of this discussion. For our narrow purposes, however, equity compensation professionals should be aware of the following points.

9.7.1   When Are Options Treated as Parachute Payments?

To be a parachute payment under Section 280G(b)(2), a payment must first be "in the nature of compensation." The regulations make it clear that options are considered to be compensation.[24] Second, the payment must be made "contingent on a change in control"—i.e., the payment would not, in fact, have been made had no change in ownership or control occurred. The easiest case would be when unvested options accelerate and become fully vested on a change in control, or when vested options are granted in connection with a change in control.[25] Things become more difficult when options are only partially accelerated at the time of the change, or when there is evidence that the option grants (or accelerated vesting) would have occurred anyway in connection with ongoing services; e.g., that the payments constitute "reasonable compensation" rather than parachute payments. Analyzing this issue is one of the trickiest aspects of the rules.[26]

9.7.2   How Are Options Valued for Purposes of Section 280G?

Once it is determined that an option-related payment is a parachute payment, the payment must be valued as part of the overall excess parachute payment calculation. If the full amount of the option is deemed to be a parachute payment, it is valued as of the date it becomes fully vested. If only the accelerated portion of the payment is a parachute payment, that portion must be calculated as a present-value and included

---

24. Treas. Reg. § 1.280G-1 Q/A-11. Treas. Reg. § 1.280G-1 Q/A-13 clarifies that the treatment of both nonstatutory and statutory options for these purposes is identical.

25. Treas. Reg. § 1.280G-1 Q/A 22-23.

26. Ibid. See also Treas. Reg. § 1.280G-1 Q/A 25-26 (parachute payment presumption); Q/A 9, 38-44 (when is a payment "reasonable compensation").

separately. Treas. Reg. § 1.280G, Q/A 13, specifically requires valuation of transferred options and Rev. Proc. 2003-68 elaborates on the rules, providing that options may be valued using any valuation method that is (i) consistent with generally accepted accounting principles (GAAP) (such as Accounting Standards Codification Topic 718), and (ii) that takes into account the factors set out in Treas. Reg. § 1.280G, Q/A 1 (i.e., the spread, the probability of the stock increasing or decreasing in value, and the length of the exercise period). Further, section 4 of Rev. Proc. 2003-68 sets out a safe-harbor valuation method for these purposes.[27] Care must be taken in performing these valuations, as option-related payments are often large enough to transform a parachute payment into an excess parachute payment.

For planning purposes, both payees and payors will want to ensure that option-related payments are carefully scrutinized as early as possible to avoid unanticipated golden parachute issues. The goal, of course, is to keep the base amount as large as possible (i.e., to maximize the type and amount of payments that go into that number) while keeping parachute payments to a minimum (i.e. to structure compensation so as to avoid characterization as parachute payments). In many cases, advance planning will result in more "reasonable compensation" and less "excess parachute payments."

9.8 Domestic Mobile Employees

Income recognized by optionees is frequently subject to state income taxes. As state budgets have tightened in recent years, many states have become more aggressive about collecting taxes from employees who live—or even just work—there during the vesting period, regardless of whether they remain residents at the time of exercise. This trend is likely to intensify as states attempt to address budget gaps.

---

27. The safe harbor method essentially uses a modified Black-Scholes model, *generally* based on the following factors: (1) the volatility of the underlying stock, (2) the exercise price of the option, (3) the value of the stock at the time of valuation, and (4) the term of the option on the valuation date. See also Rev. Proc. 98-34, 1998-1 C.B. 983 (valuation methods for compensatory stock options for purposes of gift, estate, and generation-skipping transfer taxes).

California and New York have been particularly aggressive about tax collection. While most states do not regard income earned while temporarily working in the state to be taxable until an employee has worked there for a certain period of time, California regards any income earned while working in the state as taxable—even if an employee is dispatched to a California work site for just one day in a tax year. This applies both to regular pay and to unvested equity compensation.

Domestic mobility poses many issues for employers, who may face withholding and reporting requirements in multiple states, and must deal with sometimes conflicting allocation rules.[28] In fact, each option exercise may require the employer to evaluate in which state the optionee resided at grant, during the vesting period, and at exercise. Different states may require income tax withholding based on grant date, vesting period, or exercise date. As a result, multiple states may require withholding on the same option. Employers who track employee mobility may wish to keep summaries of different scenarios as they occur so that they have something to refer back to when similar situations arise.

---

28. International mobility also carries many issues, but is outside the scope of this discussion. For a discussion of international mobility see *GPS: Global Stock Plans* (Santa Clara, CA: Certified Equity Professional Institute, 2009).

Chapter 10

Basic Accounting Issues

Pam Chernoff and Elizabeth Dodge[1]

Contents

---

1.   Elizabeth Dodge is the founder of and a principal for Equity Plan Solutions, LLC (EPS), which provides equity compensation consulting services to companies from startups to large public corporations. She started EPS at the beginning of 2016 and has been in equity compensation since 1998. She has held her CEP designation since 1999. Elizabeth is a frequent speaker on equity compensation topics, including accounting and stock plan best practices, serves on the Executive Advisory Committee for the NASPP, and received the NASPP Achievement Award in 2012.

    This chapter is a broad overview. For an in-depth explanation of equity compensation accounting, see Barbara A. Baksa, *Accounting for Equity Compensation,* 14th ed. (Oakland, CA: NCEO, 2017); and Takis Makridis, *Advanced Topics in Equity Compensation Accounting,* 7th ed. (Oakland, CA: NCEO, 2017).

Equity compensation awards are treated as an expense on a company's income statement. Before 2005, it was possible to grant stock options that did not result in an accounting expense, even though restricted stock and other kinds of equity awards did. But those days ended with the 2005 and 2006 implementation of a revised accounting standard for equity compensation.

The impetus behind the accounting changes was to enhance the information in financial statements in order to give shareholders a better idea of just how much equity awards actually "cost" the company. The Financial Accounting Standards Board (FASB), which is the private-sector body that sets U.S. accounting standards, wanted this form of compensation to appear on the income statement, just as other compensation does. This was a controversial project that took many years to complete. Many companies argued that options have no cost to the company (they contended the cost to shareholders consists purely in dilution to share value) or are a balance sheet, not an income statement, issue. However, the FASB did ultimately implement the changes.

One of the largest issues in accounting for options and ESPPs is the need to assess (often at the time of grant) a current value for awards whose ultimate value to the participant (if any) is known only years later. Calculating a value often requires challenging assumptions and formulas, but the core idea is simple: What would an investor pay today for an award with the same characteristics? What is the "fair value" of the award?

The standard that required that options be expensed was called Statement of Financial Accounting Standards 123 (revised 2004), or FAS 123(R), until September 2009, when the FASB shifted U.S. generally accepted accounting principles (GAAP) to a codified system that led to the renumbering of all authoritative standards and guidance. Under codification, most of FAS 123(R) became Accounting Standards Codification Topic 718 (ASC 718), while EITF 96-18, relating to awards granted to nonemployees, became part of ASC 505. The numbering change did not affect the basic content of the standard but did consolidate many different interpretations and other accounting pronouncements into a single source.

At about the same time that the FASB released FAS 123(R), the International Accounting Standards Board (IASB) proposed an accounting standard that was similar, but not identical. The IASB is an independent standards-setting body whose member countries are free to adopt its standards, known as international financial reporting standards (IFRS). The IASB does not have the authority to set accounting standards for individual countries, but its member countries have sought to standardize their accounting requirements to make it easier for investors and others to assess company financials across country lines. The FASB has a stated goal of shifting the U.S. from U.S. GAAP to international accounting standards, but progress has been slow and many issues remain to be addressed. Until such time as adoption by the U.S. takes place, many companies must still grapple with the requirements of IFRS for foreign subsidiaries reporting in countries that have adopted the standards while continuing to use GAAP at the U.S.-company level.

In March 2016, the FASB released Accounting Standards Update 2016-09 (ASU 2016-09), which amended ASC 718 in several key areas. Under it, companies are allowed to account for forfeitures as they occur instead of estimating expected forfeitures. The update also changes tax accounting and diluted EPS calculations. Public companies must adopt the changes for the first fiscal period that begins after December 15, 2016. Private companies must adopt for the first fiscal period that begins after December 15, 2017. Companies can choose to adopt sooner and in an interim period. More details on some of the changes and the required transition methods are included later in this chapter.

Accounting issues are a concern for public companies or privately held companies that plan on a liquidity event in the future. Other closely held companies must make sure they account for their equity compensation properly, but they often do not consider accounting issues in plan or program design. In 2012, the Financial Accounting Foundation created the Private Company Council, which is reviewing whether privately held companies should be exempt from or subject to modified GAAP requirements in certain areas. Any recommendations made by the new board will be subject to approval by the FASB. Equity compensation accounting is included in the areas under review. Companies that qualify as emerging growth companies under the JOBS Act of 2012 can take advantage of an extended transition period whenever FASB issues new rules or modifies existing ones.

10.1 Fair Value and Measurement Date

ASC 718 requires companies to record the fair value of their equity award grants as an expense on their income statements. "Fair value" is defined as the worth of the award itself on the measurement date, with all caveats and requirements (such as the expected amount of time until the option is exercised, any consideration that must be paid for it at grant, etc.). Theoretically, it is what an option or other award would sell for if there were an open market for it, as there is for options in commodity futures. The fair value of an award is determined on its "measurement date." However, the standard treats awards to employees that pay out (or "settle") in stock differently than awards that pay out in cash or those that are granted to nonemployees.

For employee awards that settle in stock, the measurement date is generally the grant date. If the award is made in the form of stock options, SARs, or a Section 423 qualified ESPP, the company must use an option-pricing model to determine the grant date fair value of the award. The grant date fair value of time-based, stock-settled options, SARs, and ESPP shares is not adjusted during the life of the award even if the assumptions used in the option-pricing model turn out to be incorrect. (The fair value may change if the original terms of the award are modified, but a discussion of modification accounting is outside the scope of this chapter.)

In contrast, the measurement date for cash-settled awards is the settlement date, meaning the date of exercise, vesting, or expiration. Therefore, the fair value of cash-settled awards is not finally determined until the award is settled. The fair value is determined each reporting period by calculating the current fair value of the grant, i.e., using an option-pricing model to estimate the fair value just as with stock-settled awards (for RSUs, the current market value is used). If the company is publicly traded, the current trading price must be used; if private, the company may choose to use either the current value of the underlying stock or its intrinsic value (i.e., the difference between the exercise price of the option or SAR and the current market value of the underlying stock).

For stock-settled awards granted to nonemployees, the measurement date is the vest date. The company must recalculate the fair value each quarter and recognize expense based on these estimates between the grant date and each vesting date. For stock options, generally the "expected term" to be used in calculating the nonemployee fair values should be the remaining contractual life of the option—the time until the option expires. Private companies may choose whether to do this by recognizing the award's intrinsic value or fair value in the reporting periods before the award is settled. In June 2016, the FASB decided to change accounting for nonemployees to simplify it and align it with accounting for employees. However, since the proposed changes have not yet been drafted, the nonemployee accounting treatment currently specified in ASC 505-50 will remain in effect for some time to come.

Denominating an equity award in a currency other than the one in which the employer company conducts its daily business does not affect the method of determining expense so long as a substantial portion of the company's stock trades in that currency.[2] So, for example, a U.S.-based company whose stock was traded on the Nasdaq could recognize the expense for U.S.-dollar denominated options granted to Canadian employees the same way it accounted for similar options granted to U.S.-based employees.

Exhibit 10-1 gives an overview of some of the accounting rules that apply to varying types of equity compensation.

Exhibit 10-1

Award type	Accounting Treatment
Stock options and stock-settled SARs (time-based vesting)	Employees: Fair value determined at grant date and recognized over service period. Nonemployees: Fair value recalculated for each reporting period, finalized at vest date. Expense recognized over service period. Fair value calculated using an option-pricing model.
Stock options and stock-settled SARs (performance-based vesting)	Fair value determined at grant date and recognized over expected service period. Fair value calculated using an option-pricing model.

---

2. Accounting Standards Update 2010-13.

Section 423 ESPPs	Result in expense if discount greater than cost of raising capital (5% safe harbor) or if plan includes a look-back feature. Expense recognized over offering period. Fair value determined at grant date and recognized over service period.
	Fair value calculated using an option-pricing model with three components: discount, put and call, based on different plan features.
Restricted stock and restricted stock units (RSUs) subject to time-based vesting	Fair value of award on grant date recognized over vesting period.
	Fair value is the fair market value of underlying stock minus any amount paid by recipient and adjusted for any dividends not paid to recipient.
Cash-settled SARs	Fair value estimated and recognized over life of award, finalized upon settlement or expiration.
	Fair value calculated using an option-pricing model on the reporting date and the intrinsic value on settlement date.
Phantom stock paid in cash (cash-settled RSU)	Fair value estimated and recognized over life of award, finalized upon settlement.
	Fair value calculated as the intrinsic value of the instrument on the reporting or settlement date.

10.2 Option-Pricing Models

The "fair value" arrived at through an option-pricing model is distinct from "fair market value," or FMV (also known simply as "market value" or "stock price"). FMV is the price a willing buyer would pay a willing seller for the underlying stock in an arm's-length transaction. For public companies, FMV is the dollar value for which the stock trades on a stock exchange. Option-pricing models are used to determine fair values for stock options, SARs, and ESPPs. ASC 718 requires that option-pricing models used to determine an equity award's fair value include, at a minimum:

- *The award's exercise price.*
- *The underlying stock's fair market value.* For public companies, this is the price for which the stock is trading on an exchange. For private companies, the board sets the fair market value. For tax reasons, this should be set using standards set by Internal Revenue Code Section 409A, which is discussed in section 2.5.

- *The award's expected term.* Companies are required to project the amount of time grants will remain outstanding. For options granted to employees, this is generally shorter than the award's contractual term but longer than the vesting period. For options granted to nonemployees, this is generally the award's contractual term. Private companies and recently public companies generally use the SAB 107 simplified method.

- *The underlying stock's expected volatility.* For public companies, this is a best estimate of the market volatility over the expected term of the option. Public companies often use historic volatility rates to assist in this determination. They may also use implied volatilities or a blend of historic and implied. Private companies that cannot produce a reliable estimate of their stock volatility generally use peer company volatility (often the same peer companies that were used for 409A valuation purposes) or industry indices. Public companies are not allowed to use industry indices.

- *The underlying stock's expected dividend yield.* Again, this is over the expected term of the grant.

- *The risk-free interest rate.* Generally, companies use the current Treasury rate applying to bills or bonds with terms equal to the award's expected term, as the prescribed zero-coupon rate on U.S. government issues is not as readily accessible. When there is no corresponding Treasury rate for the expected term, for example a six-year expected term, the existing rates are usually interpolated to derive an interest rate for that term.

The accounting standard does not require the use of any particular option-pricing model. In fact, it gives broad leeway for companies to choose which model they wish to use as long as all of the above inputs are included in the model. Historically, companies have largely relied on the Black-Scholes option-pricing model, which has the advantages of being clearly defined, broadly available, and easily auditable.

The Black-Scholes model was developed to value exchange-traded stock options.[3] Since exchange-traded options vary significantly from

---

3. Investors can buy options on many different commodities, including company stock—pork belly futures are a common example used. These options, which provide rights to acquire or dispose of underlying shares or other rights at a

compensatory stock options, Black-Scholes has been criticized as an imperfect method of valuing compensatory stock options, which typically have much longer terms, are subject to vesting, and can be exercised (and usually are exercised) before expiration. Despite these objections, the Black-Scholes option-pricing model continues to be the most commonly used way of valuing compensatory stock options and SARs.

Other models that also incorporate the required inputs include lattice models, sometimes called binomial or trinomial models. These models employ a statistical technique that creates a tree of possible outcomes. For example, in a binomial model, two possibilities are projected for each possible occurrence (for example, the stock price may go up or down). The fair value is then arrived at by considering all of the possibilities, giving a greater weight to the more probable outcomes. Lattice models can also be constructed to consider more data about a grant, such as the vesting schedule, blackout periods, and the probability that the participant will terminate after vesting, thereby reducing the allowable time to exercise, the expected term, and ultimately the fair value of the grant. Unlike the Black-Scholes option-pricing model, there is no single, standard lattice model. The models are usually created to suit the unique needs of the plan or instrument. Therefore, they are also generally more difficult to audit. In addition, their use will not always result in a lower fair value for the award.

Exhibit 10-2 gives a summary of the required option-pricing model inputs and their impact on the fair value of an award.

Exhibit 10-2

Input	Impact on Fair Value	Other Information
Exercise price	Higher FMV increases fair value of at-the-money awards; setting exercise price higher than grant date FMV reduces fair value.	
Fair market value of underlying shares	Increase in FMV increases the fair value of the award.	Generally the closing market value on the grant date is used.

set price, typically expire after a relatively short period of time (often a year or less) and can be traded freely, but they are generally not exercisable before their expiration date. An investor can sell his option in pork belly futures to someone else before it is exercised.

Exhibit 10-2

Expected term	Increase in expected term increases the fair value of the award.	This is the projection of how long the option will be outstanding before it is exercised. The longer the expected term, the higher the fair value since a longer life is more likely to result in a higher market value at exercise. This is one of the more difficult inputs to calculate. For nonemployee awards, the contractual term of the award is used.
Volatility	Increase in volatility increases the fair value of the award.	The estimated volatility over the expected term of the option. This input is generally derived via an analysis of historic stock prices, sometimes in combination with implied volatility (the volatility of exchange-traded options on the company's stock). Private companies generally derive this using peer company volatility.
Dividend yield	Increase in dividend yield reduces the fair value of the award.	This is the expected dividend yield for the company's stock over the expected term of the option. Zero is used if the company does not pay dividends on its common stock. The higher the dividend rate, the lower the fair value of the option since option holders do not receive dividends whereas holders of common stock do.
Risk-free interest rate	Increase in the risk-free interest rate increases the fair value of the award.	The risk-free interest rate over the expected term of the option. Publicly available interest rates are generally used to determine this input.

10.3 Definition of Employee

For purposes of determining which award recipients are employees, ASC 718 applies the principles used to determine employment status for tax purposes. Since these same principles are used to determine who should be issued a Form W-2 (rather than a Form 1099), an initial assessment of employee status can generally be made on the basis of who is issued a Form W-2. Under this test, consultants, advisors, and independent contractors are generally not considered employees. Outside directors are a notable exception to this rule; although outside directors are considered nonemployees for tax purposes and compensation paid to them is reported on a Form 1099-MISC, their awards receive the same accounting treatment as awards to employees under ASC 718 as long as their equity awards were granted to them because of their service as a director. Awards granted for other services receive nonemployee treatment.

10.4 Recognition of Expense and Application of Estimated Forfeiture Rate

Under ASC 718, companies are required to recognize the expense for each grant over its service period (i.e. the period over which the award is earned). For time-based awards this is generally the vesting schedule. This kind of award is considered to have an "explicit" service period. For example, if a grant of 100 options is made on Jan. 1, 2017, the fair value is determined to be $4 per share, and the final vest date is on Dec. 31, 2020, the company will generally book a portion of the $400 of total expense each quarter, recognizing approximately $100 per year and therefore $25 per quarter from Jan. 1, 2017, through Dec. 31, 2020. If the employee leaves the company before the grant vests, then the company is allowed to reverse any expense recognized in connection with the unvested portion of the grant. The cancellation of unvested shares is known as a forfeiture.

For time-based grants, two different approaches to the amortization of this expense are acceptable under ASC 718. By far the most commonly used amortization approach is the "straight-line" approach, in which the total expense for the grant is recognized evenly over the service period, regardless of the number of vesting tranches in the award or how the shares are distributed among vesting tranches.

An important caveat to this approach is that the company must recognize expense equivalent to the shares vested at any point in time. So if 50 shares vested in the first six months of the grant and the remaining 50 shares vested over the two years following, a straight-line amortization approach would not be appropriate, because less than 20% of expense would have been recognized at the six-month point, when in fact a full 50% of the shares had vested. This issue also arises in some cases if straight-line amortization is used and the vesting commencement date precedes the grant date.

Another acceptable approach is to amortize each vesting tranche individually. This approach was known as FIN 28 amortization prior to the FASB codification. For example, if an award had three vesting tranches vesting annually over three years, the fair value for the first vesting tranche would be completely recognized during the first year; the fair value for the second vesting tranche would be recognized over the first two years; and the fair value for the third vesting tranche would be recognized over three years, as illustrated in exhibit 10-3. It usually leads to a greater part of the fair value of the grant being recognized early in the life of the grant. For this reason, this approach has also been referred to as "accelerated" amortization.

Until ASU 2016-09 was released, ASC 718 also required companies to estimate the percentage of awards they believed would be forfeited versus those that would vest. Under this method, forfeiture means cancellation *before* vesting. (In contrast, grants that do vest but expire unexercised are not considered forfeited, and the expense is not reversed.) With the adoption of ASU 2016-09, companies may now choose whether to apply an estimated forfeiture rate or to simply true up for forfeitures as they occur. Choosing which of the two approaches to take is a one-time policy election made by the company upon adoption of the ASU.

Companies that choose to true up for forfeitures as they occur when they adopt ASU 2016-09 must adopt using the modified retrospective approach and perform a one-time true up in the period of adoption.

For companies that apply an estimated forfeiture rate, the expense recognized for the grants may be reduced by the estimated forfeiture rate so that only a portion of the fair value is recognized over the service period. If an estimated forfeiture rate is applied, the company adjusts the expense recognized for actual forfeitures. For instance, if a company assumed at the outset that 20% of a group of grants would be forfeited, but in fact 30% were forfeited, the company would ultimately recognize only 70% of the fair value of that group of grants. Several methodologies exist for reducing the amortization of expense by the estimated forfeiture rate, many using an annualized forfeiture rate and applying the rate based on the service period of the award. However, a more simplistic approach such as a flat rate applied to the expense can also be used as long as the expense is ultimately trued up to the actual forfeitures and vestings of the awards.

10.5 Equity Compensation Vehicles

10.5.1 Stock Options and Stock-Settled SARs with Time-Based Vesting

The accounting for stock options and stock-settled SARs that vest based only on time is relatively straightforward. The company uses an option-pricing model to determine the awards' fair value on the grant date and recognizes that cost over the service period (generally the vesting period). The inputs into the option-pricing model must include all of the six factors listed above.

The amount ultimately expensed must be adjusted to reflect actual forfeitures of awards that never vest. This adjustment is not an input into the model; rather, it is an adjustment to the proportion of the awards' fair value that must be recognized over the service period. Note that only awards that are cancelled prior to vest are treated as having been forfeited. The expense for awards that vest but then expire or are cancelled unexercised cannot be reversed.

10.5.2 Stock Options with Performance Vesting

The accounting for options and SARs that vest based on the achievement of a performance target is similar to the accounting for those with time-based vesting. However, there are some key differences, one of which is that the expense must be recognized individually for each vesting tranche using FIN 28 or accelerated amortization. Straight-line recognition is not permitted.[4]

---

4.   There are circumstances in which a delayed service inception date for subsequent tranches will mimic straight-line expense; however, that is a discussion outside the scope of this chapter.

With performance-based awards, meaning grants that have performance targets not related to stock price, the recognition of expense is based on the likelihood of the achievement of the goal. For example, if the performance-based award is likely to pay out 80% of the underlying shares, only 80% of the fair value would be recognized and a cumulative adjustment made. If, during the next quarter, the best estimate of likely payout rises to 90%, then 90% of the fair value would be recognized. Although the grant date fair value of the award does not change, the expense recognized from period to period may vary widely. The amount ultimately expensed must be adjusted to reflect actual forfeitures of awards that never vest, whether because of employee terminations or failure to achieve the performance goal.

If, instead, the grant is market-based, meaning the performance target is related to stock price or uses metrics that are based on stock price (such as total shareholder return), then the company will calculate the fair value for the award at the grant date via a sophisticated option-pricing model such as a Monte Carlo simulation (a type of lattice-based model) and recognize that amount over the service period. If a market-based award is forfeited due to a failure to achieve the market-based goal, the expense is not reversed. The expense is reversed only if the award fails to vest due to a termination of service (failure to meet the requisite service period). The option-pricing model itself will consider when and if the goal is likely to be met and incorporate that estimate into the resulting fair value. In this case, the expected term for the award is an output of the option-pricing model rather than an input. The service period over which expense is recognized is referred to as a "derived" service period, because it is based on the option pricing model's estimate of the amount of time that will pass before the stock price goal is met.

10.5.3 Section 423 ESPPs

Most tax-qualified ESPPs result in an accounting expense. Under ASC 718, a plan that offers a purchase date discount greater than the company's cost of raising capital or a plan that has "option-like features"—most notably a look-back feature in which the purchase price is based on the lower of the stock's fair market value on the first or last day of the offering period—is considered to be a "compensatory plan" and thus results in expense under ASC 718. Five percent is considered the "safe harbor" discount since the plan may not include a discount that is not available to all shareholders and that is greater than the cost of raising capital in a public offering.

Bear in mind, however, that the accounting rule does nothing to change Section 423 of the Internal Revenue Code. Companies may still offer Section 423 ESPPs that provide both a 15% discount and a look-back feature, and participants in such plans are still eligible for preferential tax treatment. This is solely an issue of whether an expense for the plan must be reflected in the income statement.

If the company wishes to avoid incurring an ESPP-related expense in its financial statements, then employees may be allowed no more than 31 days after the purchase price has been fixed to enroll in the plan (in addition to the plan satisfying the prescribed discount limits discussed above).[5] If the purchase price is based solely on the stock's price on the last day of the purchase period, then employees may be allowed to withdraw from the offering and have their money returned to them any time before the purchase date without giving rise to an accounting expense. In addition, substantially all employees must be able to participant on an "equitable basis." A Section 423 ESPP that does not result in an accounting expense is referred to as a "non-compensatory plan."

For Section 423 ESPPs that do result in an accounting expense, the fair value is set on the grant date. It is generally determined using a Black-Scholes model, but may include up to three separate components, depending on the features of the plan (see exhibit 10-3 below). Even for plans that have multiple purchases within a single offering period, a fair value will be assigned to each purchase period (as with each vesting tranche of an option) on the grant date. Then, generally, the expense for each tranche will be expensed from the offering date to the purchase date. To arrive at a fair value, the company must also estimate the amount that will be contributed to the plan and therefore how many shares are likely to be purchased during the offering period. The expense is trued up to the actual shares purchased after the purchase occurs in two circumstances:

1. The number of shares changes due to a change in salary, bonus, etc.

---

5. ASC Subtopic 718-50-25-1(c).

2. The participant terminates employment prior to the purchase date and does not participate in the purchase.

If a participant withdraws from the plan voluntarily or reduces his or her contribution rate after the start of the offering period, expense may not be reversed. This is analogous to a choice not to exercise a stock option. Only in cases where the requisite service period is not completed should the expense be reversed. If the participant increases their contribution rate during the offering period, or if the plan provides for a reset or rollover feature when the market value of the stock is lower on a purchase date that it was on the first day of the offering period, modification accounting is required. (A discussion of modification accounting is outside the scope of this chapter.)

Exhibit 10-3

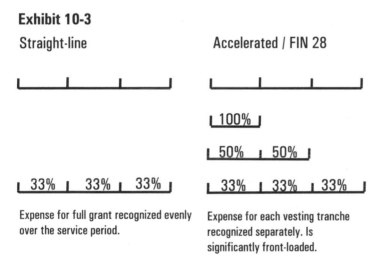

Expense for full grant recognized evenly over the service period.

Expense for each vesting tranche recognized separately. Is significantly front-loaded.

Exhibit 10-4 provides a summary of the possible components required for determining the fair value of a Section 423 qualified ESPP.

Exhibit 10-4

Plan Feature	Fair Value Component
Discount	Value of discount on enrollment date
Look-back	Black-Scholes call option (allows stock to be purchased at an unknown discount)
No beginning price limit	Black-Scholes put option (allows more shares to be purchased if the price decreases during the period)

10.5.4 Restricted Stock Awards and Restricted Stock Units

Unlike stock options and SARs, the full grant date fair value of RSAs and RSUs must be recorded as an expense if the shares are granted at no cost to employees. The grant date fair value is the stock's full FMV on the grant date, minus any amount the recipient must pay for the shares, and is recognized over the service period. If the underlying stock pays dividends, but the grant itself does not provide for dividend payments before vesting—as is sometimes the case with RSUs—then the grant's fair value may be reduced to reflect any dividends expected to be paid to shareholders between grant and vesting. This does not affect RSA grants that are eligible for dividend payments before vesting.

Because fewer shares of restricted stock or RSUs are generally granted than would be the case for stock options or SARs, the accounting expense for grants of restricted stock awards and RSUs may be similar to that recognized for grants of options and SARs. As with options, the expense is recognized over the service period, or expected vesting period in the case of a performance-based award, and can be adjusted for forfeitures unless the performance condition is market-based. In the case of a market-based performance award, a complex option pricing model must be used to determine the fair value of the award. And, as with options, if a market-based performance award is forfeited because a performance target is not achieved, expense is not reversed.

10.5.5 Cash-Settled SARs

An award of SARs that is settled in cash is treated as a liability under ASC 718, which means that the fair value is not finalized until the award is exercised or expires. The amount ultimately recognized will equal the award's intrinsic value on the settlement or expiration date. In the interim, the company must use an option-pricing model to estimate the fair value of the award at the end of each reporting period until the settlement (private companies can instead choose to record expense based on the award's current intrinsic value). The company must recognize the difference between the current estimate and the previous period's estimate—either as additional expense or as a reversal of previously recognized expense—in the current period.

10.5.6 Phantom Stock

Phantom stock awards, also known as cash-settled RSUs, are also subject to liability treatment because they pay out in cash. Thus, the fair value is not finalized until settlement (i.e., the vesting date). The intrinsic value is recalculated each reporting period and the recognition of expense is based upon the latest fair value. The full fair market value of the shares underlying the award must ultimately be treated as an expense unless the award is forfeited.

10.6 Tax Accounting

Under ASC Subtopic 718-740, an expense for equity compensation awards should be offset (must be reduced) by the anticipated tax benefit that may be realized in the future from those awards. Companies generally receive tax deductions for amounts that employees recognize as ordinary income, usually upon settlement of an award. For equity compensation awards that are not tax-qualified (i.e., everything except ISOs and Section 423 ESPPs), the company calculates its expected future tax deduction for the expense recognized for the award and, as the expense is recognized, records the anticipated tax savings, thus reducing its reported tax expense during each period during which expense is recognized. This recognition of a future tax benefit is referred to as a deferred tax asset (DTA) and is simply the fair value of the award multiplied by the corporate tax rate of the company.

For example, using our example from earlier in which a grant of 100 NSOs is made on Jan. 1, 2017, the fair value is determined to be $4 per share and the final vest date is Dec. 31, 2020 (four years later), the company will generally book a portion of the $400 of total expense each quarter, approximately $100 per year and therefore $25 per quarter from Jan. 1, 2017, to Dec. 31, 2020. During the same period in which the company is recognizing the $400 expense associated with the award, the DTA booked will be $400 times a 40% corporate tax rate, or $160 at the rate of approximately $10 per quarter.

When the grant is ultimately settled, the DTA that has been booked must be trued up to match the actual tax benefit received by the company. To determine the actual tax benefit, the income recognized by the participant at exercise or vest/delivery of restricted stock/RSUs is multiplied by the corporate tax rate at that time. This is compared to the DTA for the shares being settled.

If the actual tax benefit is larger than the DTA recorded, the company records the difference (called a "windfall" or "excess tax benefit") as a decrease to tax expense on the income statement in the period in which it occurs. In our example, let's say the gain on exercise was $1,000; therefore, the actual tax benefit to the company is $400, and the windfall tax benefit is $240 ($400 less $160). Prior to the release of ASU 2016-09, windfall tax benefits did not impact the income statement, but instead were credited to a pool of additional paid in capital (APIC). After adoption of the ASU, the windfall will reduce tax expense in the period in which the option is exercised.

If the actual tax benefit is less than the DTA recorded, the transaction is considered to produce a tax "shortfall" or "deficiency." Prior to the ASU, shortfalls reduced the APIC pool. If not enough APIC pool existed to absorb the shortfall, then tax expense was increased on the income statement. ASU 2016-09 eliminated the concept of an APIC pool and requires that all shortfalls and windfalls be reflected on the income statement.

In our example, let's say the gain on exercise was $250; therefore, the actual tax benefit to the company is $100, and the shortfall is $60 ($100 less $160). The difference between the DTA and the actual tax benefit is recorded as additional tax expense on the company's income statement. Generally, nonqualified option or SAR expirations result in shortfalls since the participant recognizes no income and therefore the company recognizes no tax benefit. Thus, at the time of expiration, the company must reverse the DTA and record a corresponding increase to tax expense.

For the adoption of this part of ASU 2016-09, companies must use the prospective method, simply reflecting windfalls and shortfalls on the income statement for any transactions that occur after the company adopts.

10.7 Earnings Per Share: Diluted and Basic

Earnings per share (EPS) is yet another accounting calculation on which equity compensation awards have an impact. Basic EPS is simply the amount of revenue earned by the company divided by the number of common stock shares outstanding. Why do equity awards affect this calculation? Because when options are exercised or RSUs vest, those grants become common stock, often moving from an "authorized but unissued" pool into common, freely tradable stock. So exercises and vesting obviously affect basic EPS, because each one increases the number of shares by which the revenue is divided.

To account for this increase in common stock driven by equity compensation transactions during a reporting period, the number of shares of new common stock included in the denominator is weighted for the time they were common stock during the period. For example, if a participant exercised 1,000 options halfway through the period, only 500 shares would be included when calculating basic EPS.

Diluted EPS is a more complicated topic and this chapter will not attempt to summarize it completely, but simply provide a brief overview. Diluted EPS is a measure of how much dilutive potential exists based on other types of arrangements that involve the issuance of common stock, such as options, restricted stock and units, warrants, and some forms of debt securities. If a company has $1 million in earnings this quarter and it has 1 million shares of common stock outstanding, its basic EPS would be $1. Now let's say that the stock price increases suddenly and a large number of employees choose to exercise their shares, resulting in 100,000 newly issued shares becoming common stock. Suddenly the company's basic EPS has dropped to approximately $0.91 ($1 million/1.1 million shares). Diluted EPS is meant to measure the potential for dilution that a company's "convertible securities" (including options and restricted stock and units) have on its basic EPS.

The basic premise behind the diluted EPS calculation is to first assume that all options and awards are suddenly vested and exercised or delivered. Obviously this is a worst-case scenario and ignores the very obvious constraints of the vesting schedule and the fact that all participants are unlikely to exercise on the same day. To mitigate this worst-case (and unrealistic) scenario, the standard requires the calculation of "assumed proceeds" from the hypothetical exercise/delivery of shares and treats those funds as if they would all be used to buy back shares on the open market. These "buy back shares" are then subtracted from the shares outstanding to arrive at the number of shares to include in the diluted EPS calculation. The sources of proceeds for these hypothetical transactions include the:

- company's receipt of the exercise price from the hypothetical option exercises; and
- average unamortized expense during the period.

Prior to ASU 2016-09, hypothetical tax benefits/windfalls or deficiencies/shortfalls were also a source of assumed proceeds (or a reduction to assumed proceeds) included in the calculation of buyback shares.

Underwater options are excluded from the calculation because the company would be able to buy back more shares than are currently outstanding, thereby making them "anti-dilutive." (Awards that are not underwater can also become anti-dilutive if the number of shares that could be bought back via the assumed proceeds calculation is greater than the number of shares outstanding.) Note: unvested restricted stock is included in the diluted EPS calculations until the shares are vested, even if the shares have voting and dividend rights. Once they vest, they are included in the basic EPS calculation.

Tax Treatment of Options on Death and Divorce

Contents

Special rules apply for the tax treatment of options when disposition of the option or optioned stock occurs as a result of death or divorce. Please note that in addition to the income tax rules cited below, estate and gift tax implications will also arise for the individual or decedent's estate. Those implications are not discussed in this chapter.

11.1   Death

The Code makes exceptions from the statutory stock option rules for dispositions and transfers with respect to death. However, plan administrators should be careful to require proof of death before applying the rules. The company should have a policy of requesting a death certificate and (where indicated by state law) appropriate testamentary documents supporting the transfer.[1]

---

1.   For specific information on the roles of the stock option administrator and the estate administrator during probate, see Michael J. Album, "Handling Death

- *Statutory Stock Options:* Statutory options are nontransferable except to an optionee's estate or beneficiaries and, as described in chapter 3, are subject to strict rules governing exercise.[2] Ordinarily, the holders of ISOs and ESPP options must satisfy both holding period and employment requirements to remain eligible for preferential tax treatment under Sections 422 and 423 of the Code. However, under the regulations to Section 421(a) of the Code, neither of these requirements will apply in the case of statutory options held or exercised by an estate or beneficiary of the optionee. Stock acquired before death under an ESPP or ISO can be transferred to the optionee's estate (or beneficiary) without resulting in a disqualifying disposition. The estate will have a stepped-up basis in the stock for income tax purposes.[3] Where an unexercised option is transferred to an estate, the tax consequences to the estate or beneficiary on exercise will be the same as if the option had been exercised by the decedent—e.g., AMT may apply on exercise. Unless otherwise stated in the company's option plan, the option's expiration date is the only time limit on post-death exercise. Generally, such exercise occurs only in the case of ISOs, as ESPPs are usually designed to refund cash in the event of an employee termination (for any reason) before the next scheduled purchase date.

- *NSOs:* If the company's plan permits transferable options, exercise by the estate (or beneficiary) will result in wages with respect to the decedent. The amount must be reported by the company on a Form 1099-MISC but is not subject to income tax withholding. FICA/FUTA withholding will be required only if the exercise occurs in the same calendar year as the employee's death.[4]

- *Tax Treatment for Disposition of Section 423 Stock by Estate:* Note that the tax treatment for disposition of Section 423 stock by an estate depends on whether the optionee or the estate purchased the shares. If the optionee purchased the stock and died before its disposition,

---

Under an Equity Compensation Plan," in *Selected Issues in Equity Compensation,* 12th ed. (Oakland, CA: NCEO, 2015).

2. Sections 422(b)(5) and 423(b)(9) of the Code.

3. Treas. Reg. § 1.421-5.

4. Rev. Rul. 86-109.

the optionee will have ordinary income in the year of death equal to the lesser of the offering date discount or the difference between the purchase price and the market value of the stock at the date of death. Regardless of the amount of the inclusion, the estate will take a stepped-up basis in the shares equal to the market value at the date of death. If the estate both purchases and disposes of the shares after the employee's death, the disposition will be treated as a qualifying disposition—i.e., the estate or beneficiary will have ordinary income equal to the lesser of the offering date discount or the actual proceeds of the sale. The amount included in the gross income of the estate is allowed as an estate tax deduction to the estate (or beneficiary) as if it were an item of income in respect of a decedent within the meaning of Section 691 of the Code.[5]

- *A Note on Section 409A:* In general, NSOs that might otherwise be treated as nonqualified deferred compensation under Section 409A should be exempt from such treatment upon death if the option agreement specifies death as a distribution event. Section 409A(a)(2)(A)(iii) specifically provides that death is a permissible distribution event that will not result in the acceleration of deferred compensation, to the extent provided in the plan documents. In addition, the six-month delay of distribution rule for specified employees of public companies will not apply if the plan documents provide for immediate payout at the time of death. Regulations proposed in 2016 allow payment through December 31 of the year following the year of death, with the beneficiary allowed to elect the year of payment. The previous deadline was March 15 of the year following the year of death. Although the regulations are not yet final, plan sponsor are allowed to rely on them.

11.2 Divorce

As with transfers due to death, the Code provides some special rules for a transfer "incident to divorce," which is defined as a transfer that occurs not more than one year after the date the marriage ceases or a

---

5. The Code sets out the rules for post-death dispositions in Sections 421(c), 423(c), and 424(c); see also Treas. Reg. § 1.423-2(k)(2).

transfer pursuant to a divorce decree and no more than six years after the date the marriage ceases.[6]

For federal tax law purposes, a valid marriage is determined based on the law of the state in which the marriage ceremony takes place, so the plan administrator must take care to ascertain the validity of the divorced couple's marriage (which is usually confirmed in the court order or copy of the divorce decree). In addition, the application of the tax laws can become particularly tricky when the parties have litigated over the division of vested and unvested options (including options earned after a divorce—an issue that comes up with surprising frequency in state courts across the country).

11.2.1 Option Transfers

After a divorce, the employer company is frequently asked to split an outstanding option between its employee and a nonemployee former spouse (NEFS). The company's ability to effect a split depends on: the state the couple lived in, the type of option being split, and the terms contained in the plan document. Without specific authorization in the plan or option grant, the company cannot legally permit the transfer of a nontransferable option to the NEFS, even pursuant to a divorce decree without an amendment to the plan documents, which generally would require compensation committee approval. Where the property settlement directs the transfer of nontransferable options, the company may need to request clarification from the appropriate court. In situations where the option is not transferrable, the ex-spouses should agree that the employee spouse will exercise on behalf of the NEFS, with a subsequent transfer of the stock (see below). The company may deposit the stock issued on exercise directly to the account of the NEFS if the employee and NEFS are in contact with the company prior to exercise and complete any required paperwork.

ISOs pose a particularly tricky case in that unexercised ISOs transferred incident to divorce decree or domestic relations order are automatically disqualified and treated as NSOs, even though a similar

---

6.   See Section 1041 of the Code (transfers between spouses generally); Section 424(c) of the Code (ISOs).

transfer of stock that was acquired upon exercise of an ISO is not a disqualifying disposition.

To address this issue, the IRS has recognized that in community property states, the former spouses may agree to transfer the benefits of the ISO without actually transferring the instrument itself. In a 2007 private letter ruling,[7] the IRS allowed continuing ISO treatment for a division of community property in which the employee spouse continued to hold ISOs as trustee for the NEFS. The NEFS was entitled to direct the employee spouse as to when to exercise the option, but only the employee could actually accomplish the exercise. After the exercise, the stock would be transferred to the NEFS. The IRS affirmed that the arrangement would not violate the requirement that ISOs may be held only by employees. For reporting purposes, the NEFS would report the alternative minimum tax (AMT) income relating to the exercise of the ISO. After exercise, the transfer of the shares from the employee spouse to the NEFS would be treated as a non-event for tax purposes. From that point, the NEFS would have the benefits of ISO treatment on disposition of the shares, including with respect to AMT credits.

11.2.2 Tax Treatment on Option Exercise

For purposes of income tax withholding upon exercise of an NSO, the NEFS is treated as if he or she were the employee. This seemingly simple rule came about as the result of a series of rulings between 2002 and 2004 that considered the tax treatment of NSOs and nonqualified deferred compensation interests incident to divorce.

The IRS set out its final, comprehensive guidance on withholding, reporting, and tax issues relating to option transfers incident to a divorce in Rev. Rul. 2004-60. In it, the IRS concluded (as it had in a series of 2002 rulings) that NSOs and nonqualified deferred compensation transferred by an employee to a NEFS incident to a divorce are subject to FICA (Social Security and Medicare), FUTA (unemployment), and income tax withholding on the NEFS to the same extent as if they had been retained by the employee.[8] Citing an example in which the taxpayer

---

7. PLR 200737009 (June 15, 2007).

8. Rev. Rul. 2004-60 expanded on the conclusion and mechanics of Rev. Rul. 2002-22, that a taxpayer who transfers interests in an NSO or NQDC to a NEFS

employee transferred one-third of the total unexercised option grant to the NEFS, the IRS ruled as follows:

1. *For FICA and FUTA tax purposes:* The transfer of the options in and of itself is not considered the payment of income to the NEFS. At the date of exercise by the NEFS, however, the spread is subject to FICA just as it would be if exercised by the employee spouse. This means that if the employee spouse has already exceeded the Social Security withholding ceiling, then the exercise by the NEFS will not result in additional Social Security withholding, although Medicare withholding will still be required. The employee portion of FICA is actually deducted from the payments to the NEFS, not from payments to the employee spouse. Because the employer pays all of the FUTA tax, the NEFS obviously has no responsibility for FUTA.

2. *For federal income tax purposes:* When the NEFS exercises the options, the employer must withhold taxes. The supplemental wage flat rate (25% of amounts of $1 million or less, and 35% of amounts in excess of $1 million) may be used for this withholding. The NEFS is entitled to use this amount as a credit when computing income taxes.

3. *For reporting purposes:* Any FICA tax withholding is reported on form W-2 using the employee spouse's name, address, and Social Security number. However, no income is included in Box 1 or Box 2 with respect to these taxes. Instead, income received by the NEFS is reported in Box 3 on a Form 1099-MISC as "other income," and income tax withheld is reported in Box 4. The employer files a Form 945 to record income tax withholding for the NEFS, while FICA is reported on the employer's Form 941 and FUTA on form 940.

---

incident to divorce is not required to include an amount in gross income on the transfer or exercise. Rev. Rul. 2004-60 also revises and adopts the proposed revenue ruling originally set out in Notice 2002-31, regarding withholding and reporting, effective as of January 1, 2005. For court orders or agreements entered prior to 2005, taxpayers may show good-faith reliance on Notice 2002-31 for reporting purposes.

11.2.3 Transfers of Optioned Stock

Transfers of stock between a spouse and a NEFS are nonevents under the Code, regardless of whether the stock was purchased pursuant to exercise of an ISO or an NSO. ISO stock continues to be eligible for preferential treatment in the hands of the NEFS, so long as the original exercise was by the employee spouse.

11.2.4 Securities Law Issues

Note that the concerns highlighted under "Transferable Options" in chapter 15 with respect to TSOs apply to employee options transferred to or exercised by an NEFS or a beneficiary. In most cases, the Form S-8 is available to register such options.

11.2.5 Practical Issues

For practical purposes, these requirements can be perplexing. What happens if the NEFS refuses to provide for withholding on exercise or if the company has insufficient information to report appropriately? What if the court has ordered a split of ISOs in a separate property state? What if the employee spouse refuses to execute transfer authorizations? In each of these cases, the in-house plan administrator needs guidance from legal counsel to properly protect the company. The company may need to petition the court itself to get clarification of the order, or to get a specific ruling (e.g., a domestic relations order, or "DRO") that resolves the issue. The goal should be to do the right thing from a legal perspective but stay out of any arguments between the ex-spouses.

Post-Termination Option Issues

Contents

When an employee leaves employment for a reason other than death or disability, a number of equity-related issues can arise. For example, a company may seek to use equity as a form of severance, either by accelerating vesting or by extending the post-termination exercise period. On the other end of the spectrum, a company may attempt to create an equity-based noncompete agreement by including (and enforcing) forfeiture clauses in all option grants. In any event, employers need to look carefully at the whole picture before using equity as part of a termination strategy. Moreover, even when no special strategies are adopted, employers need to exercise care in administering the post-termination provisions of the plan or individual option grant. In recent years, allegations of unfair treatment with respect to options have increasingly formed the basis for claims in wrongful termination litigation. Litigation particularly arises with respect to disputes over vesting and exercise rights on termination. Such claims are governed by state law and generally turn on contract construction—a strong reason to draft plan documents clearly and follow them precisely. Finally, the employer must always be aware that Section 409A of the Code may apply to treat payments made upon separation from employment as a deferral of compensation under a nonqualified deferred compensation plan. Any structuring of post-termination equity compensation will need to be done carefully so as to avoid Section 409A accelerated taxation and penalties.[1]

12.1 Using Equity as Severance

A common executive severance strategy is to allow options to continue to vest for a period of time after termination and also extend the exercise period past the normal post-termination window. There are two ways to approach additional vesting. The first is to simply accelerate vesting on the date of termination as to stock that would otherwise have vested during a specific period (the "severance period") as of his termination date. The second is to require the former employee to enter into a consulting agreement with the company for the severance period, with the shares continuing to vest over that period. In creating this type of package, the company should consider the following tax and accounting issues:

12.1.1 Acceleration

From the business perspective, acceleration provides a clean break with the former employee. However, such acceleration may change the tax character of the option if it is an ISO. Under Section 424(h) of the Code, acceleration of vesting will not, in and of itself, convert the ISO to an NSO. The problem is that in operation, such acceleration can easily run afoul of the "$100,000 first exercisable" rule in Section 422 of the Code. That rule states that an ISO may be first exercisable as to no more than $100,000 worth of stock (valued as of the date of grant) in any calendar year. If the former employee is at (or near) his or her $100,000 limit on the date of termination, acceleration of vesting may exceed the limit. Under the Code, the excess options will be automatically converted from ISOs to NSOs, with the attendant tax consequences

---

1.   Treas. Reg. § 1.409A-1(b)(9). See chapter 9 for a brief summary of Section 409A.

for the optionee. If termination is near the end of a calendar year, the best way around this result is to defer the termination date into the next year and accelerate exercisability only in the new calendar year. Further, under the regulations to Section 409A of the Code, acceleration of vesting on termination will not cause an otherwise exempt option to become nonqualified deferred compensation.

Additionally, employers must be careful not to run afoul of rules under Section 162(m) of the Code that might restrict acceleration of options that would otherwise be payable on achievement of milestones. The IRS has ruled that compensation does not qualify for the performance-based exemption if it is designed to be payable automatically upon voluntary or involuntary termination even though the performance goals have not been met. This applies to any year in which such an award is outstanding—not just the year of termination. This ruling represents a significant departure from earlier IRS pronouncements on the topic and applies to performance periods that begin after January 1, 2009. It does not apply to contracts that existed before Feb. 21, 2008.[2]

Finally, for accounting purposes, Accounting Standards Codification (ASC) Section 718-10-35 provides that an outstanding option that is modified to accelerate vesting after termination will subject the option to liability accounting under FASB's ASC 480. Depending on the facts, this could be costly for the company.

12.1.2 Consulting Agreements

The consulting agreement alternative provides the company with continuing access to the former employee's knowledge base and may also be used to help negotiate a noncompete agreement or similar post-termination settlement. However, the technical tax and accounting analysis may be unattractive to both parties, particularly if the option is an ISO.

For tax purposes, the Code requires that ISOs may be granted only to employees and may be exercised only for a period of up to three months after termination of employment (more on this below). If vesting continues after the former employee is no longer an employee, the portion of the option that vests within those three months may retain

---

2.   Rev. Rul. 2008-13 (Feb. 21, 2008). See chapter 9 for a discussion of this ruling.

its ISO status during that period, provided that the ISO is also exercised within that three-month period.

12.1.3 Extension of Exercise Period

Any extension of the period within which the terminating employee may exercise the option will be a modification for both tax (ISO) and accounting purposes and will be deemed a cancellation and regrant of the ISO as of the date of the modification. For tax purposes, the new grant must meet all of the conditions for ISO treatment to retain this status. For example, if the optionee is no longer an employee, if the exercise price is below the current fair market value, or if the new grant exceeds the $100,000 limitation, the option will no longer qualify for ISO treatment. As noted above, the Code allows a maximum three-month post-termination exercise period for ISOs, but if the plan or option agreement states a shorter period, that period will govern. Any portion of the option that is exercised more than three months after the optionee ceased to be an employee will be treated as an NSO, even if the modification itself did not disqualify the option from ISO treatment. Further, ASC Section 718-10-35 provides that any extension of the exercise period will result in a modification for accounting purposes, which could cause the company to recognize incremental expense.

12.1.4 Limitations in the Document

In devising severance packages, employers should always check the plan document first for authority. Most plans have language that gives broad discretion to the board of directors to accelerate or otherwise amend options. However, planners should not take this for granted: companies should always review the sections governing the "powers of the administrator" and the individual grant documents before making any changes. If the language is too restrictive, the plan may need to be amended before the option can be accelerated. The same issue applies to the post-termination exercise period: some plans limit such periods to 90 days. If the plan has this type of limitation, it will need to be amended before the board can extend the right to exercise the option.

12.1.5 Tax Deductions

Note that the above analysis assumes that the company wants to give the former employee a chance to retain ISOs and the preferential tax treatment accorded such ISOs. This may not, however, be the best choice for the company. As noted above, the company gets a tax deduction on the exercise of NSOs, but not on the exercise of ISOs (unless such ISOs are disposed of in a disqualifying disposition). In order to take the deduction, the employer will be required to withhold on the former employee's exercise.[3] Note also that in the event the acceleration and severance is part of a change in control package, both the company and the former employee must be alert to potential golden parachute issues under Sections 280G and 4999 of the Code as well.[4]

12.1.6 Inadvertent ERISA Severance Plans

It is important to make sure that any severance-based acceleration is limited to key employees on a case-by-case basis. If too many former employees' options are accelerated upon termination, and if such acceleration becomes known to employees in general, there may be an argument that acceleration is a severance benefit of the company for purposes of the Employee Retirement Income Security Act of 1974 (ERISA).

12.1.7 Related Change-in-Status Issues

As noted above, ASC 718 applies to changes in status from employee to consultant. Issues also arise when full-time employees become part-time employees. Is it permissible to adjust options to reduce vesting in accordance with the number of hours worked? Although few plans address this concern directly, the right answer is that changes in vesting for reduced hours should follow company policy. To avoid allegations that such adjustments unilaterally take away benefits from optionees, companies should amend their plans to refer to such policies (and ensure that the company actually adopts them).

3.　Treas. Reg. § 1.83-6. See section 9.1 of chapter 9; exhibit 9-1.

4.　See section 9.6 of chapter 9.

Another question that may arise is whether a change in status from employee to consultant will relieve the company of its withholding obligation on an option exercised by a former employee. If the former employee is granted a new option as a consultant at the time of the change, it is possible that there would be an argument that his services as an employee were unrelated to stock compensation earned under the consulting agreement. However, as a general rule if the terms of the option (for example, pricing or vesting) could only have been derived as a result of the employment relationship, the employer should assume that withholding will be required. Treas. Reg. § 31.3401(a)-1(a)(5) specifically provides that remuneration for services, unless such remuneration is specifically excepted by statute, constitutes wages *even though at the time paid the relationship of employer and employee no longer exists* between the person in whose employ the services are performed and the individual who performed them. As a general rule, payroll tax obligations will also apply with respect to any payments that would have been paid if the former employee had remained employed. If the consulting agreement is really a form of severance (i.e., no real services are expected), the answer is even clearer, as there is extensive IRS authority indicating that severance payments are subject to withholding.[5]

---

5. See generally Sections 3121(a)(13)(FICA); 3306(b)(10)(FUTA). See also Rev. Rul. 90-72, 1990-2 C.B. 211 (lump-sum payments for involuntary separation made under employer plan do not qualify as supplemental unemployment benefits and were "wages" for purposes of FICA, FUTA, and federal income tax withholding); Rev. Rul. 74-252, 1974-1 C.B. 287 (involuntary separation from service payments were in the nature of dismissal payments and were "wages" for purposes of FICA, FUTA, and income tax withholding); Rev. Rul. 73-166, 1973-1 C.B. 411 (lost pay to striking employee not re-employed after settlement of strike was dismissal payment subject to FICA, FUTA, and income tax withholding); Rev. Rul. 72-572, 1972-2 C.B. 535 (payment made in settlement of a discrimination claim brought by employee whose services were involuntarily terminated constituted "wages" for purposes of FICA, FUTA, and income tax withholding); Rev. Rul. 71-408, 1971-2 C.B. 340 (dismissal payments made to employees whose services were terminated were "wages" for purposes of FICA, FUTA, and federal income tax withholding).

12.2 Forfeiture Clauses: A Note of Caution to Companies That Do Business in California

Commentators have aggressively argued that employers should include forfeiture provisions (also known as "clawbacks") in their stock option grants as a method of ensuring that former employees refrain from competition during a post-termination period.[6] Forfeiture clauses have been used successfully by large companies (most notably IBM) to force former employees to disgorge option profits in the event a noncompete is violated.[7] Further, events on the public company scene over the past few years have made forfeiture clauses look increasingly attractive as companies seek (or are forced to seek) recovery of compensation paid to executives. The convergence of the clawback features of Sections 304 and 1003 of the Sarbanes-Oxley Act, the increasing enforcement action by the SEC in connection with financial restatements, the SEC proxy disclosure rules requiring information on clawbacks to be included as part of the CD&A, the adoption of clawback mechanisms for executives in industries benefitting from the Troubled Asset Relief Program (TARP) created by the 2008 financial rescue legislation, the surge in shareholder derivative lawsuits over option backdating and executive compensation issues, and the Dodd-Frank Act of 2010's requirement that companies institute and disclose clawback policies tied to financial restatements,[8] all combine to suggest that option clawbacks are not merely protective, but are necessary—at least at the top executive level.

Companies that employ California residents, however, need to be aware that it is generally illegal in California to require an employee to agree to a post-employment restraint on trade. Notwithstanding some years of confusion on this issue, in August 2008 the California Supreme Court held in *Edwards v. Arthur Andersen LLP*[9] that section 16600 of

---

6. For an example of this argument, see the *Corporate Counsel*, September-October 1999.

7. See *IBM v. Martson*, 37 F. Supp. 2d 613 (S.D.N.Y. 1999); and *IBM v. Bajorek*, 191 F.3d 1033 (9th Cir. 1999). The California decision was by a panel of the Ninth Circuit.

8. See chapter 13.

9. 2008 Cal. LEXIS 9618 (August 7, 2008), *aff'g* 142 Cal. App. 4th 603, 47 Cal. Rptr. 3d 788, 2006 Cal. App. LEXIS 1320 (Cal. App. 2d Dist., 2006).

California's Business & Professions Code invalidates post-employment non-compete agreements between an employer and an employee and is not subject to the so-called "narrow restraint exception" read into the law by the Ninth Circuit in several opinions. The *Edwards* restriction required the employee to agree that if he or she left the firm, "[1] for eighteen months ... you agree not to perform professional services . . . for any client on which you worked during the eighteen months [prior to leaving];" and "[2] [f]or twelve months . . . you agree not to solicit any client of the office(s) to which you were assigned during the . . . eighteen months [prior to leaving]."

As most California employment lawyers anticipated, the California Supreme Court (notwithstanding waiting two years to issue its opinion) did not find the issue difficult. It noted that for so long as section 16600 and its predecessor section have been on the books, "our courts have consistently affirmed that section 16600 evinces a settled legislative policy in favor of open competition and employee mobility." It cited earlier case law for the proposition that California "ensures that every citizen shall retain the right to pursue any lawful employment and en-terprise of their choice," and that Californians have "the important legal right ... to engage in businesses and occupations of their choosing." The court explicitly rejected the argument that a "mere limitation" on a former employee's ability to compete (such as a preclusion of working for the former employer's clients) is not the sort of "restriction" that section 16600 invalidates. The court pointed out that the statute does not speak of "prohibitions" on competition; it speaks of "restraints," which as used in the statute means *any* restraint—not just preclusions, and not just "broad" (as opposed to narrow) restraints. Thus, both the 18-month prohibition on working for Andersen clients Edwards had worked on during the 18 months prior to separation, and the 12-month prohibition on "soliciting" any clients of the offices in which he worked for the 18 months prior to separation constituted such illegal restraints.

While the result in *Edwards* was anticipated, there are a couple of points to particularly note. It is not an unknown practice in California for employers to condition severance payments—which could include post-termination rights to exercise options—on non-competition com-mitments; e.g., we'll pay your salary for six months post-employment, but if you go to work for the competition, we'll cut off the payments/

right to exercise your options." The theory seems to be that this is a self-help remedy, so the employer should be able to get away with it. There is no reason to conclude that this sort of arrangement would work. If the employer promises to pay six months of severance pay/equity compensation unless the former employee competes, it is likely that the former employee has a valid claim for the entire six months of severance, whether or not he or she competes. Indeed, in the situation in which the employer provides that severance amounts will be "offset" by amounts earned by the former employee in his or her next job, if the employee can prove that the true purpose of the provision is to restrict him or her from competing (a factual question to be determined by evidence), he or she should also prevail. The same logic applies to characterizing the restriction as a prohibition on the "solicitation" of the former employer's customers. This is simply a different way of saying "non-compete" and will not work.

At first glance, forfeiture clauses may provide some level of comfort (and even a sense of justice) to companies that wish to send a message to employees that noncompetes are serious business. In addition, there is no doubt that such clauses send a message to shareholders that the company is taking its corporate governance seriously.

However, in the authors' opinion, such clauses are ill-advised at any but the highest executive level, and—unless tied specifically to something other than post-termination competition—will be unenforceable against California employees. Although stock options are now used to enhance compensation throughout the country, they have a particularly strong presence and visibility in California's Silicon Valley. In the competitive technology community, equity compensation is viewed by employees as a necessary component of the overall salary package. Employees historically view the standard vesting restrictions as a necessary evil to equate equity compensation to cash compensation: e.g., payment for services rendered. Forfeiture clauses circumvent this reasoning.

There are many lawful ways to enforce noncompetition clauses other than to require forfeiture of already-earned income. For example, companies routinely include specific, narrowly drawn nonsolicitation provisions in employee confidentiality agreements. The California courts will, in fact, routinely uphold such provisions when they are based upon protection of trade secrets and not simply upon a desire to restrict post-termination competition. Severance and/or post-termination consulting agreements may also stipulate noncompete requirements in exchange for additional options or payments. Such techniques have the advantage of achieving their goal while respecting previous service rendered by the employee.

PART III
CURRENT ISSUES

Legislative and Regulatory Initiatives Related to Stock Options: History and Status

Stock options and the rules that affect them are a constantly changing. In recent years, new laws have affected everything from how executive compensation is structured and approved to what constitutes a reporting company that is subject to disclosure rules under the Securities Exchange Act of 1934. This chapter briefly summarizes the history of these legislative initiatives through 2013.

13.1 Legislative History: Stock Option Initiatives

Before 1991, congressional involvement with stock options was limited to enacting the implementing tax legislation for ISOs in the Economic Recovery Tax Act of 1981. Aside from those who received options, only stock plan professionals who worked with equity compensation paid much attention to their status. In fact, in 1991 the status of compensatory stock options seemed clear: the Code and its regulations governed tax treatment; Accounting Principles Board Opinion 25 (APB 25) established accounting procedures; and Section 16 of the Exchange Act dictated disclosure requirements for insiders. Even FASB, which started a review of stock option accounting in 1984, closed down the project in 1988 for lack of interest.

In the early 1990s, however, compensatory options began to get national attention in the press. A number of articles appeared that focused on big option packages for executives without noting the effectiveness of broad-based equity compensation.[1] In June 1991, Senator Carl Levin, D-Mich., picked up on the negative publicity and introduced a bill that sought to require companies to include the "cost" of options on financial statements and disclose information about unexercised options to shareholders. Under this bill, the SEC would have been required to figure out and impose a valuation method, with or without the cooperation of FASB or the Treasury Department. The bill never came up for a vote.

Over the next two years, stock options became a hot topic as a wide variety of interest groups and professional organizations loudly participated in hearings, drafted proposed legislation, and battled each

---

1. Most major newspapers, including the *New York Times* and the *Washington Post*, ran articles on the perceived abuses of stock options in the early 1990s. The *Wall Street Journal* has published an annual insert tracking executive pay since 1990. For a sense of the end-of-century views on this issue, see for example, "Stock Options are Diluting Future Earnings," which ran as the cover story in the May 18, 1998, issue of *Forbes*; and "Taking Stock: Extending Employee Ownership Through Options," *ACA Journal* (Spring 1998) (entire issue).

other in the press and on the floor of Congress. In particular, FASB was pushed back into the middle of the debate, with Senator Levin and his supporters agitating for mandatory changes to stock option valuation for financial accounting (and public disclosure) purposes. However, despite pressure from Senator Levin's committee, the SEC refused to cooperate in imposing standards on FASB. In 1995 FASB adopted Statement of Financial Accounting Standards 123 (FAS 123), requiring only that a reasonable value for outstanding options be disclosed in the footnotes to the issuer's financial statements.

With the adoption of FAS 123 and new securities disclosure rules, both of which became effective in 1996, stock plan professionals assumed that the roller coaster ride had ended. The combination of disclosure rules seemingly addressed public concern that stock options were devices for "stealth compensation." Nevertheless, in April 1997 Senator Levin revived the issue and proposed legislation that would have required any company that took a deduction for stock options under Code Section 83(h) to reflect the same expense for financial accounting purposes. An exception would have been made for certain broad-based plans. Again, Senator Levin's bill went nowhere.

In the fall of 2001, the public outrage accompanying the Enron debacle spurred a new barrage of anti-equity propaganda and proposals. Chief among these proposals was the recycled Levin-McCain bill, which once again sought to make accounting policy by limiting corporate tax deductions through the Code, an approach vigorously opposed by the administration of President George W. Bush and numerous industry and accounting groups. The bill was too contentious to become law, and ultimately the 2004 adoption of FAS 123(R) by FASB ended the debate for all but the most interested parties, although Senator Levin continues to annually introduce bills that would restrict companies' option-related tax deductions to the amounts they recognize for accounting purposes.

13.2 Recent Legislation Affecting Stock Options

Several laws passed since the start of the 21st century have affected executive compensation in terms of disclosure, shareholder rights, taxation, and corporate reporting and share registration. Equity compensation has not been the primary focus of most of these bills. However, the Sarbanes-Oxley Act of 2002, the American Jobs Creation Act of 2004 (i.e., Section 409A), the Emergency Economic Stabilization Act of 2008, the Patient Protection and Affordable Care and Dodd-Frank acts of 2010, and the Jumpstart Our Business Startups Act of 2012 all raise issues with respect to equity compensation, as further described below and elsewhere in this book. Indeed, the general public and legislative focus since 2008 on executive compensation and corporate governance will necessarily affect the use of equity compensation, especially for top executives. As the regulatory schemes associated with the most recent of these laws are put in place, we are likely to see ever-increasing limitations on when and how stock options may be used to compensate employees of public (and to some extent private) companies. The practical effects of much of this legislation are reflected in the appropriate sections of this book. This section addresses the broad outlines of these laws' effects on equity compensation and discusses provisions for which rulemaking is still under way.[2]

13.2.1 Sarbanes-Oxley Act of 2002

The Sarbanes-Oxley Act of 2002, which amended both the Securities Exchange Act of 1934 and the Securities Act of 1933, was enacted on July 30, 2002.[3] Sarbanes-Oxley was intended to combat corporate fraud by imposing rigorous new obligations for public company disclosure, reporting, and compliance with respect to financial matters and executive compensation. The law has a reach far beyond the scope of this text. For purposes of equity compensation, it is most relevant to public company insiders as a result of the following provisions:

13.2.1.1 *Loans to Executive Officers and Directors Are Prohibited*

A publicly held company may not extend, arrange for, or renew credit in the form of personal loans to its executives, officers, or members of the board of directors. This effectively curtailed the previously common practice of permitting executives to exercise stock options with promissory notes. Note that an outright cash bonus is acceptable un-

---

2.   The summaries are intended to provide general guidance only.

3.   Sarbanes-Oxley Act of 2002, P.L. 107-204, 116 Stat. 745 (July 30, 2002).

der Sarbanes-Oxley (although it will trigger disclosure on Form 8-K, discussed below), but that a bonus that is contingent on the exercise of the option would run afoul of Code Section 409A.

13.2.1.2 *Forfeiture of Compensation*

If an issuer is required to restate its financial statements due to its failure to comply with the disclosure requirements as a result of misconduct by the CEO or CFO, that executive must reimburse the company for any bonuses and incentive-based or equity-based compensation (including profits realized from sale of company stock) received within the year following the first filing or issuance of the noncompliant statement. "Misconduct" is not defined in the statute.[4] This provision was broadened substantially by the Dodd-Frank Act of 2010, discussed below.

13.2.2 American Jobs Creation Act of 2004

With the American Jobs Creation Act of 2004 (AJCA), Congress added new Section 409A to the Code, thus adopting sweeping changes to the tax treatment of deferred compensation. The impetus for Section 409A came from perceived abuses of deferred compensation by top executives in large companies. Over the years, such companies had developed many techniques for all but guaranteeing deferred compensation payments while still remaining within the technical rules exempting such funds from immediate taxation to the executive.

With Code Section 409A taking effect, those halcyon days of discretionary deferrals essentially ended. As of January 1, 2005, any compensation deferred under a "nonqualified deferred compensation plan" (NDCP) is currently taxable unless it is subject to a substantial risk of forfeiture (i.e., using the principles of Section 83 of the Code) or satisfies the rigorous requirements of Section 409A summarized in chapter 9.

13.2.3 Emergency Economic Stabilization Act of 2008

The American economy took a precipitous dive at the end of 2008. In response, The Emergency Economic Stabilization Act of 2008 (EESA) was enacted. The majority of provisions under EESA authorized the

---

4.   Sections 403 (forfeiture) and 1103 (recovery) of the Act.

Troubled Asset Relief Program (TARP), a program designed to assist certain financial institutions. Until the companies paid back the assets they received under TARP, their executives were subject to special restrictions on their compensation, including (generally) a complete ban on making parachute payments, limits on incentive compensation that encouraged risk-taking, and clawbacks where financial statements were found to be materially inaccurate.

EESA required say-on-pay resolutions at companies with outstanding funds from TARP. To that end, the Treasury Department issued its Interim Final Rule on June 10, 2009, codifying the restrictions and appointing a special master to review compensation for specific companies.[5] As noted above, these rules prohibited golden parachute payments to certain individuals, required that bonuses be paid in restricted stock, prohibited compensation that encouraged unnecessary risk, and clarified say-on-pay, clawback, and disclosure requirements. Several of these initiatives for companies that participated in TARP found their way into the Dodd-Frank bill. The SEC issued its proposed rules on say-on-pay standards for TARP recipients on July 1, 2009.

Although these complex provisions were specific to institutions that received TARP funding and therefore are not relevant to most readers, in the intervening years some of those concepts have worked their way into other new laws. In 2010 alone the Patient Protection and Affordable Care Act set stricter 162(m) limits for executives in health-care companies, and the Dodd-Frank Act requires companies to institute clawback provisions and will subject financial institutions to additional compensation-related restrictions. The Code Section 162(m) limits contained in both EESA and the 2010 health-care law are discussed in chapter 9.

Another provision in the EESA, sections 101 to 103, "Alternative Minimum Tax Relief," applied specifically to ISOs. Many optionees who exercised ISOs during the height of the dot-com boom in the 1990s found themselves in a terrible tax dilemma after the market for

---

5. On October 22, 2009, Special Master Kenneth Feinberg announced his determinations after reviewing the compensation packages of the 25 most highly paid employees at the seven firms that are receiving exceptional assistance. These determinations will significantly alter the compensation structure at the affected companies.

their stock busted: they had incurred huge AMT liability at the time of exercise, but soon afterward found themselves holding stock worth far less than its original strike price, let alone its spread at exercise. Silicon Valley taxpayer organizations had been lobbying Congress since 2001 to correct this perceived injustice; the EESA legislation did so by amending Section 53 of the Code to provide that: (1) effective for tax years beginning after December 31, 2007, the refundable AMT tax credit for 2008 and 2009 was raised by the *greater of* 50% of the unused minimum tax credit for the preceding years, or 100% of the AMT credit determined with respect to the prior tax year, regardless of the person's income (thus ensuring that all such refunds will be paid in two years); and (2) effective October 3, 2008, all liabilities associated with ISO-related AMT underpayments incurred prior to January 1, 2008, were abated in full. For these purposes, "liabilities" included the amount of the underpayment, plus any interest and penalties with respect to such underpayment.[6]

13.2.4 Dodd-Frank Act of 2010

The Dodd-Frank Act of 2010,[7] which responded to the financial crisis of 2008 and the ensuing recession, contained many provisions related to executive compensation. These provisions are just a sliver of the 2,300 page financial reform law, but include numerous new disclosure and shareholder voting requirements. The law requires a large amount of SEC rulemaking, and some of the major executive compensation provisions will not take effect until related regulations are issued. As of this writing in fall 2015, the SEC has finalized rules in connection with shareholder voting on executive compensation and golden parachute provisions,[8] compensation committee and advisor independence, and pay ratio disclosures. The SEC has issued proposed rules for prohibiting incentive compensation that encourages excessive risk-taking at financial institutions with more than $1 billion in assets; disclosure of hedging by employees, officers, and directors; disclosure of pay versus performance; and clawbacks of executive compensation.

---

6.   H.R. 1424, Title I, Secs. 101–103, pp. 99–100 (October 3, 2008).

7.   P.L. 111-203.

8.   See section 4.3.3.

13.2.4.1 *Pay Ratio Disclosure*

One of the more difficult and controversial compensation-related provisions of the Dodd-Frank Act requires companies to calculate the median annual total compensation of all company employees excluding the CEO at least once every three years in order to identify the median employee by pay. The company must then annually disclose the median employee's compensation and calculate and disclose the ratio by which the CEO's compensation exceeds that employee's compensation. Under SEC regulations finalized in 2015, companies will be required to include those numbers in their proxy statements and certain other SEC filings, including registration statements and financial statements, beginning with their 2018 proxy statement for the 2017 fiscal year.

The company can identify the median employee either by statistical sampling of the employee population or by using amounts reported in its payroll or tax records, as long as the methodology is applied consistently. The company may do this every three years unless a change at the company means the median is likely to have changed significantly. Further, if the median employee's compensation changes substantially during those three years, the company may switch to another employee whose compensation is similar to the amount that was paid to the median employee before that person's compensation changed.

The regulations require companies to calculate the total income of all employees who are employed on a company-determined date that occurs within the last three months of its fiscal year. Full-time, part-time, temporary, and seasonal employees must be included. The compensation of full-time employees who joined the company during the year may be annualized, but adjustment is not allowed for other types of employees. Companies are allowed to apply a cost-of-living adjustment to the pay of employees outside the United States.

Non-U.S. employees may be excluded from the calculation if they work in a country where data privacy laws or regulations mean the company could not legally include those employees. Additionally, companies may exclude non-U.S. employees if they make up less than 5% of the employee population. Any employees who are excluded because of data privacy rules count toward the 5%. If a company excludes any non-U.S. employees in a jurisdiction, it must exclude all non-U.S. employees in that jurisdiction.

For purposes of the disclosure, the median employee's compensation must be calculated using the same rules that apply to the CEO's annual compensation reported in the Summary Compensation table. The company must disclose its methodology in determining the median employee's compensation. If any items that would be excludable from the Summary Compensation table calculation are included in the median employee's compensation, they must also be included in the calculation of the CEO's compensation for purposes of calculating the pay ratio.

Emerging growth companies, foreign private issuers, and registered investment companies are exempt from the pay ratio disclosure requirement.

13.2.4.2   *Clawback Policies*

In July 2015, the SEC proposed rules directing the national securities exchanges to write listing standards requiring companies to create and disclose policies for clawing back incentive compensation from current and former executive officers when material noncompliance with financial reporting requirements leads to financial restatements. The amounts to be clawed back will include incentive compensation tied to accounting-related metrics, stock price, or total shareholder return (TSR). Clawbacks would not be limited to those who participated in the actions that led to the restatement.

The clawback provisions must apply to incentive compensation received in the three years preceding the date on which the company is required to prepare the restatement.

Under the proposed rules, companies would be required to file their clawback policies as exhibits to their annual reports. In their annual reports and in any proxy statement that required executive compensation disclosures, they would also be required to disclose whether a restatement requiring recovery of incentive-based compensation had been completed during that fiscal year as well as the existence of any outstanding balance of excess incentive-based compensation from a prior restatement.

This provision will not take effect until the exchanges finalize related changes to their listing standards, which they will be required to do no later than 90 days after the SEC publishes final regulations.

Public companies that fail to adopt and disclose clawback policies will be subject to delisting.

13.2.4.3 *Pay vs. Performance*

Another provision of the Dodd-Frank Act requires the SEC to issue regulations requiring companies to disclose the relationship between executive compensation actually paid and the company's financial performance as measured by stock price changes, dividends, and other distributions. In April 2015, the SEC proposed regulations that would require companies to disclose the relationship between their relative total shareholder return (TSR) over a five-year period and the compensation "actually paid" to executives.

The CEO's pay would be disclosed individually along with the average compensation paid to the remaining named executive officers (NEOs) as a group.[9] Under the proposal, the executive compensation disclosure would report two numbers each for the CEO and group of other NEOs:

- the amount already reported in the Summary Compensation table, and
- the Summary Compensation table amount adjusted to reflect the fair value of equity grants at vesting rather than at grant.[10] The SEC refers to this as the amount "actually paid."

For the purpose of calculating equity values "actually paid," the fair value of equity grants is determined in accordance with ASC 718, albeit using the vesting date rather than grant date as the measurement date. Using this method, restricted stock will generally be reported based on the vesting date fair market value, while stock options and SARs will be valued using an option-pricing model.

If more than one person serves as CEO in a year, the compensation of those individuals is aggregated in the disclosures.

---

9.   Regulation S-K, Item 402(v).

10. The amount shown is also adjusted for changes to the actuarial present value under defined benefit retirement plans that are not attributable to the applicable year of service.

TSR is measured compared to a peer group, which can be either the peer group used in the Compensation Discussion & Analysis or the peer group used in the stock performance graph that is required under Regulation S-K Item 201(e)(1)(ii). The company's cumulative TSR would be reported for each year over a five-year period (three years for smaller reporting companies), as would the TSR of the peer group for each of the five years. Smaller reporting companies could use a three-year measure. Emerging growth companies are exempt from this requirement.

The rules will become effective after final regulations are published.

13.2.4.4　*Requirements Specific to Financial Institutions*

Once regulations are finalized, covered financial intuitions that have assets of at least $1 billion will be required to disclose to regulators all of the incentive compensation they pay. This is meant to allow regulators to assess whether the institutions are encouraging excessive risk-taking or paying unreasonably large amounts of compensation. "Covered financial institutions" include, broadly, banks, broker-dealers, credit unions, investment advisers, Fannie Mae, and Freddie Mac. The SEC, together with other agencies, proposed regulations in March 2011.

13.2.4.5　*Disclosure of Hedging by Employees, Officers, and Directors*

In July 2015, the SEC proposed rules requiring enhanced disclosure of corporate hedging policies including whether employees, officers, and directors are permitted to hedge or offset any decrease in the market value of employer securities obtained by way of a compensatory award from the company.

13.2.5 Jumpstart Our Business Startups Act of 2012

The JOBS Act, passed in mid-2012, is intended to ease the raising of capital for companies with annual revenues of less than $1 billion. To that end, the act created a new category of companies called "emerging growth companies" that are exempt from many reporting and shareholder-related requirements. Emerging growth companies are defined in section 8.2.

The JOBS Act also made significant changes to Section 12(g) of the Securities Exchange Act of 1934. Before the JOBS Act, privately held companies granting stock options or other equity awards to a large number of employees could trigger rules that would require them to report to shareholders as if the company were publicly traded. In essence, the privately held company would be subject to the rules for public companies. The JOBS Act raised the number of shareholders that a private company may have and excluded from the shareholder count employees who receive equity awards pursuant to an employee compensation plan, even after they cease to be company employees. This applies to employees who have exercised their options as well as to optionees.

The exemptions from existing laws that affect these companies are described in the appropriate sections of this book.

Chapter 14

Cases Affecting Equity Compensation

Contents

As the use of equity to compensate employees has increased, so have the number of court and agency actions with respect to it. This chapter summarizes some key case law developments and agency rulings. Although this review is not comprehensive, it gives an indication of the direction of the law and the various approaches being taken by the courts (and litigants) to resolve disputes involving equity compensation. Please be aware that the following summaries are no more than that; they should not be relied upon without first consulting primary sources for details.

14.1 Tax Cases and Rulings

This section reviews recent federal and state tax cases related to equity compensation. To rise to the United States Tax Court, a taxpayer must have appealed the result of his tax audit up through all IRS administrative levels. Accordingly, the issues that arise for the federal courts frequently concern construction of difficult technical issues under the Internal Revenue Code (such as Section 83 and the alternative minimum tax). At the state level, the most common issue involves how income tax obligations must be divided between states when an employee works or has worked in one state and exercises the option in another. Generally, state courts will base their allocations on the same principles as those used to allocate foreign vs. domestic income sourcing at the federal level.

At the federal agency level, the IRS has the authority to issue rulings in both public and private determinations in writing. Please note that recent tax-related legislation and regulations (including notices relating to such regulations) are discussed in chapter 13.

14.1.1 Tax Decisions in the Courts

For many years, option-related cases that made it all the way to the circuit court level involved taxpayers' attempts to get around the unfortunate results of the dot-com boom and bust. The rapidity with which stock prices fell during this period left many taxpayers with unanticipated tax bills and disputes. While these taxpayers were frequently unsuccessful in court, The Emergency Economic Stabilization Act of 2008 finally offered relief for those who still had large AMT credits available to them and abatement for still-outstanding amounts, as discussed in section 13.2.3.

First Reported Code Section 409A Case Involves Stock Options

The first reported decision related to Code Section 409A occurred in 2013, and it involved stock options. In *Sutardja v. United States,* No. 11-724T (Fed. Cl. Feb. 27, 2013), the Federal Court of Claims granted the government's motion for partial summary judgment on February 28, 2013, holding that discounted stock options are subject to excise taxes and interest penalties under Code Section 409A. The case involved a refund claim by plaintiffs seeking to recover more than $3.1 million in

Section 409A excise taxes and more than $300,000 in interest penalties that the IRS assessed on income attributable to plaintiffs' exercise of stock options that, according to the IRS, were granted with an exercise price that was less than the fair market value of the underlying stock on the date of grant.

In arguing that the characterization of stock options as "deferrals of compensation" under IRS Notice 2005-1 (the applicable authority at the time of transactions at issue in this case) was contrary to U.S. Supreme Court precedent, the plaintiffs cited *Smith v. Commissioner,* 324 U.S. 177 (1945), the seminal case in which the Supreme Court held that the mere grant of an option is not a taxable event. The court rejected the plaintiffs' argument because the Supreme Court's holding in Smith applied explicitly to a non-discounted option and, thus, it found that IRS Notice 2005-1 was not contrary to Smith.

The plaintiffs also argued that discounted options do not constitute deferral of compensation under Code Section 409A because the definition of deferred compensation under the Federal Insurance Contributions Act (FICA) regulations explicitly excludes the grant of options for purposes of determining FICA obligations under Code Section 3121(v). The court disagreed, holding that the IRS properly disregarded the definition of deferred compensation under the FICA regulations, which, by their terms, are applicable only for purposes of determining the treatment of deferred compensation under Code Section 3121(v).

Finally, the plaintiffs argued that, even if their options were discounted options subject to Section 409A, any deferral of income would fall under the short-term deferral exception, which generally provides that payments that must be made within two-and-a-half months after the end of the year of vesting are not deferred compensation. The plaintiffs claimed that their options fell within the short-term deferral exception because they were exercised in January following the year in which they became vested. The court rejected this argument because the terms of the applicable option plan document allowed for vested options to be exercised any time within 10 years from the grant date, thus exceeding the two-and-a-half-month short-term deferral period.

After granting the government's partial motion for summary judgment on the issue of whether discounted options are subject to Code Section 409A, the court remanded the case to the trial court to determine whether the options were in fact discounted options, which is a question of fact.

14.1.2 IRS Rulings and Announcements

The Internal Revenue Service (IRS) issues a variety of rulings on tax matters in response to legislative mandates, technical audit requests by agents, and requests by individual taxpayers. There is a formal hierarchy to the rulings. Regulations, which interpret the Internal Revenue Code and are mandated by Congress, have the force of law. Public determinations are called "revenue rulings" and they state the IRS position on the interpretation of the Code and its regulations. They are frequently accompanied by IRS notices, announcements, or other interpretive documents. Revenue rulings are citable and represent the official government position on issues, but, while given deference by the courts, do not have the same definitive weight as regulations.

Another form of public ruling is known as a "revenue procedure." These rulings give technical guidance to taxpayers on the application of regulations or revenue rulings. Many revenue rulings and procedures are discussed throughout this book. The pronouncements discussed in this section are solely those that are not covered elsewhere in this work yet are significant enough to equity compensation planning to deserve mention.

Private written determinations are directed at an individual taxpayer (or the IRS field agent auditing a taxpayer) and as such may be relied upon only by that individual. Private rulings may, among other things, take the form of a private letter ruling (PLR) to an individual taxpayer, a technical advice memorandum (TAM) to a field agent, or an Advice from the Office of the IRS Chief Counsel.[1] Although such private rulings are available to the public, they are intended only to serve as an indication of the IRS position on any issue and may not be cited or relied upon as precedent.[2] Although they have no value as precedent, practitioners use them as indications of how the IRS would rule on similar issues in the future.

---

1. See Section 6110 of the Code.

2. Section 6110(k)(3) of the Code provides that written determinations may not be used or cited as precedent unless otherwise established in regulations.

14.1.2.1 *Corporate Matters*

IRS Says Option Exercises Causing 401(k) Errors

Monika Templeton, director of employee plans examination, told a 2010 IRS phone forum that about half of all 401(k) plans that have been audited have errors in calculating compensation, and that one of the most common problems is failure to include income from stock option exercises and ESPP disqualifying dispositions. The IRS, she said, is seeing cases in which different kinds of compensation are included or excluded for different purposes, rather than being consistently applied for all plan purposes. Option exercises and disqualifying dispositions are often subject to ordinary income tax treatment and must be included in calculations of deferral percentages, but the information often does not get from the stock plan administrator to the 401(k) plan administrator.

Treas. Reg. § 1.367(b)-14T Issued: No More "Killer B" Reorganizations

On May 23, 2008, the IRS issued final, temporary, and proposed regulations that implement earlier guidance intended to close a loophole that permitted multinationals to repatriate cash from foreign subsidiaries using cross-border triangular reorganizations, popularly known as "Killer B" transactions (TD 9400 and REG-136020-07). Previously, the IRS issued two notices, Notices 2006-85 and 2007-48, that discussed the different versions of the transaction and *in each case* treated repatriation of a foreign subsidiary's earnings as a taxable transaction under Code Section 367(b). Notice 2006-85 dealt with nonpublic deals and Notice 2007-48 dealt with public stock buybacks.[3]

The regulations confirm the IRS positions set out in those two notices, retroactively effective back to the dates of each notice. In the case of transactions described in Notice 2006-85, the regulations apply to transactions occurring after September 22, 2006, with some transition relief. In the case of transactions described in Notice 2007-48, the

---

3. Generally, the IRS reviewed transactions that involved a subsidiary's purchase of its parent's stock for property, where the parent or the subsidiary (or both) was foreign. In each case, the subsidiary exchanged parent stock for the stock and assets of a target corporation, taking the position that such exchange was a tax-free triangular reorganization under Section 368(a)(1)(B).

regulations apply to transactions occurring after May 31, 2007, with some transition relief.

The *new* regulations affect the use of options or other employee equity awards in any foreign subsidiary transaction that might qualify as a "Killer B" for purposes of Section 367(b) of the Code. Notably, if the parent issues stock to employees of the foreign subsidiary, the employee might then pay the parent for the exercise of the options in cash, with the subsidiary paying the spread to the parent in cash. The subsidiary has to make this payment, in most countries, to generate a deduction, but the repatriation of that money to the U.S. would then be taxable, offsetting that deduction to one extent of another (depending on the differing tax rates). This difficult technical area will remain an important tax consideration with respect to any cross-border reorganization.

14.1.2.2 *Individual Matters*

Tax Effects of Supreme Court's Same-Sex Marriage Ruling

On June 26, 2013, the United States Supreme Court issued its opinion in *United States v. Windsor*, ruling that Section 3 of the U.S. Defense of Marriage Act (DOMA) violated the Fifth Amendment to the U.S. Constitution. Under Section 3 of DOMA, only two individuals of opposite sexes could be recognized as "married" or "spouses" for purposes of construing U.S. federal laws. This provision of DOMA affected more than 1,000 laws, including the Internal Revenue Code, which regulates many aspects of employer-sponsored equity compensation plans in the United States. Windsor took effect on July 21, 2013.

On August 29, 2013, the IRS issued guidance that for purposes of federal tax law, a marriage would be valid based on the state in which the ceremony took place (the ceremony test), as opposed to the state in which the taxpayer resides (the residency test).[4] Prior to this, the IRS had traditionally relied on the residency test. As a result, for purposes of administering stock plans, tax rules applicable to spouses (mainly related to divorce) should be applied to any opposite-sex spouse and any same-sex spouse based on the state where the spouses were married.

---

4.   IR-2013-72.

As suggested above, the impact of the *Windsor* case and the IRS's subsequent guidance will for the most part affect stock plan participants only at the time of divorce. Same-sex spouses will now have access to tax transfers that occur in connection with divorce and Revenue Rulings 2002-22 and 2004-60, discussed in chapter 11, will now apply to same-sex spouses in the same way that they have always applied to opposite-sex spouses.

IRS Can Seize Non-Transferable Options

In Chief Counsel Advice No. 200926001 (Jan. 9, 2009), the IRS Chief Counsel's office concluded that the IRS can seize and sell employee stock options even if they are nontransferable. In this situation, an employee had vested ISOs and NSOs and had terminated employment with the issuing company. The IRS issued levies for taxes due against compensation, including the unexercised stock options. In the view of the IRS Chief Counsel, the restrictions on employee stock options are overridden by Section 6334(c), which gives the IRS broad collection powers.

IRS Resolves Key Uncertainties Related to Section 83(b)

In an important revenue ruling, Rev. Rul. 2007-49, 2007-31 IRB (July 30, 2007), the IRS clarified the tax consequences of a typical scenario for employee-stockholders of venture-backed companies. In such cases, investors and/or acquirers often impose a requirement in connection with a transaction that a key employee agree to accept new restrictions on his or her otherwise vested stock. Under Section 83 of the Code, the transfer of property in exchange for services is taxed at the earlier of vesting (i.e., when the property is no longer subject to a substantial risk of forfeiture or is first freely transferable) or when a Section 83(b) election is made. But what happens when fully vested property becomes subject to newly imposed restrictions? Is it vested or unvested?

Practitioners have long understood Section 83 to be inapplicable to situations in which employees contractually agree to new restrictions after their stock has already vested. Rev. Rul. 2007-49 confirms this understanding in three common fact settings:

- *Situation 1* describes a financing in which a condition of the investment is that the employee accepts a new two-year vesting schedule on his otherwise vested stock. In this situation, the IRS recognizes that under Section 83, the property transfer occurred at the initial vesting—i.e., the employee already owns the stock for tax purposes. Therefore, adding additional contractual restrictions "has no effect for purposes of § 83."

- *Situation 2* describes a tax-free (stock for stock) merger in which the employee agrees to take unvested stock in exchange for his otherwise vested stock. Again, the IRS recognizes that the initial stock is already vested under Section 83. However, the stock received in the exchange is *not* vested—it is a new grant of unvested shares that has been paid for with vested shares. Accordingly, the employee may file a Section 83(b) election at the time of the merger. Because the (old) vested stock necessarily has a fair market value equal to the (new) unvested stock, the employee has no compensation income in the year of the merger, so his basis in the new shares is the same as his basis in the old shares. When he sells the stock some years later, he will recognize capital gain in excess of his original basis only.

- *Situation 3* sets out the same facts as Situation 2, but in a taxable merger (half cash and half stock). Because the transaction is taxable, the exchange of the (old) vested shares for the (new) unvested shares results in taxable capital gain at the time of the merger equal to the difference between the employee's original basis and the fair market value of the new shares. The employee takes a tax basis in the new shares equal to the amount he paid for them (i.e., their already taxed fair market value) and may file a Section 83(b) election for the new shares. Future gain (or loss) will be capital gain (or loss).

14.1.2.3   *Stock Plan Administration*

PLR 200513012: ISO Plan with ESPP-Like Features Qualifies

In PLR 200513012 (Apr. 1, 2005), the IRS ruled that a company's ISO plan qualified under Section 422 of the Code. The plan was structured more like a Section 423 ESPP than a traditional option plan. Employees could enroll in the plan during a one-month enrollment period, during which time they could decide how much of their after-tax payroll they wanted to set aside on a regular basis to acquire shares later. The first day of the enrollment period was the grant date, on which the exercise price was set. The purchase price was the price at the end of the offering period, and the options had one-year terms. Employees could exercise at the end of one year, but they then had to transfer the shares to a bank-operated nominee account for at least one more year (which would allow them to meet ISO holding period requirements).

PLR 200418020: Reduction in Offering Period Not a "Modification"

In PLR 200418020 (Apr. 30, 2004), the IRS ruled on a shareholder approval issue for an ESPP in which the taxpayer company amended its plan because it failed to file a timely Form S-8 registration. The company offered a conventional ESPP with a 15% discount, a six-month offering period, and a look-back feature. It was required to register its ESPP stock on a Form S-8, but it missed the applicable deadline. Because the options issued under the plan must be covered by a registration statement, the company had to suspend the plan until the new statement was filed. The company thus amended its plan to extend its current offering period for an additional quarter while suspending the current purchase period until the registration was effective. The plan also was amended to require employees to notify the company of any disqualifying dispositions of stock acquired through the plan, and provided that the gain would be subject to withholding.

Under ESPP rules, a "material modification" to a Section 423 ESPP must be approved by shareholders. Because the modification at issue simply exchanged the right to exercise in the current quarter for a right to exercise in a later quarter, the IRS ruled that the amendment did not increase benefits and therefore was not a material modification for shareholder approval purposes. The changes related to disqualifying dispositions were simply minor technical changes and also did not rise to the level of material modification.

14.2 Securities-Related Matters

Between 2002 and 2009, the SEC's most important work was to implement new rules under the Sarbanes-Oxley Act, including a massive overhaul of the executive compensation disclosure rules, and to deal with the aftermath of stock option backdating. In 2010, the Dodd-Frank Act spawned a new era of SEC rulemaking that is still under way. The disclosure rules are discussed in chapter 8; the Dodd-Frank Act is discussed in chapter 13. However, a few specific rulings are worth noting.

SEC Approves Path for Monetizing Employee Options

On June 17, 2009, the SEC issued a new rule allowing employees with vested stock options to use them as collateral to sell call options on the same company's stock as a way to obtain some cash value for the shares they can exercise. Call options are the right to buy shares at a given price over some period of time. If the stock price rises, the investor "calls" the contract and purchases the shares for the agreed-upon price. If the stock price declines, the right expires and the employee stock option holder gets to keep the fee paid for the right. In effect, this strategy hedges potential losses by giving up the right to some potential gains. Until this ruling, vested options could not be used as the sole collateral to purchase call options because such transactions were considered to be "naked."

At the time of the ruling, one company (iOptions Group LLC) had a patent on a business model to do this and had been urging the SEC to allow it. Many companies do not allow executives to engage in hedging strategies on their options because they want the executives to have a continued stake in the company after exercise.[5] Under the Dodd-Frank Act, the SEC is instructed to create rules requiring companies to disclose in their proxy statements whether any employees or directors are allowed to hedge company equity securities.

SEC Issues No-Action Letter for Internal Stock Market

In a no-action letter dated October 20, 2005, to James Dvorak of Venable LLP, the SEC staff stated that an internal stock market operated by a closely held company did not have to register as a broker-dealer. The company, TEOCO, is a small technology company in Fairfax, Virginia. It is employee-owned (the name is an acronym for The Employee-Owned Company) and at the time had 64 shareholders, all of whom were cur-

---

5.   The ruling can be found at www.sec.gov/rules/sro/ise/2009/34-60127.pdf.

rent or former employees or directors, and had 130 current or former employees and directors who held options. Its plan provides for periodic trades at an appraised value, with the company acting as the go-between. The plan operates within Rule 701 under the Securities Act of 1933 (a rule that, among other things, exempts from registration requirements sales of shares equal to less than 15% of a company's total shares in any one year that are offered as part of an employee compensation plan), and no sales to or purchases by individuals otherwise disqualified from purchasing or selling shares are allowed.

TEOCO planned to arrange for periodic trades, most likely once or twice a year, with a plan committee overseeing the process. Dates are set in advance, detailed information mailed to employees, and an informational meeting held. Employees can offer to sell shares they own or buy additional shares. The company established minimums and maximums on the number of shares that must be purchased or can be sold. As submitted, the plan limits shares offered for sale to not more than 50% of what an individual owns.

The company acts as the sole buyer and seller, rather than having transactions occurring between individuals. An independent third-party appraiser sets the sale price in advance, but the price must be revisited if there are material changes in the interim. Employees indicate how many shares they want to sell or buy and submit this to the company.

In the unlikely event the number of sale and purchase offers is equal, the company buys all the shares for sale and resells them all. More likely, there will be an imbalance. If there are more purchase offers, the company buys all the shares for sale, then parcels out remaining shares based on an equitable formula designed to give preference to smaller holders. If there are more sellers, the company accepts all offers to buy and then allocates the remaining number according to the same formula.

Because the company is buying and selling for its own account, not acting as an agent (especially a commissioned agent) of the sellers or buyers, the SEC accepted the argument that it is not a broker-dealer.

In December 2013, the SEC issued a proposal intended to make it easier for companies to create internal stock markets.[6] The proposal would change Regulation A, an existing exemption from registration for small offerings of up to $5 million in securities within a 12-month

---

6.   SEC release No. 2013-265.

period and not more than $1.5 million for existing securities holders. Under the current $1.5 million limit, many employee ownership companies have too many shares on offer to qualify for the exemption. The proposal would increase the thresholds to $50 million overall and $15 million for existing holders of the issuer's securities. It would still require significant reporting, generally comparable to those for public companies, but would exempt companies from blue sky compliance in each state in which they operate. Companies that wanted to offer less than $5 million overall per 12-month period and not more than $1.5 million for employee securities holders would be subject to somewhat less onerous reporting requirements.

14.3 Contract Cases Related to Stock Options

For all its technical specificity, the law applicable to employee stock rights is essentially contract law. So it is not surprising that the bulk of equity compensation litigation arises from disagreement over the meaning of a plan, grant, or other controlling document: i.e., contract disputes. For example, an inartfully drafted or ambiguous document may give confusing guidance—or no guidance at all—as to the treatment of equity rights in a change of control situation. Key terms may be undefined or inadequately defined. Oral representations may conflict with written documentation. As with any contract, the potential issues are limitless, and judicial decisions will be based on the specific facts of each situation. Further, in most contract cases, state law—rather than federal law—will control, and so the results may differ on the same facts from jurisdiction to jurisdiction.

Whenever possible, courts do their best to defer to a written document. However, the issuer (which is generally the drafter) cannot expect to rely on its own discretion in interpreting ambiguous language: the employee's understanding of his or her rights will also be considered by the courts.[7] If a company's actions are inconsistent with its documents, those actions may well support a reading of the document that supports the actions, rather than vice versa. Ignorance of plan documents—by either party—is not an excuse.

---

7.   See, e.g., *Sanchez v. Verio, Inc.* (5th Cir. Dec. 27, 2004).

14.3.1 Waiver, Oral Modification, and Related Claims

Employment-Practices Insurance Does Not Cover Stock Redemption Liability

In *Krueger Int'l Inc. v. Royal Indemnity Co.*, No. 06-2611 (7th Cir. Apr. 9, 2007), the U.S. Court of Appeals for the Seventh Circuit upheld a lower court's summary judgment, saying that employment-practice liability insurance does not cover an oral misrepresentation of a written stock option agreement between employees and the company because the agreement was a shareholder, not employment, agreement. Moreover, the misrepresentation (about the price at which employees could exercise their options) was by an officer to whom the company had delegated this task. The company later repudiated the representation that officer made to the employee. In any event, it could not file a claim under the oral misrepresentation clause of its insurance because that insurance is meant to cover things that the employer cannot control. The repudiation was within its control.

Failure to Follow Plan Procedure by Exercising in Writing Fatal to Claim, Even If Documents Were Ambiguous as to Post-Termination Exercise Period

In *Donaldson v. Digital General Systems*, 168 S.W.3d 909 (Tex. App.-5th July 22, 2005), before plaintiff Henry Donaldson's termination of employment, he negotiated a transition agreement with employer Digital General Systems (DGS) that purported to extend his post-termination exercise period from 30 days to one year. The agreement cross-referenced the DGS option plan as the governing document with respect to option terms. The plan document provided a default post-termination exercise period of 30 days and a maximum of six months. Six months after his termination, Donaldson called the DGS option administrator to explore exercising and was advised that his options had expired one month after his termination. Donaldson argued in state court that DGS had breached its contract with him by refusing to let him exercise within the one-year period. The trial court held that while the language of the documents was ambiguous, Donaldson's failure to submit a written exercise notice in and of itself invalidated his claim that DGS had failed to honor his exercise.

    Held: On appeal to the Texas Court of Appeals, affirmed for defendant DGS. Donaldson's failure to submit a written exercise notice in accordance with the terms of the option agreement was not excused by his conversation with DGS (to the effect that his options had expired). He had previously exercised three options, each time on the same written form, and he was aware of the requirements to do so in writing.

Choice of California Law in Stock Option Agreement Governs, Notwithstanding Employment Agreement

In *Oracle Corp. v. Falotti*, 319 F.3d 1106 (9th Cir. 2003), *cert. denied*, 540 U.S. 875 (2003), plaintiff Pier Carlo Falotti was a senior vice president of Oracle working in Switzerland pursuant to an employment agreement that was governed by Swiss law. At the time of his termination, his unvested options were cancelled. However, on the purported date of termination he visited a Swiss doctor to be treated for depression. He then filed a wrongful termination action in the U.S. District Court for the Northern District of California, contending that he was terminated because of his illness. Swiss law prohibits terminating an employee because of illness and requires a two-month notice prior to termination. Falotti argued that under his employment contract, Oracle was prohibited from canceling his right to exercise options for another four months: a two-month recovery period plus the two-month statutory notice period. The additional four-month period would have resulted in his options being vested and exercisable prior to termination. The district court granted summary judgment in favor of Oracle, holding that although Swiss law governed the employment contract, the option agreement (which included a choice of law provision) was governed by California law.

Held: summary judgment affirmed on appeal to the U.S. Court of Appeals for the Ninth Circuit. The stock option agreement, not the employment agreement, governed Falotti's stock option vesting. Even if under Swiss law Falotti was entitled to a four-month notice period, there was no requirement for him to continue to be eligible for stock option vesting during that period. The court deferred to the stock option agreement's grant of exclusive authority to Oracle's compensation committee to determine when an employee ceased to be employed for purposes of the stock plan.

Employee's Continuing Employment Indicated Agreement to Modification of Option Grant

In *Cochran v. Quest Software*, 328 F.3d 1 (1st Cir. 2003), plaintiff Brian Cochran was an at-will employee who received an option grant at hire, subject to standard vesting at the rate of 25% per year under the terms of the Quest option plan. During Cochran's first year of employment (before any options had vested), he was advised that his grant was being reduced due to his poor job performance. Notwithstanding the reduction, Cochran continued to work at the company. At the end of his first year, his employment was terminated, and when he exercised his options, it was for the reduced number of vested shares. Among other things, Cochran sued for breach of contract on a theory that the options had been unilaterally rescinded by Quest. On a motion for summary judgment, the U.S. District Court for Massachusetts held in favor of the defendant on all counts and dismissed the claims.

Held: on appeal to the U.S. Court of Appeals for the First Circuit, affirmed in favor of defendant. The appellate court upheld the trial court's finding that Cochran's behavior evidenced agreement to the modification of his option agreement, i.e., he voluntarily continued his at-will employment at Quest even after he knew about the reduction. Under Massachusetts law, options are not earned until vested. Thus, the reduction of the number of shares granted before the completion of the plaintiff's first year of employment was not (without more) a breach of contract.

14.3.2 Inconsistent Documents and Ambiguous Language

Challenge to Stock Option Award in Excess of Maximum Allowed in Plan Can Proceed

In *Pfeiffer v. Leedle*, No. 7831-VCP (Nov. 8, 2013), the Delaware Chancery Court allowed a shareholder to proceed with his lawsuit against Healthways' CEO and board. The suit challenged a stock option grant to the CEO that was in excess of the maximum allowed under the plan. The defendants argued that performance clauses in the plan made the grants appropriate, but the court concluded that because the grants clearly violated the unambiguous language of the governing documents for the plan, the business judgment rule, which allows boards broad leeway in making business decisions, did not apply.

Unclear Documents Cost Company

In *Graphic Packaging Holding Co. v. Humphrey,* No. 10-12015, 2010 WL 4608775 (Nov. 16, 2010), the Court of Appeals for the 11th Circuit upheld a district court's finding that a failure of plan documents to specifically state when an award of cash-settled restricted stock units (RSUs) was to be valued for the purpose of determining the amount to be paid out was a "notable" omission. As a result, because recovery of amounts previously paid out was involved, the burden was on the company to produce sufficient evidence to support a change of valuation date. The RSUs in question paid out six months after the executive's retirement in order to comply with Section 409A's waiting period for "specified employees." The company based the payout on its stock price at the date of the executive's retirement, but later determined that the payout should have been based on the lower stock price on the date of payout. The company demanded return of the deemed overpayment, but the retired executive refused. Both courts held that in the absence of a clear valuation mandate in the award documents, the company could not provide sufficient evidence to support a finding that the original payout was a mistake.

Ambiguity in Options Language Causes Problem

In *Lewitton v. ITA Software Inc.,* No. 08-3725 F, 3d 377 (Seventh Cir., Oct. 28, 2009), a former employee successfully claimed that he should have been able to exercise options that the company argued had not yet vested because performance conditions had not been met. ITA Software hired Derek Lewitton, in part, to oversee the development of a new product and made some of his vesting contingent on meeting certain revenue targets. However, if the project did not launch in a defined period of time, the contingency would not apply. The product was delayed and eventually put on the back burner, although some work was still being done. Lewitton left and exercised his options; the company claimed some of the options had not vested because the revenue targets had not been met. It contended the project had been scrapped, not delayed.

The U.S. Court of Appeals for the Seventh Circuit found in favor of the employee, holding that vesting occurred when the product failed to timely launch.

Like many options lawsuits, this one hinged on ambiguous language. Companies need to be very clear in defining exactly what the requirements are and need to anticipate any circumstances that make the seemingly clear language not so clear.

Inconsistencies Between General Memorandum and Specific Option Agreements are Resolved in Favor of Option Agreement

In *First Marblehead Corp. v. House*, 473 F.3d 1 (1st Cir. 2006), *affirming* 401 F. Supp. 2d 152 (D. Mass. 2005), Gregory House was an executive for First Marblehead who had experience as a trader and analyst of traded stock options before joining the firm. He assisted in setting up the company's option plan and was granted options. During his employment, House received a general memorandum from company counsel that described the terms of the plan (including a 10-year exercise period) but gave no details regarding post-termination exercise. When formal documentation was ultimately adopted, both the plan document and the grant agreements expressly stated that options must be exercised within 90 days of termination.

House terminated his employment in 1998 without exercising his options. At the time of his termination, he did not review (and claimed not to have received) his option agreements. Six years later, he attempted to exercise his vested options. The company filed for declaratory relief that the exercise was invalid, and House counterclaimed for breach of contract. He alleged that the company had misrepresented his exercise period as ten years, and that if he had known the period was three months, he would have exercised with that time period.

Held: affirming summary judgment in favor of First Marblehead, reversed and remanded. The U.S. Court of Appeals for the First Circuit upheld the District Court rejection of House's argument that the company was bound by a generic overview rather than by the specific agreement. (That court also noted that House was no "babe in the woods" and should have known to inquire about when to exercise his options after termination.) However, the court sent the case back to the trial court for jury trial on the issue of negligent misrepresentation: i.e., did he rely on the company's statements in failing to timely exercise?

In the subsequent jury trial, the jury found that House had, in fact, relied on the company's negligent misrepresentations. However, based on the testimony of an expert witness, the jury also concluded that House would not have exercised those options during the 90-day post termination period, even if he had known about it. The jury's verdict on this issue was also upheld by the Court of Appeals in *First Marblehead Corp v. House (II)*, No. 27-2789 (1st. Cir. September 8, 2008).

Strange Goings-on in Texas: Unenforceable Noncompete, Enforceable Forfeiture

In the strange case of *Olander v. Compass Bank*, 363 F.3d 560 (5th Cir. 2004), plaintiff Gary Olander was barred by a broad noncompete agreement from associating with interests contrary to his employer, Compass Bank. However, the contract also stated that if the clause were ruled invalid or unenforceable, then the clawback would kick in: i.e., Compass would be entitled to claim any profits from option exercises, plus any common stock held by Olander. Olander left Compass Bank to work for another bank in 2001, violating the terms of the agreement, but he won a declaratory judgment from the trial court that the noncompete was unenforceable. Compass then filed an action for restoration of profits under the clawback, which it lost at the trial level.

Held: on appeal to the U.S. Court of Appeals for the Fifth Circuit, both for and against plaintiff. The appellate court held that (1) the noncompete was unenforceable, and (2) because the noncompete was unenforceable, the clawback provision in the same contract requiring the executive to repay profits earned from exercising options was valid. Calling Olander's victory "pyrrhic," the court noted that the noncompete was unenforceable because the options were valuable only while Olander remained an employee of Compass (an "illusory" promise because Compass could terminate him at will). Nonetheless, the agreement clearly provided that if Olander won on the noncompete issue, he would lose on the option issue.

Option Acceleration Language Resolved with Reference to Whole Agreement

In *Sanchez v. Verio, Inc.*, No. 01-11341 (5th Cir. Dec. 27, 2004) (unpublished), plaintiff Rhonda Sanchez was employed by Verio from 1998 to 2000, receiving four option grants during that period, each of which vested at the rate of 25% per year during her employment. Her option agreement provided that options would fully vest if she was "terminated by the company or related entity without cause or by the optionee with good reason within 12 months of a change in control." At the time of Sanchez's termination, Verio was in M&A discussions, but the merger was not completed until four months after Sanchez left the company. Sanchez then attempted to exercise her unvested options based on the theory that the merger occurred "within 12 months" of her termination. The company rejected the exercise, arguing that notwithstanding the use of the word "within," acceleration could occur only while Sanchez was actually an employee of the company, which was not the case at the time of the change in control. Sanchez sued for breach of contract, and the jury found that because the language was ambiguous, the option should have vested in full as of the change in control.

Held: reversed by U.S. Court of Appeals for the Fifth Circuit. The appellate court determined that notwithstanding the use of the word "within," the language regarding timing of acceleration was unambiguous. Under the terms of the option, vesting could occur only during the optionee's employment at Verio. Sanchez was not employed at the time of the change in control so no acceleration was possible.

14.4 Equity Issues Related to Employment Disputes

When an employee leaves employment for a reason other than death or disability, a number of equity-related issues can arise that lead to a dispute. Employees who sue to retain options on the basis of wrongful termination have had mixed success in the cases reported below, largely because state law varies as to whether terminations without good cause vitiate compensation promises.

14.4.1 Effects of Termination

ERISA Does Not Apply to Individual Stock Plan

Occasionally, employees try to claim rights under the Employee Retirement Income Security Act (ERISA) for stock options, stock grants, and other individual equity plans. This argument usually fails because ERISA was not intended to cover these plans unless they are broad-based and retirement-focused. In *Bell v. Pfizer*, 2010 U.S. App. LEXIS 18111 (2nd Cir., Aug. 30, 2010), the U.S. Court of Appeals for the Second Circuit held that ERISA did not apply to a stock option plan that was not designed to be a retirement plan. Here, a retiree alleged that a miscommunication about her stock options at the time of her retirement was governed by ERISA because she received retirement plan information in the same document as equity plan information. Although the court denied the plaintiff's $327 million claim, the case reminds HR professionals and plan administrators of the importance of keeping exit communications about distinct types of benefits as separate communications or at least having the legal department review them before distribution.

Executive's Failure to Pay for Options on Termination Precludes Exercise

In *Deal v. Consumer Programs, Inc.*, No. 06-1067 (8th Cir. Dec. 6, 2006), a court agreed that a former executive could be denied the right to exercise her options because she did not provide a payment for their exercise. Peggy Deal had an agreement with the company that if she were terminated pursuant to a change in control, she would receive 200% of her salary plus a bonus. She also had stock options she could exercise within 90 days of termination. When Deal was terminated after a change in control, she was never paid the severance pay under the contract. She and her lawyer sent the company a letter asking to exercise the options, but with no payment. Deal contended that the payment would have come from the contested severance pay. The letter said that she was concerned that, under the circumstances, the company would simply keep the money and not exercise the options and give her the stock. Two letters were sent; the company responded to neither one. Deal sued. The company said the severance pay and options issues were separate. A district court gave summary judgment to Deal on severance pay, but not on options.

The appeals court affirmed the lower court's conclusion that Deal was due her severance pay, but it did not agree that she was due her options. Under Missouri law, which governed this case, an option can be exercised only through strict compliance with its terms. Had Deal provided the money for the options exercise, and the company still refused, she would have had grounds for recovery, but otherwise not.

14.4.2 Equity as Wages

The law continues to be split by jurisdiction on this issue. In the last several years, the California courts (both state and federal) have overwhelmingly held that equity compensation should be considered to be "wages" or "earnings" for purposes of California employment law. This position was advanced by a significant decision reached by the California Supreme Court in November 2009. However, most courts outside of California that have considered the issue have held that equity compensation constitutes something other than a "wage" for employment law purposes.

Court Allows Illinois Claim to Proceed, but Rejects Indiana Claim

In *Rawat v. Navistar International Corp.*, No. 1:08-cv-04305 (N.D. Ill. Jan. 4, 2012), an employee who worked in Illinois and another who worked in Indiana brought suit against Navistar International Corp. over the company's stock option plan. The plan required that employees exercise their options within three months of termination from the company. However, both employees ended their employment during a blackout period that lasted for more than two years. As a result, neither was able to exercise their options in the three-month window and their options expired.

Despite the similarity of their claims, only one plaintiff survived the motion to dismiss because of how the wage laws differ in the two states. Under the Indiana wage law, wages are defined as compensation for time worked and that is not linked to the financial success of the company. Because stock options are not included in that definition, the case was dismissed as to the Indiana employee. The employee who worked in Illinois survived the motion to dismiss because Illinois has a broader wage law that requires payment of "any other compensation."

Also at issue was a release signed by the Illinois employee. The court found that the language of the release did not unambiguously cover the stock options, and that communications between the company and the Illinois employee were further evidence that the stock options were not meant to be covered.

California Supreme Court Holds That Restricted Stock Constitutes Wages

In 2009, the California Supreme Court issued an unusually significant decision in the area of employment compensation. *Schachter v. Citigroup, Inc.* (S161385), Nov. 2, 2009, concerns Citigroup's restricted stock incentive compensation plan, pursuant to which employees could elect to receive a portion of annual earned compensation in the form of restricted company stock that vested over time. The restricted stock plan provided, however, that if a participating employee resigned, he or she would forfeit rights to any unvested restricted stock (as well as to the cash the employee would have received had he or she not opted for restricted shares instead).

Schachter had opted to receive restricted shares in lieu of cash during certain years. The restricted shares were awarded at a 25% discount below market price at the time of award. Schachter quit and therefore lost the value of not-yet-vested restricted stock. He claimed the restricted stock plan violated two sections of the California Labor Code, sec. 201 (which requires unpaid earned wages to be paid upon discharge), and sec. 221 (which prohibits an employer from "collecting or receiving from an employee any part of wages theretofore paid").

The court, in a ruling that generated much laudatory comment by employment defense firms, found that Schachter had, in fact, received all of his earned compensation. He had simply voluntary agreed to exchange part of it for restricted stock that would have limited and conditional present value (the stock could be voted and would accrue dividends before vesting) and would not fully vest until two years after the date he received it. In other words, Schachter—who was not required by his employer to take any part of his compensation in restricted stock—made his own decision to gamble part of his compensation by purchasing discount restricted stock the value of which he would not obtain unless he chose to remain employed through the vesting period. The fact that stock did not vest was a function of his own decision to leave. Frankly, notwithstanding the excitement of the employment defense bar, the decision of the Supreme Court (which affirmed a decision of the Court of Appeal) was not particularly surprising. The restricted stock used in Schachter is not different in material respects from most other sorts of equity (or deferred) compensation that is subject to vesting requirements.

What the employment defense firms have not commented on—and what we see as the more significant aspect of the Supreme Court's decision—is the first absolutely clear statement by that court that shares of restricted stock (and, implicitly—but necessarily—all equity compensation) are "wages" within the meaning of the California Labor Code. In 1999 the Ninth Circuit, in *IBM v. Bajorek*, 191 F.3d 1033, had held otherwise. Bajorek's IBM equity compensation package was different from Schachter's. Bajorek was permitted to exercise stock options after his termination—but only if he agreed not to compete against IBM post-termination. Bajorek exercised stock options worth over $900,000. His agreement provided that if he went to work for a competitor of IBM within six months of termination, he would forfeit the value of the options. The Ninth Circuit ruled for IBM. In so doing, it not only applied its own judicially created "narrow restraint" doctrine to hold IBM's post-employment non-compete enforceable, despite the clear language of sec. 16600 of California's Business & Professions Code, but it held that stock options are not "wages" within the meaning of the California Labor Code. Thus, Bajorek's claim that the agreement constituted a violation of section 221 of the Labor Code (precluding an employer from compelling a kickback of earned "wages") was not applicable.

Bajorek was an astounding result, and was roundly criticized for a decade. It was, however, an effective tool for defense counsel seeking to defend post-employment non-competes, particularly when designed to be self-enforcing by operation of equity compensation forfeiture provisions. In 2008, however, in *Edwards v. Arthur Andersen LLP* (2008) 44 Cal.4th 937, the California Supreme Court emphatically ruled that the Ninth Circuit's "limited restraint" doctrine was not the law in California and that sec. 16600 invalidated all contractual restraints on competition—"limited" or otherwise—other than the (non-applicable) express statutory exceptions to 16600.

But *Edwards* did not discuss the other widely criticized Bajorek holding; that equity compensation was not "wages" under the Labor Code's definition. Schachter rectifies that omission. After discussing the Court of Appeal's specific holding that restricted stock "constituted a wage" within the meaning of the Labor Code, the Court cited its own precedent, noting that "[w]e construe the term 'wages' broadly to include not only the periodic monetary earnings of the employee but also the other benefits to which he is entitled as a part of his compensation." The Court's subsequent analysis (which determined that Schachter had received all of his earned "wages," but that he had decided to contractually "gamble" cash—which he could have retained—for qualified and contingent rights to stock that may have been worth more had he not triggered the forfeiture provision by re-signing) proceeded from the finding that the restricted stock did, in fact, comprise "wages."

Schachter's clear holding that restricted stock and other deferred equity compensation is a form of wages is extremely significant for California employees. First, a suit over rights to such deferred equity compensation is now a suit for unpaid wages—a statutory and public policy suit in California. Thus, a prevailing employee plaintiff will be awarded attorney's fees, thereby making the litigation attractive to the plaintiffs' bar, even if the amount at issue does not warrant what would otherwise be the litigation cost. Second, in the arbitration context, the employee plaintiff will be accorded the benefit of the *Armendariz* protections (the California Supreme Court's attempt to mitigate the employer advantage in employer/employee pre-dispute arbitration agreement contexts); i.e., the employer will have to pay the arbitration costs, including hefty arbitrator fees that will often exceed the amount at issue for modestly compensated employees. The *Armendariz* protections are only accorded to employee plaintiffs where they bring claims involving violation of specific statutes or fundamental public policy. Now that equity compensation has been authoritatively recognized to be "wages," an employee can bring a $75,000 stock option compensation claim in arbitration without concern that his half of a $700 per hour arbitrator's fee will exceed his likely award.

Stock Options Constitute 'Performance Bonuses' for Purposes of Calculating Disability Benefits

McAfee v. Metropolitan Life Insurance Co., No. 05-00227 (E.D. Cal. WBS KJM Dec. 11, 2008), involved an employee who participated in the company's disability insurance plan, under which employees were entitled to receive benefits in an amount based on their pre-disability earnings. At trial, the U.S. District Court for the Eastern District of California held that disability benefits should be calculated based on 12-month pre-disability earnings, including "performance bonuses." In a prior decision, the court held that the plaintiff's stock options were awarded to him through the company's executive incentive compensation plan and should be treated as a "performance bonus" for these purposes. When calculating the number of shares contemplated, MetLife used a running average number of shares over a longer historic period than 12 months, thus calculating a drastically smaller number of shares. The court held that MetLife could not rewrite the plan to suit its purposes to discount the value due the participant.

Capital Accumulation Plan, ESPP Not Covered By Massachusetts Payment of Wages Statute

In *Weems v. Citigroup Inc.*, No. 1:00-cv-11912-NG (March 31, 2011), the U.S. District Court for the District of Massachusetts ruled in favor of Citigroup, holding that the company's Capital Accumulation Plan did not violate state or federal laws despite having a forfeiture clause. Under the voluntary plan, employees could elect to have some of their wages paid in the form of restricted stock, with the condition that the shares would be forfeited if the employee voluntarily left the company or was dismissed for cause before the shares vested. While wage forfeiture clauses are generally disfavored in employment contracts, the court held that Citigroup's plan was not against public policy given its voluntary nature and unambiguous, evident forfeiture provisions. The plan has been challenged in numerous other jurisdictions with the same result.

In an earlier state case, *Weems v. Citigroup, Inc.*, No. SJC-10029 No. 993-429 (Jan. 30, 2009), the Massachusetts Supreme Judicial Court came to a similar conclusion with respect to the same plan on a labor law issue, holding that restricted stock made available to employees through an employee stock plan do not qualify as "wages" under the Massachusetts Payment of Wages statute. Under the Citigroup plan, employees could elect to use a portion of their salaries to purchase restricted stock at a discount. Stock acquired under each program was subject to a defined vesting period, meaning that employees forfeited unvested stock if they voluntarily left Citigroup's employ or were terminated for cause prior to the end of the vesting period. The plaintiffs, a group of former employees, left Citigroup voluntarily before the end of the applicable vesting periods under the plan. Citigroup thus determined that they had forfeited unvested stock under the program. The plaintiffs sued, alleging that the forfeiture violated the Payment of Wages statute. The federal district court asked the Supreme Judicial Court to clarify whether the restricted stock awarded or purchased under the plan constituted "wages" within the meaning of the statute.

The court held that it was a bona fide employee stock purchase plan (ESPP) and thus, by statute, expressly excluded from the statute. In reaching this conclusion, the court assumed that participation in the program was truly voluntary and that benefits under the plan were not illusory. In making these assumptions, the court suggested that it might have reached a different conclusion on different facts. The decision clarified that truly discretionary payments are not within the scope of the Payment of Wages statute.

Stock Options Not Wages Under Maryland Law

The plaintiff in *Varghese v. Honeywell International Inc.*, 424 F.3d 511 (4th Cir. 2005), Thomas Varghese, worked for Honeywell for 16 years before taking a leave of absence to pursue graduate studies. He vested in 4,800 options during that time. Varghese requested reinstatement at Honeywell in May 1999 but was told that his job was no longer available. After waiting until October, Varghese wrote to say he was seeking termination and severance pay. He attempted to exercise his options in October and November, but the company refused to permit him to do so, saying that it had backdated his termination to May and that the plan allowed him only three months to exercise the options after termination. Varghese sued Honeywell, claiming a violation of the Maryland Wage Payment and Collection Law (MWP&CL). The jury awarded him $337,000 in enhanced damages under that law.

Held: Reversed on appeal to the U.S. Court of Appeals for the Fourth Circuit. The appellate court construed the MWP&CL in such a way as to exclude options from the definition of "wages." After reviewing Maryland case law, the court concluded that remuneration must be guaranteed in order to be a "wage" for these purposes and that options are discretionary payments only.

14.4.3 Noncompete Agreements, Recaptures, and Stock Option Forfeitures

Texas High Court Allows Stock Options as Consideration for Noncompete Agreement

In *Marsh USA Inc. v. Cook*, No. 09-0558 (June 24, 2011), the Supreme Court of Texas held that stock options are sufficient consideration for requiring an employee to sign a noncompete agreement. This decision is significant because it provides a new avenue for companies in Texas to enforce noncompete agreements, which are generally disfavored by the courts.

No Clawback Indemnification Allowed

In *In re: DHB Industries Inc. Derivatives Litigation* (September 30, 2010), the Second Circuit Court of Appeals overturned a federal district court's approval of a settlement agreement in a consolidated derivative and class action suit under which DHB Industries agreed to indemnify its former CEO and CFO from liability under Section 304 of the Sarbanes-Oxley Act of 2002. Section 304 requires that a CEO or CFO of a public company reimburse the company for any incentive compensation received or stock sale profits recognized during the 12-month period following the filing of a financial statement that is subsequently required to be restated as a result of misconduct. The Second Circuit held that private parties may not sue to enforce Section 304, and that because only the SEC can enforce Section 304, only the SEC should be permitted to settle a Section 304 claim. Although the case involved an indemnification provision in a settlement agreement, the logic of the ruling could extend to indemnification provisions in companies' charter documents and in directors' and officers' liability insurance policies.

The ruling may also have potential implications for the compensation clawback provisions in the Dodd-Frank Act. The SEC had not yet proposed rules connected with this provision of the Dodd-Frank Act as of this writing in 2013.

Summary Judgment Denied in "Faithless Servant" Case Requiring
Executive to Forfeit Phantom Stock Benefits

In *Foley v. American Electric Power*, No. WL 571886, 37 EBC 1663 (S.D. N.Y. Mar. 7, 2006), a federal district court refused to grant summary judgment to a former executive who claimed that he was entitled to the value of his phantom stock awards even though he had been terminated for misconduct after it was revealed he made false reports of energy trading activities to trade publications. The executive did not personally benefit from the reports, but they did arguably hurt the company.

Foley had deferred 90% of his phantom equity plan income, worth more than $2 million at termination. The company later found out about the false reports and refused to pay the claim based on the "faithless servant" doctrine. The company did not contend that had it known, it would have required forfeiture of the benefit. Instead, it said that it was setting off the award against the damages due to the company. The executive contended that the plan had no specific forfeiture provision, so he was due the money. The company successfully convinced the court that it had a right to the offset. The court noted that if there had been a specific nonforfeiture provision, the issue would have been different, but, lacking that, the company had the right to recoup losses caused by employee disloyalty, whether or not the executive benefited.

The decision was only on a summary judgment motion; the case then had to be tried on the facts.

14.4.4 Treatment of Equity in Corporate Transactions

In the best of all worlds, every equity incentive plan would include a specific provision addressing what happens to outstanding employee rights at the time of a merger, acquisition, or other corporate transaction. Many plans and agreements, however, are ambiguous on how to treat such matters or fail to address them at all.

No Obligation to Make Claim for Constructive Termination

In *Sluimer v. Verity, Inc.*, 49 EBC 1238 (May 20, 2010), the U.S. Court of Appeals for the Ninth Circuit upheld a lower court's ruling that an executive displaced by a corporate change in control was not required to give notice of constructive termination (commonly required in change in control provisions attached to equity compensation awards) until after receiving sufficient detail about the proposed post-change position to determine whether the position met the "substantial reduction in responsibilities" contemplated by the award provisions. The court specifically held that, until the executive was given a clear picture of future responsibilities, there could be no finding of constructive termination by the company and, thus, no obligation for the executive to make a claim for benefits under the provisions of the award.

AT&T's Admission That Options Have Future Value Was Properly Considered

In *AT&T Corp. v. Lillis*, No. 490 (Del. March 9, 2009), the Delaware Supreme Court held that AT&T's admission that stock options have future value was properly included in granting former employees $11.3 million to compensate them for losses of benefits from the cancelation and exchange of their options pursuant to the merger of their former employer, MediaOne Corp., with AT&T. AT&T contended that the plan language was ambiguous as to whether the new options should reflect the potential future value of the old out-of-the money options when exchanged. But in the original trial, the company had admitted the options did have value. Later, the company said that the plan language was determinative and withdrew its admission. The court ruled that the former admission did show that the options in fact had value.

Employment for Stock Option Purposes Ended When Merger Closed

In *Kinsey v. Cendant Corp.*, No. 04-CV-0582-RWS (S.D.N.Y. Nov. 14, 2007), the U.S. district court for the Southern District of New York ruled that Cendant Corp. properly handled a stock option granted to an employee of Fairfield Resorts Inc. upon the close of Cendant's acquisition of Fairfield in April 2001. An employee of Fairfield was hired by Cendant upon acquisition; thus, his employment by Fairfield was terminated at that time. Under the employee's stock option agreement, he had one year to exercise his Fairfield options before they expired. The employee contended that because his employment did not terminate but transferred to Cendant, his options should not expire due to termination. The court affirmed that employment terminated when the merger closed, so the employee had only the original exercise grace period to exercise before the option expired.

Acceleration of Vesting Triggered Only If Merger Is Actually Completed

In *Bohan v. Honeywell International Inc.*, 366 F.3d 606 (8th Cir. 2004), plaintiffs argued they were entitled to full acceleration of vesting of their stock options as of the date that shareholders of Honeywell and General Electric had approved a merger agreement. Shareholder approval was obtained in January 2002, but the merger fell through in July when European regulators blocked it. The employees contended that, under the terms of the plan, shareholder approval was sufficient to trigger acceleration. At trial, the district court determined that the plan required that a merger had to be "completed"; i.e., approval was not enough. In fact, the plan specifically stated that "the Company will no longer survive as an independent publicly held corporation" and provided that option vesting would accelerate "on or following . . . a merger."

Held: affirmed by U.S. Circuit Court for the Eighth Circuit, for defendant. The plan language requiring shareholder approval could not be read separately from the language specifying that acceleration would occur only on a merger.

Transferable Options

Contents

In the late 1990s, transferable employee stock options (TSOs) generated a great deal of interest and activity, particularly among estate planners. In 2007 TSOs resurfaced, this time as a potential source of liquidity for employee optionees due to a much-watched collaboration between Google, Inc., and Morgan Stanley.[1] This chapter briefly summarizes the various issues raised by their use.

15.1   Why the Interest in TSOs?

TSOs are primarily interesting because of their estate tax implications. Companies should note that any time a Section 16 insider transfers a TSO as a gift, the indirect beneficial ownership must be reported on the insider's forms. Completed gifts need to be reported, but deferred year-end reporting on Form 5 is generally available. (Voluntary early reporting on Form 4 is permitted on Table II with transaction code

---

1.   The program, which provided for an online auction of vested stock options, began in April 2007. Complete information on the Google program can be found in its April 20, 2007, *Prospectus for Participants in the 2004 Stock Plan*, available on EDGAR at www.sec.gov. The Google program raises numerous securities law, tax, and valuation issues. For a thoughtful outline of the initial issues raised by the Google program see the May-June 2007 issues of *The Corporate Executive* and *The Corporate Counsel*. Although the auction idea generated lots of attention, we are not aware of any major public companies other than Google that have adopted similar programs on this scale.

G.) Usually, *bona fide* gifts are not treated as sales for purposes of the Section 16(b) short-swing profits recapture rule (i.e., liability purposes).[2]

Because options can be transferred without securities law penalties, TSOs offer the executive the ability to transfer high-worth options out of his or her taxable estate before death. Such a transfer has the dual benefit of reducing the total value of the estate *and* providing already taxed cash outside the estate with which to pay estate taxes.[3]

However, one should not be deceived into believing that TSOs are a panacea. As more fully explained below, statutory options are never transferable under the Code. Moreover, employee stock option plans typically reward employees for past services, provide incentive for current services, and encourage retention for future services. Accordingly, it is logical that such stock plans will continue to place limits on who can receive the benefits of an option.

15.2 Limits on TSOs

Attractive as the benefits of TSOs may be, many factors limit their use. At a minimum, the following considerations apply:

1. *Appropriate Transferees.* The Exchange Act places no limits on who may be the recipient of a transferred option, and Rule 16b-5 specifically exempts gift transfers (i.e., transfers that are not "for value"). However, for practical purposes, companies will be unlikely to permit sales of untradable options to third parties. Instead, most practitioners advise companies to use this as an estate planning tool, contractually limiting option transfers to gift transfers to a family member or trust. In fact, companies may wish to further narrow eligible transferees so as to retain better control over option exercises. Limited transferability is particularly important with respect to employee options because taxation and exercisability of the option are generally conditioned upon the employment status

---

2. See section 8.5.2.

3. The exercised TSO will have already been taxed for both gift and income tax purposes. A complete discussion of the estate and gift tax consequences of a TSO is beyond the scope of this chapter.

of the optionee. Note that this issue frequently arises in the context of options that are divided pursuant to a divorce decree.[4]

2. *Statutory Stock Options.* Under the Code, ISOs and options granted under a tax-qualified ESPP (e.g., a Section 423 plan) must be nontransferable during the lifetime of the optionee. Upon the optionee's death, the option may be exercised by the estate. Any lifetime transfer will disqualify the option for tax purposes unless the transfer is to a grantor trust controlled by the optionee and the optionee is the sole beneficial owner while the option is held in trust. An option that is transferred to a trust in a manner such that the option holder is considered the beneficiary of the trust still qualifies as a statutory option. Except in this narrow instance, only an NSO may be a TSO.[5]

3. *Gift Tax Valuation.* The transfer of a TSO as a gift (whether to an individual or a trust) is subject to gift tax for which the donor is responsible. For these purposes, the TSO will be valued as of the date of transfer, with different vesting tranches valued separately. Because employee stock options are generally not tradable, there is little guidance (and much argument!) on how such options should be valued.[6] Additional complications attach if the TSO is for both vested and unvested stock. The gift must be "complete" or the transfer will be ineffective. The IRS ruled in Rev. Rul. 98-21 that transfers of unvested options are not completed gifts for these purposes. Accordingly, a donor who transfers unvested NSOs will owe taxes on the spread at the time of vesting. If a TSO is consid-

---

4. See chapter 11.

5. See Sections 422(b) and 423(b) of the Code, and Treas. Reg. § 1.421-1(b)(2).

6. The gift tax regulations provide a general standard for valuation of property, with no specific guidance as to stock options. In addition, throughout the 1990s employee options were the subject of a heated debate among practitioners, legislators, and the SEC regarding the appropriate methodology for valuation. See also Rev. Proc. 98-34 (valuation safe harbor for gifted stock options requires nondiscounted, recognized pricing model). Valuation for gift tax purposes remains subject to its own regulations.

ered to be a grant of a future interest, it will not be eligible for the annual gift tax exclusion.[7]

4. *Income Tax Issues.* Neither the recipient nor the donor is taxed on the transfer of the TSO. Exercise by the recipient will result in income to the employee/donor (or to the employee/donor's estate, if he or she is deceased). All of the normal tax rules regarding vesting and income tax withholding will apply to the donor and the company. The recipient takes a stepped-up basis in the stock (equal to the exercise price plus the ordinary income realized by and taxed to the donor on exercise).[8] Transfers of compensatory stock options to related persons (including family members) are not dispositions of such options: i.e., the donor may not argue that for purposes of Section 83, the ordinary income component of the transaction "closed" at the date of the transfer.[9]

5. *Language of the Plan.* Most stock option plans contain language requiring all options to be nontransferable. Before granting TSOs, the plan should be reviewed and amended if necessary. State securities and/or corporate laws may also require nontransferability and should be double-checked for exemptions.[10] Amendments to permit transferability (to either the plan or an NSO) do not require shareholder approval for tax, accounting, or securities purposes. For accounting purposes, plan amendments should not have adverse consequences; however, adding a TSO feature to an already-existing option grant may result in a new measurement date.

---

7. For a thoughtful discussion of transferable options in estate planning, see P. Melcher and W. Rosenbloom, "Transferable Options: When They Work, When They Don't," *Practical Tax Lawyer* 15, no.1 (fall 2000): 5.

8. See Section 83 of the Code. If the exercise is by the estate, the spread will be subject to income tax reporting but not to withholding, although depending on timing, FICA/FUTA withholding may be required. Rev. Rul. 86-109.

9. T.D. 9067.

10. For example, the California Corporate Securities Act allows transferability similar (but not identical) to that permitted under the federal rules, including lifetime transfers to "immediate family." California Commissioner's Rules § 260.140.41(d).

6. *Tradability of TSO Stock.* The Form S-8 rules permit registration of stock received upon exercise of transferable options by family members and trusts for family members when those options were transferred pursuant to a gift or domestic relations order.[11] Such transfers must be gifts, which means that they may not be "for value." For purposes of S-8 eligibility, "family member" includes any child, stepchild, grandchild, parent, stepparent, grandparent, spouse, former spouse, sibling, niece, nephew, mother-in-law, father-in-law, son-in-law, daughter-in-law, brother-in-law, or sister-in-law, including adoptive relationships, any person sharing the employee's household (other than a tenant or employee), a trust in which these persons have more than 50% beneficial interest, a foundation in which these persons (or the employee) control the management of assets or any other entity in which these persons (and/or the employee) own more than 50% voting interests.

7. *Tracking.* The holder of the TSO must understand any plan and statutory limits on exercise and tradability. In addition, the company needs to be aware of issues related to the nonemployee optionee's lack of access to material information at the time of exercise.

15.2.1 Regulations on Option Transfers to Related Parties

Regulations governing transfers of compensatory stock options between optionees and related persons under Section 83 of the Code exclude certain family members and control group members from favorable tax treatment under the "arm's length disposition" rules otherwise set out in the regulations to Section 83.[12]

In general, Section 83 permits a taxpayer who disposes of an option to a third party to close the compensatory portion of the transaction at the time of transfer rather than at the time of exercise. Treas. Reg. § 1.83-7 is intended to address a tax-avoidance scheme that allowed optionees to take advantage of the arm's length disposition rules for options while still retaining control of the ultimate exercise. Under the terms of the scheme, the optionee would sell an unexercised NSO to

---

11. SEC Release No. 33-7646 (April 7, 1999).

12. Treas. Reg. § 1.83-7.

a relative or family limited partnership in which the optionee had a substantial interest (and implicit control). In exchange, the optionee accepted a long-term unsecured note that would come due only when the buyer exercised the option and sold the stock. This resulted in no tax to the optionee until the note was paid off, and no tax (or note payments) to the buyer until the stock was sold. In essence, the transaction created ISO deferral treatment for an NSO, minus the alternative minimum tax problem.[13]

15.3 Recommendations

While TSOs may offer opportunities for executive planning, companies need to be careful to consider all of the issues attendant to amending old options (or granting new ones) to include transferability features.

---

13. For an extensive discussion of the IRS's view on Treas. Reg. § 1.83-7, see its Coordinated Issues Paper titled "Transfer or Sale of Compensatory Stock Options or Restricted Stock to Unrelated Persons," effective October 15, 2004, and posted on the IRS website at www.irs.gov/pub/irs-utl/compensatory_final.pdf.

Reloads, Evergreens, Repricings, and Exchanges

Over the years, issuers have developed certain plan features to encourage employees to continue investing in the company's stock. The techniques described briefly below are lightning rods for opposing philosophies on equity compensation. On the one hand, the techniques ensure that shares of stock will be available for use as employee incentives on an ongoing basis. Companies generally view this as a positive long-term compensation tool. On the other hand, most of these techniques are currently viewed with suspicion by institutional shareholders and the public at large. Such critics view reloads and evergreen provisions as dilutive devices that inappropriately compensate executives at the expense of shareholders.[1] Repricings saw a resurgence in 2009 as a logical (and low-cost) response to the wholesale devaluation of employee equity after the financial collapse of late 2008. As always, however, even the most logical public company repricing requires a certain amount of public relations finesse to counter misperceptions of abuse, educate the shareholders, and avoid angering watchdog groups.

16.1 Reloads

A reload grant is intended to provide the optionee with a continuing option grant while he or she remains an employee of the company. Typically, the optionee's grant will provide that, upon exercise of an option with stock (a "stock swap"), the optionee will receive an additional option for the same number of shares that were tendered to effect the exercise.[2] The reload option will be priced at the fair market value of the stock on the date of its grant. Other terms—such as vesting restrictions, exercise schedule, and term—may be exactly the same as the original grant, or may be on an accelerated (or shorter term) basis. Reload grants are subject to the same tax, accounting, and securities rules as are any ISO or NSO. In addition, for purposes of Section 162(m) of the Code, each reload grant will count against the annual "performance-based" limit on the date of grant. For accounting purposes, under ASC 718 a reload provision does not factor into the determination of grant date fair value. When a reload option is actually granted, it is accounted for as a separate award.

Companies may provide for automatic reloads for all employees or for a class of employees such as top executives, make automatic reloads a feature of specific grants, or award reload grants at the board's discretion only. In designing reload provisions, however, it is important to

---

1. Some consulting firms and organizations publish annual surveys tracking the attitudes of shareholders on option matters, and these surveys have reflected a growing concern among larger investors. For example, Institutional Shareholder Services (ISS), a consulting company that advises institutional shareholders on proxy voting, is well-known for its negative recommendations on stock pool increases.

2. For a detailed discussion of stock swaps, see section 7.3 of chapter 7.

note that the addition of automatic reloads may be instantly rejected by institutional shareholders. As a result, they have become extremely rare.

16.2 Evergreen Provisions

In a sense, an evergreen provision is a reload for the issuer's plan rather than for an individual grant. Evergreen provisions permit an annual increase in the number of shares available under the plan with a one-time shareholder approval (i.e., at the time the evergreen provision is approved), if not otherwise required by stock exchange rules (see below). The evergreen provision may be for a specific number of additional shares or may be a percentage increase based on outstanding shares at a designated date, and it may continue for the life of the plan or for a limited period of years (i.e., five years). Note that even where the evergreen is automatic, the S-8 registration statement for the plan will need to be amended each year to reflect the annual increase.

A key advantage of an evergreen provision is that once approved, it reduces both the technical and pragmatic issues involved with going back to the shareholders to ask for additional shares. As an initial matter, the board of directors must be encouraged to use special vigilance in computing the number of shares necessary to fund its plans for a foreseeable period. In recent years, shareholders (particularly institutional shareholders) have been increasingly reluctant to approve automatic additions to employee stock plans.

Based on this reluctance, practically speaking, only privately held companies or public companies with limited institutional investors are in a position to use an evergreen. Pre-IPO companies may adopt an evergreen provision prior to the IPO for use after the IPO; however, in recent years this strategy has been used more frequently with ESPPs than with omnibus plans.

16.2.1 Tax Limitations

The statutory option rules require that a plan (whether an ISO plan or an ESPP) state at the time of shareholder approval the maximum aggregate number of shares that may be issued under the plan as statutory stock options. Such number may be either a stated number or a definite number arrived at by a percentage or formula calculation based on the number of outstanding, issued, or authorized shares at the time the plan is adopted.[3] Thus, if an evergreen provision is intended to apply to ISOs or ESPP options, that portion of the evergreen applicable to such options must comply with the tax rules. For example, a workable evergreen provision could use the following language: "1% of all shares outstanding on January 1 of each year will be added to the plan; provided that with respect to ISOs, the addition shall be 200,000 shares per year."[4]

16.2.2 Nonapproved v. Approved Plans

Both the securities laws and stock exchange rules seriously limit the availability of nonapproved plans, as noted in chapter 4. Moreover, we can assume that institutional shareholders will have the same issues with nonapproved plans as with approved plans, i.e., the dilutive effect of such plans. If shareholders are unhappy with the overall stock plan strategy, they may be loath to approve additions to the plans that require shareholder approval. For this reason, companies that decide to use nonapproved plans should take care to establish sufficient limitations to allay shareholder fears about overuse of equity compensation. For example, nonapproved plans might be used solely for defined performance rewards or divisional merit grants for non-officers. Alternatively, they might serve as a limited stopgap measure to avoid additional accounting charges on ordinary grants if the company runs out of shares before an opportunity to obtain shareholder approval.

Assuming that shareholder approval for the plan is required under the stock exchange rules, adding an evergreen provision will require additional approval, regardless of whether the plan is an ISO plan. Both Nasdaq and the NYSE also impose a 10-year term limit on any plan with an evergreen provision. If the plan has a term longer than 10 years, Nasdaq requires new approval every 10 years, and NYSE requires shareholder approval every year there is an increase.

---

3.   Treas. Reg. § 1.422-2(b)(3); Treas. Reg. § 1.423-2(c)(3).

4.   Treas. Reg. § 1.422-2(b)(3). It would also be permissible to state that the ISO addition would be 1% of the outstanding shares on the date of adoption; however, in most cases the issuer will know what that number is on the date of adoption.

16.3 Repricing Programs

Much has been said and written over the years about how to deal with options in a down-market scenario. When the market falls and anxiety over employee retention rises, companies may rush to reprice or exchange "underwater" employee stock options (options that have an exercise price above the fair market value of the underlying stock). Repricing was particularly popular—and egregious—in the months following the stock market drop in 1987 and in the panic of 2000–2001. Experience shows that despite the issues associated with adjusting option pricing, it is inevitable that issuers will wish to reassess options that are no longer "in the money" (e.g., options that no long have an exercise price that is below the fair market value of the underlying stock) any time the market is poised for a downward correction. Public companies had a similar response to the financial crisis that began in 2008, which left many employees holding options that were so far underwater that they provided no incentivizing purpose at all. From the employer perspective, if employee options (unlike investor warrants) are intended to serve as a key element of the compensation package, they lose their attractiveness once they are underwater.

Typically, in a repricing program the board of directors will set a repricing date and invite employees to trade underwater options for restricted stock or units or for new options priced as of that date. As a general rule, the repriced options will require employees to give up some of the benefits of the original grants: for example, the repriced options may be for fewer shares (i.e., one new share for two old shares) or may have a different vesting schedule from the original options. Other typical conditions are blackout periods and vesting schedule set-backs. For example, the new grant may require that the optionee (1) accept an extended vesting period and (2) agree to a six-month blackout period during which he or she may not exercise for otherwise vested shares.

16.3.1 Corporate Considerations

Before adopting a repricing program, the board of directors should carefully consider the ramifications to the shareholders and make a determination as to the overall value of repricing to the company. The courts have long considered the issue of whether inappropriate repricing might involve corporate waste. Generally, lawyers advise that when the board of directors reprices options (particularly on a large scale), it should include new conditions on the replacement grants so as to ensure sufficient consideration to counter a shareholder challenge based on corporate waste.

As noted above, many companies again turned to repricing as an answer to the devastating impact the 2008 financial crisis had on equity compensation grants held by employees. Unfortunately, given previous experience with the market perception of wholesale employee option repricing, companies must still take special care when launching a repricing program, doing so only after careful consultation with legal counsel and accounting advisors. Although the accounting consequences that discouraged repricing have largely disappeared under ASC 718, the technique frequently involves real economic costs to the company. Moreover, there may be costs in terms of perception, as shareholders—particularly institutional investors—often have serious issues with the philosophy inherent to pricing adjustments. In particular, opponents argue that options are not a guarantee of income but rather are intended to reflect the fortunes of the company and the employees' contribution to those fortunes. From the investor perspective, programs that adjust pricing offer downside protection to employees that is not otherwise available to shareholders.

Companies need to be aware that such concerns may give rise to litigation, particularly if there is a perception of wide-scale dilution as a result of the price adjustment. To this end, before adopting a protection program, the board of directors should carefully consider the ramifications to the shareholders in making a determination as to the overall value to the company. The company is best advised to ensure that the program is approved by a majority of its independent "disinterested" directors, so as to counter shareholder lawsuits based on self-dealing or breach of fiduciary duty. In fact, in view of the governance concerns expressed by the Sarbanes-Oxley Act of 2002 and Dodd-Frank Act of 2010, boards may wish to consider retaining independent counsel to advise the compensation committee with respect to any potential large-scale option offers.[5]

---

5.   For an up-to-date collection of interesting case references and comments on recent securities law litigation in this area, see the University of Denver's website www.theracetothebottom.org.

16.3.2 Tax Considerations

If the repricing affects NSOs only, there will be limited adverse tax consequences to the optionee or to the company. However, a tax issue may arise in a repricing for top executives under the Section 162(m) $1 million cap. Treas. Reg. § 1.162-27(e)(2)(vi)(B) provides that both the original option and the repriced replacement will be counted against the annual compensation limitation when computing the cap.[6] Although a single repricing to fair market value should not as a rule cause adverse tax consequences under Section 409A, companies that engage in multiple repricings should proceed with caution: if the strike price appears to be variable, it could be treated as a discount (from the initial grant) option for purposes of Section 409A.

A repricing offer will not result in a modification of an ISO unless the offer remains outstanding for more than 30 days or is accepted. Note that canceled options that were scheduled to vest in the year when the cancellation occurs continue to count against the $100,000 limit for that year.[7] Because of their earlier grant date, the canceled options will be counted before the newly granted options. Thus, if the replacement options are also scheduled to vest in the year in which the repricing occurs, any that exceed the $100,000 limit will be disqualified and treated as NSOs.

16.3.3 Securities Law Issues

Although publicly traded companies may have to seek shareholder approval to meet exchange listing requirements, no special shareholder approval requirements are connected with repricings for securities law purposes. However, the employer has many other obligations under the Exchange Act with respect to a repricing. First, any participation in the repricing by Section 16 insiders will be reportable events under Section 16(a).[8] Second, any participation by a named executive officer must be discussed in the narrative accompanying the Summary Compensation table in the company's proxy statement. Third, in the early 21st century,

---

6. See section 9.6 of chapter 9 for more on this issue.

7. Treas. Reg. § 1.422-4(b).

8. See sections 8.4 and 8.5 of chapter 8.

the SEC focused on the application of the "tender offer rules" to employee repricings and exchange offers, reasoning that such exchanges (unlike normal option grants) require optionees to make individual investment decisions. Under the Exchange Act, an issuer making a tender offer must comply with a variety of complex substantive and procedural rules relating to nondiscrimination and disclosure with respect to the terms of the offer.[9] Offers that are conducted for compensatory purposes are exempt from compliance with the nondiscrimination requirements of Rule 13e-4.[10] An issuer may take advantage of the exemption if:

1. it is eligible to use Form S-8, the options subject to the exchange offer were issued under an employee benefit plan as defined in Rule 405 of the Exchange Act, and the securities offered in the exchange offer will be issued under such employee benefit plan;

2. the exchange offer is conducted for compensatory purposes;

3. the issuer discloses in the offer to purchase the essential features and significance of the exchange offer, including the risks that optionees should consider in deciding whether to accept the offer; and

4. it otherwise complies with Rule 13e-4.

However, the issuer must still satisfy a number of hurdles to effect a valid exchange offer, including providing certain financial materials to both employees and the SEC, making various SEC filings, holding analyst calls (where appropriate), and providing a withdrawal period of at least 20 business days to offerees.[11]

---

9. Rule 13e-4 of the Exchange Act. The nondiscrimination rules are commonly referred to as the "all holders" and "best price" rules. See Rule 13e-4(f)(8)(i), (ii). In addition, Rule 13e-4 requires extensive disclosure on Schedule TO-1, which must be filed via EDGAR and distributed to optionees in accordance with specific notice periods. See discussion below.

10. For the text of the 2001 release that created the exemption, see SEC Division of Corporate Finance, "Current Issues and Rulemaking Projects Quarterly Update, March 31, 2001," Section II, available at *www.sec.gov/divisions/corpfin/cfcrq032001.htm*. In issuing the exemptive order, the SEC notes that it had previously granted relief from the Rule 13e-4(f)(8) "all-holders" and "best-price" rules for employee repricings on a case-by-case basis.

11. See generally Rule 13e-4; Schedule TO-1 and Item 10 to Schedule TO.

16.3.4 Accounting Issues

Under accounting standard ASC 718 a repricing or other modification is viewed as a cancellation of the original option and the grant of a replacement option. None of the expense previously recorded for the cancelled option is reversed and, if the option is not yet fully vested, the company continues to record the remaining unamortized expense along with the additional expense for the replacement option. The expense for the replacement option is equal to its fair value less the fair value of the cancelled option at the time of the cancellation.

For example, assume that options having a fair value of $1 million are granted on January 1, 2010. The options vest as to 100% of the underlying shares approximately three years after the date of grant, on December 31, 2012. On June 30, 2011, the company reprices the unvested options, which are underwater, by canceling them and immediately granting replacement options with a price equal to the current market value of the stock.

Under ASC 718, while the repricing is likely to result in additional expense, the amount of the expense is fixed as of the date the replacement options are granted and is not subsequently adjusted (except possibly for forfeitures). At the time of the repricing, the company has already recorded approximately $500,000 worth of expense for the underwater options (the repricing occurs exactly halfway through the three-year service period). None of this expense is reversed and the company must continue to record the remaining $500,000 of expense associated with the underwater options. The company must also compute incremental expense for the replacement options. Assume that the fair value of the replacement options is $600,000. The incremental expense for the replacement options is $100,000. As a result, the total expense the company will record for the options is $1.1 million. This includes the expense of $1 million associated with the original options and the incremental expense of $100,000 associated with the replacement options. Since $500,000 of the original expense has been recorded prior to the repricing, the expense that is recorded over the service period of the replacement options is $600,000. But the company was already planning to accrue $500,000 of this amount, so the additional cost of the repricing is only $100,000. With a relatively fixed cost associated with the repricing, the company can more easily evaluate the benefits of repricing against the financial cost.

For simplification purposes, the above example does not address the impact of forfeitures on expense associated with the repricing. The standard includes specific and complex guidance on how forfeitures of modified options and awards are accounted for, particularly where the modification results in a change in the vesting conditions applicable to the arrangement. In some cases, a portion of the expense associated with a modified option or award is not reversed upon forfeiture if the original (pre-modification) vesting conditions are met.

In many cases, publicly traded companies will design repricing programs to be cost-neutral from an accounting standpoint by granting a smaller number of new options with a fair value equal to the unrecognized expense associated with the canceled options.

Always consult your accounting advisors before initiating any modifications of outstanding options and awards. This applies not only to repricings but to other types of modifications as well, including acceleration of vesting, extension of the period in which the arrangement can be exercised, and other modifications to the terms of the arrangement.

16.3.5 Stock Exchange Listing Requirements

Under both NYSE and Nasdaq rules governing shareholder approval, a plan that does not specifically permit repricing is considered to prohibit it. Any actual repricing is thus considered a material modification that requires shareholder approval. Canceling an option and substituting a new award pursuant to a merger, acquisition, spinoff, or similar transaction does not require shareholder approval under these rules.

16.3.6 Proxy Advisory Guidelines

Repricing is an issue that has been watched closely by the proxy advisory firms that make voting recommendations to institutional shareholders. Institutional Shareholder Services (ISS), the most prominent of these companies, recommends shareholders vote against equity compensation plans that allow repricing of grants without further shareholder approval, and also recommends votes against re-electing compensation committee members when such a plan has been put forward.

In advising companies how to vote on specific proposals, ISS prefers that repricings involve only options with exercise prices that exceed the stock's 52-week high or are 50% above the current stock price, whichever is higher. It also takes into account whether the stock price decline is beyond management's control and the breadth of the employee group to which the offer will be extended.

APPENDIXES

Designing a Broad-Based Stock Option Plan

Corey Rosen[1]

Many companies seeking to provide broad-based equity compensation to employees are attracted to stock options because within the applicable legal limitations, companies have considerable discretion as to how to operate their plans. This advantage, however, means that designing these plans can be much more complex than, for instance, designing an employee stock ownership plan (ESOP), where decisions about many issues, such as eligibility and vesting, must be made within a narrow band of requirements. While companies that grant stock options can look to surveys and peers for ideas on how similar companies set up their plans, each company needs to devise a plan that is adapted to its own particular circumstances. This chapter lays out the principal areas where decisions need to be made, suggesting some considerations about how to think about making them. Because every situation is so different, however, it does not attempt to provide any universal guidelines but rather is a checklist of things to consider.

How Much to Share

The first decision is how much ownership to share. This issue will differ for closely held companies and public companies, so considerations for each kind of company are discussed separately.

---

1. Corey Rosen is the founder, senior staff member, and former executive director of the National Center for Employee Ownership (NCEO). He received his Ph.D. from Cornell University in political science in 1973, taught government at Ripon College until 1976, and then served as a Senate staff member until 1981, when he cofounded the NCEO. Mr. Rosen has coauthored several books and written more than 100 articles on various aspects of employee ownership for a variety of professional, academic, and trade publications. He has lectured on the subject across the U.S. and abroad.

Closely Held Companies

Owners of closely held companies most typically decide how much ownership to share by setting aside an amount of stock that does not exceed the maximum dilution level with which they are comfortable. (The exception to this is when the plan is an employee stock ownership plan [ESOP], in which case the goal is generally for owners to sell some or all of their stock to the plan.) This approach can create problems, however.

Typically, once this number is set, a large portion of those shares is either provided immediately to existing employees or allocated to employees over a few years. The problem with this strategy is that allocating too much too quickly leaves relatively few shares to give to new employees. In a growing company, that can create a severe problem in attracting and retaining good people. It can also create two classes of employees, some with large equity grants and some without them. Moreover, this model often does not create an explicit link between employee effort and the rewards of ownership.

A second approach focuses on what percentage of compensation must be provided in the form of equity in order to attract, retain, and motivate people. These decisions need to be based on a sense of what people can get elsewhere, as well as on discussions with employees to get a sense of how much they expect.

Rather than thinking about "how much" in terms of a total percentage of company shares or total compensation, it might make sense to use a more dynamic model based on performance. In this approach, the issue for existing owners is not "what percentage of the company do we own," but "how much is what we own worth?" Owners who use this model would rather own 10% of a $10 million company than 90% of a $1 million company. This notion can be made into an explicit plan by telling employees that if the company meets or exceeds certain targets, they will get a percentage of the incremental value created by that performance in the form of equity or something equivalent to equity, such as phantom stock. If the company exceeds its goals, then, by definition, sharing part of the surplus value leaves both the employees and the existing owners better off than they would have been. The targets can be anything—sales, profits, market penetration, or whatever else is critical to the company's future.

It is also important to consider the "internal equity" of awards. A common problem in equity plans is that employees believe they are not getting what they deserve, something they assess primarily based on what they perceive other people to be getting. Few employees would argue that everyone should get the same, but most would contend that everyone should get awards consistent with their relative contribution to the company. This problem has been starkest in relationship to executive pay, but even at rank-and-file levels, it is not uncommon for companies to pay people doing very similar jobs very different amounts of equity, perhaps because of the timing of when they came to work (more awards were available or the shares were more opportunely priced) or what it was perceived to take to hire them. Nobel Prize-winning research has shown that perceived equity in economic transactions will often trump purely "rational" economic logic. Even if you can show that giving top executives outsized grants helps everyone in the company, if employees believe that what they get is not equitable relative to what the top executives get, they will be more cynical and less motivated.

Closely held companies need to beware of the possibility of making equity grants to so many employees that the grants create legal or regulatory problems. An S corporation, for instance, cannot have more than 100 shareholders, and option holders count as shareholders (an ESOP or 401(k) plan counts as only one, however). And equity plans may be subject to securities laws. This issue is described in more detail in the chapter on securities law considerations.

Publicly Traded Companies

Publicly traded companies face many of the same design issues as their closely held counterparts and may want to use some of the same decision guidelines. Their principal constraint is investor concern about dilution. Dilution is usually measured by "overhang," the number of awards outstanding plus the number of shares available to be issued divided by all of the company's outstanding common shares. "Run rate," another common measure of dilution, is the annual percentage of shares outstanding that need to be issued each year to satisfy equity awards. This amount varies by company. In broad-based equity plans, we find that most companies fall in the 5% to 15% range, with very large public companies often in the lower end of the range and technology companies and younger companies in the higher end. Many large investors and investor advisory services have rules of thumb for dilution or run rates from equity grants, usually at dilution under 10% and run rates under 3%.

Simple calculations of overhang and run rates do have an important flaw in estimating the dilutive effect of equity awards, however. One option counts the same as one share of restricted or other full-value stock award. Phantom stock and stock appreciation rights not settled in shares do not count at all. Stock-settled stock appreciation rights (SARs) result in dilution only once the shares are paid out. Thus, a grant of 1,000 stock-settled SARs would likely have a less dilutive effect than the grant of 1,000 stock options because only enough shares to cover the appreciation of the SARs will be issued upon exercise, even though the economic effect for the award recipient is the same with SARs as it is with stock options. One share of restricted stock is typically worth about three options, so restricted stock generates only one-third the measured dilution. Simply focusing on share dilution as measured by overhang and run rates, therefore, can be misleading. The real issue ultimately is overall economic dilution. Institutional Shareholder Services (ISS), the largest shareholder advisory service, handles this by weighting the number of full-value awards depending on a company's volatility. A company with very volatile stock must count each full-value award such as restricted stock as 1.5 option shares, while companies with low volatility must weight each full-value award the same as four option shares.

ISS uses what it calls its Equity Plan Scorecard to evaluate equity plans. According to the ISS 2016 U.S. Equity Compensation Plans FAQ, plans are scored based on:

- "The projected cost of the plan, in dollar terms ("shareholder value transfer" or SVT), including in combination with other continuing equity plans and outstanding grants, relative to the company's market and industry peers.

- "Various features of the plan.

- "The company's historical grant practices, including its average annual burn rate relative to market and industry peers."[2]

What Kinds of Equity?

Which equity vehicles a company chooses depends largely on the purposes of the plan. While that may seem obvious, it is far too common for companies to pick an equity vehicle because "that's what other people do," or "that's what my advisor understood best," or "I didn't know there were other ways to do it." Beware too of advisors whose discouragement of one kind of plan or another may really be a way of saying, "I don't know how to do the other types."

ESOPs are the vehicle of choice for closely held companies whose owners want to use ownership sharing for business continuity. These plans also make sense in companies that have a strong commitment to sharing ownership broadly and find the ESOP rules acceptable, given the tax benefits the plans provide. ESOPs do not work for companies that want to discriminate in terms of who gets awards or (in most cases) where the philosophy is that employees should have to buy stock to become owners. Contributing company stock to employees' 401(k) plan accounts makes sense for companies that want to share ownership broadly and are comfortable with the allocation and diversification rules. Companies that want to provide a tax-favored way for employees to invest can make company stock an investment option in their 401(k) plans but can no longer force employees to buy company stock with their own contributions. Generally, ESOPs and 401(k) plans are not means for providing incentives for individual behavior; instead, they provide incentives for employees as a group. Employee stock purchase plans (ESPPs) are a terrific benefit, but only a few companies will have active or substantial enough participation to make them a key element of their ownership cultures on their own. They are also less incentive plans than a way to reward employees.

Very small companies with no plans to be acquired or go public often want to use cash-settled SARs or phantom stock because they can be used to track equity changes but are simple and do not require the issuance of actual stock. They lack some of the connotation of ownership, however, and offer no favorable tax treatment.

---

2.   https://www.issgovernance.com/file/policy/1_us-equity-compensation-plans-faq-dec-2015.pdf.

Stock options and restricted stock, in contrast, deliver actual shares but also require that the company provide some form of liquidity for the shares, often through a public offering or sale to another company, although companies can also arrange to repurchase the shares.

Unlike stock options and SARs, restricted stock and restricted stock units (RSUs) deliver actual shares to employees even if the stock price declines after they are granted. There are pros and cons to this approach. On the one hand, employees do not end up with nothing just because share prices decline in the market generally. On the other hand, some have argued that restricted stock just provides "pay for pulse," and that it is thus less of an incentive than options or SARs. Restricted stock can cause more economic dilution (that is, the company has less free cash flow and presumably thus a lower share price) than options or SARs because options are exercisable only if the price of the stock goes up. But restricted stock and RSUs cause less dilution in terms of the number of shares outstanding because grant sizes are smaller. That is because the risk protection of restricted stock means that each share granted is worth more than each option or SAR. A ratio of one restricted stock share to three or four stock options or SARs is not uncommon, for instance. Stock-settled SARs also pay out in shares, but are usually less dilutive in terms of shares outstanding (if not necessarily in economic dilution) than stock options, because only the number of shares needed to cover the appreciation in the stock price between grant and exercise must be issued, usually minus whatever amount is need to pay taxes.

Stock option plans can allow for the granting of nonqualified stock options (NSOs), just incentive stock options (ISOs), or some of each. Most broad-based option plans provide NSOs for rank-and-file employees because few of these employees will be able or want to meet the buy-and-hold conditions that make ISOs eligible for favorable tax treatment. Many of those who do hold onto the shares, moreover, will not get a large benefit from being able to pay taxes at capital gains rather than ordinary income rates. Companies reason that, because the employees will not use the benefits of ISOs anyway, they might as well grant NSOs and get a more certain corporate tax deduction.

Many companies do, however, grant ISOs to highly paid employees, who can greatly benefit from capital gains treatment and who may demand such options to come to work for or stay with a company. ISO plans are also common in startup companies that are not worried about tax deductions (because there are no profits) and thus are willing to give all employees the possibility of capital gains treatment on their options. ISOs also work well where the share price is low and thus the company is not likely to run up against the $100,000 limit on ISOs becoming exercisable in a year.

One problem with options and any form of SARs is that, as valuation models show, volatility is the single most important factor in determining their value. To understand this, imagine two companies with stock price movements as shown below:

	Up & Down Inc.	Stolid Corporation
Price at vesting date	$10.00	$10.00
Price one year later	$17.75	$11.20
Price two years later	$9.00	$12.00
Price three years later	$14.50	$13.30
Price four years later	$21.00	$15.00
Price five years later	$10.00	$16.20

Stolid has had steady, if unexciting, performance. Up & Down's performance has been exciting, but the company has done less well for long-term investors. If Stolid's CFO Joe Smith had 1,000 vested options at the start of year one and at least another five years to exercise, he would have done reasonably well, but not great, in any year if he had exercised and sold the stock. If Up and Down's CFO Mary Jones had 1,000 vested options with the same terms as Joe's, she would be in a much better situation if she had been astute or lucky enough to exercise and sell the shares in three of the five years. So valuation models say Mary's options are worth more at grant than Joe's even though, long-term, Mary's company is an unimpressive performer. Mary and other top officers are being rewarded for movements in the company's stock, not for long-term growth.

This has a number of insidious effects. First, it can encourage excessive risk-taking by top decision-makers, especially if their expected time horizon with the company is short (as it tends to be these days). Second, it introduces a lottery effect into the incentive structure. If Joe goes to work when the stock is at $7, and Mary joins a little later when it is at $14, Joe has a chance to make a lot of money, but Mary can only make a fraction as much. Finally, it can engender cynicism among employees who view options as a lottery whose benefits may go to the lucky and to the insiders who know best when to exercise.

This does not mean options or SARs are never appropriate. They can make sense for companies with rapidly appreciating share prices or where boards want employees to benefit only from increases in stock value. By issuing options in smaller amounts more often, moreover, much of the lottery effect described here can be ameliorated or avoided.

Who Is Eligible and Who Will Actually Get Equity?

To many people, the answer to the question of who is eligible is very simple: just the "key" people. While that view has become conventional wisdom among most compensation consultants (who, it must be said, are paid by the same key people), for many companies, everyone is a key person. Many companies are pushing down more decision-making to all levels of the company, asking employees to make business decisions on a regular basis. Managers at these companies reason that if they want people to think and act like owners, they should make them owners.

At the same time, for some companies in some labor markets, it is necessary to provide options at all levels just to attract and retain people. The research on this question could not be more decisive: broad-based plans work much better in terms of corporate performance and employee retention than narrowly focused ones do.

In fact, despite the conventional wisdom, broad-based equity grant plans are still very common, and many companies just make all employees eligible for awards. Other companies choose more complex approaches that take several criteria into account. This discussion is only for plans other than ESOPs, 401(k)s, and Section 423 ESPPs, for which there are specific rules about eligibility.

One set of issues that some companies consider, but that they probably should not, is the so-called "1/n" or "free rider" effect, and the related "line-of-sight" problem. The argument here is that an equity award cannot be much of an incentive to an employee who cannot see (has no line of sight to) just how his or her work actually affects stock prices. This is especially problematic in larger organizations where employees not only don't have clear lines of sight to the awards but also figure they can "free ride" on the efforts of others.

These arguments are appealing but empirically wrong. Research shows that motivation at work is much more complicated than a simple economic calculation. Few employees go to work each day thinking, "If I do x, I get y, but if I do x + a, I get y + b, so if y + b is large enough, I'll do x + a." A good test is to ask yourself whether anyone you know well really thinks this way. Research shows again and again that most people's efforts at work are a function of how well their job functions fit their skills, whether they have opportunities for meaningful input into decisions affecting their jobs, how much they trust management and management trusts them, whether they find the job engaging, and whether they believe what they and the company do has value.

Equity sharing becomes important in this context not so much as an incentive for behavior but as a reward. If people are asked to act like owners and are treated like owners, they will be more productive and make larger contributions in terms of new ideas and information. If they then are denied an opportunity to benefit from what they add, they will feel manipulated and back away. If, on the other hand, they feel they are equitably rewarded relative to what others contribute or that they are all part of a team sharing in the results, they are much more likely to stay committed. So the question of who gets equity should be based on who you want thinking and acting like an owner.

The research on who should get equity is unequivocal: broader ownership works better. That may come as a surprise to many decision-makers. Consultants often refer to the "80-20" rule that 80% of the performance in an organization is attributable to 20% of the people, so at most 20% should get equity or other incentives. This is more urban myth than empirically validated best practice. Because it is repeated so much, it has taken on a kind of iconic status, even though there is actually no research validating it. The largest and most comprehensive study of who should get options was performed by Yael V. Hochberg of the Kellogg School of Management at Northwestern University and Laura Lindsey at the W. P. Carey School of Business at Arizona State University. Looking at 1,500 companies over a 17-year period, they found that companies that granted options broadly to their employees showed a significant improvement in industry-adjusted return on assets (ROA), while companies that granted options more narrowly showed a decline in performance. The study, "Incentives, Targeting and Firm Performance: An Analysis of Non-Executive Stock Options," appeared in the November 2010 (vol. 23, no. 11) issue of the *Review of Financial Studies*. Joseph Blasi, and Douglas Kruse of Rutgers and Richard Freeman of Harvard found similar patterns in an initial assessment of more than 300,000 employee surveys at more than 700 companies that applied for the Best Places to Work awards. The authors explain that providing broad-based equity helps reinforce a culture of participation and reduces turnover, both of which are strongly linked to performance.

Tenure

At the simplest level, companies can require that people work a minimum amount of time, often one year, before they become eligible for equity. This assures the employee has at least some commitment to the company. This is typical in plans aimed at rank-and-file employees. Some companies have even longer tenure requirements. Companies seeking to lure new employees with critical skills, however, usually offer equity as part of the initial contract.

Full-Time/Part-Time

In the past, it was unusual to provide equity to part-time employees. Innovators like Starbucks, however, have provided options to everyone, arguing that many of their part-time people are (or if properly rewarded could be) long-term employees.

Performance or a Universal Rule?

Equity can be granted according to some kind of merit judgment; on a regular, universal schedule such as annually, or upon hiring or promotion; or it can be granted or vest upon the achievement of an individual, group, or corporate objective. These methods are not mutually exclusive; many companies use a combination of these techniques.

The core issue here is that, on the one hand, including everyone who is eligible according to some formula rules out discretion, which employees may see as arbitrary or political. It also may help foster a team atmosphere in which everyone sees that they have a stake. On the other hand, some employees may feel cheated if they think they have been exceptional performers but get unexceptional rewards. That can make some combination appealing, provided the basis for rewarding excellence is one that most or all employees see as reasonably fair—a tricky business, but one many companies have done well at, albeit in a variety of ways. Some companies, for instance, use 360-degree performance reviews in which everyone reviews everyone else, others use very specific and transparent financial or other measurable targets, and others seek employee input in designing rating systems.

A typical merit-based approach would provide work unit managers (or a single manager in a smaller company) with a number of awards that can be granted to employees in the group based on a performance appraisal. An alternative to individual merit judgments is to provide that a pool of equity awards will be given to a work team on the achievement of their own goals. Many companies, of course, will simply name specific individuals, usually top managers, who will get equity, but the company will define how much they get based on some merit assessment.

At the other end of the spectrum is an automatic formula based on compensation, seniority, promotion, or some other work-related, measurable construct. This can be for one employee or every employee. For instance, a number of larger companies provide all employees who meet basic service requirements with a fixed percentage of pay every year in stock options. The argument behind such formulas is that compensation reflects management's judgment of an employee's contribution to the company, and equity is simply another form of compensation.

Many companies provide awards on hiring, then make additional grants periodically or upon promotion. Linking additional grants to promotion gives employees an incentive to improve their skills and rewards those people the organization believes are making greater contributions. On the other hand, an overemphasis on promotion-related grants can mean that employees who are very good performers but who are not in jobs that can easily lead to promotion are overlooked.

Refresher grants give employees additional awards when they exercise some of the options or other equity benefits they were previously granted. For instance, if an employee has 1,000 options and exercises 200, then the employee would be given new options on another 200 shares at exercise. The goal here is to maintain a constant level of equity interest in the company. Similarly, refresher awards might be granted when the company issues additional shares so that an employee maintains the same percentage of potential ownership as was held before the dilution (this feature is more common in executive plans). While these automatic additional grants help to keep the employee's equity interest high, shareholders might object to the ongoing dilution.

When Will Employees Be Able to Use the Awards?

There are two principal issues in deciding when employees will be able to translate their equity into cash: vesting and exercise periods. Vesting generally provides that an employee accrues an increasing right to the awards granted based on the number of years worked. However, companies also sometimes use performance vesting, in which vesting is a function of company, group, or individual performance. As various targets are met, the equity awards become increasingly vested. The exercise period is the time between an award's vesting and its expiration.

By far the most common exercise period for stock options is 10 years; there are no data on SARs. Some exercise periods are shorter, but they are rarely longer.

There is nothing magical about 10 years for NSOs, but for ISOs, the exercise period cannot exceed 10 years. The more volatile a company's stock, the more important a longer exercise period is so that employees can weather the downturns.

As for vesting, the patterns on time-based vesting are fairly consistent across companies, with three- to five-year graduated vesting the most common schedule. Sales or profit targets are the most common performance triggers. A few companies allow employees to exercise their awards only when a defined event occurs, such as the achievement of a certain stock price or earnings goal. This accomplishes two things. First, it provides an incentive to meet the goal, and second, it reassures investors that dilution will occur only if the company meets certain targets. Once these targets are met, employees are normally given a certain amount of time to exercise the award, anywhere from a few months to several years. Alternatively, a company could provide that awards can be exercised only upon the occurrence of an event such as a sale or going public.

Deciding whether to provide for immediate vesting upon an IPO or the sale of the company, even if the awards would not otherwise be vested, can be difficult. This clearly provides a good benefit for employees, but it may make it more difficult to sell a company or take one public, especially if buyers perceive that employees will now have fully vested options that, if the underlying stock can also then be sold, may be valuable enough so that some people will just walk away.

In closely held companies, allowing exercise of an option or the right to sell shares only upon sale of the company or an IPO is a very common approach. If a company allows exercise of an option or stock-settled SAR or allows restricted stock to vest before then, employees end up owning stock and having a tax obligation. Unless the company can provide a market for the shares (an issue discussed below), this combination may not seem like much of a reward. Companies and employees have to weigh just how likely these events are to occur, however. Management is often excessively optimistic about how marketable their company is.

It is also important to consider that if equity compensation awards all become exercisable upon sale or an IPO, buyers of the stock may not find the company so valuable. A minority of closely held companies are thus now restricting exercise to sometime after a sale or an IPO (in a sale situation, this requires the acquiring company to provide options in the new employer).

Finally, the plan design should be specific in its compliance with applicable securities laws, stock exchange rules, and/or underwriter requirements that can restrict certain employees from exercising equity awards or selling stock acquired from them for a specified period around an IPO.

Providing a Market for the Shares

For publicly traded companies, providing a market for shares obtained through stock option exercises is not an issue, but for employees of closely held companies, it is one of the most important of all design issues. The majority of closely held companies solve the problem by limiting the exercise of options to when the company is sold or goes public. This makes sense for companies that realistically see these alternatives as likely to happen in the foreseeable future. Some company leaders who call us, however, assume that they can *only* provide for marketability upon these events because a closely held company, for one reason or another, cannot provide a market itself. These companies at least should be aware of the other alternatives. Moreover, some companies prefer to stay closely held. There are a variety of ways these companies can provide a market.

Purchases by Other Employees

Other employees can purchase the shares directly, although this is not likely to provide enough of a market for all the shares. When an employee purchases shares, the purchase is normally done with after-tax dollars. It can also be subject to securities laws (see the section below for more details). Companies can help employees buy the shares by loaning them the money, although the interest subsidy on loans that are on less than arm's-length terms could involve taxation to the employee. A few large closely held companies even provide their own internal stock markets, creating periodic trading days for the buying and selling of shares. This requires establishing in-house broker dealers and complying with complex securities rules in each state where the company does business.

One way employees can purchase shares with pretax dollars is through their 401(k) plans. Shares acquired through options could then be sold to employees in the 401(k) plan who wanted to purchase them. The plan would have to provide that employees can make this choice, which can add expense and complexity to the plan's administration. These purchases would also be subject to the same securities rules as any plan. (Note that employees cannot hold options themselves in the 401(k) plan; Travelers Corp. tried to do this but ultimately was prevented from doing so by government rulings.) Although companies can do this, that does not mean they should. Fiduciary concerns about employer stock in 401(k) plans have become much more important in the post-Enron era, and a very good argument can be made that 401(k) plans should limit the percentage of company stock an employee can hold. The Pension Protection Act of 2006 also provides that employees must be allowed to diversify their holdings in company stock in 401(k) plans and that employers must provide them with educational materials about the importance of diversification.

Closely held companies can also set up internal stock markets. A handful of companies do this. Until recently, the process seemed too daunting for all but the largest employers. But a small Fairfax, Virginia, company called TEOCO (an acronym for The Employee-Owned Company) has found a way to make this more practical. In its internal market, TEOCO will arrange for periodic trades, most likely once or twice a year. A plan committee will oversee the process. Dates will be set in advance, detailed information mailed to employees, and an informational meeting held. Employees can offer to sell shares they own or buy additional shares. The company established minimums and maximums on the number of shares that must be purchased or can be sold. The company acts as the sole buyer and seller, rather than the transactions occurring between individuals. An independent third-party appraiser sets the sale price in advance, but it must be revisited if there are material changes in the interim. Employees indicate how many shares they want to sell or buy and submit this to the company. In the unlikely event the number of sale and purchase offers is equal, the company buys all the shares for sale and resells them all. More likely, there will be an imbalance. If there are more purchase offers, the company buys all the shares for sale, then parcels them out based on an equitable formula designed to give preference to smaller holders. If there are more sellers, the company accepts all offers to buy then allocates the remaining number according to the same formula. Because the company is buying and selling for its own account, not acting as an agent (especially a commissioned agent) of the sellers or buyers, the SEC accepted the argument that it is not a broker-dealer. The company also will not need to register the shares because of an exemption for sales to employees under Rule 701, which exempts from registration offers of less than 15% of a company's equity in a 12-month period to employees.

Company Redemption

For a closely held company, the most practical method in most cases is for the company to buy back the shares, either directly or through an ESOP or 401(k) plan. If the company redeems the shares, the redemption is not a tax-deductible expense. If the company sets up an ESOP, however, it can make tax-deductible cash contributions to the plan (within certain limits) that can then be used to buy back the shares. While sellers to an ESOP that owns 30% or more of a closely held company can normally defer taxation on the gain from the sale by reinvesting in qualified replacement securities, owners who hold their shares as a result of stock options cannot get this benefit. The sale of their shares to the ESOP would be treated in the same way as a sale to any other buyer.

Secondary Markets and Outside Investors

Some entrepreneurial companies may be able to attract investors who will purchase some of the shares held by employees, although many investors would prefer that their stock purchases be used to help the company grow. Secondary markets such as SecondMarket and SharesPost provide markets for certain investors to buy shares in private companies, often shares resulting from employee equity awards. While this market has grown, only a small number of companies likely to do a substantial IPO or sale are likely to attract buyers for their shares.

In recent years, outside investors have become more willing to buy shares in closely held companies with the idea that they will hold them for several years and then sell them to other investors. Companies may go through a few rounds of such investors before selling or going public.

Valuation of the Shares

Companies whose shares are "readily tradable on an established market" get off easy on this issue; the value of their shares is set every day by the market. Closely held companies, however, must determine how they will set a value for the shares subject to options. In the past, it appeared that private companies could use almost any method of setting a value without much risk of legal or tax problems. However, the 2004 American Jobs Creation Act (AJCA) created Internal Revenue Code Section 409A, which governs the tax treatment of deferred compensation. Under Treasury regulations that apply to that section, rules for valuations of stock options and stock appreciation rights (SARs) in closely held companies have become much stiffer. These rules state that stock options and SARs will be treated as deferred compensation—and thus the recipient will be subject to steep taxes—if issued at less than fair market value. The regulations set out four alternatives for determining fair market value that won't lead to deferred compensation treatment:

1. following the established standards for ESOP valuations;

2. using a formula valuation that establishes fair market valuation for purposes of Treas. Reg. § 1.83-5 and that is used on a consistent basis for other transactions;

3. using a price at which any recent equity sales were made in an arm's-length transaction; or

4. if in business less than 10 years, using a formula valuation that meets somewhat (but not much) less rigorous guidelines.

Restricted stock is not specifically covered, but the prudent course would be to follow these rules. If the rules are not followed, the compensation could be considered deferred compensation subject to Section 409A of the Code. Section 409A and its regulations require that any deferrals beyond the vesting date of an award be made not later than the end of the year prior to the year in which the awards vest (so the end of 2008 for an award vesting in 2010, for instance), or, if performance based, six months before. Deferrals are considered to be short-term and thus not subject to 409A if the payout is made no later than 2½ months after the end of the service provider's taxable year or service recipient's taxable year in which the award ceases to be subject to a substantial risk of forfeiture, whichever is later. For first-time grants, the deferral must be made within 30 days in of the award. Restricted stock that pays out upon vesting would not run afoul of the rules. If the rules are violated, the tax penalties are significant.

The safest course is to value equity awards at grant and exercise using an independent appraiser. The technicalities of how shares are valued in closely held companies are beyond the scope of this chapter. Suffice it to say that a formal appraisal of a closely held company would first involve an estimate of what a willing buyer would pay a willing seller for the entire enterprise. These estimates are set primarily by looking at comparable companies, discounted earnings or cash flow, and book value. Discounts for the lack of marketability (shares of public companies are easier to sell and therefore worth more) and lack of control (the enterprise value assumes a buyer is purchasing control of a company, which is a valuable additional right not gained from holding shares that constitute a minority interest) are then applied to determine the value of an individual share.

Having a formal appraisal performed is clearly the best way to set a value. Nonetheless, most closely held companies will choose to set a value internally, usually by having the board rely on a formula, such as a multiple of earnings, book value, or some other rule of thumb. That formula, under the new rules, needs to be very carefully set, preferably with professional advice. Companies value stock in-house mostly to avoid the costs of an appraiser (typically $5,000 to $10,000 for this kind of assessment), but if their rule-of-thumb appraisal is off by just a small percentage, they could create at least two problems. If the appraisal is too high, then when employees exercise the options, they will be getting more value than the shares are really worth. If the shares are valued too low, then the options could be considered deferred compensation for tax purposes and be subject to immediate taxes and penalties. While some might shrug off these problems, saying that one will offset the other, formula-based values can produce a value both too low at grant and too high at exercise if the essentials of the industry move in the right way for this to happen over time. As any appraiser would note, a formula that is appropriate in 2008 will probably not be appropriate a few years later. Moreover, appraisals that are off substantially could lead to tax problems or lawsuits by employees or other shareholders.

Finally, companies need to be careful that they do not grant options at too low a price and then go public. The closer to an IPO underpriced options are issued, the more of a potential problem they become. Because this so-called "cheap stock" can raise tax and securities law issues upon an IPO, companies at the very least should get an independent appraisal about 18 months before an IPO.

How Often Should Awards Be Granted?

Equity inherently involves risk, but the design of plans can accentuate that risk. Companies that provide one-time grants of stock options or SARs or grant them only upon an event, such as hiring, promotion, or meeting some corporate target, wind up with employees whose ownership interest in the company is based on the price of stock at a single point in time. This is not a problem with full-value awards, which do not have an exercise price based on the stock's trading price on the grant date.

Granting options or SARs infrequently accelerates the risk of equity both for the employee and the company because equity granted at a high price may never be "in the money"; awards granted at a low price may cost the company more than it intended when they are redeemed. Employees who happen to get their chunk of equity when the share price is low end up doing very well, while those who get their grants when the price is much higher don't do well at all. Creating an ownership culture of "we're all in this together" can be very difficult in these circumstances.

For many companies, the best way to deal with these potential problems is to provide grants in smaller amounts but more frequently or to grant full-value awards such as restricted stock or phantom stock. Frequent grants work best for companies using equity as a compensation strategy. Startups whose stock value is close to zero anyway or that use large initial grants to attract people away from other opportunities may find this less appropriate. It also won't work for companies that want simply to make grants at the occasional discretion of the company, often on the attainment of some corporate milestone. These companies see equity more as a symbolic reward than as ongoing ownership strategy.

Smaller but more frequent grants are easiest to do in public companies where the share price is readily ascertainable and where share prices change continually. In a closely held company, there is no point in granting equity more frequently than the stock is valued. Giving an employee a grant three times a year when the price per share is determined annually, for instance, would give the employee three sets of awards all at the same price.

Periodic allocation "dollar-cost averages" the awards, smoothing bumps in volatile markets. This approach also gives employees more of a long-term, ongoing stake in the company. With the vesting schedules attached to the repeated grants of awards, employees are provided an even longer-term interest in the company's performance. Finally, there will be fewer big winners and losers among employees with otherwise similar jobs.

Frequent grants are not all good news, of course. The more often awards are granted, the more complex their administration becomes. Even with the best software, there is much more data entry, many more forms to file and disseminate, and many more errors that can be made.

Securities Law Issues

The granting of options does not in itself raise federal securities law considerations (although it may raise securities law issues at the state level, as in California, for example), but when employees exercise their options, that is considered a sale by the company and hence is subject to securities laws. This chapter is not intended to provide a primer on the complicated issues involved with state and federal securities laws, but rather to describe briefly the general issues so that plan designs can be created that will not lead to unexpected regulatory burdens.

The two key elements of securities laws are registration and disclosure. Registration means the filing of documents with the state and/or federal securities agencies concerning the employer whose stock is being sold. The federal Securities Act of 1933 requires that securities be registered before they are sold. However, the act's regulations offer several exemptions from registration, which are frequently used by privately held companies.

Disclosure refers to providing information to buyers about what they are getting, similar to, but frequently less detailed than, what would be in a prospectus. At times, there are specific state and federal rules about what needs to go in these documents, including objective discussions of risks, the financial condition of the firm, officers' and directors' salaries, and other information. In the absence of requirements for the registration of the securities, disclosure is intended to satisfy the anti-fraud requirements of federal and state laws. Whenever stock is offered for sale, the company generally still needs to provide appropriate financial disclosure to satisfy anti-fraud rules.

The Jumpstart Our Business Act of 2012 (JOBS Act) created a number of changes for entrepreneurial companies. Generally, offers to sell securities (stocks, bonds, etc.) require registration of those securities unless there is a specific exemption. In addition, companies that have more than 2,000 shareholders (no more than 500 of whom are nonaccredited investors) and more than $10 million in assets are considered public firms under federal law and must comply with the reporting requirements of the Securities Exchange Act of 1934 even if they do not have to register under the 1933 Act. People who receive shares pursuant to an employee compensation plan are not considered to be shareholders for these purposes. The act created a new category of companies called "emerging growth companies," defined as those with $1 billion or less in revenue. Such companies are allowed more time to phase into regulatory requirements, including accounting rules and voting rules on executive pay.

Under the JOBS Act:

- Companies can use "crowdfunding" to raise a maximum of $1 million (or $2 million if they provide audited financial statements) in privately sourced sales to investors who invest up to $10,000 or 10% of their income, if less. These sales might be through website solicitations, personal solicitations, or other direct approaches. Companies must warn investors about risks, require them to answer questions showing they understand the risks, and provide the SEC with a notice of the offering.

- Companies qualifying under Section 506 of Regulation D of the 1933 Securities Act are allowed to use advertisements to solicit investors, a practice previously banned by regulation. Section D allows unlimited offerings to accredited investors (basically, high-income investors, certain institutional investors, employee benefit plans, and certain key insiders) and up to 35 other purchasers without having to file a registration statement.

- Companies can raise up to $50 million in share sales under Regulation A before triggering SEC registration requirements, up from the $5 million level set 20 years ago.

Public companies can use the relatively simple Form S-8 to issue shares pursuant to a stock option plan. However, because registration requires the filing of audited financial statements and continuing reporting obligations to the Securities and Exchange Commission (SEC) and appropriate state agencies, private companies generally issue stock to employees pursuant to exemptions from registration. The effect of this is that the stock holder cannot freely resell without in turn using an exemption from registration. There are registration exemptions for small offerings of up to $1 million or $5 million of stock, depending on the exemption, and for larger offerings made to a small number of sophisticated investors.

Under Rule 701 of the Securities Act of 1933, offers to a company's employees, directors, general partners, trustees, officers, or consultants can be made under a written compensation agreement. The maximum amount that can be sold under Section 701 in a 12-month period cannot exceed the greater of (1) $1 million; (2) 15% of the issuer's total assets as of the most recent balance sheet date; or (3) 15% of the outstanding securities of that class as of the most recent balance sheet date. The offerings must be discrete (not included in any other offer, generally considered to be at least six months from the prior offer).

Another exemption is available under Section 4(a)(2) of the Securities Act of 1933, which has been interpreted to allow for exemptions from federal registrations of offerings of stock to a limited number of investors who have access to the same information normally provided in a public offering and who are accredited investors or sophisticated enough both to assess and to bear the risks. This exemption has been interpreted in different ways by the courts. Whether it allows such approaches as offering stock to more than just a company's "key employees" is unclear.

Another set of exemptions is available under the SEC's Regulation D, which provides exemptions for small offerings in Rules 504 and 506. Rule 504 exempts offerings up to $5 million to an unlimited number of people, with no limits of their being sophisticated or accredited. Rule 506 exempts offerings of any size made to as many as 35 sophisticated investors and an unlimited number of accredited investors, although if general solicitation is used to attract buyers, then the shares may be sold only to accredited investors.

"Accredited investors" include directors, partners, or executives of the issuing company; anyone with a net worth (including that of their spouses) of over $1 million; and anyone with an income over $200,000 (or whose joint income with a spouse is more than $300,000) who has made that amount for the preceding two years and is likely to continue to make it; and financial institutions, business development companies, or other companies with total assets exceeding $5 million. "Sophisticated investors" are people who, on their own or with the aid of a representative such as an accountant, are able to judge the risks, merits, and disadvantages of a particular investment. Finally, offerings that are made only to residents of the state in which the offering is made may be exempt from federal registration if the offeror is incorporated in that state, gets 80% of its gross revenue from business conducted in the state, and has 80% of its assets in the state.

These exemptions from registration are available under federal law. Some states track federal exemptions; some do not. Most states have "blue sky laws" (the general name for state securities laws) that comply with the Uniform Securities Act, which is partly based on federal law. Perhaps most important for offerings to employees, however, states that have a specific exemption parallel to the federal Rule 701 exemption (for offerings to employees) are the exception rather than the rule. State registration for such offerings may be needed, therefore, unless other exemptions are met. Some states have limited offering exemptions for sales to up to 35 non-accredited investors and an unlimited number of accredited investors. Unless the buyers are sophisticated investors, issuers must believe the offering is suitable for the purchasers in terms of the purchasers' financial condition, including other securities holdings. Note, however, that even if all these exemption requirements are met, some states require companies to pay filing fees to operate their plans.

Public Company Issues

Public companies cannot use Rule 701 for an exemption from securities registration. Instead, most use Form S-8, a simplified registration form that can be used to comply with securities laws in conjunction with an offering of options. Public companies do not have to offer formal prospectuses to potential buyers, as closely held companies would. They are, however, required to provide information to employee stock purchasers about the company and its option plan. The Form S-8 registration statement allows that to be done by reference to already available public documents or the dissemination of the required information.

Public companies must also make sure their plan design and its execution comply with trading restrictions that apply to corporate insiders. This requires the filing of various reports and the restriction of some trading activity, among other things. These issues are too technical for adequate discussion here. Public companies should consult with their legal counsel on these matters before designing their plans.

Design Issues Raised by Securities Laws

Because of the expense and complexity of dealing with securities registration, some closely held companies prohibit the exercise of options until the company is sold or goes public, when either the acquirer must deal with these issues or the public offering makes most of them go away. (Note that this discussion does not include a description of special rules that public companies must meet for the exercise of options that are primarily focused on "insiders," a term whose definition would almost always exclude rank-and-file workers.)

Most closely held companies, however, will be able to avoid securities registration requirements at the federal level even with a broad-based option plan; some will have to meet state requirements, but these are generally much less onerous. Anti-fraud disclosure statements will raise cost issues, however, and some companies may not want to divulge the required information. When designing a plan, therefore, these issues need to be considered carefully with qualified counsel to assure that the operation of the plan will not trigger requirements the company does not want to meet.

Methods of Exercising Options

There are a variety of ways employees can exercise their options. These must be specified in the plan's documents if employees are to be able to exercise their options. Some of these methods will work only for public companies, however.

Cash

The most straight-forward approach is that the employee simply pays for the exercise of the option in cash. However, simplicity has its cost. If an employee is exercising a substantial amount of options, it could require a large amount of up-front cash that some people may not have.

Stock Swaps

Many companies allow employees who own shares in the company to exchange those shares for the shares to be acquired by the exercise of the option. One benefit of a stock swap is the ability to purchase shares with pretax appreciation in already owned shares. The complex tax effects of stock swaps are discussed in the chapter titled "Financing the Purchase of Stock Options."

Cashless Exercise

This approach is intended for public companies. Its mechanics can be a bit complicated, but the concept is simple: an employee exercises options on a given number of shares, and at the same time has a broker (one working with the company) sell the number of shares needed to pay the exercise price and usually also the withholding taxes due at exercise. This approach is referred to as a "sell-to-cover" exercise if only the shares that cover the exercise price and taxes are sold or a "same-day sale" if all of the shares underlying the option are sold. The broker buys the shares up front and the employee gets the spread between the stock's fair market value on the exercise date and the exercise price upon the settlement of the trade. The spread could be delivered in shares or cash.

Cashless Exercise in a Closely Held Company

A closely held company could arrange a transaction in which the employee purchases the shares only in the most technical sense. The employee buys the shares and the company immediately repurchases them, giving the employee the cash value of the difference, minus applicable taxes. A variation on this approach would give the employee shares equal to the value of the spread.

Note, however, that any form of exercise in which the employee sells shares sooner than two years after grant and one year after exercise will not qualify for incentive stock option treatment.

Accounting, Corporate, and Communications Issues

In designing a plan, it is important to consider a variety of other issues. For instance, the accounting treatment of equity compensation means it shows up as an expense on the company's income statement. Will this cause adverse reactions from other owners? How will the present value of the options be determined for this disclosure? Are there corporate bylaws or other policies that need to be changed? Will shareholders approve the plans? Finally, how will the company communicate how equity vehicles work to employees, and, more importantly, what new roles will employees play as "owners-in-waiting?"

Conclusion

There is no single template for a broad-based equity compensation plan. Designing a plan that works for a company requires a careful assessment of at least the company's goals, culture, finances, corporate structure, demographics, and labor market situation, as well as consultation with peers and experienced advisors.

Primary Sources

Contents

This book makes use of many primary source materials, some of which are reproduced here for the reader's convenience. Readers are also encouraged to take advantage of the many websites that now offer free access to statutes, legislative history, and related authority online. To start your search, go to www.firstgov.gov (government materials only) or to any of the following sites:

- IRS website: www.irs.gov

- IRS Revenue Rulings: www.taxlinks.com

- FASB website: www.fasb.org

- IASB website: www.iasb.org.uk

- SEC website: www.sec.gov

Section 83 of the Internal Revenue Code

Property transferred in connection with performance of services

(a) **General rule.** If, in connection with the performance of services, property is transferred to any person other than the person for whom such services are performed, the excess of—

(1) the fair market value of such property (determined without regard to any restriction other than a restriction which by its terms will never lapse) at the first time the rights of the person having the beneficial interest in such property are transferable or are not subject to a substantial risk of forfeiture, whichever occurs earlier, over

(2) the amount (if any) paid for such property,

shall be included in the gross income of the person who performed such services in the first taxable year in which the rights of the person having the beneficial interest in such property are transferable or are not subject to a substantial risk of forfeiture, whichever is applicable. The preceding sentence shall not apply if such person sells or otherwise disposes of such property in an arm's length transaction before his rights in such property become transferable or not subject to a substantial risk of forfeiture.

(b) **Election to include in gross income in year of transfer.**

(1) **In general.** Any person who performs services in connection with which property is transferred to any person may elect to include in his gross income for the taxable year in which such property is transferred, the excess of—

(A) the fair market value of such property at the time of transfer (determined without regard to any restriction other than a restriction which by its terms will never lapse), over

(B) the amount (if any) paid for such property.

If such election is made, subsection (a) shall not apply with respect to the transfer of such property, and if such property is subsequently forfeited, no deduction shall be allowed in respect of such forfeiture.

(2) **Election.** An election under paragraph (1) with respect to any transfer of property shall be made in such manner as the Secretary prescribes and shall be made not later than 30 days after the date of such transfer. Such election may not be revoked except with the consent of the Secretary.

(c) **Special rules.** For purposes of this section—

(1) **Substantial risk of forfeiture.** The rights of a person in property are subject to a substantial risk of forfeiture if such person's rights to full enjoyment of such property are conditioned upon the future performance of substantial services by any individual.

(2) **Transferability of property.** The rights of a person in property are transferable only if the rights in such property of any transferee are not subject to a substantial risk of forfeiture.

(3) **Sales which may give rise to suit under section 16(b) of the Securities Exchange Act of 1934.** So long as the sale of property at a profit could subject a person to suit under section 16(b) of the Securities Exchange Act of 1934, such person's rights in such property are—

(A) subject to a substantial risk of forfeiture, and

(B) not transferable.

(d) Certain restrictions which will never lapse.

(1) **Valuation.** In the case of property subject to a restriction which by its terms will never lapse, and which allows the transferee to sell such property only at a price determined under a formula, the price so determined shall be deemed to be the fair market value of the property unless established to the contrary by the Secretary, and the burden of proof shall be on the Secretary with respect to such value.

(2) **Cancellation.** If, in the case of property subject to a restriction which by its terms will never lapse, the restriction is canceled, then, unless the taxpayer establishes—

(A) that such cancellation was not compensatory, and

(B) that the person, if any, who would be allowed a deduction if the cancellation were treated as compensatory, will treat the transaction as not compensatory, as evidenced in such manner as the Secretary shall prescribe by regulations,

the excess of the fair market value of the property (computed without regard to the restrictions) at the time of cancellation over the sum of—

(C) the fair market value of such property (computed by taking the restriction into account) immediately before the cancellation, and

(D) the amount, if any, paid for the cancellation, shall be treated as compensation for the taxable year in which such cancellation occurs.

(e) Applicability of section. This section shall not apply to—

(1) a transaction to which section 421 applies,

(2) a transfer to or from a trust described in section 401(a) or a transfer under an annuity plan which meets the requirements of section 404(a)(2),

(3) the transfer of an option without a readily ascertainable fair market value,

(4) the transfer of property pursuant to the exercise of an option with a readily ascertainable fair market value at the date of grant, or

(5) group-term life insurance to which section 79 applies.

(f) Holding period. In determining the period for which the taxpayer has held property to which subsection (a) applies, there shall be included only the period beginning at the first time his rights in such property are transferable or are not subject to a substantial risk of forfeiture, whichever occurs earlier.

(g) Certain exchanges. If property to which subsection (a) applies is exchanged for property subject to restrictions and conditions substantially similar to those to which the property given in such exchange was subject, and if section 354, 355, 356, or 1036 (or so much of section 1031 as relates to section 1036) applied to such exchange, or if such exchange was pursuant to the exercise of a conversion privilege—

> (1) such exchange shall be disregarded for purposes of subsection (a), and

> (2) the property received shall be treated as property to which subsection (a) applies.

(h) Deduction by employer. In the case of a transfer of property to which this section applies or a cancellation of a restriction described in subsection (d), there shall be allowed as a deduction under section 162, to the person for whom were performed the services in connection with which such property was transferred, an amount equal to the amount included under subsection (a), (b), or (d)(2) in the gross income of the person who performed such services. Such deduction shall be allowed for the taxable year of such person in which or with which ends the taxable year in which such amount is included in the gross income of the person who performed such services.

Section 162 of the Internal Revenue Code

Trade or Business Expenses
Subsections (a) and (m) only

(a) In general. There shall be allowed as a deduction all the ordinary and necessary expenses paid or incurred during the taxable year in carrying on any trade or business, including-—

> **(1)** a reasonable allowance for salaries or other compensation for personal services actually rendered;

> **(2)** traveling expenses (including amounts expended for meals and lodging other than amounts which are lavish or extravagant under the circumstances) while away from home in the pursuit of a trade or business; and

> **(3)** rentals or other payments required to be made as a condition to the continued use or possession, for purposes of the trade or business, of property to which the taxpayer has not taken or is not taking title or in which he has no equity.

For purposes of the preceding sentence, the place of residence of a Member of Congress (including any Delegate and Resident Commissioner) within the State, congressional district, or possession which he represents in Congress shall be considered his home, but amounts expended by such Members within each taxable year for living expenses shall not be deductible for income tax purposes in excess of $3,000. For purposes of paragraph (2), the taxpayer shall not be treated as being temporarily away from home during any period of employment if such period exceeds 1 year. The preceding sentence shall not apply to any Federal employee during any period for which such employee is certified by the Attorney General (or the designee thereof) as traveling on behalf of the United States in temporary duty status to investigate or prosecute, or provide support services for the investigation or prosecution of, a Federal crime.

* * *

(m) Certain excessive employee remuneration.

(1) In general. In the case of any publicly held corporation, no deduction shall be allowed under this chapter for applicable employee remuneration with respect to any covered employee to the extent that the amount of such remuneration for the taxable year with respect to such employee exceeds $1,000,000.

(2) Publicly held corporation. For purposes of this subsection, the term "publicly held corporation" means any corporation issuing any class of common equity securities required to be registered under section 12 of the Securities Exchange Act of 1934.

(3) Covered employee. For purposes of this subsection, the term "covered employee" means any employee of the taxpayer if—

(A) as of the close of the taxable year, such employee is the chief executive officer of the taxpayer or is an individual acting in such a capacity, or

(B) the total compensation of such employee for the taxable year is required to be reported to shareholders under the Securities Exchange Act of 1934 by reason of such employee being among the 4 highest compensated officers for the taxable year (other than the chief executive officer).

(4) Applicable employee remuneration. For purposes of this subsection—

(A) In general. Except as otherwise provided in this paragraph, the term "applicable employee remuneration" means, with respect to any covered employee for any taxable year, the aggregate amount allowable as a deduction under this chapter for such taxable year (determined without regard to this subsection) for remuneration for services performed by such employee (whether or not during the taxable year).

(B) Exception for remuneration payable on commission basis. The term "applicable employee remuneration" shall not include any remuneration payable on a commission basis solely on account of income generated directly by the individual performance of the individual to whom such remuneration is payable.

(C) Other performance-based compensation. The term "applicable employee remuneration" shall not include any remuneration payable solely on account of the attainment of one or more performance goals, but only if—

(i) the performance goals are determined by a compensation committee of the board of directors of the taxpayer which is comprised solely of 2 or more outside directors,

(ii) the material terms under which the remuneration is to be paid, including the performance goals, are disclosed to shareholders and approved by a majority of the vote in a separate shareholder vote before the payment of such remuneration, and

(iii) before any payment of such remuneration, the compensation committee referred to in clause (i) certifies that the performance goals and any other material terms were in fact satisfied.

(D) Exception for existing binding contracts. The term "applicable employee remuneration" shall not include any remuneration payable under a written binding contract which was in effect on February 17, 1993, and which was not modified thereafter in any material respect before such remuneration is paid.

(E) Remuneration. For purposes of this paragraph, the term "remuneration" includes any remuneration (including benefits) in any medium other than cash, but shall not include—

(i) any payment referred to in so much of section 3121(a)(5) as precedes subparagraph (E) thereof, and

(ii) any benefit provided to or on behalf of an employee if at the time such benefit is provided it is reasonable to believe that the employee will be able to exclude such benefit from gross income under this chapter.

For purposes of clause (i), section 3121(a)(5) shall be applied without regard to section 3121(v)(1).

(F) Coordination with disallowed golden parachute payments. The dollar limitation contained in paragraph (1) shall be reduced (but not below zero) by the amount (if any) which would have been included in the applicable employee remuneration of the covered employee for the taxable year but for being disallowed under section 280G.

(5) Special rule for application to employers participating in the Troubled Assets Relief Program

(A) In general. In the case of an applicable employer, no deduction shall be allowed under this chapter—

(i) in the case of executive remuneration for any applicable taxable year which is attributable to services performed by a covered executive during such applicable taxable year, to the extent that the amount of such remuneration exceeds $500,000, or

(ii) in the case of deferred deduction executive remuneration for any taxable year for services performed during any applicable taxable year by a covered executive, to the extent that the amount of such remuneration exceeds $500,000 reduced (but not below zero) by the sum of—

(I) the executive remuneration for such applicable taxable year, plus

(II) the portion of the deferred deduction executive remuneration for such services which was taken into account under this clause in a preceding taxable year.

(B) Applicable employer. For purposes of this paragraph—

(i) In general. Except as provided in clause (ii), the term "applicable employer" means any employer from whom 1 or more troubled assets are acquired under a program established by the Secretary under section 101(a) of the Emergency Economic Stabilization Act of 2008 if the aggregate amount of the assets so acquired for all taxable years exceeds $300,000,000.

(ii) Disregard of certain assets sold through direct purchase. If the only sales of troubled assets by an employer under the program described in clause (i) are through 1 or more direct purchases (within the meaning of section 113(c) of the Emergency Economic Stabilization Act of 2008), such assets shall not be taken into account under clause (i) in determining whether the employer is an applicable employer for purposes of this paragraph.

(iii) Aggregation rules. Two or more persons who are treated as a single employer under subsection (b) or (c) of section 414 shall be treated as a single employer, except that in applying section 1563 (a) for purposes of either such subsection, paragraphs (2) and (3) thereof shall be disregarded.

(C) Applicable taxable year. For purposes of this paragraph, the term "applicable taxable year" means, with respect to any employer—

(i) the first taxable year of the employer—

(I) which includes any portion of the period during which the authorities under section 101(a) of the Emergency Economic Stabilization Act of 2008 are in effect (determined under section 120 thereof), and

(II) in which the aggregate amount of troubled assets acquired from the employer during the taxable year pursuant to such authorities (other than assets to which subparagraph (B)(ii) applies), when added to the aggregate amount so acquired for all preceding taxable years, exceeds $300,000,000, and

(ii) any subsequent taxable year which includes any portion of such period.

(D) Covered executive. For purposes of this paragraph—

(i) In general The term "covered executive" means, with respect to any applicable taxable year, any employee—

(I) who, at any time during the portion of the taxable year during which the authorities under section 101(a) of the Emergency Economic Stabilization Act of 2008 are in effect (determined under section 120 thereof), is the chief executive officer of the applicable employer or the chief financial officer of the applicable employer, or an individual acting in either such capacity, or

(II) who is described in clause (ii).

(ii) Highest compensated employees An employee is described in this clause if the employee is 1 of the 3 highest compensated officers of the applicable employer for the taxable year (other than an individual described in clause (i)(I)), determined—

(I) on the basis of the shareholder disclosure rules for compensation under the Securities Exchange Act of 1934 (without regard to whether those rules apply to the employer), and

(II) by only taking into account employees employed during the portion of the taxable year described in clause (i)(I).

(iii) Employee remains covered executive If an employee is a covered executive with respect to an applicable employer for any applicable taxable year, such employee shall be treated as a covered executive with respect to such employer for all subsequent applicable taxable years and for all subsequent taxable years in which deferred deduction executive remuneration with respect to services performed in all such applicable taxable years would (but for this paragraph) be deductible.

(E) Executive remuneration. For purposes of this paragraph, the term "executive remuneration" means the applicable employee remuneration of the covered executive, as determined under paragraph (4) without regard to subparagraphs (B), (C), and (D) thereof. Such term shall not include any deferred deduction executive remuneration with respect to services performed in a prior applicable taxable year.

(F) Deferred deduction executive remuneration. For purposes of this paragraph, the term "deferred deduction executive remuneration" means remuneration which would be executive remuneration for services performed in an applicable taxable year but for the fact that the deduction under this chapter (determined without regard to this paragraph) for such remuneration is allowable in a subsequent taxable year.

(G) Coordination. Rules similar to the rules of subparagraphs (F) and (G) of paragraph (4) shall apply for purposes of this paragraph.

(H) Regulatory authority. The Secretary may prescribe such guidance, rules, or regulations as are necessary to carry out the purposes of this paragraph and the Emergency Economic Stabilization Act of 2008, including the extent to which this paragraph applies in the case of any acquisition, merger, or reorganization of an applicable employer.

(6) **Special rule for application to certain health insurance providers**

(A) In general- No deduction shall be allowed under this chapter—

(i) in the case of applicable individual remuneration which is for any disqualified taxable year beginning after December 31, 2012, and which is attributable to services performed by an applicable individual during such taxable year, to the extent that the amount of such remuneration exceeds $500,000, or

(ii) in the case of deferred deduction remuneration for any taxable year beginning after December 31, 2012, which is attributable to services performed by an applicable individual during any disqualified taxable year beginning after December 31, 2009, to the extent that the amount of such remuneration exceeds $500,000 reduced (but not below zero) by the sum of—

(I) the applicable individual remuneration for such disqualified taxable year, plus

(II) the portion of the deferred deduction remuneration for such services which was taken into account under this clause in a preceding taxable year (or which would have been taken into account under this clause in a preceding taxable year if this clause were applied by substituting "December 31, 2009" for "December 31, 2012" in the matter preceding subclause (I)).

(B) Disqualified taxable year- For purposes of this paragraph, the term "disqualified taxable year" means, with respect to any employer, any taxable year for which such employer is a covered health insurance provider.

(C) Covered health insurance provider- For purposes of this paragraph—

(i) In general- The term "covered health insurance provider" means—

(I) with respect to taxable years beginning after December 31, 2009, and before January 1, 2013, any employer which is a health insurance issuer (as defined in section 9832(b)(2)) and which receives premiums from providing health insurance coverage (as defined in section 9832(b)(1)), and

(II) with respect to taxable years beginning after December 31, 2012, any employer which is a health insurance issuer (as defined in section 9832(b)(2)) and with respect to which not less than 25 percent of the gross premiums received from providing health insurance coverage (as defined in section 9832(b)(1)) is from minimum essential coverage (as defined in section 5000A(f)).

(ii) Aggregation rules- Two or more persons who are treated as a single employer under subsection (b), (c), (m), or (o) of section 414 shall be treated as a single employer, except that in applying section 1563(a) for purposes of any such subsection, paragraphs (2) and (3) thereof shall be disregarded.

(D) Applicable individual remuneration- For purposes of this paragraph, the term "applicable individual remuneration" means, with respect to any applicable individual for any disqualified taxable year, the aggregate amount allowable as a deduction under this chapter for such taxable year (determined without regard to this subsection) for remuneration (as defined in paragraph (4) without regard to subparagraphs (B), (C), and (D) thereof) for services performed by such individual (whether or not during the taxable year). Such term shall not include any deferred deduction remuneration with respect to services performed during the disqualified taxable year.

(E) Deferred deduction remuneration- For purposes of this paragraph, the term "deferred deduction remuneration" means remuneration which would be applicable individual remuneration for services performed in a disqualified taxable year but for the fact that the deduction under this chapter (determined without regard to this paragraph) for such remuneration is allowable in a subsequent taxable year.

(F) Applicable individual- For purposes of this paragraph, the term "applicable individual" means, with respect to any covered health insurance provider for any disqualified taxable year, any individual—

(i) who is an officer, director, or employee in such taxable year, or

(ii) who provides services for or on behalf of such covered health insurance provider during such taxable year.

(G) Coordination- Rules similar to the rules of subparagraphs (F) and (G) of paragraph (4) shall apply for purposes of this paragraph.

(H) Regulatory authority- The Secretary may prescribe such guidance, rules, or regulations as are necessary to carry out the purposes of this paragraph.

Section 280G of the Internal Revenue Code

Golden parachute payments

(a) **General rule.** No deduction shall be allowed under this chapter for any excess parachute payment.

(b) **Excess parachute payment.** For purposes of this section—

(1) **In general.** The term "excess parachute payment" means an amount equal to the excess of any parachute payment over the portion of the base amount allocated to such payment.

(2) **Parachute payment defined.**

(A) In general. The term "parachute payment" means any payment in the nature of compensation to (or for the benefit of) a disqualified individual if—

(i) such payment is contingent on a change—

(I) in the ownership or effective control of the corporation, or

(II) in the ownership of a substantial portion of the assets of the corporation, and

(ii) the aggregate present value of the payments in the nature of compensation to (or for the benefit of) such individual which are contingent on such change equals or exceeds an amount equal to 3 times the base amount.

For purposes of clause (ii), payments not treated as parachute payments under paragraph (4)(A), (5), or (6) shall not be taken into account.

(B) Agreements. The term "parachute payment" shall also include any payment in the nature of compensation to (or for the benefit of) a disqualified individual if such payment is made pursuant to an agreement which violates any generally enforced securities laws or regulations. In any proceeding involving the issue of whether any payment made to a disqualified individual is a parachute payment on account of a violation of any generally enforced securities laws or regulations, the burden of proof with respect to establishing the occurrence of a violation of such a law or regulation shall be upon the Secretary.

(C) Treatment of certain agreements entered into within 1 year before change of ownership. For purposes of subparagraph (A)(i), any payment pursuant to—

(i) an agreement entered into within 1 year before the change described in subparagraph (A)(i), or

(ii) an amendment made within such 1-year period of a previous agreement,

shall be presumed to be contingent on such change unless the contrary is established by clear and convincing evidence.

(3) Base amount.

(A) In general. The term "base amount" means the individual's annualized includible compensation for the base period.

(B) Allocation. The portion of the base amount allocated to any parachute payment shall be an amount which bears the same ratio to the base amount as—

(i) the present value of such payment, bears to

(ii) the aggregate present value of all such payments.

(4) Treatment of amounts which taxpayer establishes as reasonable compensation. In the case of any payment described in paragraph (2)(A)—

(A) the amount treated as a parachute payment shall not include the portion of such payment which the taxpayer establishes by clear and convincing evidence is reasonable compensation for personal services to be rendered on or after the date of the change described in paragraph (2)(A)(i), and

(B) the amount treated as an excess parachute payment shall be reduced by the portion of such payment which the taxpayer establishes by clear and convincing evidence is reasonable compensation for personal services actually rendered before the date of the change described in paragraph (2)(A)(i).

For purposes of subparagraph (B), reasonable compensation for services actually rendered before the date of the change described in paragraph (2)(A)(i) shall be first offset against the base amount.

(5) Exemption for small business corporations, etc.

(A) In general. Notwithstanding paragraph (2), the term "parachute payment" does not include—

(i) any payment to a disqualified individual with respect to a corporation which (immediately before the change described in paragraph (2)(A)(i)) was a small business corporation (as defined in section 1361(b) but without regard to paragraph (1)(C) thereof), and

(ii) any payment to a disqualified individual with respect to a corporation (other than a corporation described in clause (i)) if—

(I) immediately before the change described in paragraph (2)(A)(i), no stock in such corporation was readily tradeable on an established securities market or otherwise, and

(II) the shareholder approval requirements of subparagraph (B) are met with respect to such payment.

The Secretary may, by regulations, prescribe that the requirements of subclause (I) of clause (ii) are not met where a substantial portion of the assets of any entity consists (directly or indirectly) of stock in such corporation and interests in such other entity are readily tradeable on an established securities market, or otherwise. Stock described in section 1504(a)(4) shall not be taken into account under clause (ii)(I) if the payment does not adversely affect the shareholder's redemption and liquidation rights.

(B) Shareholder approval requirements. The shareholder approval requirements of this subparagraph are met with respect to any payment if—

(i) such payment was approved by a vote of the persons who owned, immediately before the change described in paragraph (2)(A)(i), more than 75 percent of the voting power of all outstanding stock of the corporation, and

(ii) there was adequate disclosure to shareholders of all material facts concerning all payments which (but for this paragraph) would be parachute payments with respect to a disqualified individual.

The regulations prescribed under subsection (e) shall include regulations providing for the application of this subparagraph in the case of shareholders which are not individuals (including the treatment of nonvoting interests in an entity which is a shareholder) and where an entity holds a de minimis amount of stock in the corporation.

(6) Exemption for payments under qualified plans. Notwithstanding paragraph (2), the term "parachute payment" shall not include any payment to or from—

(A) a plan described in section 401(a) which includes a trust exempt from tax under section 501(a),

(B) an annuity plan described in section 403(a),

(C) a simplified employee pension (as defined in section 408(k)), or

(D) a simple retirement account described in section 408(p).

(c) Disqualified individuals. For purposes of this section, the term "disqualified individual" means any individual who is—

(1) an employee, independent contractor, or other person specified in regulations by the Secretary who performs personal services for any corporation, and

(2) is an officer, shareholder, or highly-compensated individual.

For purposes of this section, a personal service corporation (or similar entity) shall be treated as an individual. For purposes of paragraph (2), the term "highly-compensated individual" only includes an individual who is (or would be if the individual were an employee) a member of the group consisting of the highest paid 1 percent of the employees of the corporation or, if less, the highest paid 250 employees of the corporation.

(d) Other definitions and special rules. For purposes of this section—

(1) Annualized includible compensation for base period. The term "annualized includible compensation for the base period" means the average annual compensation which—

(A) was payable by the corporation with respect to which the change in ownership or control described in paragraph (2)(A) of subsection (b) occurs, and

(B) was includible in the gross income of the disqualified individual for taxable years in the base period.

(2) Base period. The term "base period" means the period consisting of the most recent 5 taxable years ending before the date on which the change in ownership or control described in paragraph (2)(A) of subsection (b) occurs (or such portion of such period during which the disqualified individual performed personal services for the corporation).

(3) Property transfers. Any transfer of property—

(A) shall be treated as a payment, and

(B) shall be taken into account as its fair market value.

(4) **Present value.** Present value shall be determined by using a discount rate equal to 120 percent of the applicable Federal rate (determined under section 1274(d)), compounded semiannually.

(5) **Treatment of affiliated groups.** Except as otherwise provided in regulations, all members of the same affiliated group (as defined in section 1504, determined without regard to section 1504(b)) shall be treated as 1 corporation for purposes of this section. Any person who is an officer of any member of such group shall be treated as an officer of such 1 corporation.

(e) **Regulations.** The Secretary shall prescribe such regulations as may be necessary or appropriate to carry out the purposes of this section (including regulations for the application of this section in the case of related corporations and in the case of personal service corporations).

Section 421 of the Internal Revenue Code

General rules [stock options]

(a) **Effect of qualifying transfer.** If a share of stock is transferred to an individual in a transfer in respect of which the requirements of section 422(a) or 423(a) are met—

(1) no income shall result at the time of the transfer of such share to the individual upon his exercise of the option with respect to such share;

(2) no deduction under section 162 (relating to trade or business expenses) shall be allowable at any time to the employer corporation, a parent or subsidiary corporation of such corporation, or a corporation issuing or assuming a stock option in a transaction to which section 424(a) applies, with respect to the share so transferred; and

(3) no amount other than the price paid under the option shall be considered as received by any of such corporations for the share so transferred.

(b) **Effect of disqualifying disposition.** If the transfer of a share of stock to an individual pursuant to his exercise of an option would otherwise meet the requirements of section 422(a) or 423(a) except that there is a failure to meet any of the holding period requirements of section 422(a)(1) or 423(a)(1), then any increase in the income of such individual or deduction from the income of his employer corporation for the taxable year in which such exercise occurred attributable to such disposition, shall be treated as an increase in income or a deduction from income in the taxable year of such individual or of such employer corporation in which such disposition occurred. No amount shall be required to be deducted and withheld under chapter 24 with respect to any increase in income attributable to a disposition described in the preceding sentence.

(c) Exercise by estate.

(1) In general. If an option to which this part applies is exercised after the death of the employee by the estate of the decedent, or by a person who acquired the right to exercise such option by bequest or inheritance or by reason of the death of the decedent, the provisions of subsection (a) shall apply to the same extent as if the option had been exercised by the decedent, except that—

(A) the holding period and employment requirements of sections 422(a) and 423(a) shall not apply, and

(B) any transfer by the estate of stock acquired shall be considered a disposition of such stock for purposes of section 423(c).

(2) Deduction for estate tax. If an amount is required to be included under section 423(c) in gross income of the estate of the deceased employee or of a person described in paragraph (1), there shall be allowed to the estate or such person a deduction with respect to the estate tax attributable to the inclusion in the taxable estate of the deceased employee of the net value for estate tax purposes of the option. For this purpose, the deduction shall be determined under section 691(c) as if the option acquired from the deceased employee were an item of gross income in respect of the decedent under section 691 and as if the amount includible in gross income under section 423(c) were an amount included in gross income under section 691 in respect of such item of gross income.

(3) Basis of shares acquired. In the case of a share of stock acquired by the exercise of an option to which paragraph (1) applies—

(A) the basis of such share shall include so much of the basis of the option as is attributable to such share; except that the basis of such share shall be reduced by the excess (if any) of (i) the amount which would have been includible in gross income under section 423(c) if the employee had exercised the option on the date of his death and had held the share acquired pursuant to such exercise at the time of his death, over (ii) the amount which is includible in gross income under such section; and

(B) the last sentence of section 423(c) shall apply only to the extent that the amount includible in gross income under such section exceeds so much of the basis of the option as is attributable to such share.

Section 422 of the Internal Revenue Code

Incentive stock options

(a) In general. Section 421(a) shall apply with respect to the transfer of a share of stock to an individual pursuant to his exercise of an incentive stock option if—

(1) no disposition of such share is made by him within 2 years from the date of the granting of the option nor within 1 year after the transfer of such share to him, and

(2) at all times during the period beginning on the date of the granting of the option and ending on the day 3 months before the date of such exercise, such individual was an employee of either the corporation granting such option, a parent or subsidiary corporation of such corporation, or a corporation or a parent or subsidiary corporation of such corporation issuing or assuming a stock option in a transaction to which section 424(a) applies.

(b) Incentive stock option. For purposes of this part, the term "incentive stock option" means an option granted to an individual for any reason connected with his employment by a corporation, if granted by the employer corporation or its parent or subsidiary corporation, to purchase stock of any of such corporations, but only if—

(1) the option is granted pursuant to a plan which includes the aggregate number of shares which may be issued under options and the employees (or class of employees) eligible to receive options, and which is approved by the stockholders of the granting corporation within 12 months before or after the date such plan is adopted;

(2) such option is granted within 10 years from the date such plan is adopted, or the date such plan is approved by the stockholders, whichever is earlier;

(3) such option by its terms is not exercisable after the expiration of 10 years from the date such option is granted;

(4) the option price is not less than the fair market value of the stock at the time such option is granted;

(5) such option by its terms is not transferable by such individual otherwise than by will or the laws of descent and distribution, and is exercisable, during his lifetime, only by him; and

(6) such individual, at the time the option is granted, does not own stock possessing more than 10 percent of the total combined voting power of all classes of stock of the employer corporation or of its parent or subsidiary corporation.

Such term shall not include any option if (as of the time the option is granted) the terms of such option provide that it will not be treated as an incentive stock option.

(c) Special rules.

(1) Good faith efforts to value of stock. If a share of stock is transferred pursuant to the exercise by an individual of an option which would fail to qualify as an incentive stock option under subsection (b) because there was a failure in an attempt, made in good faith, to meet the requirement of subsection (b)(4), the requirement of subsection (b)(4) shall be considered to have been met. To the extent provided in regulations by the Secretary, a similar rule shall apply for purposes of subsection (d).

(2) Certain disqualifying dispositions where amount realized is less than value at exercise. If—

(A) an individual who has acquired a share of stock by the exercise of an incentive stock option makes a disposition of such share within either of the periods described in subsection (a)(1), and

(B) such disposition is a sale or exchange with respect to which a loss (if sustained) would be recognized to such individual,

then the amount which is includible in the gross income of such individual, and the amount which is deductible from the income of his employer corporation, as compensation attributable to the exercise of such option shall not exceed the excess (if any) of the amount realized on such sale or exchange over the adjusted basis of such share.

(3) Certain transfers by insolvent individuals. If an insolvent individual holds a share of stock acquired pursuant to his exercise of an incentive stock option, and if such share is transferred to a trustee, receiver, or other similar fiduciary in any proceeding under title 11 or any other similar insolvency proceeding, neither such transfer, nor any other transfer of such share for the benefit of his creditors in such proceeding, shall constitute a disposition of such share for purposes of subsection (a)(1).

(4) Permissible provisions. An option which meets the requirements of subsection (b) shall be treated as an incentive stock option even if—

(A) the employee may pay for the stock with stock of the corporation granting the option,

(B) the employee has a right to receive property at the time of exercise of the option, or

(C) the option is subject to any condition not inconsistent with the provisions of subsection (b).

Subparagraph (B) shall apply to a transfer of property (other than cash) only if section 83 applies to the property so transferred.

(5) 10-percent shareholder rule. Subsection (b)(6) shall not apply if at the time such option is granted the option price is at least 110 percent of the fair market value of the stock subject to the option and such option by its terms is not exercisable after the expiration of 5 years from the date such option is granted.

(6) Special rule when disabled. For purposes of subsection (a)(2), in the case of an employee who is disabled (within the meaning of section 22(e)(3)), the 3-month period of subsection (a)(2) shall be 1 year.

(7) Fair market value. For purposes of this section, the fair market value of stock shall be determined without regard to any restriction other than a restriction which, by its terms, will never lapse.

(d) **$100,000 per year limitation.**

(1) In general. To the extent that the aggregate fair market value of stock with respect to which incentive stock options (determined without regard to this subsection) are exercisable for the 1st time by any individual during any calendar year (under all plans of the individual's employer corporation and its parent and subsidiary corporations) exceeds $100,000, such options shall be treated as options which are not incentive stock options.

(2) Ordering rule. Paragraph (1) shall be applied by taking options into account in the order in which they were granted.

(3) Determination of fair market value. For purposes of paragraph (1), the fair market value of any stock shall be determined as of the time the option with respect to such stock is granted.

Section 423 of the Internal Revenue Code

Employee stock purchase plans

(a) **General rule.** Section 421(a) shall apply with respect to the transfer of a share of stock to an individual pursuant to his exercise of an option granted after December 31, 1963, under an employee stock purchase plan (as defined in subsection (b)) if–

(1) no disposition of such share is made by him within 2 years after the date of the granting of the option nor within 1 year after the transfer of such share to him; and

(2) at all times during the period beginning with the date of the granting of the option and ending on the day 3 months before the date of such exercise, he is an employee of the corporation granting such option, a parent or subsidiary corporation of such corporation, or a corporation or a parent or subsidiary corporation of such corporation issuing or assuming a stock option in a transaction to which section 424(a) applies.

(b) Employee stock purchase plan. For purposes of this part, the term "employee stock purchase plan" means a plan which meets the following requirements:

(1) the plan provides that options are to be granted only to employees of the employer corporation or of its parent or subsidiary corporation to purchase stock in any such corporation;

(2) such plan is approved by the stockholders of the granting corporation within 12 months before or after the date such plan is adopted;

(3) under the terms of the plan, no employee can be granted an option if such employee, immediately after the option is granted, owns stock possessing 5 percent or more of the total combined voting power or value of all classes of stock of the employer corporation or of its parent or subsidiary corporation. For purposes of this paragraph, the rules of section 424(d) shall apply in determining the stock ownership of an individual, and stock which the employee may purchase under outstanding options shall be treated as stock owned by the employee;

(4) under the terms of the plan, options are to be granted to all employees of any corporation whose employees are granted any of such options by reason of their employment by such corporation, except that there may be excluded—

(A) employees who have been employed less than 2 years,

(B) employees whose customary employment is 20 hours or less per week,

(C) employees whose customary employment is for not more than 5 months in any calendar year, and

(D) highly compensated employees (within the meaning of section 414(q));

(5) under the terms of the plan, all employees granted such options shall have the same rights and privileges, except that the amount of stock which may be purchased by any employee under such option may bear a uniform relationship to the total compensation, or the basic or regular rate of compensation, of employees, and the plan may provide that no employee may purchase more than a maximum amount of stock fixed under the plan;

(6) under the terms of the plan, the option price is not less than the lesser of—

(A) an amount equal to 85 percent of the fair market value of the stock at the time such option is granted, or

(B) an amount which under the terms of the option may not be less than 85 percent of the fair market value of the stock at the time such option is exercised;

(7) under the terms of the plan, such option cannot be exercised after the expiration of—

(A) 5 years from the date such option is granted if, under the terms of such plan, the option price is to be not less than 85 percent of the fair market value of such stock at the time of the exercise of the option, or

(B) 27 months from the date such option is granted, if the option price is not determinable in the manner described in subparagraph (A)

(8) under the terms of the plan, no employee may be granted an option which permits his rights to purchase stock under all such plans of his employer corporation and its parent and subsidiary corporations to accrue at a rate which exceeds $25,000 of fair market value of such stock (determined at the time such option is granted) for each calendar year in which such option is outstanding at any time. For purposes of this paragraph—

(A) the right to purchase stock under an option accrues when the option (or any portion thereof) first becomes exercisable during the calendar year;

(B) the right to purchase stock under an option accrues at the rate provided in the option, but in no case may such rate exceed $25,000 of fair market value of such stock (determined at the time such option is granted) for any one calendar year; and

(C) a right to purchase stock which has accrued under one option granted pursuant to the plan may not be carried over to any other option; and

(9) under the terms of the plan, such option is not transferable by such individual otherwise than by will or the laws of descent and distribution, and is exercisable, during his lifetime, only by him.

For purposes of paragraphs (3) to (9), inclusive, where additional terms are contained in an offering made under a plan, such additional terms shall, with respect to options exercised under such offering, be treated as a part of the terms of such plan.

(c) Special rule where option price is between 85 percent and 100 percent of value of stock. If the option price of a share of stock acquired by an individual pursuant to a transfer to which subsection (a) applies was less than 100 percent of the fair market value of such share at the time such option was granted, then, in the event of any disposition of such share by him which meets the holding period requirements of subsection (a), or in the event of his death (whenever occurring) while owning such share, there shall be included as compensation (and not as gain upon the sale or exchange of a capital asset) in his gross income, for the taxable year in which falls the date of such disposition or for the taxable year closing with his death, whichever applies, an amount equal to the lesser of—

(1) the excess of the fair market value of the share at the time of such disposition or death over the amount paid for the share under the option, or

(2) the excess of the fair market value of the share at the time the option was granted over the option price.

If the option price is not fixed or determinable at the time the option is granted, then for purposes of this subsection, the option price shall be determined as if the option were exercised at such time. In the case of the disposition of such share by the individual, the basis of the share in his hands at the time of such disposition shall be increased by an amount equal to the amount so includible in his gross income. No amount shall be required to be deducted and withheld under chapter 24 with respect to any increase in income attributable to a disposition described in the preceding sentence.

Section 424 of the Internal Revenue Code
Definitions and special rules [stock options]

(a) Corporate reorganizations, liquidations, etc. For purposes of this part, the term "issuing or assuming a stock option in a transaction to which section 424(a) applies" means a substitution of a new option for the old option, or an assumption of the old option, by an employer corporation, or a parent or subsidiary of such corporation, by reason of a corporate merger, consolidation, acquisition of property or stock, separation, reorganization, or liquidation, if—

(1) the excess of the aggregate fair market value of the shares subject to the option immediately after the substitution or assumption over the aggregate option price of such shares is not more than the excess of the aggregate fair market value of all shares subject to the option immediately before such substitution or assumption over the aggregate option price of such shares, and

(2) the new option or the assumption of the old option does not give the employee additional benefits which he did not have under the old option.

For purposes of this subsection, the parent-subsidiary relationship shall be determined at the time of any such transaction under this subsection.

(b) Acquisition of new stock. For purposes of this part, if stock is received by an individual in a distribution to which section 305, 354, 355, 356, or 1036 (or so much of section 1031 as relates to section 1036) applies, and such distribution was made with respect to stock transferred to him upon his exercise of the option, such stock shall be considered as having been transferred to him on his exercise of such option. A similar rule shall be applied in the case of a series of such distributions.

(c) Disposition.

(1) **In general.** Except as provided in paragraphs (2), (3), and (4), for purposes of this part, the term "disposition" includes a sale, exchange, gift, or a transfer of legal title, but does not include -

(A) a transfer from a decedent to an estate or a transfer by request or inheritance;

(B) an exchange to which section 354, 355, 356, or 1036 (or so much of section 1031 as relates to section 1036) applies; or

(C) a mere pledge or hypothecation.

(2) **Joint tenancy.** The acquisition of a share of stock in the name of the employee and another jointly with the right of survivorship or a subsequent transfer of a share of stock into such joint ownership shall not be deemed a disposition, but a termination of such joint tenancy (except to the extent such employee acquires ownership of such stock) shall be treated as a disposition by him occurring at the time such joint tenancy is terminated.

(3) **Special rule where incentive stock is acquired through use of other statutory option stock.**

(A) Nonrecognition sections not to apply. If—

(i) there is a transfer of statutory option stock in connection with the exercise of any incentive stock option, and

(ii)the applicable holding period requirements (under section 422(a)(1) or 423(a)(1)) are not met before such transfer,

then no section referred to in subparagraph (B) of paragraph (1) shall apply to such transfer.

(B) Statutory option stock. For purpose of subparagraph (A), the term "statutory option stock" means any stock acquired through the exercise of an incentive stock option or an option granted under an employee stock purchase plan.

(4) **Transfers between spouses or incident to divorce.** In the case of any transfer described in subsection (a) of section 1041—

(A) such transfer shall not be treated as a disposition for purposes of this part, and

(B) the same tax treatment under this part with respect to the transferred property shall apply to the transferee as would have applied to the transferor.

(d) Attribution of stock ownership. For purposes of this part, in applying the percentage limitations of sections 422(b)(6) and 423(b)(3)—

(1) the individual with respect to whom such limitation is being determined shall be considered as owning the stock owned, directly or indirectly, by or for his brothers and sisters (whether by the whole or half blood), spouse, ancestors, and lineal descendants; and

(2) stock owned, directly or indirectly, by or for a corporation, partnership, estate, or trust, shall be considered as being owned proportionately by or for its shareholders, partners, or beneficiaries.

(e) **Parent corporation.** For purposes of this part, the term "parent corporation" means any corporation (other than the employer corporation) in an unbroken chain of corporations ending with the employer corporation if, at the time of the granting of the option, each of the corporations other than the employer corporation owns stock possessing 50 percent or more of the total combined voting power of all classes of stock in one of the other corporations in such chain.

(f) **Subsidiary corporation.** For purposes of this part, the term "subsidiary corporation" means any corporation (other than the employer corporation) in an unbroken chain of corporations beginning with the employer corporation if, at the time of the granting of the option, each of the corporations other than the last corporation in the unbroken chain owns stock possessing 50 percent or more of the total combined voting power of all classes of stock in one of the other corporations in such chain.

(g) **Special rule for applying subsections (e) and (f).** In applying subsections (e) and (f) for purposes of section 422(a)(2) and 423(a)(2), there shall be substituted for the term "employer corporation" wherever it appears in subsection (e) and (f) the term "grantor corporation" or the term "corporation issuing or assuming a stock option in a transaction to which section 424(a) applies" as the case may be.

(h) **Modification, extension, or renewal of option.**

(1) **In general.** For purposes of this part, if the terms of any option to purchase stock are modified, extended, or renewed, such modification, extension, or renewal shall be considered as the granting of a new option.

(2) **Special rule for section 423 options.** In the case of the transfer of stock pursuant to the exercise of an option to which section 423 applies and which has been so modified, extended, or renewed, the fair market value of such stock at the time of the granting of the option shall be considered as whichever of the following is the highest—

(A) the fair market value of such stock on the date of the original granting of the option,

(B) the fair market value of such stock on the date of the making of such modification, extension, or renewal, or

(C) the fair market value of such stock at the time of the making of any intervening modification, extension, or renewal.

(3) Definition of modification. The term "modification" means any change in the terms of the option which gives the employee additional benefits under the option, but such term shall not include a change in the terms of the option—

(A) attributable to the issuance or assumption of an option under subsection (a);

(B) to permit the option to qualify under section 423(b)(9); or

(C) in the case of an option not immediately exercisable in full, to accelerate the time at which the option may be exercised.

(i) Stockholder approval. For purposes of this part, if the grant of an option is subject to approval by stockholders, the date of grant of the option shall be determined as if the option had not been subject to such approval.

(j) Cross references. For provisions requiring the reporting of certain acts with respect to a qualified stock option, an incentive stock option, options granted under employer stock purchase plans, or a restricted stock option, see section 6039.

Section 1041 of the Internal Revenue Code

Transfers of property between spouses or incident to divorce

(a) General rule.—No gain or loss shall be recognized on a transfer of property from an individual to (or in trust for the benefit of)—

(1) a spouse, or

(2) a former spouse, but only if the transfer is incident to the divorce.

(b) Transfer treated as gift; transferee has transferor's basis.—In the case of any transfer of property described in subsection (a)—

(1) for purposes of this subtitle, the property shall be treated as acquired by the transferee by gift, and

(2) the basis of the transferee in the property shall be the adjusted basis of the transferor.

(c) Incident to divorce.—For purposes of subsection (a)(2), a transfer of property is incident to the divorce if such transfer—

(1) occurs within 1 year after the date on which the marriage ceases, or

(2) is related to the cessation of the marriage.

(d) Special rule where spouse is nonresident alien.—Subsection (a) shall not apply if the spouse (or former spouse) of the individual making the transfer is a nonresident alien.

(e) Transfers in trust where liability exceeds basis.—Subsection (a) shall not apply to the transfer of property in trust to the extent that—

(1) the sum of the amount of the liabilities assumed, plus the amount of the liabilities to which the property is subject, exceeds

(2) the total of the adjusted basis of the property transferred.

Proper adjustment shall be made under subsection (b) in the basis of the transferee in such property to take into account gain recognized by reason of the preceding sentence.

Section 4999 of the Internal Revenue Code
Golden parachute payments

(a) Imposition of tax.—There is hereby imposed on any person who receives an excess parachute payment a tax equal to 20 percent of the amount of such payment.

(b) Excess parachute payment defined.—For purposes of this section, the term "excess parachute payment" has the meaning given to such term by section 280G(b).

(c) Administrative provisions.—

(1) Withholding.—In the case of any excess parachute payment which is wages (within the meaning of section 3401) the amount deducted and withheld under section 3402 shall be increased by the amount of the tax imposed by this section on such payment.

(2) Other administrative provisions.—For purposes of subtitle F, any tax imposed by this section shall be treated as a tax imposed by subtitle A.

Section 6039 of the Internal Revenue Code
Returns required in connection with certain options

(a) Requirement of Reporting

Every corporation –

(1) which in any calendar year transfers to any person a share of stock pursuant to such person's exercise of an incentive stock option, or

(2) which in any calendar year records (or has by its agent recorded) a transfer of the legal title of a share of stock acquired by the transferor pursuant to

his exercise of an option described in section 423(c) (relating to special rule where option price is between 85 percent and 100 percent of value of stock),

shall, for such calendar year, make a return at such time and in such manner, and setting forth such information, as the Secretary may by regulations prescribe.

(b) Statements To Be Furnished to Persons With Respect to Whom Information Is Reported.—Every corporation making a return under subsection (a) shall furnish to each person whose name is set forth in such return a written statement setting forth such information as the Secretary may by regulations prescribe. The written statement required under the preceding sentence shall be furnished to such person on or before January 31 of the year following the calendar year for which the return under subsection (a) was made.

(c) Special rules

For purposes of this section –

(1) Treatment by employer to be determinative

Any option which the corporation treats as an incentive stock option or an option granted under an employee stock purchase plan shall be deemed to be such an option.

(2) Subsection (a)(2) applies only to first transfer described therein

A statement is required by reason of a transfer described in subsection (a)(2) of a share only with respect to the first transfer of such share by the person who exercised the option.

(3) Identification of stock

Any corporation which transfers any share of stock pursuant to the exercise of any option described in subsection (a)(2) shall identify such stock in a manner adequate to carry out the purposes of this section.

(d) Cross references

For definition of –

(1) the term "incentive stock option", see section 422(b), and

(2) the term "employee stock purchase plan" see section 423(b).

Section 16 of the Securities Exchange Act of 1934

Directors, Officers, and Principal Stockholders

(a) Disclosures required

(1) Directors, officers, and principal stockholders required to file—Every person who is directly or indirectly the beneficial owner of more than 10 percent of any class of any equity security (other than an exempted security)

which is registered pursuant to section 78l of this title, or who is a director or an officer of the issuer of such security, shall file the statements required by this subsection with the Commission.

(2) Time of filing—The statements required by this subsection shall be filed—

(A) at the time of the registration of such security on a national securities exchange or by the effective date of a registration statement filed pursuant to section 78l (g) of this title;

(B) within 10 days after he or she becomes such beneficial owner, director, or officer, or within such shorter time as the Commission may establish by rule;

(C) if there has been a change in such ownership, or if such person shall have purchased or sold a security-based swap agreement involving such equity security, before the end of the second business day following the day on which the subject transaction has been executed, or at such other time as the Commission shall establish, by rule, in any case in which the Commission determines that such 2-day period is not feasible.

(3) Contents of statements—A statement filed—

(A) under subparagraph (A) or (B) of paragraph (2) shall contain a statement of the amount of all equity securities of such issuer of which the filing person is the beneficial owner; and

(B) under subparagraph (C) of such paragraph shall indicate ownership by the filing person at the date of filing, any such changes in such ownership, and such purchases and sales of the security-based swap agreements or security-based swaps as have occurred since the most recent such filing under such subparagraph.

(4) Electronic filing and availability—Beginning not later than 1 year after July 30, 2002—

(A) a statement filed under subparagraph (C) of paragraph (2) shall be filed electronically;

(B) the Commission shall provide each such statement on a publicly accessible Internet site not later than the end of the business day following that filing; and

(C) the issuer (if the issuer maintains a corporate website) shall provide that statement on that corporate website, not later than the end of the business day following that filing.

(b) Profits from purchase and sale of security within six months—For the purpose of preventing the unfair use of information which may have been obtained by such beneficial owner, director, or officer by reason of his relationship to the issuer, any profit realized by him from any purchase and sale, or any sale and purchase, of any equity security of such issuer (other than an exempted security) or a security-based swap agreement involving any such equity security within any period of less than six months, unless such security or security-based swap agreement was acquired in good faith in connection with a debt previously contracted, shall inure to and be recoverable by the issuer, irrespective of any intention on the part of such beneficial owner, director, or officer in entering into such transaction of holding the security or security-based swap agreement purchased or of not repurchasing the security or security-based swap agreement sold for a period exceeding six months. Suit to recover such profit may be instituted at law or in equity in any court of competent jurisdiction by the issuer, or by the owner of any security of the issuer in the name and in behalf of the issuer if the issuer shall fail or refuse to bring such suit within sixty days after request or shall fail diligently to prosecute the same thereafter; but no such suit shall be brought more than two years after the date such profit was realized. This subsection shall not be construed to cover any transaction where such beneficial owner was not such both at the time of the purchase and sale, or the sale and purchase, of the security or security-based swap agreement or a security-based swap involved, or any transaction or transactions which the Commission by rules and regulations may exempt as not comprehended within the purpose of this subsection.

(c) Conditions for sale of security by beneficial owner, director, or officer— It shall be unlawful for any such beneficial owner, director, or officer, directly or indirectly, to sell any equity security of such issuer (other than an exempted security), if the person selling the security or his principal

(1) does not own the security sold, or

(2) if owning the security, does not deliver it against such sale within twenty days thereafter, or does not within five days after such sale deposit it in the mails or other usual channels of transportation; but no person shall be deemed to have violated this subsection if he proves that notwithstanding the exercise of good faith he was unable to make such delivery or deposit within such time, or that to do so would cause undue inconvenience or expense.

(d) Securities held in investment account, transactions in ordinary course of business, and establishment of primary or secondary market—The provisions of subsection (b) of this section shall not apply to any purchase and sale, or sale and purchase, and the provisions of subsection (c) of this section shall not apply to any sale, of an equity security not then or theretofore held by him in an investment account, by a dealer in the ordinary course of his business and incident to the establishment or maintenance by him of a primary or secondary market (otherwise than on a national securities exchange or an exchange exempted from registration under section 78e of this title) for such security. The Commission may, by such rules and regulations as it deems necessary or appropriate in the public interest, define and prescribe terms and conditions with respect to securities held in an investment account and transactions made in the ordinary course of business and incident to the establishment or maintenance of a primary or secondary market.

(e) Application of section to foreign or domestic arbitrage transactions— The provisions of this section shall not apply to foreign or domestic arbitrage transactions unless made in contravention of such rules and regulations as the Commission may adopt in order to carry out the purposes of this section.

(f) Treatment of transactions in security futures products—The provisions of this section shall apply to ownership of and transactions in security futures products.

(g) Limitation on Commission authority—The authority of the Commission under this section with respect to security-based swap agreements shall be subject to the restrictions and limitations of section 78c–1 (b) of this title.

SEC Rule 144

Preliminary Note: Certain basic principles are essential to an understanding of the registration requirements in the Securities Act of 1933 (the Act or the Securities Act) and the purposes underlying Rule 144:

1. If any person sells a non-exempt security to any other person, the sale must be registered unless an exemption can be found for the transaction.

2. Section 4(1) of the Securities Act provides one such exemption for a transaction "by a person other than an issuer, underwriter, or dealer." Therefore, an understanding of the term "underwriter" is important in determining whether or not the Section 4(1) exemption from registration is available for the sale of the securities.

The term "underwriter" is broadly defined in Section 2(a)(11) of the Securities Act to mean any person who has purchased from an issuer with a view to, or offers or sells for an issuer in connection with, the distribution of any security, or participates, or has a direct or indirect participation in any such undertaking, or participates or has a participation in the direct or indirect underwriting of any such undertaking. The interpretation of this definition traditionally has focused on the words "with a view to" in the phrase "purchased from an issuer with a view to * * * distribution." An investment banking firm which arranges with an issuer for the public sale of its securities is clearly an "underwriter" under that section. However, individual investors who are not professionals in the securities business also may be "underwriters" if they act as links in a chain of transactions through which securities move from an issuer to the public.

Since it is difficult to ascertain the mental state of the purchaser at the time of an acquisition of securities, prior to and since the adoption of Rule 144, subsequent acts and circumstances have been considered to determine whether the purchaser took the securities "with a view to distribution" at the time of the acquisition. Emphasis has been placed on factors such as the length of time the person held the securities and whether there has been an unforeseeable change in circumstances of the holder. Experience has shown, however, that reliance upon such factors alone has led to uncertainty in the application of the registration provisions of the Act.

The Commission adopted Rule 144 to establish specific criteria for determining whether a person is not engaged in a distribution. Rule 144 creates a safe harbor from the Section 2(a)(11) definition of "underwriter." A person satisfying the applicable conditions of the Rule 144 safe harbor is deemed not to be engaged in a distribution of the securities and therefore not an underwriter of the securities for purposes of Section 2(a)(11). Therefore, such a person is deemed not to be an underwriter when determining whether a sale is eligible for the Section 4(1) exemption for "transactions by any person other than an issuer, underwriter, or dealer." If a sale of securities complies with all of the applicable conditions of Rule 144:

1. Any affiliate or other person who sells restricted securities will be deemed not to be engaged in a distribution and therefore not an underwriter for that transaction;

2. Any person who sells restricted or other securities on behalf of an affiliate of the issuer will be deemed not to be engaged in a distribution and therefore not an underwriter for that transaction; and

3. The purchaser in such transaction will receive securities that are not restricted securities.

Rule 144 is not an exclusive safe harbor. A person who does not meet all of the applicable conditions of Rule 144 still may claim any other available exemption under the Act for the sale of the securities. The Rule 144 safe harbor is not available to any person with respect to any transaction or series of transactions that, although in technical compliance with Rule 144, is part of a plan or scheme to evade the registration requirements of the Act.

(a) *Definitions.* The following definitions shall apply for the purposes of this rule:

(1) An "affiliate" of an issuer is a person that directly, or indirectly through one or more intermediaries, controls, or is controlled by, or is under common control with, such issuer.

(2) The term "person" when used with reference to a person for whose account securities are to be sold in reliance upon this rule includes, in addition to such person, all of the following persons:

(i) Any relative or spouse of such person, or any relative of such spouse, any one of whom has the same home as such person;

(ii) Any trust or estate in which such person or any of the persons specified in paragraph (a)(2)(i) of this section collectively own 10 percent or more of the total beneficial interest or of which any of such persons serve as trustee, executor or in any similar capacity; and

(iii) Any corporation or other organization (other than the issuer) in which such person or any of the persons specified in paragraph (a)(2)(i) of this section are the beneficial owners collectively of 10 percent or more of any class of equity securities or 10 percent or more of the equity interest.

(3) The term "restricted securities" means:

(i) Securities acquired directly or indirectly from the issuer, or from an affiliate of the issuer, in a transaction or chain of transactions not involving any public offering;

(ii) Securities acquired from the issuer that are subject to the resale limitations of Rule 502(d) under Regulation D or Rule 701(c);

(iii) Securities acquired in a transaction or chain of transactions meeting the requirementsof Rule 144A;

(iv) Securities acquired from the issuer in a transaction subject to the conditions of Regulation CE;

(v) Equity securities of domestic issuers acquired in a transaction or chain of transactions subject to the conditions of Rule 901 or Rule 903 under Regulation S;

(vi) Securities acquired in a transaction made under § 230.801 to the same extent and proportion that the securities held by the security holder of the class with respect to which the rights offering was made were, as of the record date for the rights offering, "restricted securities" within the meaning of this paragraph (a)(3);

(vii) Securities acquired in a transaction made under § 230.802 to the same extent and proportion that the securities that were tendered or exchanged in the exchange offer or business combination were "restricted securities" within the meaning of this paragraph (a)(3); and

(viii) Securities acquired from the issuer in a transaction subject to an exemption under section 4(6) (15 U.S.C. 77d(6)) of the Act.

(4) The term *debt securities* means:

(i) Any security other than an equity security as defined in § 230.405;

(ii) Non-participatory preferred stock, which is defined as non-convertible capital stock, the holders of which are entitled to a preference in payment of dividends and in distribution of assets on liquidation, dissolution, or winding up of the issuer, but are not entitled to participate in residual earnings or assets of the issuer; and

(iii) Asset-backed securities, as defined in § 229.1101 of this chapter.

(b) *Conditions to be met.* Subject to paragraph (i) of this section, the following conditions must be met:

(1) *Non-Affiliates.*

(i) If the issuer of the securities is, and has been for a period of at least 90 days immediately before the sale, subject to the reporting requirements of section 13 or 15(d) of the Securities Exchange Act of 1934 (the Exchange Act), any person who is not an affiliate of the issuer at the time of the sale, and has not been an affiliate during the preceding three months, who sells restricted securities of the issuer for his or her own account shall be deemed not to be an underwriter of those securities within the meaning of section 2(a)(11) of the Act if all of the conditions of paragraphs (c)(1) and (d) of this section are met. The requirements of paragraph (c)(1) of this section shall not apply to restricted securities sold for the account of a person who is not an affiliate of the issuer at the time of the sale and has not been an affiliate during the preceding three months, provided a period of one year has elapsed since the later of the date the securities were acquired from the issuer or from an affiliate of the issuer.

(ii) If the issuer of the securities is not, or has not been for a period of at least 90 days immediately before the sale, subject to the reporting requirements of section 13 or 15(d) of the Exchange Act, any person who is not an affiliate of the issuer at the time of the sale, and has not been an affiliate during the preceding three months, who sells restricted securities of the issuer for his or her own account shall be deemed not to be an underwriter of those securities within the meaning of section 2(a)(11) of the Act if the condition of paragraph (d) of this section is met.

(2) *Affiliates or persons selling on behalf of affiliates.* Any affiliate of the issuer, or any person who was an affiliate at any time during the 90 days immediately before the sale, who sells restricted securities, or any person who sells restricted or any other securities for the account of an affiliate of the issuer of such securities, or any person who sells restricted or any other securities for the account of a person who was an affiliate at any time during the 90 days immediately before the sale, shall be deemed not to be an underwriter of those securities within the meaning of section 2(a)(11) of the Act if all of the conditions of this section are met.

(c) *Current public information.* Adequate current public information with respect to the issuer of the securities must be available. Such information will be deemed to be available only if the applicable condition set forth in this paragraph is met:

(1) *Reporting Issuers.* The issuer is, and has been for a period of at least 90 days immediately before the sale, subject to the reporting requirements of section 13 or 15(d) of the Exchange Act and has filed all required reports under section 13 or 15(d) of the Exchange Act, as applicable, during the 12 months preceding such sale (or for such shorter period that the issuer was required to file such reports), other than Form 8–K reports (§ 249.308 of this chapter); or

(2) *Non-reporting Issuers.* If the issuer is not subject to the reporting requirements of section 13 or 15(d) of the Exchange Act, there is publicly available the information concerning the issuer specified in paragraphs (a)(5)(i) to (xiv), inclusive, and paragraph (a)(5)(xvi) of § 240.15c2–11 of this chapter, or, if the issuer is an insurance company, the information specified in section 12(g)(2)(G)(i) of the Exchange Act (15 U.S.C. 78*l*(g)(2)(G)(i)).

Note to § 230.144(c). With respect to paragraph (c)(1), the person can rely upon:

1. A statement in whichever is the most recent report, quarterly or annual, required to be filed and filed by the issuer that such issuer has filed all reports required under section 13 or 15(d) of the Exchange Act, as applicable, during the preceding 12 months (or for such shorter period that the issuer was required to file such reports), other than Form 8–K reports (§ 249.308 of this chapter), and has been subject to such filing requirements for the past 90 days; or

2. A written statement from the issuer that it has complied with such reporting requirements.

3. Neither type of statement may be relied upon, however, if the person knows or has reason to believe that the issuer has not complied with such requirements.

(d) *Holding Period For Restricted Securities.* If the securities sold are restricted securities, the following provisions apply:

(1) *General rule.*

(i) If the issuer of the securities is, and has been for a period of at least 90 days immediately before the sale, subject to the reporting requirements of section 13 or 15(d) of the Exchange Act, a minimum of six months must elapse between the later of the date of the acquisition of the securities from the issuer, or from an affiliate of the issuer, and any resale of such securities in reliance on this section for the account of either the acquiror or any subsequent holder of those securities.

(ii) If the issuer of the securities is not, or has not been for a period of at least 90 days immediately before the sale, subject to the reporting requirements of section 13 or 15(d) of the Exchange Act, a minimum of one year must elapse between the later of the date of the acquisition of the securities from the issuer, or from an affiliate of the issuer, and any resale of such securities in reliance on this section for the account of either the acquiror or any subsequent holder of those securities. (iii) If the acquiror takes the securities by purchase, the holding period shall not begin until the full purchase price or other consideration is paid or given by the person acquiring the securities from the issuer or from an affiliate of the issuer.

(2) *Promissory Notes, Other Obligations or Installment Contracts.* Giving the issuer or affiliate of the issuer from whom the securities were purchased a promissory note or other obligation to pay the purchase price, or entering into an installment purchase contract with such seller, shall not be deemed full payment of the purchase price unless the promissory note, obligation or contract:

(i) Provides for full recourse against the purchaser of the securities;

(ii) Is secured by collateral, other than the securities purchased, having a fair market value at least equal to the purchase price of the securities purchased; and

(iii) Shall have been discharged by payment in full prior to the sale of the securities.

(3) *Determination of Holding Period.* The following provisions shall apply for the purpose of determining the period securities have been held:

(i) *Stock dividends, splits and recapitalizations.* Securities acquired from the issuer as a dividend or pursuant to a stock split, reverse split or recapitalization shall be deemed to have been acquired at the same time as the securities on which the dividend or, if more than one, the initial dividend was paid, the securities involved in the split or reverse split, or the securities surrendered in connection with the recapitalization.

(ii) *Conversions and exchanges.* If the securities sold were acquired from the issuer solely in exchange for other securities of the same issuer, the newly acquired securities shall be deemed to have been acquired at the same time as the securities surrendered for conversion or exchange, even if the securities surrendered were not convertible or exchangeable by their terms.

Note to § 230.144(d)(3)(ii). If the surrendered securities originally did not provide for cashless conversion or exchange by their terms and the holder provided consideration, other than solely securities of the same issuer, in connection with the amendment of the surrendered securities to permit cashless conversion or exchange, then the newly acquired securities shall be deemed to have been acquired at the same time as such amendment to the surrendered securities, so long as, in the conversion or exchange, the securities sold were acquired from the issuer solely in exchange for other securities of the same issuer.

(iii) *Contingent Issuance of Securities.* Securities acquired as a contingent payment of the purchase price of an equity interest in a business, or the assets of a business, sold to the issuer or an affiliate of the issuer shall be deemed to have been acquired at the time of such sale if the issuer or affiliate was then committed to issue the securities subject only to conditions other than the payment of further consideration for such securities. An agreement entered into in connection with any such purchase to remain in the employment of, or not to compete with, the issuer or affiliate or the rendering of services pursuant to such agreement shall not be deemed to be the payment of further consideration for such securities;

(iv) *Pledged Securities.* Securities which are *bona fide* pledged by an affiliate of the issuer when sold by the pledgee, or by a purchaser, after a default in the obligation secured by the pledge, shall be deemed to have been acquired when they were acquired by the pledgor, except that if the securities were pledged without recourse they shall be deemed to have been acquired by the pledgee at the time of the pledge or by the purchaser at the time of purchase;

(v) *Gifts of Securities.* Securities acquired from an affiliate of the issuer by gift shall be deemed to have been acquired by the donee when they were acquired by the donor;

(vi) *Trusts.* Where a trust settlor is an affiliate of the issuer, securities acquired from the settlor by the trust, or acquired from the trust by the beneficiaries thereof, shall be deemed to have been acquired when such securities were acquired by the settlor;

(vii) *Estates.* Where a deceased person was an affiliate of the issuer, securities held by the estate of such person or acquired from such estate by the estate beneficiaries shall be deemed to have been acquired when they were acquired by the deceased person, except that no holding period is required if the estate is not an affiliate of the issuer or if the securities are sold by a beneficiary of the estate who is not such an affiliate.

Note to § 230.144(d)(3)(vii). While there is no holding period or amount limitation for estates and estate beneficiaries which are not affiliates of the issuer, paragraphs (c) and (h) of this section apply to securities sold by such persons in reliance upon this section.

(viii) *Rule 145(a) Transactions.* The holding period for securities acquired in a transaction specified in § 230.145(a) shall be deemed to commence on the date the securities were acquired by the purchaser in such transaction, except as otherwise provided in paragraphs (d)(3)(ii) and (ix) of this section.

(ix) *Holding company formations.* Securities acquired from the issuer in a transaction effected solely for the purpose of forming a holding company shall be deemed to have been acquired at the same time as the securities of the predecessor issuer exchanged in the holding company formation where:

> (A) The newly formed holding company's securities were issued solely in exchange for the securities of the predecessor company as part of a reorganization of the predecessor company into a holding company structure;

> (B) Holders received securities of the same class evidencing the same proportional interest in the holding company as they held in the predecessor, and the rights and interests of the holders of such securities are substantially the same as those they possessed as holders of the predecessor company's securities; and

> (C) Immediately following the transaction, the holding company has no significant assets other than securities of the predecessor company and its existing subsidiaries and has substantially the same assets and liabilities on a consolidated basis as the predecessor company had before the transaction.

(x) *Cashless exercise of options and warrants.* If the securities sold were acquired from the issuer solely upon cashless exercise of options or warrants issued by the issuer, the newly acquired securities shall be deemed to have been acquired at the same time as the exercised options or warrants, even if the options or warrants exercised originally did not provide for cashless exercise by their terms.

Note 1 to § 230.144(d)(3)(x). If the options or warrants originally did not provide for cashless exercise by their terms and the holder provided consideration, other than solely securities of the same issuer, in connection with the amendment of the options or warrants to permit cashless exercise, then the newly acquired securities shall be deemed to have been acquired at the same time as such amendment to the options or warrants so long as the exercise itself was cashless.

Note 2 to § 230.144(d)(3)(x). If the options or warrants are not purchased for cash or property and do not create any investment risk to the holder, as in the case of employee stock options, the newly acquired securities shall be deemed to have been acquired at the time the options or warrants are exercised, so long as the full purchase price or other consideration for the newly acquired securities has been paid or given by the person acquiring the securities from the issuer or from an affiliate of the issuer at the time of exercise.

(e) *Limitation on amount of securities sold.* Except as hereinafter provided, the amount of securities sold for the account of an affiliate of the issuer in reliance upon this section shall be determined as follows:

(1) If any securities are sold for the account of an affiliate of the issuer, regardless of whether those securities are restricted, the amount of securities sold, together with all sales of securities of the same class sold for the account of such person within the preceding three months, shall not exceed the greatest of: (i) one percent of the shares or other units of the class outstanding as shown by the most recent report or statement published by the issuer; or (ii) the average weekly reported volume of trading in such securities on all national securities exchanges and/or reported through the automated quotation system of a registered securities association during the four calendar weeks preceding the filing of notice required by paragraph (h), or if no such notice is required the date of receipt of the order to execute the transaction by the broker or the date of execution of the transaction directly with a market maker; or (iii) the average weekly volume of trading in such securities reported through the consolidated transaction reporting system contemplated by Rule 11Aa3-1 under the Securities Exchange Act of 1934 during the four-week period specified in subdivision (ii) of this paragraph.

(2) If the securities sold are debt securities, then the amount of debt securities sold for the account of an affiliate of the issuer, regardless of whether those securities are restricted, shall not exceed the greater of the limitation set forth in paragraph (e)(1) of this section or, together with all sales of securities of the same tranche (or class when the securities are nonparticipatory preferred stock) sold for the account of such person within the preceding three months, ten percent of the principal amount of the tranche (or class when the securities are nonparticipatory preferred stock) attributable to the securities sold.

(3) *Determination of amount.* For the purpose of determining the amount of securities specified in paragraph (e)(1) of this section and, as applicable, paragraph (e)(2) of this section, the following provisions shall apply:

(i) Where both convertible securities and securities of the class into which they are convertible are sold, the amount of convertible securities sold shall be deemed to be the amount of securities of the class into which they are convertible for the purpose of determining the aggregate amount of securities of both classes sold;

(ii) The amount of securities sold for the account of a pledgee of those securities, or for the account of a purchaser of the pledged securities, during any period of three months within six months (or within one year if the issuer of the securities is not, or has not been for a period of at least 90 days immediately before the sale, subject to the reporting requirements of section 13 or 15(d) of the Exchange Act) after a default in the obligation secured by the pledge, and the amount of securities sold during the same threemonth period for the account of the pledgor shall not exceed, in the aggregate, the amount specified in paragraph (e)(1) or (2) of this section, whichever is applicable;

Note to § 230.144(e)(3)(ii). Sales by a pledgee of securities pledged by a borrower will not be aggregated under paragraph (e)(3)(ii) with sales of the securities of the same issuer by other pledgees of such borrower in the absence of concerted action by such pledgees.

(iii) The amount of securities sold for the account of a donee of those securities during any three-month period within six months (or within one year if the issuer of the securities is not, or has not been for a period of at least 90 days immediately before the sale, subject to the reporting requirements of section 13 or 15(d) of the Exchange Act) after the donation, and the amount of securities sold during the same threemonth period for the account of the donor, shall not exceed, in the aggregate, the amount specified in paragraph (e)(1) or (2) of this section, whichever is applicable;

(iv) Where securities were acquired by a trust from the settlor of the trust, the amount of such securities sold for the account of the trust during any threemonth period within six months (or within one year if the issuer of the securities is not, or has not been for a period of at least 90 days immediately before the sale, subject to the reporting requirements of section 13 or 15(d) of the Exchange Act) after the acquisition of the securities by the trust, and the amount of securities sold during the same three-month period for the account of the settlor, shall not exceed, in the aggregate, the amount specified in paragraph (e)(1) or (2) of this section, whichever is applicable;

(v) The amount of securities sold for the account of the estate of a deceased person, or for the account of a beneficiary of such estate, during any three-month period and the amount of securities sold during the same threemonth period for the account of the deceased person prior to his death shall not exceed, in the aggregate, the amount specified in paragraph (e)(1) or (2) of this section, whichever is applicable: *Provided,* that no limitation on amount shall apply if the estate or beneficiary of the estate is not an affiliate of the issuer;

(vi) When two or more affiliates or other persons agree to act in concert for the purpose of selling securities of an issuer, all securities of the same class sold for the account of all such persons during any three-month period shall be aggregated for the purpose of determining the limitation on the amount of securities sold;

(vii) The following sales of securities need not be included in determining the amount of securities to be sold in reliance upon this section:

(A) Securities sold pursuant to an effective registration statement under the Act;

(B) Securities sold pursuant to an exemption provided by Regulation A (§ 230.251 through § 230.263) under the Act;

(C) Securities sold in a transaction exempt pursuant to section 4 of the Act (15 U.S.C. 77d) and not involving any public offering; and

(D) Securities sold offshore pursuant to Regulation S (§ 230.901 through § 230.905, and Preliminary Notes) under the Act.

(f) *Manner of sale.*

(1) The securities shall be sold in one of the following manners:

(i) *Brokers' transactions* within the meaning of section 4(4) of the Act;

(ii) Transactions directly with a *market maker*, as that term is defined in section 3(a)(38) of the Exchange Act; or

(iii) *Riskless principal transactions* where:

(A) The offsetting trades must be executed at the same price (exclusive of an explicitly disclosed markup or markdown, commission equivalent, or other fee);

(B) The transaction is permitted to be reported as riskless under the rules of a self-regulatory organization; and

(C) The requirements of paragraphs (g)(2)(applicable to any markup or markdown, commission equivalent, or other fee), (g)(3), and (g)(4) of this section are met.

Note to § 230.144(f)(1): For purposes of this paragraph, a *riskless principal transaction* means a principal transaction where, after having received from a customer an order to buy, a broker or dealer purchases the security as principal in the market to satisfy the order to buy or, after having received from a customer an order to sell, sells the security as principal to the market to satisfy the order to sell.

(2) The person selling the securities shall not:

(i) Solicit or arrange for the solicitation of orders to buy the securities in anticipation of or in connection with such transaction, or

(ii) Make any payment in connection with the offer or sale of the securities to any person other than the broker or dealer who executes the order to sell the securities.

(3) Paragraph (f) of this section shall not apply to:

(i) Securities sold for the account of the estate of a deceased person or for the account of a beneficiary of such estate provided the estate or estate beneficiary is not an affiliate of the issuer; or

(ii) Debt securities.

(g) *Brokers' Transactions.* The term "brokers' transactions" in Section 4(4) of the Act shall for the purposes of this rule be deemed to include transactions by a broker in which such broker:

(1) Does no more than execute the order or orders to sell the securities as agent for the person for whose account the securities are sold;

(2) Receives no more than the usual and customary broker's commission;

(3) Neither solicits nor arranges for the solicitation of customers' orders to buy the securities in anticipation of or in connection with the transaction; *Provided,* that the foregoing shall not preclude:

(i) Inquiries by the broker of other brokers or dealers who have indicated an interest in the securities within the preceding 60 days;

(ii) Inquiries by the broker of his customers who have indicated an unsolicited bona fide interest in the securities within the preceding 10 business days;

(iii) The publication by the broker of bid and ask quotations for the security in an inter-dealer quotation system provided that such quotations are incident to the maintenance of a bona fide inter-dealer market for the security for the broker's own account and that the broker has published bona fide bid and ask quotations for the security in an inter-dealer quotation system on each of at least twelve days within the preceding thirty calendar days with no more than four business days in succession without such two-way quotations; or

(iv) The publication by the broker of bid and ask quotations for the security in an alternative trading system, as defined in § 242.300 of this chapter, provided that the broker has published bona fide bid and ask quotations for the security in the alternative trading system on each of the last twelve business days; and

Note to § 230.144(g)(3)(ii). The broker should obtain and retain in his files written evidence of indications of bona fide unsolicited interest by his customers in the securities at the time such indications are received.

(4) After reasonable inquiry is not aware of circumstances indicating that the person for whose account the securities are sold is an underwriter with respect to the securities or that the transaction is a part of a distribution of securities of the issuer. Without limiting the foregoing, the broker shall be deemed

to be aware of any facts or statements contained in the notice required by paragraph (h) below.

Notes. (i) The broker, for his own protection, should obtain and retain in his files a copy of the notice required by paragraph (h).

(ii) The reasonable inquiry required by paragraph (g)(4) of this section should include, but not necessarily be limited to, inquiry as to the following matters:

a. The length of time the securities have been held by the person for whose account they are to be sold. If practicable, the inquiry should include physical inspection of the securities;

b. The nature of the transaction in which the securities were acquired by such person; c. The amount of securities of the same class sold during the past three months by all persons whose sales are required to be taken into consideration pursuant to paragraph (e) of this section;

d. Whether such person intends to sell additional securities of the same class through any other means;

e. Whether such person has solicited or made any arrangement for the solicitation of buy orders in connection with the proposed sale of securities;

f. Whether such person has made any payment to any other person in connection with the proposed sale of the securities; and

g. The number of shares or other units of the class outstanding, or the relevant trading volume.

(h) *Notice of proposed sale.*

(1) If the amount of securities to be sold in reliance upon this rule during any period of three months exceeds 5,000 shares or other units or has an aggregate sale price in excess of $50,000, three copies of a notice on Form 144 (§ 239.144 of this chapter) shall be filed with the Commission. If such securities are admitted to trading on any national securities exchange, one copy of such notice also shall be transmitted to the principal exchange on which such securities are admitted.

(2) The Form 144 shall be signed by the person for whose account the securities are to be sold and shall be transmitted for filing concurrently with either the placing with a broker of an order to execute a sale of securities in reliance upon this rule or the execution directly with a market maker of such a sale. Neither the filing of such notice nor the failure of the Commission to comment on such notice shall be deemed to preclude the Commission from taking any action that it deems necessary or appropriate with respect

to the sale of the securities referred to in such notice. The person filing the notice required by this paragraph shall have a bona fide intention to sell the securities referred to in the notice within a reasonable time after the filing of such notice.

(i) *Unavailability to securities of issuers with no or nominal operations and no or nominal non-cash assets.*

(1) This section is not available for the resale of securities initially issued by an issuer defined below:

(i) An issuer, other than a business combination related shell company, as defined in § 230.405, or an asset-backed issuer, as defined in Item 1101(b) of Regulation AB (§ 229.1101(b) of this chapter), that has:

(A) No or nominal operations; and

(B) Either:

(*1*) No or nominal assets;

(*2*) Assets consisting solely of cash and cash equivalents; or

(*3*) Assets consisting of any amount of cash and cash equivalents and nominal other assets; or

(ii) An issuer that has been at any time previously an issuer described in paragraph (i)(1)(i).

(2) Notwithstanding paragraph (i)(1), if the issuer of the securities previously had been an issuer described in paragraph (i)(1)(i) but has ceased to be an issuer described in paragraph (i)(1)(i); is subject to the reporting requirements of section 13 or 15(d) of the Exchange Act; has filed all reports and other materials required to be filed by section 13 or 15(d) of the Exchange Act, as applicable, during the preceding 12 months (or for such shorter period that the issuer was required to file such reports and materials), other than Form 8-K reports (§ 249.308 of this chapter); and has filed current "Form 10 information" with the Commission reflecting its status as an entity that is no longer an issuer described in paragraph (i)(1)(i), then those securities may be sold subject to the requirements of this section after one year has elapsed from the date that the issuer filed "Form 10 information" with the Commission.

(3) The term "Form 10 information" means the information that is required by Form 10 or Form 20-F (§ 249.210 or § 249.220f of this chapter), as applicable to the issuer of the securities, to register under the Exchange Act each class of securities being sold under this rule. The issuer may provide the Form 10 information in any filing of the issuer with the Commission. The Form 10 information is deemed filed when the initial filing is made with the Commission.

SEC Rule 701

Exemption for offers and sales of securities pursuant to certain compensatory benefit plans and contracts relating to compensation.

Preliminary Notes

1. This section relates to transactions exempted from the registration requirements of section 5 of the Act (15 U.S.C. 77e). These transactions are not exempt from the antifraud, civil liability, or other provisions of the federal securities laws. Issuers and persons acting on their behalf have an obligation to provide investors with disclosure adequate to satisfy the antifraud provisions of the federal securities laws.

2. In addition to complying with this section, the issuer also must comply with any applicable state law relating to the offer and sale of securities.

3. An issuer that attempts to comply with this section, but fails to do so, may claim any other exemption that is available.

4. This section is available only to the issuer of the securities. Affiliates of the issuer may not use this section to offer or sell securities. This section also does not cover resales of securities by any person. This section provides an exemption only for the transactions in which the securities are offered or sold by the issuer, not for the securities themselves.

5. The purpose of this section is to provide an exemption from the registration requirements of the Act for securities issued in compensatory circumstances. This section is not available for plans or schemes to circumvent this purpose, such as to raise capital. This section also is not available to exempt any transaction that is in technical compliance with this section but is part of a plan or scheme to evade the registration provisions of the Act. In any of these cases, registration under the Act is required unless another exemption is available.

(a) **Exemption**. Offers and sales made in compliance with all of the conditions of this section are exempt from section 5 of the Act (15 U.S.C. 77e).

(b) **Issuers eligible to use this section**.

(1) **General**. This section is available to any issuer that is not subject to the reporting requirements of section 13 or 15(d) of the Securities Exchange Act of 1934 (the "Exchange Act") (15 U.S.C. 78m or 78o(d)) and is not an investment company registered or required to be registered under the Investment Company Act of 1940 (15 U.S.C. 80a-1 et seq.).

(2) **Issuers that become subject to reporting**. If an issuer becomes subject to the reporting requirements of section 13 or 15(d) of the Exchange Act (15 U.S.C. 78m or 78o(d)) after it has made offers complying with this section,

the issuer may nevertheless rely on this section to sell the securities previously offered to the persons to whom those offers were made.

(3) Guarantees by reporting companies. An issuer subject to the reporting requirements of section 13 or 15(d) of the Exchange Act (15 U.S.C. 78m, 78o(d)) may rely on this section if it is merely guaranteeing the payment of a subsidiary's securities that are sold under this section.

(c) Transactions exempted by this section. This section exempts offers and sales of securities (including plan interests and guarantees pursuant to paragraph (d)(2)(ii) of this section) under a written compensatory benefit plan (or written compensation contract) established by the issuer, its parents, its majority-owned subsidiaries or majority-owned subsidiaries of the issuer's parent, for the participation of their employees, directors, general partners, trustees (where the issuer is a business trust), officers, or consultants and advisors, and their family members who acquire such securities from such persons through gifts or domestic relations orders. This section exempts offers and sales to former employees, directors, general partners, trustees, officers, consultants and advisors only if such persons were employed by or providing services to the issuer at the time the securities were offered. In addition, the term "employee" includes insurance agents who are exclusive agents of the issuer, its subsidiaries or parents, or derive more than 50% of their annual income from those entities.

(1) Special requirements for consultants and advisors. This section is available to consultants and advisors only if:

(i) They are natural persons;

(ii) They provide bona fide services to the issuer, its parents, its majority-owned subsidiaries or majority-owned subsidiaries of the issuer's parent; and

(iii) The services are not in connection with the offer or sale of securities in a capital-raising transaction, and do not directly or indirectly promote or maintain a market for the issuer's securities.

(2) Definition of "Compensatory Benefit Plan." For purposes of this section, a compensatory benefit plan is any purchase, savings, option, bonus, stock appreciation, profit sharing, thrift, incentive, deferred compensation, pension or similar plan.

(3) Definition of "Family Member." For purposes of this section, family member includes any child, stepchild, grandchild, parent, stepparent, grandparent, spouse, former spouse, sibling, niece, nephew, mother-in-law, father-in-law, son-in-law, daughter-in-law, brother-in-law, or sister-in-law, including adoptive relationships, any person sharing the employee's household (other than a tenant or employee), a trust in which these persons have more than fifty percent of the beneficial interest, a foundation in which these persons (or the employee) control the management of assets, and any other entity in which these persons (or the employee) own more than fifty percent of the voting interests.

(d) Amounts that may be sold.

(1) Offers. Any amount of securities may be offered in reliance on this section. However, for purposes of this section, sales of securities underlying options must be counted as sales on the date of the option grant.

(2) Sales. The aggregate sales price or amount of securities sold in reliance on this section during any consecutive 12-month period must not exceed the greatest of the following:

(i) $1,000,000;

(ii) 15% of the total assets of the issuer (or of the issuer's parent if the issuer is a wholly-owned subsidiary and the securities represent obligations that the parent fully and unconditionally guarantees), measured at the issuer's most recent balance sheet date (if no older than its last fiscal year end); or

(iii) 15% of the outstanding amount of the class of securities being offered and sold in reliance on this section, measured at the issuer's most recent balance sheet date (if no older than its last fiscal year end).

(3) Rules for calculating prices and amounts.

(i) Aggregate sales price. The term aggregate sales price means the sum of all cash, property, notes, cancellation of debt or other consideration received or to be received by the issuer for the sale of the securities. Non-cash consideration must be valued by reference to bona fide sales of that consideration made within a reasonable time or, in the absence of such sales, on the fair value as determined by an accepted standard. The value of services exchanged for securities issued must be measured by reference to the value of the securities issued. Options must be valued based on the exercise price of the option.

(ii) Time of the calculation. With respect to options to purchase securities, the aggregate sales price is determined when an option grant is made (without regard to when the option becomes exercisable). With respect to other securities, the calculation is made on the date of sale. With respect to deferred compensation or similar plans, the calculation is made when the irrevocable election to defer is made.

(iii) Derivative securities. In calculating outstanding securities for purposes of paragraph (d)(2)(iii) of this section, treat the securities underlying all currently exercisable or convertible options, warrants, rights or other securities, other than those issued under this exemption, as outstanding. In calculating the amount of securities sold for other purposes of paragraph (d)(2) of this section, count the amount of securities that would be acquired upon exercise or conversion in connection with sales of options, warrants, rights or other exercisable or convertible securities, including those to be issued under this exemption.

(iv) Other exemptions. Amounts of securities sold in reliance on this section do not affect "aggregate offering prices" in other exemptions, and amounts of securities sold in reliance on other exemptions do not affect the amount that may be sold in reliance on this section.

(e) Disclosure that must be provided. The issuer must deliver to investors a copy of the compensatory benefit plan or the contract, as applicable. In addition, if the aggregate sales price or amount of securities sold during any consecutive 12-month period exceeds $5 million, the issuer must deliver the following disclosure to investors a reasonable period of time before the date of sale:

(1) If the plan is subject to the Employee Retirement Income Security Act of 1974 ("ERISA") (29 U.S.C. 1104 - 1107), a copy of the summary plan description required by ERISA;

(2) If the plan is not subject to ERISA, a summary of the material terms of the plan;

(3) Information about the risks associated with investment in the securities sold pursuant to the compensatory benefit plan or compensation contract; and

(4) Financial statements required to be furnished by Part F/S of Form 1-A (Regulation A Offering Statement) (§239.90 of this chapter) under Regulation A (§§230.251 - 230.263). Foreign private issuers as defined in §230.405 must provide a reconciliation to generally accepted accounting principles in the United States (U. S. GAAP) if their financial statements are not prepared in accordance with U. S. GAAP (Item 17 of Form 20-F (§249.220f of this chapter)). The financial statements required by this section must be as of a date no more than 180 days before the sale of securities in reliance on this exemption.

(5) If the issuer is relying on paragraph (d)(2)(ii) of this section to use its parent's total assets to determine the amount of securities that may be sold, the parent's financial statements must be delivered. If the parent is subject to the reporting requirements of section 13 or 15(d) of the Exchange Act (15 U.S.C. 78m or 78o(d)), the financial statements of the parent required by Rule 10-01 of Regulation S-X (§210.10-01 of this chapter) and Item 310 of Regulation S-B (§228.310 of this chapter), as applicable, must be delivered.

(6) If the sale involves a stock option or other derivative security, the issuer must deliver disclosure a reasonable period of time before the date of exercise or conversion. For deferred compensation or similar plans, the issuer must

deliver disclosure to investors a reasonable period of time before the date the irrevocable election to defer is made.

(f) No integration with other offerings. Offers and sales exempt under this section are deemed to be a part of a single, discrete offering and are not subject to integration with any other offers or sales, whether registered under the Act or otherwise exempt from the registration requirements of the Act.

(g) Resale limitations.

(1) Securities issued under this section are deemed to be "restricted securities" as defined in §230.144.

(2) Resales of securities issued pursuant to this section must be in compliance with the registration requirements of the Act or an exemption from those requirements.

(3) Ninety days after the issuer becomes subject to the reporting requirements of section 13 or 15(d) of the Exchange Act (15 U.S.C. 78m or 78o(d)), securities issued under this section may be resold by persons who are not affiliates (as defined in §230.144) in reliance on §230.144 without compliance with paragraphs (c) and (d) of §230.144, and by affiliates without compliance with paragraph (d) of §230.144.

Glossary

Acceleration: With respect to unvested shares, speeding up the vesting schedule (that is, decreasing the period over which vesting restrictions lapse).

Accounting Standards Codification Topic 718 (ASC 718): Accounting provision mandating that compensation expense for options and awards granted to employees is determined at grant, and is generally not adjusted for subsequent events (with the exception of forfeitures), provided that the option or award can only be settled in stock. This was called FAS 123(R) until it was recategorized as part of FASB's 2009 codification of authoritative accounting literature.

Affiliate: Under Rule 144, a person who directly or indirectly controls, is controlled by, or is under common control with the issuer. As a rule, executive officers and directors are deemed to be affiliates. Affiliates are subject to certain limitations as to volume and timing with respect to sale of unregistered (restricted) stock of the issuer.

Alternative Minimum Tax (AMT): Alternative tax system to federal income tax intended to recapture certain tax preference or adjustment items (such as the spread on exercise of an ISO); the tax is assessed on "alternative minimum taxable income" and, to the extent it is greater than regular taxable income, must be paid in the year computed. AMT is treated as a credit against regular income tax and may be carried forward to future years.

Backdating: The practice (whether or not fraudulent) of setting an option exercise price that is less than fair market value on the grant date. The term has been used to describe practices as varied as intentional discounting (i.e., intentionally stating that the option was granted on a date different than the actual grant date), misdating (unintentionally stating the incorrect grant date price), "spring-loading" (granting options before good news breaks), "bullet-dodging" (granting options after bad news breaks), "forward-dating" (approving options with a grant date set after approval), and 30-day pricing (approving options with grant price to be set at average or best price in a 30-day window). Backdating may raise accounting, SEC disclosure, and tax issues (particularly under Section 409A of the Code).

Black-Scholes Valuation: A mathematical formula used for valuing stock options that considers such factors as the volatility of returns on the underlying securities, the risk-free interest rate, the expected dividend rate, the relationship of option price to the price of the underlying securities, and expected option life. Developed in 1973 by three economists, the model was originally created to value options traded on European commodity exchanges.

Blue Sky Laws: State securities laws governing the purchase and sale of securities. The phrase "blue sky" originates from a federal case that described such laws as aimed against "speculative schemes which hold no more basis than so many feet of blue sky."

Board of Directors: Board elected by a corporation's shareholders to set policies and oversee the affairs of the corporation, generally elected on an annual basis.

Cashless Exercise: Form of stock option exercise in which the option price for the number of shares of stock being purchased is paid with consideration other than cash. Common cashless exercise methods include broker-assisted same-day-sale transactions and stock swaps.

California Commissioner's Rules: Regulations implementing the California Securities Act of 1968.

Change in Control: A transaction that alters the ownership of a corporation, including a merger, consolidation, stock sale, or asset sale. With respect to options, events that constitute a change in control are generally defined in the plan.

Code: See "Internal Revenue Code (Code)."

Collateral: Property given to secure a promissory note.

Common Stock: Basic ownership interest in a corporation that typically confers on the holder of the security the right to vote, select directors, receive dividends, and share in residual assets upon the dissolution or winding up of the business.

Compensation Committee: A committee of the board of directors that evaluates and approves executive compensation (including equity compensation plans).

Compensation Expense: *For financial reporting purposes,* the cost recognized by a corporation on its financial statements with respect to the issuance of its securities in connection with stock-based compensation. If pursuant to ASC 718, it is measured based on the fair value of the shares. *For tax purposes,* the amount realized on exercise of an option that is potentially deductible by a corporation on its income tax return as a trade or business expense under Section 162 of the Code (generally limited to the amount included in income by the employee at the time of exercise or disposition).

Cost Basis (Tax Basis): A tax concept representing the actual and constructive cost of property to a taxpayer; for purposes of stock purchased under an option, the cost basis is equal to the amount paid on exercise plus any amount included in ordinary income prior to disposition.

Director: Member of a corporate board of directors. Independent (or outside) directors may not be employed by the corporation.

Discount Option: Option with an exercise price below fair market value on date of grant.

Disposition: Sale, gift, or other transfer of stock purchased pursuant to an option.

Disqualifying Disposition: For purposes of stock purchased pursuant to a statutory stock option, a disposition made within two years from grant or one year from exercise (pursuant to Section 421 of the Code).

Early Exercise: With respect to stock purchased under an option, a purchase made subject to ongoing vesting restrictions (i.e., on a different schedule than the vesting schedule).

EDGAR (Electronic Data Gathering Analysis and Retrieval System): The automated computer system developed and implemented by the SEC for filing registration statements, periodic reports, and other federal securities law filings.

Employee: An individual who performs services for an employer, subject to the control of the employer as to the type of work and manner of performance.

Employee Stock Purchase Plan (ESPP): Type of stock option plan that provides for ongoing stock purchases by employees pursuant to a subscription agreement. May be a tax-qualified statutory option plan under Section 423 of the Code, or may result in nonstatutory option treatment under Section 83. Tax-qualified plans generally include a discount from market price, determined either as of the first or last day of the applicable exercise period. See "Section 423 Plan."

Employment Tax: A general term used to describe taxes imposed under FICA and FUTA.

Evergreen Provision: A replenishment feature in a stock plan that automatically increases at regular intervals the number of shares reserved under the plan.

Exchange Act: See "Securities Exchange Act of 1934 (Exchange Act)."

Exercise: Purchase of stock pursuant to an option.

Exercise Price: The price at which an option may be exercised, stated in the option agreement. Also called the "strike price."

Fair Market Value: For tax and accounting purposes, the value of a share of stock on any given date. In a privately held company, fair market value is determined by the corporation's board of directors. In a public company, fair market value is determined with reference to the price posted on the applicable stock market (generally this is closing price, but it depends on how the plan was drawn up).

Fair Value: For accounting purposes, the value of an option determined in accordance with ASC 718, using a pricing model such as Black-Scholes or a lattice model.

FAS 123(R): Statement of Financial Accounting Standards No. 123 (revised 2004), "Share-Based Payment." The Financial Accounting Standards Board's revision of its FAS 123 accounting standard. The majority of FAS 123(R) was recategorized as Accounting Standards Codification Topic 718 (ASC 718) as part of a 2009 codification of authoritative accounting literature. See entry under "Accounting Standards Codification Topic 718 (ASC 718)" for full description.

Federal Insurance Contributions Act (FICA): A series of employment taxes imposed on employees and employers with respect to employee wages, including Social Security and Medicare taxes.

Federal Unemployment Tax Act (FUTA): An employment tax imposed on employers with respect to employee wages.

Financial Accounting Standards Board (FASB): A private-sector organization recognized by the SEC as the source for GAAP for corporations that offer and sell securities in the U.S.

Financial Industry Regulatory Authority (FINRA): A self-regulatory organization subject to the Exchange Act, comprising brokers and dealers. Created in 2007 to incorporate oversight of U.S. securities markets into one organization. Among the organizations incorporated was the National Association of Securities Dealers (NASD), which comprised brokers and dealers in the over-the-counter (OTC) securities market.

Generally Accepted Accounting Principles (GAAP): Substantive rules for the practice of accounting as established by the body of opinions and decisions issued by the FASB.

Golden Parachute: Under Section 280G of the Code, a package of compensation-related benefits (including options) awarded to an employee contingent upon a change in control of the employer corporation.

Grant Date: The date upon which an employee stock option is approved by the company's board of directors.

Holding Period: *For tax purposes,* the length of time stock must be held before transfer in order for any gain to be eligible for capital gain treatment. For statutory option purposes, the period is one year from exercise and two years from grant (set out in Section 421 of the Code); for general capital gains purposes, the period is more than one year from the date of transfer of capital property (Sections 1221–1223 of the Code). The tax holding period begins on the date the property is first transferred (regardless of whether purchased with a note or subject to contractual restrictions). *For Rule 144 purposes,* the length of time unregistered stock must be held before transfer. If purchase is with a note, the securities holding period begins only when the note is paid off or fully collateralized with property other than the underlying stock.

IASB: See "International Accounting Standards Board (IASB)."

Immaculate Exercise: See "Net Exercise."

In the Money: Term used to describe an employee stock option where the current fair market value of the shares of stock subject to the option is greater than the exercise price.

Incentive Stock Option (ISO): A statutory stock option described in Section 422 of the Code.

Independent Contractor: A service provider who is not an employee.

Insider: A general term referring to persons who, by virtue of their positions within a corporation, have access to confidential information about a corporation. Frequently used to denote directors, officers, 10% shareholders, and persons otherwise subject to the Exchange Act.

Insider Trading: A person's wrongful use or wrongful communication, whether directly or indirectly, of confidential information to purchase or sell securities.

Institutional Investor: A large non-bank investor, frequently representing an institution such as a finance company, pension fund, or mutual fund.

Internal Revenue Code (Code): The Internal Revenue Code of 1986, as amended; the key federal statute providing for taxation of individuals, corporations, and other persons.

Internal Revenue Service (IRS): An agency of the federal government, under the supervision of the Department of the Treasury, that is responsible for administering the federal tax laws.

International Accounting Standards Board (IASB): Voluntary global accounting standards-setting organization whose member nations include the U.S., Australia, Canada, France, Germany, Japan, New Zealand, and the U.K. IASB standards are intended to establish GAAP on an international basis.

Intrinsic Value: For accounting purposes, the compensation cost of an option computed in accordance with APB 25; equal to the difference (if any) between the exercise price and the fair market value of a share of the underlying stock on the measurement date.

Lattice Models: Models for determining the fair value of employee stock options that use a decision-tree approach of possible future outcomes. A value is arrived at based on the weighted probability of all possible future outcomes. There are many different kinds of lattice models including binomial models and trinomial models, among many others.

Measurement Date: For accounting purposes, the first date on which both the number and the price of shares subject to an option is known. The measurement date for a fixed award is the date of grant, while the measurement date for a variable award is the date of vesting (or expiration).

Modification: *For purposes of a statutory option,* a beneficial change to the terms of an option (including by way of example, the number of shares, an extension of the term, pricing, or the method of financing). Under Section 424 of the Code, the underlying option will be disqualified from statutory option treatment unless it is treated as a new option as of the date of the modification.

Nasdaq: The largest computerized stock market in the U.S., Nasdaq was originally the National Association of Securities Dealers' network showing quotations and transaction information with respect to securities traded in the over the counter market.

National Association of Securities Dealers (NASD): A self-regulatory organization subject to the Exchange Act, comprised of brokers and dealers in the over-the-counter (OTC) securities market. The NASD was established in the late 1930s to regulate the OTC market. It was incorporated into the Financial Industry Regulatory Authority (FINRA) in 2007.

Net or Immaculate Exercise: An exercise technique that permits the optionee to buy shares with no cash down by agreeing to allow the issuer to withhold (at exercise) that number of shares with a value equal to the full exercise price plus withholding taxes. The optionee receives only the balance of the shares.

New York Stock Exchange (NYSE): The oldest organized stock exchange.

No-Action Letter: Interpretive letter issued by the SEC to a specific requestor, indicating the SEC staff's advice regarding the application of specific securities forms or rules; available to the public.

Nonapproved Plan: A stock option plan that has not been approved by the shareholders.

Nonstatutory (or Nonqualified) Stock Option (NSO): Any option other than a statutory stock option; its tax treatment is governed by Section 83 of the Code.

One Million Dollar Cap: Under Section 162(m) of the Code, the maximum amount of compensation paid to "covered employees" that may be deducted by a publicly traded corporation.

Optionee: An individual who has been granted an option.

Ordinary Income: Income, such as compensation income, taxed at ordinary rather than capital gains rates under the Code.

PLR: See "Private Letter Ruling (PLR)."

Preferred Stock: Equity securities of a corporation that carry certain rights, preferences, and privileges superior to common stock. Preferred stock generally receives an investment return at a specific rate whenever dividends are declared, and has priority to the earnings and assets in the event of a sale or liquidation of the corporation before distributions may be made to common shareholders.

Private Letter Ruling (PLR): A ruling issued by the IRS to a specific taxpayer, indicating the IRS interpretation of tax law with respect to a stated set of facts. PLRs include private letter rulings and technical advice memoranda, and are available to the public, although they may not be cited as precedent and do not bind the IRS other than as to the taxpayer requesting the ruling. Other forms of non-precedential IRS rulings include field service memoranda and IRS Chief Counsel Advisory memoranda.

Privately Held Company (Closely Held Company): A company whose stock is not publicly traded.

Promissory Note: A written promise to pay a specified amount of money at a specified time in the future; may be unsecured or secured with collateral acceptable to the holder of the note; if recourse is not limited specifically to the underlying collateral, holder will be entitled to recourse against all of the assets of the maker.

Public Company: A company whose stock is publicly traded on a recognized stock exchange; subject to the registration, disclosure, and related rules enforced by the SEC.

Public Offering: An offering of securities to the general public under a registration statement prepared and filed with the SEC in accordance with the 1933 Act and any applicable blue sky laws.

Qualifying Disposition: For purposes of stock purchased pursuant to a statutory stock option, a disposition made after a minimum of two years from grant and one year from exercise (pursuant to Section 421 of the Code).

Registration: The formal process for the issuance of securities under federal and/ or state securities laws that permit public sale of securities.

Reload Option: A stock option granted to an individual who has exercised an option (typically by a stock swap) that restores the original number of shares under option; the terms of the option (e.g., the price) need not be the same as those of the swapped option.

Repricing: A program under which a board of directors will typically set a repricing date and invite employees to trade underwater options for restricted stock or units or for new options priced as of that date. As a general rule, the repriced options will require employees to give up some of the benefits of the original grants: for example, the repriced options may be for fewer shares (i.e., one new share for two old shares) or may have a different vesting schedule from the original options.

Restricted Securities: Shares of stock issued in a transaction that was not registered under the 1933 Act in reliance on an exemption. Resale of such shares is generally subject to Rule 144 (or subsequent registration).

Revenue Procedure: A notice published by the IRS giving administrative guidance on the application of tax laws; intended to be relied upon by taxpayers.

Revenue Ruling: A ruling published by the IRS that states the IRS audit position on the application of the tax law to specific facts; establishes precedent that may be relied upon.

Rule 144: Rule promulgated by the Securities and Exchange Commission as a "safe harbor" for the resale of "restricted securities" (that is, securities that were acquired other than in a public offering) and "control securities" (that is, securities owned by affiliates of the corporation).

SAR/SSAR: See "Stock Appreciation Right (SAR)."

Section 423 Plan: An ESPP that complies with statutory option rules under Section 423 of the Code. See "Employee Stock Purchase Plan."

Securities Act of 1933 (1933 Act): A federal statute governing the offer and sale of securities in interstate commerce; prescribes registration, disclosure, and fraud rules.

Securities and Exchange Commission (SEC): An agency of the federal government created under the Exchange Act that administers the federal laws regulating the offer and sale of securities within the U.S.

Securities Exchange Act of 1934 (Exchange Act): A federal statute that requires stock exchanges to register with (or obtain an exemption from) the SEC as a prerequisite to doing business; includes reporting, proxy solicitation, tender offer, and insider trading rules.

Shareholder/Stockholder: A person who owns one or more of the outstanding shares of stock of a corporation.

Shareholder/Stockholder Approval: Authorization by shareholders of a corporate transaction or event.

Spread: For any share purchased under an option, the difference between the option price and the fair market value of a share of stock on the date of exercise.

Statutory Stock Option: An employee option accorded favorable tax treatment under Sections 421–424 of the Code; that is, an ISO or Section 423 ESPP option.

Strike Price: See "Exercise Price."

Stock Appreciation Right (SAR)/Stock-Settled Stock Appreciation Right (SSAR): A contractual right granted to an individual that gives the recipient the right to receive a cash amount equal to the appreciation on a specified number of shares of stock over a specified period of time. An SSAR pays out the appreciation in the form of stock rather than cash.

Stock Option: A contract right granted to an individual to purchase a certain number of shares of stock at a certain price (and subject to certain conditions) over a defined period of time.

Stock Swap: A transaction in which already owned stock is exchanged in lieu of cash to pay the option price for the exercise of an employee stock option.

Tax Withholding: The retention of certain amounts from an employee's wages or compensation by a corporation to satisfy income tax and/or employment tax obligations.

Transferable Stock Option: An NSO that permits the optionee to transfer the option to one or more third parties.

Underwater or "Out of the Money": Terms used to describe an employee stock option where the current fair market value of the shares of stock subject to the option is less than the exercise price.

Vesting: With respect to an option, the process of earning shares of stock over the term of the option; the process by which shares under option become first transferable or not subject to a substantial risk of forfeiture under Section 83 of the Code (e.g., by satisfying continuing service or performance-based conditions).

Vesting Period: With respect to an option, period over which shares subject to the option vest.

Wages: Under Section 3401 of the Code, remuneration (in any form) paid to an employee in connection with services rendered to the employer.

Bibliography

Books

Baksa, Barbara A. *Accounting for Equity Compensation*, 14th ed. Oakland, CA: NCEO, 2017.

Benderly, Danielle, et al. *Executive Compensation Disclosure Handbook*, 2010 ed. Chicago: R.R. Donnelley, updated May 2010.

Certified Equity Professional Institute. *GPS: Global Stock Plans*. Santa Clara, CA: Certified Equity Professional Institute, 2009.

Hicks, J. William. *Resales of Restricted Securities*. 2012 ed. Eagan, MN: Thomson West, 2012.

Makridis, Takis. *Advanced Topics in Equity Compensation Accounting*, 7th ed. Oakland, CA: NCEO, 2017.

Rodrick, Scott, ed. *Selected Issues in Equity Compensation*, 14th ed. Oakland, CA: NCEO, 2017.

Romeo, Peter J., and Alan L. Dye. *Section 16 Treatise and Reporting Guide*. 4th ed. Concord, CA: Executive Press, 2012. Also available online at www.section16treatise.net.

Rosen, Corey, et al. *Equity Alternatives: Restricted Stock, Performance Awards, Phantom Stock, SARs, and More*. 15th ed. Oakland, CA: NCEO, 2017.

_____. *The Decision-Maker's Guide to Equity Compensation*, 2nd ed. Oakland, CA: NCEO, 2011.

Wilson, Bill C., and Diane M. McGowan. *Golden Parachutes*. Tax Management Portfolio 396. Washington: BNA.

Articles

Dash, Eric. "Inquiry into Stock Option Pricing Casts A Wide Net." *New York Times* (June 19, 2006).

Henning, Peter J. "Behind the Fade-Out of Options Backdating Cases," *New York Times DealBook White Collar Watch* (April 30, 2010).

Heron, Randall, and Erik Lie. "What Fraction of Stock Option Grants to Top Executives Have Been Backdated or Manipulated?" (July 14, 2006).

Hochberg, Yael, and Laura Anne Lindsey, "Incentives, Targeting and Firm Performance: An Analysis of Non-Executive Stock Options," *Review of Financial Sutdies* vol. 23, no. 11 (November 2010).

369

Lattman, Peter. "Backdating Scandal Ends with a Whimper," New York Times (November 11, 2010).

Lie, Erik. "On the Timing of CEO Stock Option Awards." *Management Science* (May 2005).

Melcher, Peter J., and Warren Rosenbloom. "Transferable Options: When They Work, When They Don't." *Practical Tax Lawyer* 15, no. 1 (Fall 2000): 5.

Pender, Kathleen. "Hidden Victims of Stock Option Backdating." *San Francisco Chronicle* (October 26, 2006).

Surveys

Equilar. "2015 Equity Trends Report."

National Association of Stock Plan Professionals (NASPP). Multiple equity compensation-related surveys.

NCEO, NASPP, and CEP Institute. "2016 ESPP Survey."

Periodicals

Corporate Counsel and *Corporate Executive* (Executive Press)

Employee Ownership Report (NCEO)

The Stock Plan Advisor (NASPP)

WorldatWork Journal (WorldatWork)

Websites

www.bakermckenzie.com/nlnagescountrymatrix (Baker & McKenzie, Selected Tax & Legal Consequences: 40-Country Matrix)

www.fasb.org (Financial Accounting Standards Board)

www.fwcook.com (Frederic W. Cook & Co.)

www.globalequity.org (Global Equity Organization)

www.ifrs.org (International Accounting Standards Board)

www.irs.gov (Internal Revenue Service)

www.issgovernance.com (Institutional Shareholder Services)

www.mystockoptions.com (myStockOptions.com)

www.naspp.com (National Association of Stock Plan Professionals)

www.nceo.org (National Center for Employee Ownership)

www.sec.gov (Securities and Exchange Commission)

www.thecorporatecounsel.net (Executive Press)

www.theracetothebottom.org (University of Denver)

www.usa.gov (U.S. government web portal)

Index

Symbols

$1 million cap. *See* Internal Revenue Code: Section 162(m)
$100,000 limit. *See* Incentive stock options (ISOs)
401(k) plans, 61, 176, 245, 293, 294, 296, 301, 302

A

Accounting, 189–208
  codification, 10
Accounting Principles Board Opinion No. 25 (APB 25), 230
Accounting Standards Codification (ASC) Topics,
ASC 480, 219
ASC 505, 10, 190
  Subtopic 505-50, 193
ASC 718, 10, 22, 76, 159–60, 192–205, 220, 221, 278, 285–86, 359
  backdating, 76
  cash-settled SARs, 115, 194, 204
  employee, definition of, 197–98
  ESPPs, 94, 194, 201–3
  estimated volatility, 195, 197, 295–96
  expected term, 193, 195–97, 201
  expense, recognition of, 198–200
  extension of exercise period, 220
  fair value, 159, 160, 192–94
  forfeitures, 198–200, 204, 205
  liability, 204

measurement date, 192–94
modifications, 94, 203, 219, 220, 285–86
NSOs, 22
option-pricing models and inputs, 192–97, 200, 201, 204, 238
performance conditions, 109
phantom stock, 194, 205
recognition of expense, 198–200
reloads, 278–79
repricings, 285–86
restricted stock and RSUs, 194, 204
Section 718-10-35, 219, 220
service period, 193–94, 198–200, 201, 203, 204, 285
stock options, 193–96, 200–201
stock-settled SARs, 192, 193, 200
Subtopic 718-740 (formerly FAS 109), 205–6
tax accounting, 205–6
termination, 218–22
ASC Subtopic 505-50. *See* Accounting Standards Codification Topics: ASC 505: Subtopic 505-50
Accounting standards updates (ASU), 10, 176, 191, 193, 199, 206, 208
ASU 2010-13, 193
ASU 2016-09, 176, 191, 199, 206, 208
Accredited investors, 307
Acquisitions. *See* Changes in control

About the Authors

Alison E. Wright is a partner in the Employee Benefits Group at the law firm of Hanson Bridgett LLP, resident in the firm's San Francisco office. Her practice focuses on the tax, securities, and ERISA aspects of executive and equity compensation, including nonqualified deferred compensation plans, stock compensation plans, employee stock purchase plans, change-in-control plans, perquisite programs, and executive employment and severance agreements. She also advises clients regarding their traditional employee benefit plans, including 401(k) and other retirement plans, health and welfare plans, and cafeteria plans. Alison has experience assisting clients with compensation and benefits issues raised in mergers and acquisitions, including golden parachute payments, COBRA responsibilities, and due diligence review.

She is a member of the American Bar Association, the State Bar of California, the National Center for Employee Ownership (NCEO), the National Association of Stock Plan Professionals (NASPP), and the Western Pension & Benefits Council. She received her BA from Colby College in 1989 and her JD from the University of California at Davis School of Law in 1995. She received her LLM from New York University School of Law in 1996. Alison is admitted to practice in California.

Alison is a member of the board of directors of the NCEO and the Orinda Association. She is the chair of the Brown Bag Lunch Committee and a member of the board of directors of the San Francisco chapter of the Western Pension & Benefits Council. She has written for several publications and has presented at webinars and in-person events for the NCEO, NASPP, and Western Pension & Benefits Council.

Alisa J. Baker, a partner at the law firm of Levine & Baker LLP, is a nationally recognized equity/executive compensation expert who specializes in counseling individuals and companies on the full range of compensation-related matters, including:

- Preparation and negotiation of executive employment agreements, severance/separation agreements, consulting agreements, and individual equity arrangements, including representation of partners and company founders.

- Representation of senior executives, company founders, and employee-stockholders on their rights in merger & acquisition (M&A) transactions and venture capital financings, including group and individual representation with respect to "golden parachute," deferred compensation, and equity structuring matters.

- Representation of senior lawyers, including corporate chief legal officers and general counsel, as well as law firm partners, with respect to individual employment, compensation, and severance matters.

- Counseling on employee rights with respect to compensation matters, including stock option/restricted stock plans, non-equity performance plans, nonqualified deferred compensation arrangements and fringe benefits, executive compensation assessment, and compensation committee review procedures.

- Expert witness and consulting services for equity-related litigation.

Alisa is the coauthor of two books on equity compensation: *The Stock Options Book* (17th ed., 2016), a comprehensive overview (used as a core text for Santa Clara University's Certified Equity Professional Institute [CEPI] credentialing program), and *The Law Of Equity Compensation* (2006, coauthored with Corey Rosen), a treatise on equity compensation-related litigation from 2001 to 2005. Her articles have appeared in publications ranging from the *Wall Street Journal* to the *Journal of Taxation*, and she is a frequent contributor to online and print journals in her field. Alisa is regularly quoted in, and sourced by, such news outlets as the *San Jose Mercury News*, the *San Francisco Chronicle*, the *Recorder*, and *Bloomberg News*. A popular speaker, her engagements have included numerous appearances before industry groups, including the National Association of Stock Plan Professionals (NASPP), the National Center for Employee Ownership (NCEO), the E*Trade Business

Solutions Group, and the Society for Human Resource Management. She is a founding member of the CEPI board of advisors and currently serves on the MyStockOptions board of advisors and the NCEO stock option advisory board. Alisa is also on the board of directors of the San Francisco Child Abuse Prevention Center.

Alisa received her BA and MA in English with honors, and her MS in higher education with distinction from the University of Pennsylvania in Philadelphia. She earned her JD with honors from Georgetown University Law Center in Washington, D.C., where she was an associate editor of the Georgetown Law Journal. She has been a teaching fellow at Stanford Law School and an adjunct lecturer in executive compensation at Golden Gate University. In 2009, Alisa was elected a fellow of the American College of Employee Benefits Counsel, a recognition by her peers of her distinguished accomplishments in the field.

Before establishing Levine & Baker LLP with partner Richard E. Levine, Alisa was a partner with the Mountain View law firm GCA Law Partners LLP (formerly General Counsel Associates), and before that practiced with the employee benefits group at Wilson Sonsini Goodrich & Rosati and the tax group at Fenwick & West. During 2000–2001, she served as executive vice president/general counsel of Snapfish.com Corporation in San Francisco.

Pam Chernoff, CEP, is a freelance technical writer and editor specializing in equity compensation-related topics. She is curriculum coordinator for the Certified Equity Professional Institute at Santa Clara University and spent eight years as a project director at the National Center for Employee Ownership. She is a coauthor and editor of *The Decision-Maker's Guide to Equity Compensation* (2nd ed.) Before that, she was copy desk chief at *Pensions & Investments* newspaper. She has a master's degree in journalism from Northwestern University.

About the NCEO

The National Center for Employee Ownership (NCEO) is widely considered to be the leading authority in employee ownership in the U.S. and the world. Established in 1981 as a nonprofit information and membership organization, it now has more than 3,000 members, including companies, professionals, unions, government officials, academics, and interested individuals. It is funded entirely through the work it does.

The NCEO's mission is to provide the most objective, reliable information possible about employee ownership at the most affordable price possible. As part of the NCEO's commitment to providing objective information, it does not lobby or provide ongoing consulting services. The NCEO publishes a variety of materials on employee ownership and participation; holds dozens of seminars, webinars, and conferences on employee ownership annually; and offers online courses. The NCEO's work also includes extensive contacts with the media.

Membership Benefits

NCEO members receive the following benefits:

- The members-only newsletter *Employee Ownership Report*.
- Access to the members-only area of the NCEO's website, including the NCEO's member-only Document Library.
- Free access to live webinars.
- Discounts on books and other NCEO products and services.
- The right to contact the NCEO for answers to questions.

An introductory one-year membership is $90 for U.S. residents. To join or order publications, visit our website at www.nceo.org or telephone us at 510-208-1300.